Daniel Wolsey Voorhees, Thomas B. Long

Forty Years of Oratory

Vol. II

Daniel Wolsey Voorhees, Thomas B. Long

Forty Years of Oratory
Vol. II

ISBN/EAN: 9783337176198

Printed in Europe, USA, Canada, Australia, Japan

Cover: Foto ©ninafisch / pixelio.de

More available books at **www.hansebooks.com**

FORTY YEARS OF ORATORY

DANIEL WOLSEY VOORHEES

LECTURES, ADDRESSES AND SPEECHES

COMPILED AND EDITED BY HIS THREE SONS AND HIS DAUGHTER
HARRIET CECILIA VOORHEES

A BRIEF SKETCH OF HIS LIFE BY
JUDGE THOMAS B. LONG
OF INDIANA

Knowledge is power, the power to maintain free government and preserve constitutional liberty.

IN TWO VOLUMES

Volume II

Illustrated with Portraits, Historical Scenes, Etc.

INDIANAPOLIS AND KANSAS CITY
THE BOWEN-MERRILL COMPANY
1898

ILLUSTRATIONS

Vol. II

	PAGE.
Daniel W. Voorhees, When He Entered the House of Representatives	Frontispiece.
John E. Cook	379
Mary Harris	403
Hallet Kilbourn	449
Daniel W. Voorhees, at the Age of Sixty	637
Benjamin Franklin	645
Robert Fulton	653
Francis Bacon	660
Thomas A. Hendricks	667
The Farragut Statue at Washington	686
The Engagement of the Bon Homme Richard and Serapis	692
David G. Farragut	701
James D. Williams	706
James A. Garfield	718
The Memphis Bridge	722
Oliver P. Morton	747
Constantino Brumidi	749
John Marshall	753
Samuel F. B. Morse	777

CONTENTS

VOL. II.

DEFENSE OF JOHN E. COOK.
    An argument to a jury, delivered at Charles Town, Virginia, November 8, 1859. The circumstances calling forth this moving appeal for mercy, which gave Mr. Voorhees, then a young man, a national reputation, were tragic, fatal, and most harrowing. Cook was little more than a boy and had followed John Brown into Virginia to free the slaves. He was taken after the killing and fight at Harper's Ferry, indicted for murder and treason, and tried at Charles Town. He was the brother of the wife of Governor Ashbel P. Willard of Indiana, and Mr. Voorhees' appearance in his behalf was due to the strong friendship existing between Governor Willard and himself............................379

DEFENSE OF MARY HARRIS.
    An argument to a jury, delivered on July 18, 1865, in the supreme court of the District of Columbia. Insanity as a defense for homicide. The facts in this case were laden with woe, and the power of pathos in the speaker was fully shown. On the 30th of January, 1865, Mary Harris, a young lady of eighteen or nineteen years of age, shot and killed Adoniram J. Burroughs in the treasury building at Washington, D. C. She was indicted for murder, tried and acquitted. The proof showed that Burroughs had been engaged to Miss Harris, but had, with many cruel attending circumstances, abruptly, without explanation, deserted her and married another lady, and that this heartless conduct of the deceased produced in the defendant paroxysmal insanity, in one of which paroxysms she was at the time of the killing...............403

THE KILBOURN CASE.
    Argument on writ of *habeas corpus*, April 24, 1876, before Chief Justice David K. Cartter of the supreme court of the District of Columbia. The house of representatives of the United States not the final judge of its powers where the rights and liberty of the citizen are concerned. The courts have jurisdiction. The right of the people, under the constitution, "to be secure in their persons, houses, papers and effects against unreasonable searches and seizures." On March 14, 1876, Hallet Kil-

(v)

bourn was arrested by order of the house of representatives of the United States and imprisoned for an alleged contempt of the house in refusing to produce, for examination by its committee, certain of his private books and papers pertaining to his business as a real estate broker. He applied for a writ of *habeas corpus* upon which he was released. Mr. Voorhees making this the closing argument. The views of Andrew Jackson, Thomas Jefferson, Alexander H. Stephens and Jeremiah S. Black 449

FIRST TRIAL OF KILBOURN VS. THOMPSON.

The closing argument to a jury, made in the supreme court of the District of Columbia, April 21, 1882. Human liberty. Its value. The measure of damages for its loss. Based on his unlawful imprisonment by the house of representatives, Mr. Kilbourn brought suit for $150,000 damages against John G. Thompson, who, as sergeant-at-arms of the house, and acting by its order, had arrested and imprisoned him. The jury returned a verdict for Mr. Kilbourn for the enormous sum of $100,000. This the court set aside as excessive, stating that the jury had been unduly influenced by "the powerful appeal" made to them by Mr. Voorhees, and that they were "moved by his eloquence and inspired by the magnanimity of his sentiments." 508

DEFENSE OF CAPTAIN EDWARD T. JOHNSON.

An argument to a jury, delivered June 23, 1885, at Greeneville, Tennessee. The sanctity of home, and the right of man to defend its purity. On September 23, 1884, Captain Edward T. Johnson shot and killed Edwin Henry, near Greeneville, Tennessee, for the betrayal of his wife and the destruction of his home. He was indicted for murder, tried and acquitted. The plea entered by the defense was insanity. Tribute to John Howard Payne, and the home coming of the author of "Home, Home! Sweet, Sweet Home!" 531

DEFENSE OF HARRY CRAWFORD BLACK.

An argument to a jury, delivered at Frederick, Maryland, April 21, 1871. The law of self-defense. The right of the assaulted party to stand his ground. The old law of retreat to the ditch or wall. The establishment by sacred history, by the uses of civilization, by the common action of mankind, and by universal consent as shown by the unvarying uniformity of the verdicts of juries, of the death penalty for the seducer. The value of family honor. On October, 17, 1870, Harry Crawford Black shot and killed Colonel W. W. McKaig, Jr., in a street duel in the city of Cumberland, Maryland, for the ruin of his sister. He was indicted for murder, tried and acquitted 598

INFLUENCE OF THE PHYSICAL SCIENCES ON THE PROGRESS OF CIVILIZATION.

An address delivered before the Athenian and Union Literary Societies of the University of Missouri, June 22, 1874. The right of man to dominion over the earth. Failure of all prior civilizations to exercise it through want of knowledge. Physical sciences unknown to ancient civilizations. The vast conquests, power and gorgeous splendor of ancient Rome, and their ephemeral character. Christopher Columbus; the ignorance of his time and his struggle against it. The key to scientific knowledge and why the ancients lacked it. Modern civilization the reign of utility. The Baconian philosophy. Its comparison with those of the ancients. The permanency of the fruits of useful scientific invention..637

TRIBUTE TO VICE-PRESIDENT HENDRICKS.

An address on the death of Hon. Thomas A. Hendricks, of Indiana, delivered in the senate of the United States, January 26, 1886. A sketch of the life and public services of Mr. Hendricks, with incidents, and an analysis of his character. Containing also brief delineations of his character as a lawyer, by the late Hon. Walter Q. Gresham, the late Hon. Joseph E. McDonald, and by the Hon. David Turpie.....................667

THE FLAG ON THE SEA.

An address delivered at the unveiling of the Farragut statue in Farragut Square, Washington, D. C., on April 25, 1881. The life and achievements of Admiral David G. Farragut. The infancy and development of the American navy and its valor and glory in three wars. Its rescue in its infancy of the United States from humiliation abroad and the maintenance of the national dignity among the nations of the earth by it in its splendid maturity. John Paul Jones and the action of the Bon Homme Richard and Serapis. Commodore David Porter and the action of the Essex with the Phœbe and Cherub. Farragut in the Hartford. The honors still owing by the United States to the heroes of the navy 686

TRIBUTE TO GOVERNOR JAMES D. WILLIAMS.

Delivered at Wheatland, Indiana, July 4, 1883, at the unveiling of the monument over the tomb of the Hon. James D. Williams, governor of Indiana. A sketch of the life and an analysis of the character of Governor Williams. The birth of the state of Indiana, its infancy and growth. The formation of its government and the pioneers in its development to wealth and dignity. A picture of early times.....................706

TRIBUTE TO PRESIDENT GARFIELD.

Delivered September 21, 1881, to a meeting of citizens at Terre Haute, Indiana, gathered to testify their grief, at the most melancholy death of President James A. Garfield, and their sympathy with those left desolate in his home. A contribution to his memory of respect and personal regard, and an estimate of his character...........................718

THE LOUISIANA PURCHASE AND THE SOUTHLAND OF THE REPUBLIC.

An address delivered at Memphis, Tennessee, May 12, 1892, at the opening of the great bridge over the Mississippi river. Wealth, power and destiny of the Mississippi valley. The bridge. The Mississippi in 1801 the western boundary of the United States. Jefferson's efforts to secure the vast Louisiana territory beyond. Napoleon forced to cede it. Its mighty influence on the subsequent greatness of our country. The southland of the republic. Its recuperation and giant resources. Our relations with the peoples of South America. Nicaragua canal and Monroe doctrine. The Memphis of the Nile and the Memphis of the Mississippi 722

TRIBUTE TO SENATOR MORTON.

An address on the death of the Hon. Oliver P. Morton, a senator from Indiana, delivered in the senate of the United States, January 17, 1878. An estimate of his character... 747

CONSTANTINO BRUMIDI.

Remarks made in the senate of the United States, February 24, 1880. A tribute to this great artist, and a description of his beautiful works in the capitol at Washington.. 749

MAGNA CHARTA.

An address delivered before the State Bar Association of South Carolina, at Charleston, April 29, 1892. Review of the laws of ancient powers and the survival of their principles. The chief glory of the law belongs to the English speaking people. Origin of trial by jury. Runnimede and the Great Charter. Its provisions the foundation of our liberties. The mystery of its authorship. The petition of right. The bill of rights. The great writ of *habeas corpus*. Its origin. The power under the constitution to suspend it. The extraordinary omission of a bill of rights from the constitution as originally adopted. The supreme court of the United States and John Marshall the interpreter of the constitution... 753

TRIBUTE TO PROFESSOR MORSE.

Delivered April 16, 1872, at a meeting in the house of representatives of the United States in commemoration of the philosopher and inventor, Samuel F. B. Morse. A eulogy upon his genius and the grandeur of his scientific achievements.. 777

FORENSIC

JOHN E. COOK.

DEFENSE OF JOHN E. COOK

An argument delivered at Charles Town, Virginia, November 8, 1859, upon the trial of John E. Cook, indicted for treason, murder, and inciting slaves to rebel, in the Harper's Ferry insurrection.

John E. Cook was a brother-in-law of Ashbel P. Willard, then governor of Indiana. He was misled into this fatal enterprise and became one of the lieutenants of John Brown.

The trial took place in the circuit court of Jefferson county, Judge Richard Parker presiding.

The defense was conducted by Mr. Voorhees, Governor Willard, and Hon. Joseph E. McDonald of Indiana, and Thomas C. Green and Lawson Botts of Virginia.

The commonwealth was represented by Hon. Andrew Hunter.

The following jurors were impaneled and sworn: Lorenzo Etchison, William M. Lemon, George Show, Michael S. Hansecker, Charles T. Butler, Martin Swimley, Henry Selby, Joseph Hout, Thomas Chapline, Jacob S. Sheetz, John Snyder and Charles Huyett.

The jury returned a verdict of guilty of murder only, acquitting him of the charge of treason. It thus became possible for the governor to exercise the pardoning power. Every effort was made to induce the governor, Hon. Henry A. Wise, to exercise such power, but without avail, and John E. Cook was, in December, 1859, hanged at Charles Town.

With the Permission of the Court:

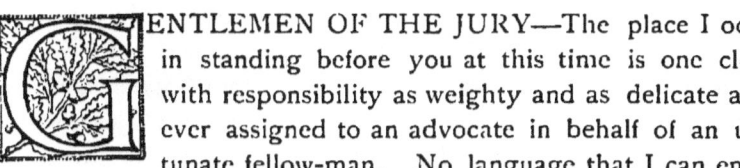ENTLEMEN OF THE JURY—The place I occupy in standing before you at this time is one clothed with responsibility as weighty and as delicate as was ever assigned to an advocate in behalf of an unfortunate fellow-man. No language that I can employ could give any additional force to the circumstances by which I am surrounded, and which press so heavily upon the public mind as well as on my own. I come, too, as a stranger to each one of you. Your faces I know only by the common image we bear to our Maker; but in your exalted character of citizens of the ancient

and proud commonwealth of Virginia, and of the American Union, I bear to you a passport of friendship and a letter of introduction.

I come from the sunset-side of your western mountains—from beyond the rivers that now skirt the borders of your great state; but I come not as an alien to a foreign land, but rather as one who returns to the home of his ancestors, and to the household from which he sprang. I come here not as an enemy, but as a friend, with interests common with yourselves, hoping for your hopes, and praying that the prosperity and glory of Virginia may be perpetual.

Nor do I forget that the very soil on which I live in my western home was once owned by this venerable commonwealth as much as the soil on which I now stand. Her laws there once prevailed, and all her institutions were there established as they are here. Not only my own state of Indiana, but also four other great states in the northwest, stand as enduring and lofty monuments of Virginia's magnanimity and princely liberality. Her donation to the general government made them sovereign states; and since God gave the fruitful land of Canaan to Moses and Israel, such a gift of present and future empire has never been made to any people. Coming from the bosom of one of these states, can I forget the fealty and duty which I owe to the supremacy of your laws, the sacredness of your citizenship, or the sovereignty of your state? Rather may the child forget its parent, and smite with unnatural hand the author of its being.

The mission on which I have visited your state is to me, and to those who are with me, one full of the bitterness and poison of calamity and grief. The high, the sacred, the holy duty of private friendship for a family fondly beloved by all who have ever witnessed their illustrations of the purest social virtues, commands, and alone commands, my presence here. And, while they are overwhelmed by the terrible blow which has fallen upon them through the action of the misguided young man at the bar, yet I speak their sentiments as well as my own when I say that one gratification, pure and unalloyed, has been afforded us since our melancholy arrival in your midst. It has been to witness the progress of this court, from day to day, surrounded by all that is calculated to bias the minds of men, but pursuing with calmness, with dignity, and impartiality the true course of the law and the even pathway of justice. I would not be true to the dictates of my own heart and judgment did I not bear voluntary and emphatic witness to the wisdom and patient kindness of his honor on the bench; the manly and generous spirit which has characterized the counsel for the prosecution; the true, devoted, and highly professional manner of the local counsel here for the defense; the scrupulous truthfulness of the witnesses who have testified, and the decorum and justness of the juries who have acted their parts from the first hour of this court to the present time—I speak in the hearing of the country. An important and memorable page in history is being written. Let it not be omitted that Virginia has thrown around a band of deluded men, who invaded her soil with treason and murder, all the safeguards of her constitution and laws, and placed them in her courts upon an equality with her own citizens. I know of what I speak, and my love of truth and sense of right forbid me to be silent on this point.

Gentlemen, I am not here on behalf of this pale-faced, fair-haired wanderer from his home and the paths of duty, to talk to you about technicalities of law born of laborious analysis by the light of the midnight lamp. I place him before you on no such ground. He is in the hands of friends who abhor the conduct of which he has been guilty. But does that fact debar him of human sympathy? Does the sinful act smite the erring brother with a leprosy which forbids the touch of the hand of affection? Is his voice of repentance and appeal for forgiveness stifled in his mouth? If so, the meek Saviour of the world would have recoiled with horror from Mary Magdalene, and spurned the repentant sorrow of Peter, who denied him. For my client I avow every sympathy. Fallen and undone, broken and ruined as he is by the fall, yet, from the depths of the fearful chasm in which he lies, I hear the common call which the wretched make for sympathy more clearly than if it issued from the loftiest pyramid of wealth and power. If he who made the earth, and hung the sun and moon and stars on high to give it light, and created man a joint heir of eternal wealth, and put within him an immortal spark of the celestial flame which surrounds his throne, could remember mercy in executing justice when his whole plan of divine government was assailed and deranged; when his law was set at defiance and violated; when the purity of Eden had been defiled by the presence and counsels of the serpent—why, so can I, and can you, when the wrong and the crime stand confessed, and every atonement is made to the majesty of the law which the prisoner has in his power to make.

Let us come near to each other and have a proper understanding. I am laboring with you for an object. I think I know something of the human heart, and of the leading attributes by which it is governed throughout the world. By virtue of those attributes, I feel that we may annihilate the distance that separates our homes, sweep away all blinding excitement, and sit down together and reason upon this most tragic and melancholy affair as becomes citizens of the same government, proud of the same lineage, actuated by the same interests, and forever linked to the same destiny.

You are not merely impaneled in your capacity as jurors to pass upon the life of this erratic youth before you, but the nation can not be divorced from a deep and permanent interest in your deliberations. The crime for which the law claims his life as forfeit is one connected with a question of the weightiest national import—a question which, without any fault of yours, has rudely strained and shaken the bonds which embrace and hold together the states of this Union. This trial is incident to that question, and must be met in the face of the whole nation, and in the view of the American people, as a matter of universal interest and concern. The very nature of the offense now under discussion lifts us all to a point of observation on which statesmen and patriots have long bent their anxious looks. And the pressing, ever present, and determined question of the hour which now sits with you in the jury-box, and will retire with you to your deliberations on your verdict, is, how shall you most fully meet the requirements of the American people at large; best conduce to the peace and repose of the Union; allay the rushing winds that are abroad on the face of the great deep; say peace, be still, to the angry elements of passion and treasonable agitation, and at the same time do all your duty as honest and conscientious men administering the laws of your state?

If it shall be in my power, in some measure, to point out the course by which these great objects may be attained, I shall mark this otherwise sad day on which I address you as the brightest to me in the calendar of time. And, further, if these objects are to be attained on your part by invoking into your midst, and following the winning counsels of the meek-eyed and gentle angel of mercy—if you can faithfully discharge your oath as jurors, and, at the same time, best meet the obligations which rest upon you as American citizens, by tempering the bitter cup which justice commends to the lips of the prisoner, with the ingredient of clemency, I know you, by the universal law of the human heart, will rejoice in such an opportunity, and join in the public and private happiness which will flow from your verdict. By the help of God, and appealing to him for the purity of the motives which animate my breast, I now proceed to demonstrate such a course as both just and wise in the case of John E. Cook.

First of all things, gentlemen of the jury, is your duty to Virginia. Whatever she requires at your hands, that you are to give. Your first love belongs to her; she is the matron who has nursed you, and the queen mother to whom you owe allegiance. As an advocate and defender at home of the doctrines of the state-rights men of the school of 1798, I do not come here to ask you to abate one jot or tittle of your affection and jealousy for the honor and interest of Virginia. Indeed, were such an invocation necessary, which I know it is not, I would invoke you by the great names of your history, by the memory of your ancient renown, by the thrilling associations of the classic soil on which we stand, and by the present commanding attitude which your commonwealth holds before the world, to be true and loyal to what she has been, what she is, and what she hopes to be.

But how stands Virginia in reference to the assault which was made upon her citizens and her soil at Harper's Ferry on the 17th day of October, 1859; and what vindication does she need at your hands for the outrage? Are the circumstances such as to require of her re-enactment of the Mosaic law, repealed by the benign teachings of the Nazarene on the shores of Galilee? Is she required to say, in a stern and inexorable spirit:

> And if any mischief follow, then thou shalt give life for life,
> Eye for eye, tooth for tooth, hand for hand, foot for foot,
> Burning for burning, wound for wound, stripe for stripe?

Not so. She asks nothing of the kind at your hands. Punishment has already been swift and sure. The measure of her vengeance for the great wrong committed against her is full, and her vindication is ample before the world. She met her invaders on the spot, and those who lifted their hands against her are, most of them, in the graves to which Virginians consigned them; a few bound in her prisons, and a few others wanderers and fugitives on the face of the earth. The executive and citizens of your state guided the bolt which fell upon this mad offspring of a loathsome fanaticism, and the invasion perished at a single blow. And in the spirit of the answer of Cushi to King David, I would say to you: "The enemies of the state of Virginia, and all that rise against her to do her hurt, be as these men are." But as the great King of Israel rose up and went to his chamber, and wept over the untimely fall of Absalom, the rebellious son of his own loins, who had lifted his paricidal hand against the life of an indulgent father, may not the world commend a similar emotion in the breast of a jury of Virginians over the sorrowful fate of the youthful prisoner at the bar! You will probably say that the lives of your citizens have been sacrificed. I answer that it is lamentably true; but it is also true that life has been taken already to atone for life; that the blood of murderers, older and wiser than the prisoner, has been poured out in response to the cry of the blood of your citizens from the ground.

You will say that your state has been polluted by the foot of the traitor. I answer that the footstep rested but as for a moment on your border, and was swept away by a whirlwind of patriotic indignation. You will say that your law has been violated; your dignity and honor as a free people insulted. I answer that, alas! it is too true; but I answer, also, that it is equally true that your laws have been fully, thoroughly, and justly vindicated. Here in this court, again and again, the sword of justice, wielded by an even hand, has fallen upon the miserable remnant of the confederated band who impiously mocked the integrity of the American Union by assailing the institutions of Virginia. The leader stands at the foot of the gallows, and its heights will expiate many crimes against the peace and laws of the country—not least amongst which is the crime of enlisting young men, such as the prisoner, in a cruise of piracy against you and me, and all law-abiding citizens of this happy Union. Let the leader of the mutiny on ship-board perish; but if it appears that young men have followed false guidance, and been bound in the despotism of an iron will, order them back to duty, and give them one more chance to show whether they are worthy of life or death. Virginia can thus afford to act. It is one of the chief blessings of power that it can extend mercy to the weak, and the crown jewel of courage is magnanimity to the fallen.

But there is another point on which Virginia, though mourning for the death of her citizens, has triumphantly met the aspersions and calumnies of the enemies of her domestic institutions by reason of the late outbreak at Harper's Ferry. The institution of domestic slavery to-day stands before the world more fully justified than ever before in the history of this or, indeed, perhaps, of any other country. The liberator, urged on by false and spurious philanthropy, deceitful and sinister in its origin, and selfish and corrupt in its practice, came into your midst to set the bondsman free, and though violence tore him from his master, though liberty was sounded in his ear, though a leader was proclaimed to lead him to the promised land, though an impiously self-styled Moses of deliverance came in the might of the sword and placed arms of bold attack and strong defense in his hands, yet what a spectacle do we behold! The bondsman refuses to be free; drops the implements of war from his hands; is deaf to the call of freedom; turns against his liberators; and, by instinct, obeys the injunction of Paul by returning to his master! Shall this pass for nothing? Shall no note be made of this piece of the logic of our government? Shall the voice of the African himself die unheard on the question of his own freedom? No. It shall be perpetuated. It shall be put in the record.

The slave himself, under circumstances the most tempting and favorable to his love of freedom, if he has any, surrounded by men and scenes beckoning him on to vengeance, to liberty, and dominion, with the power of life and death over his master in his hands, and the world open before him, with the manacle and chain, which was never forged or welded except in the heated furnace of a riotous and prurient imagination, stricken from his body, turns eagerly and fondly to the condition assigned him by the laws, not merely of Virginia, not merely of legislatures and law-makers, but by the law of his being, by the law which governs his relation to a white man wherever the contact exists, by the law which made the hewers of wood and drawers of water under a government formed by God himself, and which, since the world began down to the present time, has made the inferior subordinate to the superior whenever and wherever two unequal races have been brought together. Let this fact go forth to the country. Let it be fully understood by those men and women who languish and sigh over the condition of your institutions that their sympathy is repudiated, and that they themselves are despised by both races in the South. This, too, Virginia has proven.

Is there anything left to be done by your verdict in peremptorily taking the life of the prisoner, and offering it a sacrifice to heal the wrongs of your state? I humbly conceive that Virginia in no respect needs such a sacrifice. This much I think I have shown.

And now let us turn to the prisoner. If Virginia, through you, can afford to be clement, your inquiry will then be, is the object on whom you are asked to bestow your clemency worthy to receive it? I know the field on which I now enter is filled with preconceived ideas, but in the spirit of truth I shall explore it, and by the truth of what I say I am willing that my unfortunate client may be judged by you, and, moreover, by that God in whose presence no hidden things exist, and before whom, at no distant day, you and I shall stand with him and see him and know him as he is, and not as we see him and know him now, encompassed by the dread and awful calamities of the present hour.

Who is John E. Cook? He has the right himself to be heard before you; but I will answer for him. Sprung from an ancestry of loyal attachment to the American government, he inherits no blood of tainted impurity. His grandfather an officer of the Revolution, by which your liberty as well as mine was achieved, and his gray-haired father, who lives to weep over him, a soldier of the war of 1812, he brings no dishonored lineage into your presence. If the blood which flows in his veins has been offered against your peace, the same blood in the veins of those from whose loins he sprang has been offered in fierce shock of battle and foreign invasion in behalf of the people of Virginia and the Union. Born of a parent stock occupying the middle walks of life, and possessed of all those tender and domestic virtues which escape the contamination of those vices that dwell on the frozen peaks, or in the dark and deep caverns of society, he would not have been here had precept and example been remembered in the prodigal wanderings of his short and checkered life. Poor deluded boy! wayward, misled child! An evil star presided over thy natal hour and smote it with gloom. The hour in which thy mother bore thee and blessed thee as her blue-eyed babe upon her knee is to her now one of bitterness as she stands near the bank of the chill river of death and looks back on a name hitherto as unspotted and as pure as the unstained snow. May God stand by and sustain her, and preserve the mothers of Virginia from the waves of sorrow that now roll over her!

Not only the ancestry of John E. Cook, but all with whom his life is now bound up, stand before the country as your friends, and the friends of the constitution as handed down to us by the valor and wisdom of Washington. I will not shrink from the full and absolute recognition of my position. You and I, gentlemen of the jury, can have no secrets in this case from one another. We will withdraw the curtains, and look each other fully in the face. A citizen of the state in which I live, who, by virtue of his brilliant and commanding intellect, and because of his sound and national principles, has been placed at an early period of his life in the highest position in the power of a state to give, is here beside me, and wears near his heart a sister's likeness to this boy. And there is not in the wide world, on the broad green face of the earth, a man, whose heart is not wholly abandoned to selfish depravity, who will not say that his presence here is commanded by honor, love, duty, and fidelity to all that ennobles our poor, fallen race. Let poor, miserable, despised, loathed, spurned, and abhorred miscreants cavil and revile at this proud act of painful duty. The true and eternal impulses of the human heart, the world over, constitute our appellate court.

But the governor of the state of Indiana needs neither vindication nor defense as a statesman of catholic opinions, nor as a man fully appreciating the duties of domestic life. Rather do I allude to his presence here and his position on the agitating questions of the day, to show that something else besides ancestral inheritance or the teachings of family connections has given the fatal bias to the prisoner's mind, which led him away from the worship of his own household gods, and into the communion of idolators, aliens, and enemies of the pure faith of an American citizen. And it seems to me, in view of the services which those who love this boy have rendered to their country, and in view of their devotion to the true construction of the constitution and the injunctions of our fathers, I might rehearse and quote to you with propriety a passage from the history of the latter years of the wisest king Israel ever had:

> For it came to pass when Solomon was old that his wives turned away his heart after other gods; and his heart was not perfect with the Lord his God as was the heart of David, his father. For Solomon went after Ashtoreth, the goddess of the Zidonians, and after Milcom, the abomination of the Ammonites.
> And Solomon did evil in the sight of the Lord, and went not fully after the Lord as did David, his father.
> And the Lord was angry with Solomon because his heart was turned from the Lord God of Israel which had appeared unto him twice.
> And had commanded him concerning this thing that he should not go after other gods; but he kept not that which the Lord commanded.
> Wherefore the Lord said unto Solomon, forasmuch as this is done of thee, and thou hast not kept my covenant and my statutes which I commanded thee, I will surely rend the kingdom from thee, and will give it to thy servant.
> Notwithstanding, in thy days I will not do it for David, thy father's sake.

The king, who was forgiven, and spared not merely his life, but his kingdom also, and his glory during his lifetime because of the loyalty of his father who had gone before him, was old and very wise and full of experience. The prisoner before you has done no more than to disobey your covenants and statutes, and pleads that it has been done in the early morning of life, his first offense, and under the baneful influence of a school of philosophy which he once thought sincere and right, but which he now here, once and forever, to you, and before the world, renounces as false, pernicious and pestilential. Shall man be more intolerant than God? Shall you be less merciful than he, in whose presence your only plea will be mercy! mercy! mercy! Will you say you dare not recommend mercy to John E. Cook, when divine examples and the appeals of your own conscience are on your side? I will never believe it until the appalling fact is announced by you.

But let us advance. I have spoken of Cook, his parentage, and connections. Again comes the question, who is he? And now I proceed to answer it with reference to the transactions at Harper's Ferry, and with reference to the facts of the case. Let us spread broad and wide before us the moving panorama of evil which reaches its denouement at Harper's Ferry.

There are hearts and feelings woven in the destiny of the prisoner which will be relieved and solaced as far as truth dragged up from the depths of this misfortune can relieve and solace them. In an evil hour—and may it be forever accursed!—John E. Cook met John Brown on the prostituted plains of Kansas. On that field of fanaticism, three years ago, this fair and gentle youth was thrown into contact with the pirate and robber of civil warfare. To others whose sympathies he has enlisted I will leave the task of transmitting John Brown as a martyr and hero to posterity. In my eyes he stands the chief of criminals, the thief of property stolen—horses and slaves—from the citizens of Missouri, a falsifier here in this court, as I shall yet show, and a murderer not only of your citizens, but of the young men who have already lost their lives in his bloody foray on your border. This is not pleasant to say, but it is the truth, and as such ought to be and shall be said.

You have seen John Brown, the leader. Now look on John Cook, the follower. He is in evidence before you. Never did I plead for a face that I was more willing to show. If evil is there, I have not seen it. If murder is there, I am to learn to mark the lines of the murderer anew. If the assassin is in that young face, then commend me to the look of an assassin. No, gentlemen, it is a face for a mother to love, and a sister to idolize, and in which the natural goodness of his heart pleads trumpet-tongued against the deep damnation that estranged him from home and its principles.

Let us look at the meeting of these two men. Place them side by side. Put the young face by the old face; the young head by the old head. We have seen somewhat of the history of the young man. Look now for a moment at the history of the old man. He did not go to Kansas as a peaceable settler with his interests linked to the legitimate growth and prosperity of that ill-fated territory. He went there, in the language of one who has spoken for him since his confinement here, as the Moses of the slaves' deliverance. He went there to fulfill a dream, which had tortured his brain for thirty years, that he was to be the leader of a second exodus from bondage. He went there for war and not for peace. He went there to call around him the wayward and unstable elements of a society in which the bonds of order, law, and religion were loosened, and the angry demon of discord was unchained. Storm was his element by his own showing. He courted the fierce tempest. He sowed the wind that he might reap the whirlwind. He invoked the lightning and gloried in its devastation. Sixty summers and winters had passed over his head, and planted the seeds of spring and gathered the harvests of autumn in the fields of his experience. He was the hero, too, of battles there. If laurels could be gained in such a fratricidal war as raged in Kansas, he had them on his brow. Ossawatomie was given to him, and added to his name by the insanity of the crazy crew of the North as Napoleon conferred the names of battle-fields on his favorite marshals. The action of Black Jack, too, gave him consideration, circumstance and condition with philanthropists of bastard quality, carpet-knight heroes in Boston, and servile followers of fanaticism throughout the country. His courage is now lauded to the skies by men who have none of it themselves. This virtue, I admit, he has—linked, however, with a thousand crimes. An iron will, with which to accomplish evil under the skillful guise of good, I also admit to be in his possession—rendering his influence over the young all the more despotic and dangerous.

Imagine, if you please, the bark on which this young man at the bar and all his hopes were freighted, laid alongside of the old weather-beaten and murderous man-of-war whose character I have placed before you.

The one was stern and bent upon a fatal voyage. Grim-visaged war, civil commotion, pillage and death, disunion and universal desolation thronged through the mind of John Brown. To him law was nothing, the Union was nothing, the peace and welfare of the country were nothing, the lives of the citizens of Virginia were nothing. Though a red sea of blood rolled before him, yet he lifted up his hand and cried " Forward!" Shall he now shrink from his prominence, and attempt to shrivel back to the grade of his recruits and subalterns? Shall he deny his bad pre-eminence, and say that he did not incite the revolt which has involved his followers in ruin? Shall he stand before this court and before the country, and deny that he was the master spirit, and gathered together the young men who followed him to the death in this mad expedition? No! his own hand signs himself "commander-in-chief," and shows the proper distinction which should be made between himself and the men who, in an evil moment, obeyed his orders.

Now turn to the contrast again and behold the prisoner. Young and new to the rough ways of life, his unsandaled foot tender and unused to the journey before him, a waif on the ocean, at the mercy of the current which might assail him, and unfortunately endowed with that fearful gift which causes one to walk as in a dream through all the vicissitudes of a lifetime; severed and wandering from the sustaining and protecting ties of kindred, he gave, without knowing his destination or purpose, a pledge of military obedience to John Brown, "commander-in-chief."

Gentlemen of the jury, there is one character which, in the economy of God's providence, has been placed upon the earth, but perhaps has never been fully drawn, and is most difficult to draw. It is the character of him who glides down the stream of life in a trance, dreams as he floats along, and sees visions on either shore. Realities exist in this world, no doubt. Practical views are certainly the best. But that impalpable, airy, and unsubstantial creations of the busy imagination come now and then, and lure the children of men to chase the "will-o'-the-wisp" over the dangerous morasses of life, is as true as that we have our allotted pilgrimage of threescore years and ten. Who has not beheld the young man of strict moral culture, impressed with high principles of right, and gifted with good intellect, start out upon the dusty and well-beaten highway which millions have trod before him, only to turn aside at the first inviting grove of pleasure, the first call of some fanciful wood nymph, or to follow over the falls of ruin and death some meandering stream whose beautiful surface caught his eye? To such a one right and wrong are utter abstractions, and have no relation whatever to things that exist. Give to such a mind a premise, however false, and from it will spring a castle in the air with proportions as true and just as the most faultless architecture ever framed by mathematical skill. Some lay the foundation of their actions on the rock and are never overthrown. Some build upon the shifting sand, and fall when the storm comes. But in each instance the building may be the same in its symmetry. So with the deductions of the mind. All depends, not upon the reasoning, but upon the basis on which thought rests, and which supports the edifice of our conclusions. The enthusiast and visionary takes his standpoint, and fixes the premises of his conduct from caprice and the circumstances which have obtained the ascendency over his mind. That such has been the character and such the conduct of the prisoner, without one spark of malignity of heart, or a single impulse of depravity, all the evidence in this case clearly establishes.

Some general ideas gilded over by the alluring title of freedom were held out to him by Brown, and formed the basis of what seemed to him duty and honor. If ever man charged with crime was lifted up by the evidence of his case above the ignoble traits of the ordinary felon, the prisoner is thus distinguished. Instead of the eager and willing bandit, anxious to join a hoary leader bent on mischief—instead of the outlaw in mind and character gloomily and fiercely pondering revenge against his fellow-men for fancied or real injuries—we see from the evidence a kind though wayward heart, a cheerful, obliging, though visionary mind. With children everywhere he has been a favorite; and since little children crept upon the knee of the Saviour eighteen hundred years ago, they have been the most infallible judges of a gentle and affectionate heart. Amiability and sweetness of temper he has carried with him through the world; and he brings that trait now before you to show that strong inducements and powerful incentives must have been brought to bear in order to engage him in an enterprise so desperate as that for which his life is now so sadly imperiled.

What motive controlled him to this action? A crime without a motive can not exist. Was it a motive of bloodshed? His character forbids the thought. Was it the motive of disloyalty to a government cemented by the blood of his ancestors, and defended by all who are near to him by ties of kindred? Not a syllable of proof warrants such a conclusion. Was his motive robbery or unholy gain? Other fields are more inviting to the land pirate; but the thought of plunder never crossed a mind like his. One answer, and one alone, is to be given to all these questions. John Brown was the despotic leader and John E. Cook was an ill-fated follower of an enterprise whose horror he now realizes and deplores. I defy the man, here or elsewhere, who has ever known John E. Cook, who has ever looked once fully into his face and learned anything of his history, to lay his hand on his heart and say that he believes him guilty of the origin or the results of the outbreak at Harper's Ferry.

Here, then, are the two characters whom you are thinking to punish alike. Can it be that a jury of Christian men will find no discrimination should be made between them? Are the tempter and the tempted the same in your eyes? Is the beguiled youth to die the same as the old offender who has pondered his crimes for thirty years? Are there no grades in your estimation of guilt? Is each one, without respect to age or circumstance, to be beaten with the same number of stripes? Such is not the law, human or divine. We are all to be rewarded according to our works, whether in punishment for evil, or blessings for good that we have done. You are here to do justice, and if justice requires the same fate to befall Cook that befalls Brown, I know nothing of her rules, and do not care to learn. They are as widely asunder in all that constitutes guilt as the poles of the earth, and should be dealt with accordingly. It is in your power to do so, and by the principles by which you yourselves are willing to be judged hereafter, I implore you to do it!

Come with me, however, gentlemen, and let us approach the spot where the tragedy of the 17th of October occurred, and analyze the conduct of the prisoner there. It is not true that he came as a citizen to your state and gained a home in your midst to betray you. He was ordered to take his position at Harper's Ferry in advance of his party for the sole purpose of ascertaining whether Colonel Forbes, of New York, had divulged the plan. This order came from John Brown, the "commander-in-chief," and was doubtless a matter of as much interest to others of prominent station as to himself. Cook simply obeyed—no more. There is not a particle of evidence that he tampered with your slaves during his temporary residence. On the contrary, it is admitted on all hands that he did not. His position there is well defined. Nor was he from under the cold, stern eye of his leader. From the top of the mountain his chief looked down upon him, and held him as within a charmed circle. Would Cook have lived a day had he tried to break the meshes which environed him?

Happy the hour in which he had made the attempt even had he perished, but, in fixing the measure of his guilt, the circumstances by which he was surrounded must all be weighed. At every step we see him as the instrument in the hands of other men, and not as originating or advising anything

His conduct toward that elegant and excellent gentleman, Colonel Washington, is matter of sore regret to his friends, and also to himself. It is the one act most difficult of all others to reconcile with the well-known character of the man. But even there his offense is palliated by the dictatorship which governed him. At the first glance we see a high-toned gentleman's hospitality abused. This has been used to aggravate his acknowledged offenses. But the truth is, that when Cook first visited Colonel

Washington's house and received from him various acts of kindness, the thought that soon he was to be ordered back over that threshold in a hostile manner had never entered his brain. The act was not Cook's but Brown's. The mere soldier is never punished for the outrages of his commander. And when you allow that the prisoner's great error was the enlistment under the leadership of Brown in the first place, then you must admit that everything else has followed in logical sequence. Obedience and fidelity to a leader in a false and pernicious cause are entitled to offset, in some measure at least, the evil that has flown from them.

But the prisoner took certain weapons hallowed by great and sacred associations from the possession of Colonel Washington. Ah! in this he is once more consistent with the visionary and dreamy cast of his mind. The act was not plunder, for he pledged their safe return to their owner, and has faithfully kept that pledge to the full extent of his power. But his wayward fancy was caught with the idea that a spell of enchantment hung around them, and that, like the relics of a saint, they would bless and prosper any cause in which they were invoked. The sword of Frederick the Great and the pistols of Lafayette linked to the name and family of Washington! With what a charm such associations would strike the poetic temperament of a young enthusiast embarked in an enterprise presenting to his perverted imagination the incentives of danger and glory; and if a new order of things was to be inaugurated, and storm and revolution were to shake the country and the world, like the heart of the Bruce, or the eagles of Napoleon, these warlike incentives of heroes were to fascinate and allure followers, and hallow the battles in which they were lifted. The mind of the prisoner is fully capable of dreaming such dreams, and nursing such visions.

But it has been said that Cook left the scene at Harper's Ferry at an early hour to avoid the danger of the occasion, and thus broke faith with his comrades in wrong. Even this is wholly untrue. Again we find the faithful, obedient subaltern carrying out the orders of his chief, and when he had crossed the river and fulfilled the commands of Brown, he did what Brown's own son would not do—by returning and exposing himself to the fire of the soldiers and citizens for the relief of Brown and his party. We see much, alas! too much, to condemn in his conduct, but nothing to despise; we look in vain for an act that belongs to a base or malignant nature. Let the hand of chastisement fall gently on the errors of such as him, and reserve your heavy blows for such as commit crime from motives of depravity.

Up to this point I have followed the prisoner and traced his immediate connection with this sad affair. You have everything before you. You have heard his own account of his strange and infatuated wanderings up and down the earth with John Brown and his coadjutors; how like a fiction it all seems, and yet how lamentably true; how unreal to minds like ours; how like the fever dream of a mind warped and disordered to the borders of insanity does the part which the prisoner has played seem to every practical judgment! Is there nothing in it all that affords you the dearest privilege which man has on earth—the privilege of being merciful? Why, the very thief on the cross, for a single moment's repentance over his crimes, received absolute forgiveness, and was rewarded with paradise.

But, gentlemen, in estimating the magnitude of this young man's guilt, there is one fact which is proven in his behalf by the current history of the day which you can not fail to consider. Shall John E. Cook perish, and the real criminals who for twenty years have taught the principles on which he acted hear no voice from this spot? Shall no mark be placed on them? Shall this occasion pass away, and the prime felons who attacked your soil and murdered your citizens at Harper's Ferry escape? The indictment before us says that the prisoner was "seduced by the false and malignant counsels of other traitorous persons." Never was a sentence written more just and true. "False and malignant counsels" have been dropping for years, as deadly and blighting as the poison of the Bohun Upas tree, from the tongues of evil and traitorous persons in that section of the Union to which the prisoner belongs. They have seduced not only his mind, but many others, honest and misguided like him, to regard the crime at Harper's Ferry as no crime, your rights as unmitigated wrongs, and the constitution of the country as a league with hell and a covenant with death. On the skirts of the leaders of abolition fanaticism in the North is every drop of blood shed in the conflict at Harper's Ferry; on their souls rests the crime of murder for every life there lost; and all the waters of the ocean could not wash the stains of slaughter from their treacherous and guilty hands.

A noted Boston abolitionist (Wendell Phillips), a few days ago, at Brooklyn, New York, in the presence of thousands, speaking of this tragic occurrence, says: "It is the natural result of anti-slavery teaching. For one, I accept it. I expected it." I, too, accept it in the same light, and so will the country. Those who taught, and not those who believed and acted, are the men of crime in the sight of God. And to guard other young men, so far as in my power, from the fatal snare which has been tightened around the hopes and destiny of John E. Cook, and to show who are fully responsible for his conduct, I intend to link with this trial the names of wiser and older men than he; and, if he is to be punished and consigned to a wretched doom, they shall stand beside him in the public stocks; they shall be pilloried forever in public shame as "the evil and traitorous persons who seduced him to his ruin by their false and malignant counsels."

The chief of these men, the leader of a great party, a senator of long standing, has announced to the country that there is a higher law than the constitution, which guarantees to each man the full exercise of his own inclination. The prisoner before you has simply acted on the law of Wm. H. Seward, and not the law of his fathers. He has followed the Mahomet of an incendiary faith. Come forth, ye sages of abolitionism, who now cower and skulk under hasty denials of your complicity with the bloody result of your wicked and unholy doctrines, and take your places on the witness stand. Tell the world why this thing has happened. Tell this jury why they are trying John E. Cook for his life. You advised his conduct and taught him that he was doing right. You taught him a higher law and then pointed out to him the field of action. Let facts be submitted. Mr. Seward, in speaking of slavery, says: "It can and must be abolished, and you and I must do it." What worse did the prisoner attempt?

Again, he said, upon this same subject, "Circumstances determine possibilities;" and doubtless the circumstances with which John Brown had connected his plans made them possible in his estimation, for it is in evidence before the country, unimpeached and uncontradicted, that the great senator of New York had the whole matter submitted to him, and only whispered back, in response, that he had better not been told. He has boldly announced an irrepressible conflict between the free and slave states of this Union. These seditious phrases, "higher law" and "irrepressible conflict," warrant and invite the construction which the prisoner and his young deluded companions placed upon them. Yet they are either in chains, with the frightful gibbet in full view, or sleep in dishonored graves, while the apostle and master spirit of insurrection is loaded with honors and fares sumptuously every day. Such is poor, short-handed justice in this world.

An old man, and for long years a member of the national congress from Ohio, next shall testify here before you that he taught the prisoner the terrible error which now involves his life. Servile insurrections have forever been on the tongue and lips of Joshua R. Giddings. He says "that when the contest shall come, when the thunder shall roll and the lightning flash, and when the slaves shall rise in the South, in imitation of the horrid scenes of the West Indies, when the southern man shall turn pale and tremble, when your dwellings shall smoke with the torch of the incendiary, and dismay sit on each countenance, he will hail it as the approaching dawn of that political and moral millennium which he is well assured will come upon the world." The atrocity of these sentiments chills the blood of honest patriots, and no part of the prisoner's conduct equals their bloody import. Shall the old leader escape and the young follower die? Shall the teacher, whose doctrines told the prisoner that what he did was right, go unscathed of the lightning which he has unchained? If so, Justice has fled from her temples on earth, and awaits us only on high to measure out what is right between man and man.

The men who have misled this boy to his ruin shall here receive my maledictions. They shrink back from him now in the hour of his calamity. They lift up their hands and say, Avaunt! to the bloody specter which their infernal orgies have summoned up.

You hear them all over the land ejaculating through false, pale, coward lips, "Thou canst not say I did it," when their hands are reeking with all the blood that has been shed and which yet awaits the extreme penalty of the law. False, fleeting, perjured traitors, false to those who have acted upon your principles, false to friends as well as country, and perjured before the constitution of the republic—ministers who profess to be of God who told this boy here to carry a Sharps rifle to Kansas instead of his mother's Bible—shall this jury, this court, and this country forget their guilt and their infamy because a victim to their precepts is yielding up his life before you? May God forget me if I here, in the presence of this pale face, forget to denounce with the withering, blighting, blasting power of majestic truth, the tall and stately criminals of the northern states of this Union.

The visionary mind of the prisoner heard from a member of congress from Massachusetts that a new constitution, a new Bible, and a new God were to be inaugurated and to possess the country. They were to be *new*, because they were to be anti-slavery, for the old constitution, and the old Bible, and the God of our fathers, the ancient Lord God of Israel, the same yesterday, today, and forever, were not on the side of abolitionism. Is there no mitigation for his doom in the fact that he took his life in his hand, and aimed at that which a coward taught him, but dared not himself attempt.

Base, pusillanimous demagogues have led the prisoner to the bar, but while he suffers—if suffer he must—they, too, shall have their recreant limbs broken on the wheel. I will not leave the soil of Virginia, I will not let this awful occasion pass into history, without giving a voice and an utterance to its true purport and meaning, without heaping upon its authors the load of execration which they are to bear henceforth and forever.

Day after day and year after year has the baleful simoon of revolution, anarchy, discord, hostility to the South and her institutions swept over that section of the country in which the lot of the prisoner has been cast. That he has been poisoned by its breath should not cut him off from human sympathy; rather should it render every heart clement toward him. He never sought place or station, but sought merely to develop those doctrines which evil and traitorous persons had caused him to believe were true. Ministers, editors, and politicians—Beecher, Parker, Seward, Giddings, Sumner, Hale, and a host of lesser lights of each class—who in this court-room, who in this vast country, who in the wide world who shall read this trial, believes them not guilty as charged in the indictment in all the counts to a deeper and far more fearful extent than John E. Cook. Midnight gloom is not more somber in contrast with the blazing light of the meridian sun than is the guilt of such men in comparison with that which overwhelms the prisoner. They put in motion the maelstrom which has engulfed him. They started the torrent which has borne him over the precipice. They called forth from the caverns the tempest which wrecked him on a sunken reef. Before God, and in the light of eternal truth, the disaster at Harper's Ferry is their act, and not his. May the ghost of each victim to their doctrines of disunion and abomination sit heavy on their guilty souls! May the fate of the prisoner, whatever it may be, disturb their slumbers and paralyze their arms when they are again raised against the peace of the country and the lives of its citizens!

I know by the gleam of each eye into which I look in this jury-box, that if these men could change places with young Cook, you would gladly say to him, "Go, erring and repentant youth, our vengeance shall fall on those who paid their money, urged on the attack, and guided the blow." Let me appeal to you, gentlemen of the jury, in the name of eternal truth and everlasting right, is nothing to be forgiven to youth, to inexperience, to a gentle, kind heart, to a wayward and peculiar though not vicious character, strangely apt to be led by present influences? I have shown you what those influences, generally and specially, have been over the mind of the prisoner. I have shown you the malign influence of his direct leader. I have shown you, also, the "false and malignant counsels" in behalf of this sad enterprise, emanating from those in place, power, and position. It might have been your prodigal son borne away and seduced by such counsels, as well as my young client. Do with him as you would have your own child dealt by under like circumstances. He has been stolen from the principles of his ancestors and betrayed from the teachings of his kindred. If he was your own handsome child, repentant and confessing his wrong to his conntry, what would you wish a jury of strangers to do? That do yourselves. By that rule guide your verdict; and the poor boon of mercy will not be cut off from him. He thought the country was about to be convulsed; that the slave was pining for an opportunity to rise against his master; that two-thirds of the laboring population of the country, North and South, would flock to the standard of revolt; that a single day would bring ten, fifty—yea, a hundred thousand men—to arms in behalf of the insurrection of the slaves. This is in evidence. Who are responsible for such terribly false views, and what kind of a visionary and dreaming mind is that which has so fatally entertained them?

That the prisoner's mind is pliant to the impressions, whether for good or for evil, by which it is surrounded, let his first interview in his prison with Governor Willard, in the presence of your senator, Colonel Mason, bear witness. His error was placed before him. His wrong to his family and his country was drawn by a patriotic, and, at the same time, an affectionate hand. His natural being at once asserted its sway. The influence of good, and not of evil, once more controlled him as in the days of his childhood; and now here before you he has the merit at least of a loyal citizen, making all the atonement in his power for the wrong which he has committed. That he has told strictly the truth in his statement is proven by every word of evidence in this cause.

Gentlemen, you have this case. I surrender into your hands the issues of life and death. As long as you live, a more important case than this you will never be called to try. Consider it, therefore, well in all its bearings. I have tried to show you those facts which go to palliate the conduct of the prisoner. Shall I go home and say that in justice you remembered not mercy to him? Leave the door of clemency open; do not shut it by a wholesale conviction. Remember that life is an awful and a sacred thing; remember that death is terrible—terrible at any time, and in any form.

> Come to the bridal chamber, Death!
>   Come when the mother feels
> For the first time, her first-born's breath;
>   Come when the blessed seals
> That close the pestilence are broke,
> And crowded cities wail its stroke;
> Come in consumption's ghastly form,
> The earthquake's shock, the ocean's storm;
> Come when the heart beats high and warm
>   With banquet, song, and dance, and wine,
> And thou art terrible. The groan,
> The knell, the pall, the bier,
> And all we know, or dream, or fear
>   Of agony, are thine.

But when to the frightful mien of the grim monster, when to the chill visage of the spirit of the glass and scythe, is added the hated, dreaded specter of the gibbet, we turn shuddering from the accumulated horror. God spare this boy, and those who love him, from such a scene of woe.

I part from you now, and most likely forever. When we next meet—when I next look upon your faces and you on mine—it will be in that land and before that tribunal where the only plea that will save you or me from a worse fate than awaits the prisoner, will be mercy. Charity is the paramount virtue; all else is as sounding brass and a tinkling symbol. Charity suffereth long, and is kind. Forbid it not to come into your deliberation; and, when your last hour comes, the memory that you allowed it to plead for your erring brother, John E. Cook, will brighten your passage over the dark river, and rise by your side as an interceding angel in that day when your trial as well as his shall be determined by a just but merciful God.

I thank the court and you, gentlemen, for your patient kindness, and I am done.

MARY HARRIS.

DEFENSE OF MARY HARRIS

Mary Harris was indicted, in the supreme court of the District of Columbia, for killing Adoniram J. Burroughs, on January 30, 1865, in the treasury department, at the city of Washington.

The killing grew out of Burrough's inhuman and brutal disregard of his promise of marriage to Miss Harris, producing in her a marked type of paroxysmal insanity.

The trial began in said court, sitting as a criminal court, at the city of Washington, the Honorable Andrew Wylie, associate justice, presiding, on July 3, 1865, the government being represented by E. C. Carrington, Esquire, district attorney, and Nathaniel Wilson, assistant district attorney, and the prisoner by Mr. Voorhees, Jos. H. Bradley, Esquire, of the District of Columbia, Judge James Hughes, of Indiana, Judge Mason, of Iowa, and William Y. Fendall, of the District of Columbia.

Moses T. Parker, Thomas H. Barron, Francis Ballenger, Michael R. Coombs, Alexander Lammond, Thomas A. Tolson, John Scrivenner, Butler Baker, Donald McCathran, and Zach. B. Brooke, were selected and sworn as jurors.

On July 18th Mr. Voorhees made the closing argument for the defense, which follows, and after the closing argument for the government, by the district attorney, the case was given to the jury, which returned a verdict of "not guilty" after five minutes deliberation.

May It Please the Court, and You, Gentlemen of the Jury:

IT is not necessary for me to attempt to increase your sense of the solemnity of the issue which is placed in your hands. Nor need I dwell upon the fact that this is one of the most remarkable cases ever submitted to a jury for trial. In many of its aspects it wears features more startling and extraordinary than we have hitherto met with in the annals of jurisprudence. There is no man in this court-room, no one throughout this broad land, whatever his experience or profession may be, who has ever seen its like in all respects before.

A few months ago, in open day, in one of the public buildings of this capital, and in the presence of numerous observers, a human being was shot down by the frail hand of the prisoner at the bar, and sent to his final, dread account. The homicide mentioned in the indictment was thus committed; and, if it was deliberate, rational murder, then the blood of innocence is crying unappeased from the ground. But what are the elements which constitute this baleful crime? From that hour presaging woe to the human race, when the first man born of woman became a murderer, down to the present time, we have on record the frightful characteristics of the murderer. He is a being in whose heart the fires of malice and hate glow in perpetual flames, in whose face the image of God is blotted out, in whose eyes the light of mercy and love is forever quenched, who lies in wait like the tiger for his prey, and who strikes his unsuspecting and unoffending victim from motives of revenge or the lust of gain. Around such a being there centers every conception of horror which the human mind can embrace. All nature, animate and inanimate, the very earth and sky, recoil from him who bears the primal curse, and there is no communion for his blackened spirit this side of the abodes of the lost.

But turn from this faint picture of a real murderer to the delicate, gentle being before you. We are told that deliberate and atrocious murder has been committed, and that the criminal is in court. We are told that a brutal assassination has been accomplished, and that the lurking and ferocious assassin is in our presence. Where, gentlemen, where? Am I to be told that this heart-broken young girl, with her innocent, appealing face, and look of supplicating dependence on you, is the fierce and malignant monster of guilt which is described in the indictment and in the inflammatory language of the prosecution? Am I to be told that her heart conceived and her hand executed that crime for which the Almighty marked the brow of Cain?

Let us pause and reason together for a few moments on a primary question in this case. The life of this defendant, from the days of her early and happy childhood to the present hour, has been investigated and laid open before you. Every trait of her character, all the general incidents of her conduct since she was ten years old, have been elucidated and detailed in your hearing. Of what vice has she ever been guilty? In what immorality has she ever indulged? Not one, at no time, and under no circumstances. Her life has been amiable, kind, affectionate, blameless and pure. Troops of friends, of the best and most irreproachable in the land, have gathered about her in her quiet sphere at every stage of her checkered existence. These files of depositions, declaring all her ways for nearly ten years past, attest these facts. Then, at the very threshold of this case, you are to answer this question: Can a young and generous mind, wholly uncontaminated with vice, unsullied and unstained by contact with the evil practices of life, without previous training even in the contemplation of crime, at once, while in a healthy state, in the undisturbed enjoyment of all its faculties, incur that awful grade of guilt at which civilized human nature in all ages stands aghast? Is it within your experience that the soil of virtue bears spontaneously the hideous fruits of vice? Are there no gradations in human character and conduct? Where is the hardened criminal who ever ascended the gibbet in expiation of his offenses who has not marked his downfall from small beginnings, increasing gradually and swelling in volume until he was hurled onward to the commission of those gigantic crimes for which the law claimed his life as forfeit? And yet you are called on to believe that this defendant, at one single bound, sprang from the paths of virtue, gentleness, and purity, without any intervening preparation, to the highest and most revolting grade of guilt and ferocity known to human society. Those who have predetermined her guilt and passed a verdict in advance of the evidence and the law may indulge in this absurd and repulsive philosophy. They may cherish this libel on human nature; and, in doing so, they may as well go further. Let the school-houses be torn down and the churches abandoned. The instruction and moral culture of youth are useless and in vain. The precepts of morality and the principles of religion afford no security to the minds of their possessors from the sudden, instantaneous development of the most appalling wickedness.

In the name of reason and universal experience I utterly repudiate this shocking theory, which the prosecution is forced to embrace before it can proceed a single step against the life of this girl. In the name of undefiled and virtuous human nature, I repel it. In the name of innocent childhood and unstained womanhood, in the name of your own dear ones at home, I pronounce it a slander upon those holy attributes of the human heart which tend upward and ally us with heaven. I deny that Mary Harris is a criminal. I deny that any murder has been committed. I deny that this young prisoner is responsible for the death of A. J. Burroughs. I assert that his death was not a crime. He was not slain in violation of law, for offenses against the law can only come by those who possess a sound mind and an unimpaired intelligence. And now, invoking your attention, I shall proceed to show you, from the story of her life, which must constitute her defense, that it is not your duty to lay your hands in further punishment on the suffering head of Mary Harris, but that it will rather be your pleasing task to open her prison doors and bid her go free, attended by the charitable blessings of all Christian people.

Who is this unfortunate defendant, and whence came she, when her weary feet bore her still more weary heart to this crowded capital? A short time since, and but few here could have answered; but now all is known. We see at a single glance a gliding, panoramic view of the life of an earnest, devoted girl. Our eyes first rest upon a point nearly ten years ago. At this time Mary Harris was a beautiful and happy child, some ten years of age, in the town of Burlington, Iowa. In that hour of tender childhood, the evidence shows that Burroughs first met her; and would to God that in that hour she had died! Gentle memories would have clustered around her peaceful grave, and this bitter cup, whose very dregs she is now drinking, would have been spared her. There is a mercy at times in death, for which the stricken soul longs and gasps as the parched and feverish earth does for the cooling rain. But he who notes the sparrow fall, and has a design in all the ways of men, ordered it otherwise; and she is here to-day, weary and heavily laden, but humbly submitting to the Providence by which her own will has been overruled and her actions guided.

Burroughs, at this time, gentlemen, was a man of comparatively mature age, more than twice her senior—as he afterward in his letters declares—almost old enough to be her father. She sat upon his knee in the purity of unconscious childhood. I speak now from the evidence furnished by his own letters of a later period, and also from the testimony of those who witnessed at that time their constant intercourse. He proposed to mold and fashion her mind by the superior force of his own age, experience, and will, in order that she might, at a future period, make him a suitable wife. There is no room to doubt upon this point. Let those ninety-two letters here produced in court make their appeal. They speak in no uncertain tone. They show us robust, developed manhood, seeking the ascendency over a confiding child. They show us maturity and strength striving for the mastery over inexperience and weakness. He assumes even a paternal interest, and teaches her young heart literally to leave father and mother and cleave unto him. We hear it stated that no marriage engagement ever existed between them. The miserable desire to inflict indiscriminate punishment upon the innocent as well as the guilty would even deny this plain fact, which is established by almost every line of the evidence to which you have listened. The prosecution itself proved that at one time the very day was fixed for the fulfillment of their oft-repeated vows.

Under these circumstances, need I dwell at length upon the imperious nature of the influence which he obtained over her? The child became absorbed in the man. What else could happen? They walked the pathway of life hand in hand for many long years of hope and fond anticipation. He taught her to regard him as her future destiny. He was all the world to her. Her heart opened and expanded under the influence of his smile, as the bud becomes a flower beneath the rays of the sun. She grew up to womanhood in unquestioning obedience to his will. The ties by which she was bound to him were the growth of years, and embraced all the strength of her whole being. And did all this have no effect on the subsequent condition of her mind when disaster came? He had carried her to the highest pinnacle of happiness and hope. She stood upon the summit of joyous expectations, and all around her was sunshine and gladness. Well might she exclaim to my learned and eminent brother, as she paced her prison floor, "Oh! Mr Bradley, you should have seen me then; I was so happy!" Yes, though poor and humble, yet she loved and was beloved, and it was enough; she was content. For in that hour, when a virtuous woman feels for the first time that she possesses the object of her devotion, there comes to her a season of bliss which brightens all the earth before her. The mother watching her sleeping babe has an exclusive joy beyond the comprehension of all hearts but her own. The wife who is graced by her husband's love is more beautifully arrayed than the lilies, and envies not the diadems of queens. But to the young virgin heart, more than all, when the kindling inspiration of its first and sacred love is accompanied by a knowledge that for it in return there burns a holy flame, there comes an ecstasy of the soul, a rapturous exaltation, more divine than will ever again be tasted this side of the bright waters and perennial fountains of paradise. The stars grow brighter, the earth more beautiful, and the world for her is filled with a delicious melody. This, peculiarly, is woman's sphere of happiness. There she concentrates all the wealth, the unsearchable riches of her heart, and stakes them all upon the single hazard. If she loses, all is lost; and night and thick darkness settle down upon her pathway. It is not so with man. His theater is broader. No single passion can so powerfully absorb him. A variety of interests appeal to him at every step. If disappointment overtakes him, a wide and open horizon invites him to new enterprises, which will relieve him of that still, deep, brooding intensity which is the pregnant parent of woe, insanity, and death to woman.

I am speaking now of general principles; but every word that I have said is applicable to the case of Mary Harris. For when her parents, distrusting Burroughs, and fearing that very treachery which afterward blasted her life as well as his own, endeavored to break off the connection and wed her to another, who, from their previous history, could for a moment doubt the result? He went to Chicago, and advised her to do the same in order to be near him. Gentlemen, the language which faithful woman holds to the object of her love when the hour of separation is threatened is very old and very beautiful:

> Entreat me not to leave thee, or to return from following after thee; for whither thou goest I will go, where thou lodgest I will lodge.
> Thy people shall be my people, thy God my God; where thou diest there I will be buried.
> May the Lord do so to me and more also if aught but death part thee and me.

It was in this spirit and under these circumstances that she came to Chicago and resided with the Misses Jane and Louisa Devlin. It was Burroughs still shaping her destiny. It was the man still pointing the course for the child to follow. And shall this be imputed to her as a fault? Will this prosecution, fed as I believe it to be from the springs of private malice, assail her because she trusted Burroughs and confided in his honor? Had Burroughs been faithful to his vows, as he was called on to be, by every attribute which ennobles manhood, by every law human and divine, then this unhappy girl would have been to-day his respected wife, and the world would have applauded her sublime devotion to him when the truth between them was sought to be poisoned by whispering tongues. Now, because he was false and broke her heart, you are called on to believe that this act abased her virtuous brow into the dust of shame. I repel this calumny. Not only do I pronounce it a slander upon Mary Harris, but it is equally a slander upon the truth, fidelity, and virtue of womanhood. She did no more than what the proudest, the purest, and the best have done in all countries and at all times. She endowed him upon whose arm she leaned with the principles of justice and honor; she crowned his brow with a constellation of all the virtues and then trusted him. She turned her back on home, kindred, and friends, and with him faced the world alone

We are told that no stain shall rest on the name of the deceased. The leading counsel for the government, at the very opening of this trial, announced, with singular emphasis, as if anticipating your conclusion, that he was a Christian who had lived and died without a blemish or reproach to that sacred character. His brother, the Rev. John C. Burroughs, says that his object here is to relieve his name from the slightest opprobrium. Thus we see the purpose of this unnatural struggle for a conviction, in the face of law and evidence which for more than two hundred years have prevailed in the defense of the children of misfortune and providential affliction. Mary Harris is to be condemned, to be carried to the horrid gibbet—that appalling machinery of death, terror, and lasting ignominy—in order that the conduct of A. J. Burroughs shall stand triumphantly vindicated! I do not wish to assail the dead; but is it expected that this monstrous assumption in favor of crime shall be passed in silence? Shall this trial impress upon the public mind, as a lesson for future action, that it is a part of the Christian character to win the love and confidence of a child, to cultivate her affections as years advance, engage to become her husband, induce her to leave her home in order to enjoy his society, and to escape from another proposal of marriage; and then, after seven years of hope deferred, to dispel all her bright dreams of life by quitting her in a moment, by dropping all connection with her without a word of explanation, by marrying another woman and turning his back on her forever?

Government and its officials, churches and their ministers, the press and its editors, are all powerful auxiliaries of public opinion, and I have heard their loud and clamorous notes throughout this trial; but when they ask me to subscribe to this idea of Christian grace and human excellence, I shall confidently appeal to you against them all.

I am now leaving out of view the darkest aspect of the conduct of the deceased toward this defendant. I am presenting it on grounds where there is no dispute. No honest man can dispute the courtship of the child, the subsequent engagement, the allurement from home, and the final, unexplained, silent desertion, and the sudden marriage of another. His own handwriting, in letters whose genuineness is not called in question, attest these facts. And even if there was nothing but their long and peculiar relation to each other proven, you would easily understand that I have stated the case correctly. Then this is the model without a flaw, the character without a stain, the name without a blemish! According to this new theology, falsehood has become respectable, treachery noble, and the base, cowardly betrayal of a young, inexperienced female confidence, a qualification for a seat with the just made perfect. I can join in no such wretched blasphemy.

I cling to the old and homely virtues according to whose teachings such conduct has been loaded with infamy from the earliest dawn of civilized human society; and taking my stand on this universal verdict of all ages, this irreversible judgment of enlightened mankind, I say that such conduct is more injurious to morality than murder, that it is worthy of the punishment of death, and that he who is guilty of it ought to die. I do not, it is true, place this defense on that ground; but when the prosecution sees fit to tender an issue upon the character of the deceased in the face of the black and revolting record of his guilt, it is proper that it should be met. When an effort is openly made to debauch the public mind into the belief that vice is virtue, that turpitude is morality, and that crime against unsuspecting innocence is one of the adornments of the christian religion, then I conceive that the voice of truth should be heard.

But to proceed. Time passed on with this defendant, bearing her onward to a region of horrors, to the scene of her dismay and ruin; and I must move along on the melancholy tide and approach the sorrowful hour. We have now traced these parties for years. Burroughs had carried her hopes to the highest elevation. She was looking forward to a future filled with honor and with delight. It was of his creation, and there was not a cloud within the scope of her vision. In such a serene and happy moment as this, with no note of preparation to her tender and susceptible mind, with no sign of warning, the blow descended upon her naked head, shivering every hope with which her heart was tenanted, and dashing the temple of reason itself into ruins. Is this statement the work of fancy on my part? Is it not the sad, literal truth? I appeal to you who have heard the evidence. Counsel have seen fit to attribute powers of eloquence to me which I neither possess nor affect. I can only repeat to you a plain and simple story of wrong, misery, and madness which you already know, and which is far more eloquent in itself than any words I can employ. Seven years of love were spurned in an instant. Seven years of patient hope were turned in a moment to despair. He had lifted her up almost to celestial heights, only that her fall might be sufficiently great to dash her to pieces. Though without sin, yet she was cast out from her place of blissful abode, and fell, like the son of the morning, to hope no more forever. In order to understand the effect of disappointment and misfortune, we must fully consider the condition of the mind when the shock came. Adopting this rule in the present instance, and we shudder at the bare contemplation of the mental agony of the defendant when she realized that she was abandoned by him for whom she had abandoned all but her honor.

I am aware that the suffering of helpless woman, under such circumstances, are too often discussed with a sneer. There are those, who go in the catalogue for men, who aspire to be thought wise in the ways of the world, by talking and writing in flippant and witty strains in regard to woman, her sorrows and misfortunes. To such sage and philosophic minds there is no such thing as mental derangement, growing out of disappointed love or broken marriage vows. They are not thus to be imposed upon. The defense of insanity in such cases is merely a cunning device of counsel. Well, gentlemen, I am consoled with the belief that there is nowhere in this court, either on the bench or in the jury-box, one of these ready-made critics of human motives and human conduct, who are always deaf to law, to evidence, and to reason.

I have endeavored, during my humble career in life, to study somewhat the causes which most deeply afflict the human breast, and instill into it the bitterest and most intolerable memories. I think I can sympathize, to some extent at least, with those sensitive natures which are most susceptible to emotions of pain, and which at times wander in realms of gloom, and pray madly to be released from the unsatisfying scenes of the world. You have heard the character of the defendant in this respect fully delineated. She has been endowed by her Creator with the highest capacity for enjoyment or anguish. It is with her a land of sunshine or a land of darkness. She has but few, if any, medium traits. Dr. Nichols, with the hand of a master, has drawn a picture of those invisible substances known as the mind and moral affections. He has applied his learning and science to the case of this poor girl, and we see the very pulsations of her heart laid bare before us. And, with this plain view of her mental and moral organization, and in the presence of the evidence as I now present it, without its further most cruel and harrowing features, I pronounce the calamity which befell her, by the mere act of his abandonment and desertion, as one of the heaviest that ever broke on the head of youth and confiding innocence. Is there no cause for insanity here? Do these things work no madness in the brain? Do they not rather plant in the ardent mind of woman the corroding canker, which no balm can cure—a consuming fire, which no lethean waters can quench? I appeal to human experience. It is said that we are manufacturing a defense for this girl. This charge means that we are assuming facts in her behalf which do not exist; that her condition, at the time of the homicide, was not such as we represent it. Is it not, therefore, a most essential ingredient of this defense to show that Mary Harris had been visited by those causes which have been recognized in all ages as the most prolific sources of insanity to her sex? Must we be told that we are standing on doubtful ground? Do men of sense gape and stare, because we show that the conduct of Burroughs made Mary Harris insane? Did such a thing never happen before? Is all this something so new, that we are to be styled visionary explorers and reckless adventurers? Why, gentlemen, we are simply following a broad, sorrowful, and well-beaten track. It is thickly strewn with the wrecks of human happiness—with broken hearts and ruined intellects. Go to the asylums for the insane — those awful tombs of living death! See that once-beautiful, but now pallid and shrunken face, pressed against the bars of her cell. See the scorching frenzy of her restless and anxious eye. Her parched lips move, and she calls upon a name which is strange to our ears. She prays sadly, perhaps, to be allowed to go to him. She murmurs the broken lines of some song which they sang together in the days of old. And then upon a sudden, as if a serpent's tooth had struck her bleeding heart, she shrieks out maledictions, and calls down the curses of God on his head. At last she cowers down shudderingly in her corner, where, chained to the barren rock of the past, her one perpetual memory, with beak and talons sharper and more ruthless than the vulture's, preys with ceaseless rage upon her vitals. The name she has called upon is borne by one who is the favorite of fortune, who wears the honors of the world on his brow, who has wife and children blooming under his roof, who has a high seat in the sanctuary—is a "Christian without a stain"—who has forgotten his victim, and is happy. His name may not be Burroughs; but his conduct was not more false, and the ruin which he wrought was not more fatal to peace and life.

Turn to the books which record the experience of the world on this subject, and see whether this is picture or dreadful reality. I might detain you hour after hour reading cases of insanity produced by causes similar in kind to those which disordered the reason of the defendant. I shall content myself with but few. I read from Sir W. C. Ellis, page 79:

> E. C., a female about thirty years of age ; how long she has been insane is not exactly known. This case, like the preceding, was the consequence of offended pride. She was a fine young woman, but of ambitious views. She, too, had become attached to a person in a more elevated situation of life than herself; and the mortification of being rejected on account of the difference of rank was a wound to her pride which she could not brook ; she became incurably insane.

We are not told what became of the man of rank. He most likely wore purple and fine linen, and fared sumptuously every day, while she lived and died forgotten by him; simply "incurably insane." But again:

> M. T., aged thirty, has been insane four months. Cause of the attack, disappointment in love. She formed an attachment with a young man about six years ago; and he left her after promising marriage. She says she has never been comfortable in her mind since, though she has worked regularly until within a few weeks. But she has shown evident symptoms of derangement; she neglected her business and returned to her friends, saying her state of mind would not permit her to work. About a week before her admission she passed a whole night in the street, and she has since meditated self-destruction.

How like the case on trial this sounds, only that M. T had far less to crush her to the depths of despair than Mary Harris. In the case cited by the author, she was a woman when she first formed her disastrous attachment. In the case here in court, her love was ingrafted on the tender stalk of childhood, and it grew with her growth and strengthened with her strength until it became a component part of life itself. In the case from the book he left her, and that was all. It was not all in the case we are trying; no, not all.

But one more case to illustrate this question:

> M. D., thirty years of age, had been insane only a few weeks. She had been brought up as a dressmaker, but unhappily had been seduced by an officer, to whom she was very much attached; after living with him for some time he deserted her for another. Grief, mortified pride, and jealousy, all combined, produced a state of excitement which ultimately ended in insanity. She had sleepless nights, the natural secretions were disordered, and violent mania was the consequence.

It is true that in this case the additional crime of seduction occurred; but I deny that this fact tends to increase the susceptibility of the female mind to insanity when laboring under grief from disappointed affection. While it brings its load of shame, yet it likewise blunts the fine edge of female pride. While it scalds and blisters the very soul with a sense of degradation, yet the standard of honor is lowered, and the fires of a former virtuous indignation are turned to ashes. The woman is humbled in her own estimation, and no longer chafes as formerly under the burden of her wrongs. She has submitted to her own dishonor, and she abandons thereafter the claim which a virtuous woman has to complain of man's injustice. Pride, honor, and indignation at wrong, are all attributes of virtue, and when they are assailed and aroused to an unnatural action, they are the copious springs from which insanity takes it rise. Let it not then be said that because Mary Harris is pure her wrongs are less. I have even heard it urged that because, through all the long and intimate years which she passed with Burroughs, she kept the vestal fires of chastity alive in her heart, that therefore her sufferings could not have been so great, when he abandoned her and attempted to stain her name with pollution, as if she had fallen. This is not my theory of female character. The just, the pure, the good, those who have never consented unto iniquity, are those who, as a general rule, are unable to relieve themselves from those burning memories of cruelty and injustice which so often bring distraction.

But while I have shown, by authority, that the mere abandonment of the defendant by the deceased, under their peculiar circumstances, would have sufficiently accounted for the deplorable condition in which we afterward find her, yet, as I have said, this was not all. No; gladly would I be convinced that it was. But I now approach a scene of turpitude which brightens all his former conduct by the contrast. He not merely left this girl alone in the world, robbing her of all the priceless treasures of hope which she had laid up in the future, but he endeavored, in the very wantonness of wickedness, to trample her in the mire under his feet; to make her an object of scorn; to taint her name with moral leprosy, and to consign her to odium and shame.

I am aware that it is to be urged that Burroughs was not the author of the infamous Greenwood letters. I am ready for that issue. Tell me, first, is there anybody else in the world likely to have approached Mary Harris in that way? Does a stranger thus approach a woman whose name is unsullied? Does a mere casual acquaintance seek thus to gain an intimacy with one whose virtue was never called in question? And who but Burroughs was intimate with the prisoner? If there was another it would have been shown. The brother, Dr. Burroughs, has not slept on the track of the accused. He has spared neither labor nor money to bring before you every item of her brief and now miserable life which might bear hard upon her in this trying hour. He wrote to a brother divine at Burlington to engage his assistance. He went to Janesville to bring every hidden thing to light. He hunted up all those who had ever known her. He associated with policemen, and took them into his confidence. He labored day and night to rake together every grain of evidence which would weigh against her life in the scales of justice which you now hold. And if any one had ever sustained such a relation toward her, except Burroughs, as would have rendered it even remotely reasonable that he wrote these letters, would he not have been discovered and held up in this investigation? If she had ever borne herself toward any one else in such a manner as to warrant a reasonable being in such an advance, that fact would have been proven.

And again, who would have used the language to Ellen Mills, at 94 Quincy street, but Burroughs? The evening on which he waited and watched for the meeting which his letter had requested, he said to the keeper of this abode of sin and shame that he would sit near the window, where he could observe the approach of his victim, and that he would himself go to the door and let her in. Why did he assume this task? Because, as he said, she knew him so well that she would trust him and come in. Whom else but Burroughs did Mary Harris know so well? Whom else could she so implicitly trust? Whom but him, who had fostered the growth of her confidence from childhood up to womanhood? Whom but him, on whose arm she had leaned so long and so fondly? And above all, who else could so confidently assert his power over her? "She knows me so well, that she will trust me and come in." This alone fixes the paternity of the Greenwood letters. This alone discloses who was that night waiting for this girl, as plainly as if a beam of light had at that moment fallen on him, and made his guilty face visible to every eye in Chicago. I appeal to the candid judgments of all. Was there more than one person in the world who would have spoken and proceeded in this deed of infamy as it is shown that this man did? Look, too, at the phraseology of these letters: "My dear Molly." "Come; do come." Whose language is that? Is it not the peculiar voice of Jacob, though the hand may be the counterfeited hand of Esau?

But still more on this point. It has been well known for months what our defense would be. It has been well known that we would prove that Ellen Mills, the woman of 94 Quincy street, identified Burroughs as the man who plotted and watched at her house, in pursuance of the plans of these letters. It was known to all here concerned as counsel for the government, and it was known to Dr. Burroughs, within a few weeks after his brother's death, that this woman had minutely and accurately described the deceased to Miss Devlin and the accused, and had also recognized his photograph. It was equally well known that a clerk in the post-office had done the same. For when these letters were received, the defendant, outraged by their character, took prompt measures to ascertain their depraved origin. A letter was written in reply, addressed to J. P. Greenwood, and the clerk was requested to observe with care who called for it. He identified Burroughs as the man, even to the cornelian ring on his finger, which had been given to him as a token of love by Miss Harris. I repeat, that the prosecution well knew, from almost the first step in the preparation of this case, that we would prove these facts by Louisa Devlin. They also knew then, and now know from the records of this court, that we labored for months, in every form known to the law, to obtain the testimony of these two important witnesses, Ellen Mills and the post-office clerk. They were important to us; but if Louisa Devlin is swearing falsely, they are much more important to you [turning to Dr. Burroughs]. Our efforts to procure their testimony were in vain. What efforts did you make? You say you are here to defend your brother's reputation. If the post-office clerk did not say that it was your brother who called for these Greenwood letters, and did not describe him to Mary Harris and Louisa Devlin, why did you not bring him here? If Ellen Mills never made similar statements as to the person who visited her house, why is she not on the witness stand, or her depositions on file? You have brought witnesses here from Chicago and witnesses from Janesville, whose testimony is so immaterial that it trifles with the time of the court. But here are two witnesses who, if our proof on this vital point be false, can prove that falsehood, and relieve your brother's reputation where its need is the sorest; and yet, instead of joining us to bring them here, we find you, by your own extorted admission, listening to the unscrupulous suggestions of a policeman, that one of them at least shall be carried out of sight by the corrupt use of money; and the other one escapes us, although we follow him with an order from the war department.

Gentlemen of the jury, this Christian minister by profession swears positively that his brother did not write these letters. But does he not stand before this court, before this jury, before the world, and before God, convicted, upon his own testimony, of suppressing the very evidence which would have settled that question forever? There is but one conclusion to be drawn from this fact. These two absent witnesses would have sustained Louisa Devlin; and Dr. Burroughs and this prosecution knew it. They would have described the deceased here in this court as they did in Chicago. This is no forced assumption of mine. It is a well-settled conclusion of law. The suppression of evidence is a grave and almost conclusive presumption against the party that resorts to it. This is more especially true when, as in this case, the prosecution is sustained by the treasury of the government in enforcing the attendance of witnesses. What is the object of a trial in a court of justice? We are here in search of truth. We have, each one of us, under the solemnities of an oath, invoked the name and help of God in the discharge of that duty. We stand on holy ground. Life, life, that mysterious gift of the Creator, is the issue at stake. Its awful import should inspire every breast with a religious desire to aid this court and jury in arriving, if possible, at the exact truth. Then, what shall be said of one who admits that he has not done so? I learn that it is said that no attack can injure Dr. Burroughs; that his position is so exalted that no shaft can reach him. I have no desire to indulge in personal assaults; but no position in life, no assumption of superior piety and virtue, will ever shield the character of a witness who, in a trial involving life itself, conceals material evidence, and then attempts to supply its place by his own unsupported oath. Nor need counsel in such an instance waste their time in denunciation, for no language which our tongues could utter could paint his conduct in colors so dark, in a moral deformity so hideous, as he himself has painted it by his own testimony. Such a witness becomes at once powerless for evil before an intelligent jury. He is dead by his own act. And I submit here now, in all candor, in the face of this court, in the presence of my learned brethren of the bar, and to you the final arbiters of this sad and trying hour, that Dr. Burroughs stands in contempt of this court, for his collusion with the policeman, Douglass, to hide away a witness from its process; he stands in contempt of society, which requires all its members to aid in vindicating justice; he stands in contempt of you, in refusing to bring before you all the evidence in his power to establish a point on which he asks you to find in his favor; and he stands in contempt of the teachings of the merciful Master on the Mount, by coming here with deceit and treachery in his heart to strike this helpless, feeble, sick and lonely being, to whom his very name is an unendurable misery.

But it is most confidently insisted that these letters are not in the handwriting of the deceased. They may or may not be. After he is identified as the one who called, in the name of Greenwood, at the post-office for a reply, and who waited at 94 Quincy street, for the proposed meeting, it is of no consequence whether he guided the pen or dictated to a confederate. The testimony of Mr. Danenhower is deemed material on this point. He says that the leave of absence on which the deceased went home to get married commenced September 8th, and hence he could not have been there in time to write them. My answer is, first, that nothing is more common than for clerks to leave a few days in advance of the date of their permission; and, secondly, that, in addition to the identification by Ellen Mills and the clerk at the post-office, it is in proof that Louisa Devlin and Mary Harris both saw him at times corresponding very nearly, if not exactly, with the dates of these letters. This is conclusive. There are but two witnesses in the world who could have contradicted these facts. Dr. Burroughs knew they would not contradict them, and he therefore kept them away, with the aid of "a hundred dollars or two," as suggested by the policeman, and came here himself to contradict them.

It will be asked, however, what motive Burroughs had to thus compass the destruction of one whose image, if he was human, must have been blended with his tenderest memories, with the most sacred associations of his heart? A refuge will be sought in this inquiry, from the irresistible pressure of the proof which thus far shatters all the assumptions and theories of the prosecution. Why—why did he do this deed without a name for cruelty and perfidy? You will be told that all the actions of sane people have their intelligent reasons. This is true; and the history of this case gives a ready, an instant answer to this inquiry. His motive was not the gratification of passion. Lust was not one of the elements in his calculations. Base and wretched as are such motives of action, yet, if it be possible, those that actuated Burroughs were still lower and more depraved. Look calmly at his situation. From Mary Harris he was about turning away without a word. He knew that such an act would be to her as appalling as the voice of doom. His conscience made him a coward. He could not face her with the story of his stupendous crime. He could not look into her confiding eye and tell her that his whole life toward her had been one mighty falsehood. Human nature, however depraved, was not equal to such a task. The past was filled with voices of reproach and terror to his guilty heart. The future frowned on him full of menace and warning. The present was haunted by a sense of conscious wrong from which he tried in vain to escape. He knew, too, that he was in her power. These letters which are here in court, and many others not here, arose in his memory. He recalled that one in which he says: "And Mollie, if from any reason whatever I may change my views or feelings toward you, and I should feel like entering into a matrimonial alliance with any one else than yourself, I will promptly advise you of it." He was about taking that fatal step, but he had not the manly honor to fulfill his promise. He, however, like one who plans the commission of a crime, took measures for his escape. He was to be married in a few days to the unhappy lady who now mourns in her widowed home, and whose melancholy fate I deeply commiserate; and he knew that when that fact reached the ears of Mary Harris, her cries, her sobs, her voice of wailing would ascend like perpetual lamentations in the air. She might, in her deep distress, utter his name to the world in such a way as to stain his character as a Christian. She might come near him some day and remind him that he once took a child from her parents' roof, and broke her heart. Aye, it was in her power to denounce him as false and infamous at all times and places; to pursue him, if she desired, as an avenging shadow; to rob him of peace, and to turn his days and nights into fear and alarm. But if her foot once crossed the threshold of shame, she was in the fowler's snare and at his mercy. If this defendant had ever entered 94 Quincy street, Burroughs would have breathed easy, and gone to his approaching nuptials a free and happy man, secure from molestation at her hands. Her mouth would have been closed forever. It was not her soul that he expected to pollute, but her name. He intended to have been able to prove that she was seen to enter this wretched house, and to hold that fact in terror over her. If she struggled and cried out against her cruel fate, he could silence her. Or if she refused to be still in her sufferings, he could close the ears and steel the hearts of all virtuous people against her. If she entered that house, she would come out covered with an everlasting mildew. Her heart might be as pure as before, for she was unconscious of its character, but her name would be spotted with an incurable leprosy. Burroughs had made up his mind to break his engagement, of long years' standing, with Mary Harris; and the Greenwood letters laid a plan by which he was to justify that heartless act and silence her complaints. Is there no motive in this? We find him capable of one wrong toward her. He deserts her without cause. Is he not capable of committing the other, when he has a powerful motive in his desire to escape the consequences of the first? If he could, in the hour of his desertion, render her powerless and despised, he was safe and free. The one absorbing purpose of his heart at that time was to sever the tie that bound them together, and when we find him unwilling to do so by an interview, we are prepared to believe that he attempted to do so by consigning her name to ignominy and pollution.

Gentlemen, you now have my views upon that branch of the evidence which relates to the Greenwood letters and all their criminal surroundings. I hold—

First. That it is not reasonable from the whole evidence that any one else but Burroughs wrote them.

Second. That Ellen Mills and the post-office clerk identified him fully as the man.

Third. That if he was not their author, it was in the power of this prosecution, by bringing these two last-named persons here as witnesses, to have conclusively shown that fact.

Fourth That instead of procuring the attendance of these parties, we find those who are in the interest of the prosecution—Dr.

Burroughs and Douglass, the policeman—engaged in planning the suppression of their testimony; which fact in itself creates a presumption of law in favor of my position.

Fifth. That Burroughs had a powerful and controlling motive to write them.

But now allow me to say that, for the purposes of our defense, it is only necessary to show that Mary Harris actually believed that he wrote them, and that they thus became one of the exciting causes of her mental agony and derangement. But I have preferred to show not merely that she believed him to be the author, but also to show that she had overwhelming reasons for her belief—reasons from which there was no escape. No woman who truly loves ever willingly consents to blacken and deface her own idol. She rather clings to him in blind adoration long after the proofs of his treachery have become visible to all eyes but her own. And who will say that this defendant jumped to conclusions on this point against the deceased? On the contrary, when her fears and suspicions were alarmed, with what conscientious care she proceeded. Step by step the painful truth was pressed upon her. The woman of Quincy street described him. The clerk did the same. But she did not stop there. She was perhaps convinced, for the letters in themselves to her practiced eye contained terrible proof; but she had some hope of relief, in some way, not yet well defined in her thoughts, from an interview in another quarter. This young girl, then but eighteen or nineteen years of age, gathered up the letters of the deceased, took his miniature, took all that related to her seven years of love and hope, and knowing the standing of the Rev. John C. Burroughs, knowing his religious character, went to him like a child to a father, and poured out her grief and her fears. How like the pure and noble girl that she was.

But here we are involved in a contradiction as to the day on which this call was made. Dr. Burroughs says that she came on the 16th day of September. I do not believe him. His brother was married on the 15th, and I do not believe him, because, in order to free himself from reproach, it is necessary for him to fix his interview with the defendant subsequent to his brother's marriage. I do not believe him, because Louisa Devlin swears that it took place on the 15th. I do not believe him because Jane Devlin swears it was the 15th. I learn that they are to be assailed in the interest of Dr. Burroughs, in order to sustain him. Let it be so. You have looked upon those two honest, truthful faces, and observed their patient candor under the most protracted examinations. They have been the good angels of human nature in this cause. They were the friends of Mary Harris in sunshine, and they have abided through darkness. Others may have shrunk from her side, but they have stuck closer because of her calamities. Like the petrel of the sea, their friendship has spread a stronger pinion and pursued a bolder flight in the midst of the lightning and the tempest. Are such pure and unselfish beings as these to be degraded by counsel in order to support the testimony of one who appears in this case more like a criminal than an honest man? Make the contrast between them, gentlemen. Who failed to note that damning hesitancy of manner which caused every eye in this court-room to rest upon him with suspicion? Who could fail to perceive that he was weighing the effect, not the truthfulness, of his answers before giving them? Who ever heard an equal number of qualifying adjectives, expressive of cautious doubt and uncertainty, used in the same space of time as when he was under cross-examination? No; his oath will not weigh an instant in your minds as against theirs. You will believe, from the evidence, that the defendant and Dr. Burroughs met on the 15th and not on the 16th of September.

But, if you will allow me, I will state another reason why it was on the 15th, the day of the fatal marriage. The law gives the prisoner the right to stand where I am standing, if she had the power to do so, and speak for herself. I am but speaking for her, and in that capacity I have the right to say that it was the 15th, because she says so, because that awful day has left an indelible scar on her brain that fixes her recollection. And every word that has fallen from her pallid lips on this subject has carried truth to my mind. Dr. Nichols has sworn to her exalted sense of truth and female virtue, and a mountain of oaths by Dr. Burroughs would not shake my faith in her integrity. I do not believe, at this dreadful moment, she would purchase her life by the utterance of a falsehood—no, not even to escape that death from which we shrink back in speechless horror.

Thus, then, these two persons met on the 15th of September, 1863. Dr. Burroughs says a woman came with the defendant. If we were manufacturing a defense, we would say so too, and have one of the Misses Devlin to personate this third party, and then by her testimony show what took place at this interview, and contradict Dr. Burroughs. But it is not true. Mary Harris went alone, and I am somewhat at a loss to know why this unknown woman has been conjured up. If she has a real existence, why was she not brought here, as so many others have been, to uphold, if possible, the private part of this prosecution?

Let us, however, now examine for a few moments the account which Dr. Burroughs gives of that meeting between himself and the prisoner. He admits she came to see him in regard to his brother, and that she apprised him of her long and intimate relations with him. The Greenwood letters were submitted to him, as also her reasons for believing that the deceased wrote them. She was in grief and trouble on that account. She inquired whether he was in Chicago. Dr. Burroughs admits to Judge Newman that he knew of their long correspondence; but while asserting that this interview took place on the day after his brother's marriage, he is forced to admit that he did not inform her of that fact. Why did he so carefully conceal his brother's marriage of the day previous? Why did he not tell her the truth? He admits that he did not do so. He says that he asked her if his brother had broken any engagement with her, and that she said he had not. The force of this answer will be fully appreciated when it is remembered that at this time the defendant was not aware that the deceased was married, and that this reverend witness was purposely concealing that fact from her.

But he says that Mary Harris told him that no marriage engagement had ever existed between her and his brother. Now, gentlemen, if she had made such a statement to Dr. Burroughs on that occasion it would constitute a marvel and a wonder in the history of human nature. It would stand alone as a contradiction

28

of the universal experience of the world. Here was a young girl for the first time in her life in an agony of apprehension for fear she was about to be betrayed by the man whom she loved. The fact that she was engaged to marry him does not admit of a doubt. That is all clear now. Some trouble had even at one time arisen because she was about to marry out of the church—that is, to Burroughs. You remember his own letter on that point. No one now disputes the engagement. You are called, then, to believe that this defendant, going to Dr. Burroughs on the very subject of her relations with his brother, to whom she was in fact engaged—the evidence of which she carried with her to show him, complaining also of the contemplated breach of faith—that she, under these circumstances, told an absolute falsehood, and of such character as to utterly deprive her of all claims upon the accused, or of any right to inquire of his movements or conduct! In other words, we are to believe that she bore false witness voluntarily against herself upon a subject of the most supreme and sacred moment; that while discussing her rights with the deceased, she admitted she had no rights; that while hunting for him with nearly a hundred of his letters in her pocket promising marriage, she deliberately settled the whole case against herself by informing his brother that there was nothing whatever between them except the ordinary relations of friendship. What an interview, according to Dr. Burroughs! He knew of the long intimacy and correspondence, as he told Judge Newman. She came to him on the 16th, as he asserts. She wanted to know where A. J. Burroughs was. He told her he had left the city the day before. The Greenwood letters were discussed. And then Dr. Burroughs became inquisitive. How important, too, were his questions! He must have foreseen this trial. At least he must have been qualifying himself to swear in an action for a breach of marriage promise. He asks her if any marriage engagement existed. She frankly says no, when she holds in her hands at that moment the evidence to the contrary. He asks her if his brother had ever made any dishonorable proposals to her, and she again answers no, although she at that time was painfully impressed with the fact that he had attempted to allure her into a house of ill fame. Another very comprehensive question: Had the deceased ever broken any engagement with her? And once more she gives the necessary answer in the negative. There this extraordinary interview quietly ends by Dr. Burroughs forgetting to tell this distressed girl that the object of her solicitude, and in whom indeed they were both so deeply interested, was married on the day before. This is the testimony of Dr. Burroughs, as given in your hearing. Is there a man in the world, of common intelligence, who will believe it? Is it not monstrous and most unnatural? It sounded from the witness-stand like ironical fiction, told to provoke a stare and a smile, and in that it succeeded. The defendant went to Dr. Burroughs for information, and came away almost as ignorant as she went. Dr. Burroughs, on the contrary, made that the occasion to cram himself as a witness to every phase which any judicial inquiry might ever assume between them. He says that he is here simply to protect his brother's reputation, and he certainly betrayed an early knowledge that it would need protection.

But in this connection allow me a word as to his purpose here, and the spirit in which he has testified. It has been well known for many months that we would defend Mary Harris on the ground that grief, disappointment, and despair, connected with a severe physical disease peculiar to woman, and in itself a constant source of insanity, had given rise in her mind to recurring periods of mania, and that at one of these periods she committed the act for which she is now on trial. Well, has not Dr. Burroughs entered the lists upon that issue? He says that his only care is for the character of his deceased brother. That would be commendable; but is it true? He has taken pains, in different ways, to convince the counsel for the defense, as well as this court and jury, that he does not wish to have the defendant convicted, but that "she ought to be sent home to her friends." Then why, may I ask, is this long array of witnesses brought here by him, to put up their crude and unlearned opinions against the medical evidence on the subject of her sanity? Was it essential to the Christian character of A. J. Burroughs to prove that here and there, at Chicago, at Janesville, and elsewhere, a man, a woman, or a child had met Mary Harris for a few passing moments, and did not discover that she was insane? No. This evidence can have but one purpose. It aims at the life of the prisoner. It in no wise touches the character of the deceased. It is a bold demand on the part of Dr. Burroughs for blood. It is the key which unlocks and reveals the meaning of his presence, and of all his evidence in this case. O spirit of eternal justice, what more is this poor shivering victim of man's cruel perfidy to suffer! Is it not enough that one drove her mad, and caused her to cry out—

> I am bound
> Upon a wheel of fire, that mine own tears
> Do scald like molten lead?

And must the brother come now, and struggle to drag this wan, emaciated, and stricken being to an awful and ignominious death? Is he not satisfied with the ruin already wrought? Are you not ready to exclaim, "Spare her, Dr. Burroughs; oh, spare her! Spare her for the sake of the name you bear. Enough she has suffered in that name. For the love of God and for the sake of his mercies, spare her broken life. Do not press and trample on the fallen and undone. She may meet you no more in this world. You may forget her mortal agonies in the honeyed commendations of your followers. But there comes a day when the one who murdered her peace, and the one who now seeks to murder her life, will both meet their victim in the presence of the Great Judge, and in a court above the sun, where misfortune is not a crime, and where earthly distinctions fade away; where the poor are rich, and the merciful blessed; where the feeble are strong, and the oppressor's rod is broken; and in that awful presence they will be called to answer why, at their hands, Mary Harris was beaten and scourged to madness and death. Spare her; oh, spare her! lest, if you succeed in your purpose to slay her here, she will confront you in the eternal world as a bright angel, with her fair hair dabbled in her own innocent blood, shed by your hand, and there shriek into your shrinking ear, 'False, fleeting, and perjured!'"

Alas! how often the great rules of right—eternal and unchangeable right—are perverted in man's administration of justice!

How often the accused should be the accuser! How often the unoffending sufferer bears the punishment due alone to others! What a scene is this in which we are all engaged! Here, before you, sits one of the feeblest and saddest beings ever born of woman—a mere helpless atom, buffeted and driven here by angry and malignant winds. The babe in its mother's arms was never more unconscious of the evil purposes of crime than the heart of this pale and wasted prisoner. Yet the freezing terrors of the law surround her on all sides: the judge upon the bench, with wise and patient calmness elucidating its principles; this jury, listening to the story of her blighted life, and solemnly weighing the evidence; this crowded and anxious audience watching the result; and men, bearded men, earnestly discussing the issue, whether she may live or die! And why all this? Because, as she said to you [turning to Mr. Bradley], "I have been beaten and scourged without cause." Yes; bruised, maimed, and mangled until the divine gift of human reason gave way, utterly powerless, with less than the instinct of the poorest worm, that resents in blindness the heel that tramples it to dust. And yet this is the being against whom we are to listen to a hue and cry as if she were a monster, a Borgia, or a Hecuba!

Gentlemen, I sometimes tire of life when I see wrong and injustice spreading their prosperous branches as the green and flourishing palm; when those by whom offenses come in this world, who prey upon virtue and turn it into vice, who sport with innocence in order to poison it, who make a mockery of love and a plaything of truth, go not only unscathed of the law, but even applauded by the hired panderers to a depraved and debauched public sentiment. Whatever of philosophy I have takes a painful and gloomy form, and I feel that I could say, with the great dramatist:

> Out brief candle,
> Life's but a walking shadow; a poor player
> That struts and frets his hour upon the stage,
> And then is heard no more; a tale told by an idiot,
> Full of sound and fury, signifying nothing.

Gentlemen of the jury, I have now, to the best of my ability, discussed the evidence relating to the first proposition of the defense. I am reasoning from cause to effect; and we have maintained and proven that in the case of the prisoner there existed overwhelming causes of insanity. To establish this great fact, I have thus far dwelt upon her relation to the deceased, the hopes he inspired in her breast, the power he obtained over her will and destiny, their final separation, and the aggravating circumstances by which that separation was surrounded. But although these moral causes alone more than account for her subsequent condition, yet, at this point, I wish barely to call your attention to the testimony of Dr. Fitch. He is a gentleman of standing in his profession in Chicago, and attended the prisoner in her illness soon after Burroughs had abandoned her. He states that he found her laboring under a painful disease peculiar to her sex; and every medical man in the world, and every book ever written on that subject, declare that this disease is a constant physical cause of periodical, or, as it is more properly termed, paroxysmal insanity. I shall not discuss or dwell upon this fact. It is only necessary to state it, and to remind you that it is in proof that she was suffering from one of these attacks when she entered the treasury building on the fatal 30th day of January. In this most important feature of the case there is no conflict of testimony, and no room for doubt or conjecture. Where, then, in the whole range of judicial history, was there ever shown a more powerful combination of causes, in the same person, of mental derangement? The well-known moral causes existed in malevolent force; and in fearful alliance with them was a physical disease which is recognized as one of the principal causes of mischief and malady to the female mind. Shall we, then, any longer wonder that, with her delicate nervous temperament, she fell before such a terrible combination? Would it not rather be matter for astonishment if her mind had survived, in calmness and health, all these shocks? But now, having inquired into and summed up the causes, let us explore the ground still before us, in order to discover, if we can, whether the effects of those causes actually did occur in this case. Let us lift the curtain for a few moments, and look upon that shifting scene of suffering which her life continuously presents, from the 15th day of September, 1863, to the present hour.

We behold, for once at least in our lives, a human being totally transformed. The change is complete in every respect. Physically, she is no longer the same. Her former buoyant health withers away. The bloom of her face dies out, as it were, in a single night. Her already slight frame becomes still slighter. Sleep, the gentle nurse in whose arms the peaceful invalid woos the returning spirit of health, fled from her eyes. Burroughs had murdered sleep; and her mind was fixed, with an appalling intensity, on the memory of the past, which was to her brain as a consuming fire. From this horrible spell there was no escape. Ellis, from whom I have already quoted, says:

> But in those cases where the over-action of the brain has been brought on by thinking too long and too intensely on painful truths, from which there is no escape for the patient, it is exceedingly difficult to divert the attention, and to prevent the mind from dwelling upon them so continually as to produce disease; for, although patients are conscious of the injury they are inflicting upon themselves, and of the inutility of their over-anxiety, and judge most accurately of their situations, they do not appear to possess the power of controlling their thoughts.

No; and hence we see her mind developing its changes in equal pace with her body. It is the seat of the canker which blighted her whole system, and which no medicinal balm can reach. There was lodged that perilous stuff which no drug can purge from the distracted breast. According to the evidence, she was, up to that period, the merriest and the most joyous of her circle. The world, the glad earth, the opening day, the bending sky, and the kind faces of friends were all beautiful to her, and she enjoyed the few years of her unclouded happiness. But now the laugh was gone; no merriment kindled in her eye; the future to her was dead; she lived in the past, and it was the charnel-house of all her hopes, and over it hung the mourning cypress. I am reading her condition to you by the light of the evidence alone. I am showing you that effects were following causes. She grew weary of life. Who does not, when all that gives life its value has perished? This is, in itself, one of the incipient stages of insanity. It is the offspring of that "black melancholy" which all authors designate as one of the parent springs of madness. And when this defendant rose that morning from her bed, and murmured her farewell to the friend, whom she supposed to be asleep, had she succeeded in taking her "walk by the lake shore," in the darkness before daybreak, she never would have been here on trial. The winds and waves would have sung her requiem. There might have been an inquest, and the usual verdict:

> One more unfortunate,
> Weary of breath,
> Rashly importunate,
> Gone to her death.

Perhaps there would have been an item in the papers of the next morning. Men would have read it listlessly over their coffee, and forgotten it during the breakfast. And yet in that item would have been contained the account of a wreck of more infinite and incalculable value than all the richly laden argosies that ever sunk beneath the surface of the deep. It would have told of a ruin which calls upon heaven, earth, and hell as its interested witnesses. It would have recorded a crime which rises in mountain blackness against the soul of the betrayer of innocence. But the purposes of the suicide were defeated, and we are left to still further notice her total transformation of character.

How shall I dwell upon those unnatural outbreaks of violence which occurred toward those who were the beneficent guardians of her daily life? We have found the developments of suicidal mania; and alas! we now discover the unmistakable symptoms of homicidal insanity. This whole evidence shows her natural disposition to have been most amiable, gentle, and affectionate. She now, at times, lost all these once familiar traits. Where is the man of science who does not see at a glance what all this means? Do the moral affections and the mind all undergo a sudden and radical revolution, characterized by irrational actions, while all the functions are in a healthful condition? As well ask whether the dove can change itself at pleasure to the kite, or the lamb to the ravening wolf. If Mary Harris was not insane when she aimed a large and deadly knife at the breast of her dearest friend, then human character can assume the hues of the chameleon at will, and there are no rules by which human motives can be fathomed. Again she attacks Louisa Devlin; at another period she assaults a customer in the store; at another she is so violent that her friends imprison her in her room by force; and at another she escapes and flies along the streets at night, and is secured and brought back only after great exertion and difficulty. She tears articles of domestic use to pieces, and in every way, at stated intervals, displays a morbid propensity to destroy.

This form of insanity is too well understood to require at this time a minute discussion and a full citation of authorities. I wish, however, to dwell briefly on some proper distinctions to be observed. We find the most eminent authors fully recognizing the existence of an insane impulse to commit deeds of violence by persons apparently perfectly rational on all other subjects, and acting without the slightest provocation. Ray, in his great work —Medical Jurisprudence of Insanity—uses the following language:

> The last and most important form of moral mania that will be noticed consists in a morbid activity of the *propensity to destroy ;* where the individual, without provocation or any other rational motive, apparently in the full possession of his reason, and oftentimes in spite of his most strenuous efforts to the contrary, imbrues his hands in the blood of others ; oftener than otherwise, of the partner of his bosom, of the children of his affections, of those, in short, who are most dear and cherished around him. The facts here alluded to are of painful frequency, and the gross misunderstanding of their true nature almost universally prevalent, excepting among a few in the higher walks of the profession, leads to equally painful results. In the absence of any pathological explanation of this horrid phenomenon, the mind seeks in vain among secondary causes for a rational mode of accounting for it, and is content to resort to that time-honored solution of all the mysteries of human delinquency, the instigation of the devil. Of the double homicide to which this affection gives rise, there can be no question which is most to be deplored, for, shocking as it is for one bearing the image of his Maker to take the life of his fellow-being with brutal ferocity, how shall we characterize the deliberate perpetration of the same deed under the sanction of law and of the popular approbation ? We trust, however, that the ample researches of writers of unquestionable veracity and ability, which are now just reaching the attention of the legal profession, will be soon followed by a conviction of past errors, and a more rational administration of the criminal law. * * * Esquirol, in his valuable memoir, first published in the shape of a note in the French translation of Hoffbauer's work, observes that homicidal insanity or *monomanie-homocide*, as he terms it, presents two distinct forms—in one of which the monomaniac is always influenced by avowed motives, more or less irrational, and is generally regarded as mad; in the other, there are no motives acknowledged nor to be discerned, the individual being impelled by a blind irresistible impulse.

After citing a number of cases to illustrate his views, this enlightened author further says:

> In most cases of homicidal insanity, the presence of some physical or moral disorder may be detected, and though none is mentioned in those above related, there is reason to suppose that it might have been ascertained by a more thorough examination.

In the case now under investigation in this court, both physical and moral disorders of the most painful and afflicting character have been discovered. We do not claim that this is one of those cases which, as Ray observes, have so often baffled the mind in their solution. On the contrary, we show you a person sick in mind and body, and assert that such functional disease of the brain ensued as to impel to this strange and irrational course of conduct. We are involved in no mysteries. We have the causes, and the effects have followed. A mind overstrained in the perpetual contemplation of a harrowing theme, and a body broken by painful disease, gave rise to a paroxysmal insanity, which assumed the destructive form. Ray, speaking further on this subject, says:

> In nearly all, the criminal act has been preceded, either by some well-marked disturbance of the health, originating in the head, digestive system, or uterus, or by an irritable, gloomy, dejected, or melancholy state; in short, by many of the symptoms of the incubation of mania.

In the light of these authorities, the conduct of the defendant seems no longer wonderful, and we are not compelled to look to the malicious contrivances of a depraved heart for its solution.

But we have heard it urged by the prosecution, with an air of triumph, that there is at least one act on her part which clearly proves her a rational being. She bought a pistol. Now, if any one thing in her whole history more than another proves her periods of insanity, and especially on the subject of her misfortune and bereavement, it is this act itself, and the circumstances under which the purchase was made. To one, when questioned, she replies that other ladies besides her carry pistols in Chicago; but her real reason, as you will remember she stated it, was one of those frightful ideas which pursue the startled and suspicious minds of the insane. She said that she believed there was a scheme between her false lover and his brother, Dr. Burroughs, to pick her up in the street some day and carry her away, where she would never be heard of again, and she meant to be ready to defend herself. She was haunted and pursued by this irrational fear. Says Ray again:

> In general mania, especially the early stage, the mind is filled with vague fears, suspicions, jealousy and distrust, and the thoughts are sadly confused. The pa-

tient believes that enemies encompass him around, bent on destroying his reputation or his life. With no special plan in view he arms himself with swords and pistols, and accident, or some unaccountable caprice, finally determines his victim.

Winslow, in his masterly work on the brain, in speaking of such a patient, also says:

> All objects within the range of his perverted senses are tinctured and distorted by a disordered vision, jaundiced eye, and morbidly exalted and excited fancy. In this incipient phase of mental derangement he shakes with fear at the reflection of his image; crouches with apprehension at the reverberating sound of his own footsteps; trembles at the melancholy sighing of the wind through a neighboring copse; turns pale at the echo of his voice; falls back aghast with horror at the recognition of his shadow, mistaking it for a frightful phantom or grim spectral image.
> Fierce as ten furies; terrible as hell.

Yes; and as Mary Harris hurried with feverish haste along those streets which she first visited in order to be near him whom she was now to see no more, and mingled amid those scenes which only spoke to her heart of him, she beheld a mocking specter forever at her side.

> She hears a voice we can not hear,
> Which says she must not stay;
> She sees a hand we can not see,
> Which beckons her away.

This act, then, on which reliance is placed for a conviction—the purchase of the pistol—is shown to have been induced by one of those wild delusions which are absolutely conclusive of a disordered intellect. It is the culmination of the evidence which her conduct affords while she yet remained at Chicago.

But she came to Washington, stopping a few days at Baltimore. She thought Burroughs had blackened her reputation, and that the world had turned against her. She thought to have a lawyer sue him; and when the question of damages was suggested, she simply said she did not mean that; he was poor, and she did not want his money, but she wanted to vindicate her honor. Why, says the prosecution, this is the talk of a rational woman. Certainly, the light of reason at times blazed up almost as strongly as ever, though, for a poor girl without means, except what she borrowed of Miss Devlin, to travel a thousand miles to bring suit against a man, and then refuse his money, is, in itself, an evidence of unnatural excitement.

But, let us meet this question here and now, and test it fairly by the rules of science. Let the inquiry embrace all that can be urged on this point against the defense. You say that she comes calmly into this court and does not rave in your presence. You say that, at certain times, when we catch a glimpse of her, she has exercised the attributes of reason. You have brought a number of witnesses here, from a great distance, to say that she was not mad in their unobservant presence. All this we admit, and more. We not only admit, but we assert, that there are intervals during which she is perfectly sane on all subjects.

I again quote Ray:

It is well known that many diseases, especially of the class called *nervous*, observe a law of periodicity which is not uncommon in the actions of the animal economy. One effect of this curious law consists in an intermission of the outward manifestations of the disease, so complete as to bear the appearance of a perfect cure, and this, in the present state of our knowledge, is all that we can with certainty say of it.

Dr. Reid says:

There are few cases of mania or melancholy where the light of reason does not now and then shine out between the clouds. In fevers of the mind, as well as those of the body, there occur frequent intermissions. But the mere interruption of a disorder is not to be mistaken for its cure or its ultimate conclusion. * * * Madmen may show at starts more sense than ordinary men.

But I do not stop here. I leave the question of lucid intervals, and approach the periods of the insane paroxysms. Even then the reasoning powers are often acute and accurate, defying at times the most patient skill to detect any malady of the mind.

Says Esquirol:

The insane group and arrange their ideas, carrying on a reasonable conversation, defend their opinions with subtlety, and even with a rigid severity of logic, give very rational explanations, and justify their actions by highly plausible motives.

Winslow also says:

Whilst analyzing the incipient symptoms of insanity, as manifested during the stage of exaltation and excitement, it will not be irrelevant for me to consider an important subject closely connected with the matter under consideration, but, perhaps, more immediately bearing upon a medico-legal point of great interest to the jurist, as well as to the practical psychologist. I refer to the subtlety, quickness of apprehension, ready wit, biting sarcasm, great power of self-control, extreme cunning, and extraordinary shrewdness of the insane, as well as the wonderful mastery they have occasionally been seen to exercise over their acknowledged delusions, whilst under the searching analysis of the ablest and most accomplished advocates of the day.

Of course, the prosecution here is compelled to fly in the face of all this, and insist that, in order that insanity may be proved to exist at all, it must appear so plainly that he who runs may read it, and that the wayfaring man, though a fool, may behold the fact at a single glance. We all remember the testimony of the renowned Erskine in regard to this question. He once examined a man in court with a view to the discovery of his mental alienation, and spent the entire day in propounding questions, to which the unfortunate man, who was really insane, returned answers which were perfectly correct and rational. In this case which we are now trying, Dr. Young, a very excellent physician and a worthy gentleman, says that he several times visited the prisoner in jail, and prescribed for her; that his attention was in nowise called to her mental condition, and that he did not discover any evidences of insanity. This seems conclusive to the minds of the gentlemen who represent the government; but in the light of scientific truth it is nothing; it vanishes as an imperceptible mote in the atmosphere. What strange delusions haunt the popular mind on this subject! We forget that the mind is a many-stringed instrument, and that, while it requires every chord in a healthy state to create a perfect harmony, yet one may be strained and broken, and still the others when touched give forth their own unimpaired tones. It is a matter of history that "Tasso composed his most eloquent and impassioned verses during paroxysms of insanity. Lucretius wrote his immortal poem *De Rerum Natura* when suffering from an attack of mental aberration. Alexander Cruden compiled his Concordance whilst insane. Some of the ablest articles in Aikin's Biography were written by a patient in a lunatic asylum." Sublime inventions have likewise sprung from the labors of disordered intellects, and exquisite statuary has stood up at their bidding. But in these most painful instances there was somewhere a hidden wound which would not heal, which bled at the touch. When it gaped afresh the whole instrument wailed forth in melancholy madness, and the stricken beings were irresponsible for their acts in the sight of God and man.

And now, gentlemen, as we approach the final and tragical scene where the disaster of this girl's life culminated in the death of Burroughs, let us pause a moment at Baltimore. Mrs. Fleming was called for the government, and yet all will admit that her evidence powerfully supports the defense. We see the defendant fitful, nervous, and wavering; as the witness says, not natural. At times she sinks in long and gloomy spells of abstracted silence. She gazes steadily on space and distance, all unconscious of surrounding objects. She breaks suddenly from these dismal reveries, sometimes in a ghostly and exalted glee.

Moody madness.
Laughing loud, amidst severest woe.

At other times she starts up, singing, in plaintiff strains, the broken fragments of some melancholy song which tells of disappointed love. When the witness heard her murmuring, "I loved him, but he doubted me," she heard the universal wail of woman's broken heart and wandering mind. And as the hour drew nigh for her departure to Washington, she spends a sleepless night poring over these fond letters of the deceased. The midnight is not more gloomy than her soul. She is communing with the lost—the lost hopes of other and brighter days—the lost hours of a radiant joy—the lost hours of love, of happiness and promise. She is amidst the tombs, and the demon, Memory, absorbs and binds her captive. She takes no note of time. The witness calls her, and finds her still buried in her thoughts. She starts in a hurry with a return ticket, in order to go back to Baltimore that evening. Thus this lonely being came here, and in this mood of mind she went to the treasury building. No wonder when she first reached there that the lady, whom the prosecution introduced, noticed a light in her eyes which alarmed her.

Up to this time, where are the indications or expressions of malice toward the deceased? Where is the evidence that she premeditated murder? The pistol itself is scarcely calculated to take life, and it has been shown that she obtained it under the influence of an insane delusion. She inquired for Burroughs; she wanted to see him. Was this with a desire to kill? In the instant that he fell by her hand, she implored God on her knees to spare him. Does the murderer beseech Divinity to spare his victim? She offered her life for his if he could be saved. Is this the conduct of one who lies in wait and assassinates in cold blood? As his life was ebbing away, she shrieked, "O God! I loved him better than my own soul." Is this the language of one who, in the exercise of reason, has smitten to death an object of hate and revenge? Recall that awful scene which was delineated before you by the honorable secretary of the treasury, the force and terror of which even, he declared, he could not properly describe. The rigid features, the white and ghastly face, the blazing and tearless eye, the rapid and, at times, incoherent speech, imprinted upon his mind, for the first time in his life, the dreadful reality of absolute despair. He rendered a verdict in favor of her innocence, when, with the instincts of the kind gentleman, he took Mrs. McCullough the next morning to visit her in prison. He had witnessed her state and condition, and judged the case correctly. There was neither premeditation, malice, nor design. She was incapable of either. It was the insane paroxysm to which we have already seen her subjected. We have the medical testimony, which I shall directly apply, but I will first support my position from the books.

Fodere, as quoted by Ray, uses this striking language:

> The mania, which is accompanied by fury, is very often periodical; that is, as if granting an occasional truce to the patient, it appears only at certain epochs, between which he enjoys all his reason, and seems to conduct and judge, in all respects, like other men, *if we except in regard to certain ideas the thought of which may, at any time, occasion a fresh paroxysm.*

Who ever possessed a more painful train of ideas than Mary Harris; and if the mere thought of them might, at any moment, unsettle her reason, how shall we describe the effect of the actual presence of Burroughs? For a year and more the memory of her wrongs at his hands had pressed like a hot iron on her brain, her health was broken, she was pursued by a delusion, and shook like an aspen in the wind; her nights were bereft of repose, and to her perturbed spirit day brought no rest or cheering. And thus, the feverish, drifting wreck of her former self, she met him. Mental philosophers have declared the result. It is at such a time that the beautiful language of his honor's charge is applicable. Frenzy mounts up by the side of reason, seizes it, and for the time being takes it prisoner.

Dr. Combe, one of the ablest thinkers on this subject, also says:

> But, however calm and rational the patient may appear to be during the lucid intervals, as they are called, and while enjoying the quietude of domestic society, or the limited range of a well-regulated asylum, it must never be supposed that he is in as perfect possession of his senses as if he had never been ill. In ordinary circumstances and under ordinary excitement, his perceptions may be accurate, and his judgment perfectly sound; but *a degree of irritability of brain remains behind, which renders him unable to withstand any unusual emotion, any sudden provocation, or any unexpected and pressing emergency.*

We only claim for this unfortunate defendant the demonstrations of science. We only ask that what universal experience has found true of others may be found true of her. She was very frail in mind and body, and "unable to withstand any unusual emotion, any sudden provocation, or any unexpected and pressing emergency." There was a "cause that hurt her brain," and the appearance of the deceased revived it in all its bitterness and power. The flash of the lightning is not more instantaneous and irresistible than was the awful impulse which followed. It may have been the swift avenging stroke of Nemesis. He may have beheld the spirit of retribution as he took that last, fearful glance at her unearthly face; but no attribute of reason guided her blow. It was the rebound of his own acts, which were conceived in guilt, but which now returned in madness to torment the inventor. He had laid for her a frightful train of ideas, all connected with himself. His presence applied the match, and the explosion hurled him into eternity.

But thus far, gentlemen of the jury, I have dwelt in my own feeble way upon the condition, language, and conduct of the prisoner, and the application of standard works of science, in order to reach the conclusion which is maintained by the defense. I now, however, take one further and higher step, and plant myself on sworn facts, which you can not disregard, except in violation of your oaths as jurors. We placed upon the stand a gentleman of eminent distinction as a physician of the diseased mind. Dr. Nichols has pursued this branch of science as a specialty for over twenty-five years, and has been the superintendent of the asylum for the insane in this District for the past eighteen years. His reputation is known extensively throughout the country, and I may be permitted to say that he has deeply impressed me as a gentleman of profound intellect, a vigorous and correct thinker, and a most conscientious laborer in the vineyard of truth. Life, honor, and justice are all safe in his hands. He comes before you, and relieves this case of every difficulty. He lifts a weighty responsibility from your shoulders, and makes your duties light and easy to be discharged. First, he has heard, and had submitted to him for inspection, every word of testimony in this cause to which you yourselves have listened. Secondly, he has visited the defendant in prison as often as he conceived necessary, to enable him to form a correct opinion of her condition. His means of information, therefore, embrace every source. He meets fully and completely the requirements of medical jurisprudence as an expert. No man ever stood up in a court of justice more amply qualified to give an opinion. And in view of this girl's history and early life, in view of the mental afflictions which overwhelmed her, in view of the physical disease which preyed upon her system, and in view of all the facts which her unhappy case presents to his analytical, discriminating, and scientific mind, he declares to you, as the result of his careful deliberations, that she has suffered from paroxysms of insanity, and that the act of homicide on the 30th of January arose from an insane impulse, and not from motives of hate or revenge—in his own language,"that this theory is more in harmony with the truth than the other."

THE DISTRICT ATTORNEY. He did not say that.

MR. VOORHEES. He did say it; and said it even in stronger language, I believe, than I have used, as the official record will show.

29

[The evidence of Dr. Nichols on this point was here read, and found to be as stated by the speaker.—*Reporter.*]

MR. VOORHEES. I knew that I was correct. Here, then, is the whole defense established by the highest evidence known to the law. The opinion of an expert is *a fact in the case.* No other witness can give any opinion at all. Dr. Nichols, therefore, proves as *a fact* that, from moral and physical causes combined, the defendant has labored under paroxysmal insanity, and that the act for which she is now on trial was committed during a paroxysm, and under an insane impulse. You have no legal right to find a verdict contrary to the testimony of Dr. Nichols, unless he is unworthy of belief, or has been successfully contradicted by other competent witnesses, whose opinions are entitled to greater weight than you attach to his. On this proposition I rest securely. And on the uncontradicted statement of this scientific witness I risk the life of the prisoner. He is the Saint Peter of my faith, and on this rock I build the defense; and neither the power of the public prosecution nor the gates of private malice shall prevail against it.

But we are met at this point with a proposition by the prosecution which I undertake to say is without a parallel in the courts of any country which has been blessed with the light of civilization. Utterly borne down and crushed by the evidence of Dr. Nichols, the gentlemen who represent the government boldly and without a blush declare that the opinions of men who, like him, have given their lives to the study of the mind in all its various and mysterious phases, are less reliable in the discovery of insanity than the opinions of those who have bestowed no particular attention on this great and difficult subject. The cry of "mad doctors" has been raised, and we heard an appeal against them in favor of what were styled "common-sense doctors." Gentlemen, I feel humiliated that I have listened to such language from such a source. Is there such an unappeasable rage to take the poor life of this prisoner that in order to do it these distinguished gentlemen are willing to resort to the lowest and most pernicious arts of the profession? Do they propose to deride the disciples of learning, the devotees of science? Will they stand up here in the noon-day of human progress and enter the lists as the avowed champions of ignorance?

Who are the "mad doctors" of the world at whom this persistent and systematic sneer is leveled? They are those who have made the subject of insanity a specialty, who have given their days and nights to incessant and laborious thought, who have struggled with painful toil to alleviate the direst woes of their fellow-men, to cure those wounds which the lash of misfortune inflicts, and to pluck from the diseased mind its rooted sorrows. And is it found necessary to stamp such characters with odium in order to convict Mary Harris? Shall we pluck from the scientific heavens their brightest and boldest luminaries, and accept darkness, gloom, and mist again? Shall we strike down that blazing galaxy of genius, toil, and progress, where the names of Winslow, Esquirol, Ray, Gall, Spurzheim, Rush, Combe, Prichard, Ellis, Hoffbauer, with others of the shining host, are burning as stars on the front of the sky; and into whose glorious companionship we anticipate but a few years by introducing now the name of Dr. Nichols himself?

These are they against whom the prosecutors invoke the aid of ignorance and prejudice. They have certainly mistaken the age in which they live. The district attorney is nearly two centuries in the rear of the still advancing column of human improvement. There was a period in the world's history when this assault on men of science would have relaxed the dull features of stupidity into a smile and caused blind superstition to nod its ugly head with approval. There was a time when darkness rested upon the face of the waters in the scientific world, when the voice of learning had not yet brought order out of chaos, when courts of justice were nurseries of bigotry, when mental derangement was judicially interpreted as the possession of a demon, and the sufferer declared to be in familiar communion with the prince of evil. At such a time as this the district attorney could have charged upon "mad doctors" amidst acclamations. Could he have found an enlightened man of science during such a period he could doubtless have had him hung as a sorcerer or magician, along with the party whom he declared to be insane. And even now, to-day, wherever there is a cavern in which the owls and bats of ignorance, superstition, and gangrened prejudice yet inhabit, where the rays of liberal enlightenment have not yet penetrated, and where no beautiful thing has ever grown as a sign of progress, there his voice, going forth from this court-room, in denunciation of the growth, the achievements, the accumulated treasures of ages, will be hailed as if clothed with the authority of a heathen oracle in the days of heathen supremacy. Yes, in order to ask for a conviction at your hands, he is compelled to repudiate the products of civilization, recede into the darkness of the past, and from the gloomy fortresses of barbarism shower his missiles on the head of this most unfortunate being. When Paul explained the mysteries of the redemption, the barbarian official of Rome cried out, "Much learning hath made thee mad." Dr. Nichols pours a flood of light upon the issue before this court, and the law officer of the government says, "Thou art a mad doctor." It is no part of my purpose to give offense, but in the name of bright-eyed truth, in the name of immortal science, in the name of the high, advanced banners of civilization, in the name of the stalwart, conquering spirit of gigantic progress, in the name of the greatest benefactors of suffering and diseased humanity, in the name of the liberal, humane, and learned profession of which I am an humble member, and in the name of an American court of justice, I protest against this attempt to break down and trample under foot the wisdom, the experience, and the labor of ages, and to destroy, by an unworthy appeal to the basest prejudices of mankind, those safeguards which the proudest intellects of the earth have erected around such victims of misfortune as this young prisoner.

But let us see how the prosecution, after all, has fared in the issue which it attempted to make between Dr. Nichols and those members of the medical profession who have been introduced as witnesses, under the novel title of "common-sense doctors." Upon a presentation of the case, detailing the evidence with wonderful fidelity and accuracy, every physician, without a single exception who was placed upon the stand by the government, concurred instantly and unreservedly with Dr. Nichols. Dr. May, Dr. Miller, Dr. Johnson, Dr. Howard—all very eminent, and of long experience in their profession, standing in the very front ranks—swear without hesitation that, in their opinions, the defendant was subject to paroxysmal insanity, and that the presence of Burroughs developed a maniacal impulse over which she had no control, and before which he fell. Will it be said that Mr. Bradley did not submit a fair statement of facts to these medical gentlemen? You shall judge of that. Would he fabricate a case on which to obtain their opinions? The district attorney and Mr. Wilson certainly do not mean such an imputation. Can a man at his time of life, at the head of his profession, eminent in it before some of us were born, beloved and respected by all; can he afford to attempt to practice a fraud upon you in your presence, when you have all the means of detecting it? No. He submitted the whole case, including his own accurate and most intelligent observations of her wretched condition in prison—a recital so vivid and eloquent in its faithful simplicity that thoughts of it swell the heart with emotion, and banish from our minds all idea of guilt in the conduct of the prisoner.

Let us, then, sum up the result of the medical testimony. Five eminent physicians, with Dr. Nichols at their head, in this branch of their profession, establish the irresponsibility of the defendant. Four of them were called by the government to establish the contrary. Not one has given it as his opinion that she was sane at the time of the homicide. There is absolutely no conflict of evidence on the point, and hence we hold that we have brought ourselves within the ruling of the court. The court has charged you that the burden of this issue is upon us; that it is not enough for us to raise a doubt in your minds whether she was sane or not, but that we must establish her insanity by the weight of evidence, and beyond a reasonable doubt. Favorable as this construction of the law is to the prosecution, yet it can avail nothing in behalf of a conviction, for not merely the weight of the evidence, but all, every particle of the evidence touching the question of insanity, is with the defense. The prosecution stands destitute and naked, without a shadow of support. I challenge the records of the courts of this or any other country to show a more perfect and conclusive defense, or a more powerless and utterly defeated prosecution. We hear much said in regard to the defense of insanity. Many speak of it as a plea manufactured by counsel. It is, however, in one vital respect, like all others—it must be supported by proof or it falls to the ground. Have we manufactured the positive and direct testimony of every medical witness introduced on both sides? Is this our handiwork? I submit to you and to the candid judgment of the country, that if Mary Harris can be convicted under this evidence, if Dr. Nichols can be broken down in this court, not by contradiction, but by declamatory appeals to prejudice, and if, finally, the unbroken chain of scientific testimony can be put aside as naught, then the great and settled principles of medical jurisprudence are a delusion and a snare, and the infirmities of the intellect occasioned by misfortune constitute no defense for violent and irrational conduct.

And why, without one solitary witness to support their theory of the case, do the prosecutors so hunger and thirst for the conviction of this most desolate and bereaved of sorrowing mortals! Why do they clamor so fiercely against the barriers of the law and of the evidence which encompass her about, in order to drag that sick and fragile body to a miserable death? Is it punishment they seek? She has suffered more already than the king of terrors in his most frightful form can inflict. If she had been broken on the wheel, her limbs disjointed, and her flesh torn in piecemeal by the most fiendish skill of the executioner, her tortures would have been merciful compared to the racking which sunders into fragments the immortal mind. There is no arrow in death's full quiver that can give this young breast a new sensation of agony. She has sounded all the depths and shoals of misery and pain. She has lived in

> A whirling gulf of phantasy and flame.

Restore her by your verdict to the soothing influence of friends, of home. Let her go and lay her aching head on the maternal bosom of that church which for eighteen centuries has tenderly ministered to her children in distress. Let her go and seek, in the love and mercy of the Father of us all, consolation for the cruelty and inhumanity of man.

But it is claimed that a conviction must be had for the sake of example. You have been told that the people of the District of Columbia demand it. I would not bring such an argument into court, but when here I will meet it. If it be true that you desire examples for the correction of vice and the preservation of morality, I pray you not to commence with the humblest, the feeblest, and the most helpless. But I deny that the condemnation of the defendant is demanded by the people of this capital. Who are they who ask her blood at your hands? I know this people, and to some extent I think I may speak for them. I have been the recipient of their constant kindness while in their midst, and as a representative in congress I have, in return, dealt with them in a spirit of liberality whenever I have known their wishes. You were told that the defendant came here from a distance—that the states were pouring their criminals in upon you, and therefore she must suffer as a warning to others. Such a statement is unjust to your people. You want justice, and justice alone, administered upon all: and who believes that this girl's life is required as an offering upon the altar of public justice? I repel this imputation upon the intelligence and humanity of this kind and hospitable District. When you are discharged from your protracted confinement and return to your homes, as you will in a few hours, ask those whom you meet there whether they desired you to cut the feeble thread of this girl's life by your verdict. I will abide by their answer. To no one has she appeared as the criminal, save to those who conduct and inspire the prosecution. To all others in your midst she has presented the sad spectacle of calamity and misery. Her purity, her gentleness, her guileless truth, shining out in every word and act, have won to her side in this dark hour your oldest, your best, and most honored citizens. Her prison abode has been brightened by the presence of the noblest and purest of her own sex, and delicate flowers from the loftiest station in the world have mingled their odors with the breath of her captivity.* Men, venerable in their years, and strong in their convictions of the principles of

---

*Mr. Voorhees here alludes to a beautiful bouquet sent to the prisoner by Mrs. Lincoln, before the White House had been darkened by murder, the central flower of which signified, in botanical language, " Trust in me."

immutable right, have been drawn to her assistance by an instinctive obedience to the voice of God, commanding them to succor the weak, lift up the fallen, and alleviate the distress of innocence. And now for Mary Harris, and in the name of him who showered his blessing on the merciful, who spoke the parable of the Samaritan, who gave the promise to those who feed and clothe the stranger in their gates, and who visit the sick and them that are in prison, I thank the people of the capital. Add one more obligation for her to remember until the grave opens to hide her from the world. It is in your hands to grant. The law in its grave majesty approves the act. The evidence with an unbroken voice demands it. Your own hearts press forward to the discharge of a most gracious duty. The hour is almost at hand for its performance. Unlock the door of her prison, and bid her bathe her throbbing brow once more in the healing air of liberty. Let your verdict be the champion of law, of morality, of science. Let it vindicate civilization and humanity, justice and mercy.

Appealing to the Searcher of all hearts, to that omnipresent eye which beholds every secret thought, for the integrity of my motives in the conduct of this cause, and for the sincerity of my belief in the principles which I have announced, I now, with unwavering confidence in the triumph of innocence, surrender all into your hands.

THE KILBOURN CASE

ARGUMENT ON WRIT OF HABEAS CORPUS

On the 14th day of March, 1876, Hallet Kilbourn, then a real estate broker in the city of Washington, was, by a resolution of the house of representatives of the United States, adjudged in contempt of the house for his refusal to appear before a special committee thereof, appointed to investigate an alleged real estate pool and the Jay Cooke indebtedness to the United States, and to obey a certain *subpœna duces tecum* requiring him to produce, for the inspection of the committee, certain of his private books and papers. Acting upon the authority of this resolution, John G. Thompson, sergeant-at-arms of the house, assumed the custody of Mr. Kilbourn and committed him to the common jail of the District of Columbia until such time as he should purge himself of such contempt.

On the 11th day of April, following, Mr. Voorhees, Hon. Jeremiah S. Black, Hon. Matt. H. Carpenter, Hon. Charles A. Eldredge, Gen. Noah L. Jeffries and Walter D. Davidge, Esquire, as counsel for Mr. Kilbourn, presented to the Honorable David K. Cartter, chief-justice of the supreme court of the District of Columbia, an application for a writ of *habeas corpus*, whereupon the court made an order directing the marshal of the United States for the District of Columbia to take the body of Mr. Kilbourn into his custody, and keep him safely until further order.

On the 19th day of April, the hearing proceeded upon the application, return of respondent and reply of relator, and continued throughout the 19th, 20th, 21st and 24th days of said month.

The sergeant-at-arms was represented, during the various stages of this litigation, by Hon. Samuel S. Shellabarger, Col. Robert I. Christy, Judge William Merrick, William M. Trescott, Esquire, H. Wise Garnett, Esquire, Hon. Frank Hurd, W. H. Smith, Esquire, Hon. Jeremiah M. Wilson, and District Attorney George B. Corkhill, representing the attorney-general of the United States.

On the 24th of April, Mr. Voorhees made the argument which follows.

On the 28th, the chief-justice delivered an opinion sustaining Mr. Kilbourn's contention, and ordered his discharge from the custody of the house.

Mr. Kilbourn, at the January term of the supreme court of the District of Columbia, instituted a civil action against Michael C. Kerr, John G. Thompson, John M. Glover, Jeptha D. New, Burwell B. Lewis and A. Herr Smith, to recover $150,000 for false imprisonment. A demurrer to the declaration was interposed, which was sustained and judgment rendered for the defendants.

The cause was taken, by writ of error, by Mr. Kilbourn, to the supreme court of the United States. In that tribunal the judgment of the lower court was affirmed as to all the defendants save John G. Thompson, but was reversed as to him, and the cause remanded for trial.

May it Please your Honor:

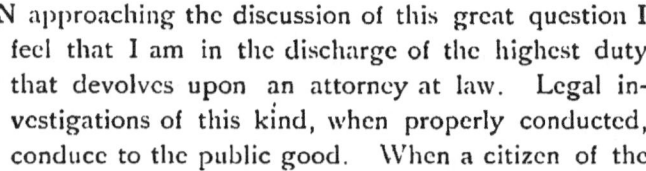

IN approaching the discussion of this great question I feel that I am in the discharge of the highest duty that devolves upon an attorney at law. Legal investigations of this kind, when properly conducted, conduce to the public good. When a citizen of the United States is in prison and asks that his imprisonment be judicially inquired into, a member of the bar who would hesitate to present his claims to a court of justice would be unworthy American citizenship. I come, therefore, to the discussion of this question with all the sincerity that arises from a sense of duty. Let there be no misunderstanding upon that point. I regard the presentation of Mr. Kilbourn's right as a citizen here as of the highest, gravest, and most transcendent importance, involving a discussion of the powers of the various departments of this government that can never be indulged in without benefit to all concerned in it, or who give intelligent attention thereto. And so, now, we will look at the beginning of this case.

When the writ under discussion was first issued, an astonishing spectacle was presented. It was deliberately proposed by the law committee of the house of representatives that it should not be obeyed. It would have been the first precedent of the kind in American history, had the proposition been adopted. In the face of the constitution of the United States, which says that the privilege of the writ of *habeas corpus* shall not be suspended, unless, when in cases of rebellion or invasion, the public safety may require it; in the face of that provision, in time of profound peace, not merely congress, but one branch of congress—not the whole of congress, but a part of congress, proposed to suspend the writ of *habeas corpus*. That was the solemn proposition made to the house of representatives, for there was nothing else in it. If the house of representatives, the president, or a military officer, or anybody else, says no to the writ of *habeas corpus*, what is it but a suspension of the writ? Can anybody tell me? Can anybody answer me what else it is? Nothing but that. And the constitution says in express and powerful words, using the fewest possible in order to make them strong, that such suspension shall not take place except when rebellion or invasion requires it for the public safety.

It has long, sir, been a question who had the power of suspending the writ of *habeas corpus* even in rebellion and invasion. I never thought anything less than the two branches of congress could do it. I denied that power to the president always, because this great writ is aimed at executive authority more than at anybody else. And allow me to say to the gentlemen on the other side here this morning, that there is not a crowned head to-day anywhere inside the boundaries of civilized government that would dare to do what it was proposed the house of representatives should do. There may be barbarian monarchs, outside of the pale of civilization, who can throw their subjects into prison and keep them there and defy judicial investigation, but the emperor of Russia can not do it. The emperor of Germany can not do it, with all the consolidated Germanic states at his feet. The queen of England, the empress of India, can not do it, either in England, Scotland, Ireland, or in India. If she should attempt it she would not stay on her throne thirty days. An attempt of this kind was one of the prime causes that expelled James II, and created the revolution of 1688, which again reasserted Magna Charta, restored *habeas corpus* and petition of rights, and settled English privileges, so that, at least, no king has ever attempted again what the house of representatives was solemnly asked to do. And the last time the British parliament, in what is called its omnipotence, dared propose such an act, is just one hundred and seventy-two years ago. The world moves. The world moves in the courts as well as in the sciences. It moves in the churches, in morality, in ethics, in law, in all the departments of thought and human action. The movements of the human race are forward, and I shall spend little time in going back a hundred years or more to follow up many of the decisions that have been produced here. In the same period those decisions were born you can find others declaring that the tax on tea was constitutional, and that our forefathers who threw it into Boston

Harbor were violating the British constitution and the common law of England.

Sir, the sober thought of the house of representatives convinced them that they could not suspend the writ of *habeas corpus*. They could not suspend it even if it had been in time of war, the senate not concurring. The writ commanded the officer of the house to bring the body of Hallet Kilbourn into court in order that it might be seen whether his commitment was according to law or not.

Let us see, then, what the house did. It acted wisely. The house, by obeying this writ and sending its officer with the body of the prisoner into court, consents to its operation. What are its functions? Its functions are those of judicial inquiry; and why was Mr. Kilbourn brought here if there was nothing to inquire into? The entire argument of the gentlemen has been that, although he is here, and although the house of representatives sent him here, they sent him here in order that they might say that you had nothing whatever to do with him. They say that you have no judicial inquiry to make at all; that the question of the power of the house to punish for contempts is *res adjudicata;* that you can not inquire whether the house had jurisdiction of the offense or of the subject. Very well, then. Why are we here? Why did the house of representatives, after full discussion, say to its officer, take Mr. Kilbourn to the supreme court of this District? If the power to punish for contempt is *res adjudicata*, and if you have no power to investigate the point of jurisdiction, I do not know what we have been here for, and I do not know why the house of representatives sent him. Those are the only things that can be inquired into, and I say the action of the house itself is the agreement of a party to this proceeding, that this court may inquire into all matters it deems proper and legitimate touching the liberty of this citizen of the United States, touching the question of whether he is legally or illegally imprisoned. The vote of the house of representatives, of one hundred and sixty-five to seventy-five, of more than two to one, sending this man here, is the solemn consent of the house of representatives that this inquiry shall be made. The argument of the gentlemen all the way through was that there was nothing to inquire into here; that the power to punish was closed, and you could not inquire into that; and that the question of jurisdiction was beyond your inquiry. Then, I repeat again, why are we here? What is all this talk and delay about, and why did the house of representatives, if that is the law, send this case here at all? If they had determined there was nothing that this court could inquire into, if they had determined that there was no jurisdictional point, then they would have adhered to the report of the judiciary committee, which said to the court, it is none of your business. But, instead of that, they have said by their return, you have something to do with this case; take it and inquire into it, as has been done in all the ages of civilized jurisprudence since liberty was established on the foundations of law.

Let us next determine what can properly be made the subject of inquiry in this court. So far as the house of representatives is concerned, it has consented that this court may inquire from top to bottom. So far as the house is concerned, it has consented in coming here, with the body of the prisoner, that there is no phase of this case that you may not investigate; but in your honor's judgment, based upon the decision of the supreme court, as interpreted by you, the inquiry is limited, and I shall discuss the question upon that limited basis. This court has held in our presence, and the supreme court's decision has been relied upon to that effect—whether I give the doctrine my assent or not, or whether you do or not, is not the question—that the question of the power of either branch of congress to punish for contempt, other than its own members, is to be taken as *res adjudicata* in this case. The next question is, whether this court can inquire whether the house of representatives had jurisdiction of this case. If that is denied, then there is nothing left for this court to do. If that is denied, this return need not have been made. If the proposition of the gentlemen here is true, that the question of the power of the house to punish for contempt is settled and that you have no power to inquire into the jurisdiction, then I should like to ask any intelligent man what restraint—where, in what way, can the house of representatives be restrained in the exercise of irresponsible and unlimited power over anybody? Will anybody answer me? If they are the judges of their own jurisdiction, and of the extent of punishment, and of the manner of it, then we have a power here far beyond that of monarchs. What answer can be made to this? Are the gentlemen ready to go to that extent, that the house has exclusive power to judge whether it has jurisdiction over you or me, and then how much, and in what way, it will punish? *Something* must be left to be inquired into by the court, or else each house of congress has a power before which the human mind stands appalled. If they have the unlimited power of punishment, and the unlimited power of jurisdiction also, need I stop to argue the question before this court, whether they may not put a man to death, just as well as to put him in prison? Why not? Oh, say the gentlemen here, we must presume that congress will not do wrong. I will not presume any such thing. I know too well the contrary. There are no presumptions of that kind. Presume that congress will not do wrong! No, a long experience with my friend from Ohio, in the house of representatives, teaches me personally the contrary. And further, no philosophic mind will assume that human nature can be intrusted with irresponsible power, on the presumption that it will not do wrong. It will always do wrong when it has unlimited power. When one of the embassadors of an Assyrian king approached the prophet of God, consulting him in regard to the condition of his master, the prophet burst into tears, and foretold an evil career for the questioner; that he would ascend the king's vacant throne when he died, and smite God's people in all their borders. And the embassador knew himself so little, was so incensed, that he exclaimed, "Is thy servant a dog, that he should do this?" Yet he did the very thing when the opportunity came.

The possession of power is like the tiger's taste of blood, it is not to be permitted. Neither presidents, nor congresses, nor courts are to be left with unlimited power. Whenever that is done, farewell to our free form of government. We are a government of checks, of restraints, and I would no more trust congress with unlimited power over the lives and liberties of citizens than I would the same number of men any place else in the United States. Therefore, if it please your honor, I yield nothing to this presumption. I repudiate it, and spurn it from me. The presumption that congress will not do wrong, and, therefore, you can trust it with unlimited powers; therefore, this court will not inquire into its jurisdiction; therefore, the court will not inquire into their cause for punishment; therefore, there is nothing for this court to do here except to turn the question back to this unlimited despot that sits in one end of the capitol, called the house of representatives! A more atrocious doctrine was never advanced in an American court, or on American soil! Let it be proclaimed as an established law throughout the United States that congress has the power to construe what is a contempt, and then the unlimited power to determine how it will punish that contempt, whether with chains or death; let that go forth, and congress will not long exist in this country. Why, if that power exists it ought to have been called in a good while ago. How comfortable a doctrine would it have been when the house of representatives desired to get rid of Andrew Johnson, when he was president of the United States! They tried him by impeachment. They were mistaken; they ought to have tried him for contempt. He had a great, a sovereign, and openly declared contempt for congress; traveled extensively, declaring it at every step. All they needed to do was to arrest him for contempt, bring him to the bar of the house, and then punish him as they pleased. Do you say they could not do it because he was president? Ah, but you have claimed the right of each house of congress to determine whether they could or not; they need have cared nothing about the fact that he was president. "We are the sole judges; we will take jurisdiction. Nobody has a right to inquire; nobody has the right to investigate." No *habeas corpus* can confer upon the court the right to determine the point of jurisdiction, and they could, by imprisoning Mr. Johnson the balance of his term, have had the president in their own hands, or if he had been an uncomfortable incumbrance in prison, they could have killed him by the same power that is claimed here. The mind of man can not meet this argument. They could have killed Mr. Johnson just as well as keep him in prison. This is a novel doctrine. It ought to have been thought of before. It would have saved much trouble, and even now, instead of proceeding by impeachment against persons, why not construe their alleged offenses into contempts of the house of representatives, and put them into prison that way? You may say that the house of representatives could only imprison a man as long as its own life lasted. Just let, then, the senate declare its sense of contempt; the senate never dies; it could keep a man there until he dies in prison. I give this illustration to show the monstrous absurdity of this doctrine, to show its atrocity, and that it has no place in the bounds of reason, and consequently can have none in the bounds of law. What is not founded in reason can not be founded in law.

Now, sir, if this question of the jurisdiction of the house belongs to it solely to determine, as well as the power to punish, and the mode, and the extent, let us look the issue squarely in the face. It has power over life and death, no limitation, no restraint, no inquiry. Nobody has a right to interfere. Let this doctrine prevail, and first one party, and then another, will rend this country into bloody atoms. Why this fear of the judiciary? Why this fear of the courts interfering with congress? The courts are not swayed by the popular passions expressed in elections every two years. They do not change with the changes of the multitude. And allow me to say that if courts had been more respected in this country, if they had been obeyed, as Mr. Webster pointed out their powers in his reply to Hayne, of South Carolina, when he demonstrated that there was but one tribunal of last resort, but one from which no appeal could be made, the supreme court of the United States; if that doctrine had been obeyed and respected there would have been no line of grave-yards from one ocean to the other across this continent. The sword would have slumbered in its scabbard, and the peaceful fields would have waved where the grain has since grown strong with the blood that enriches the soil. Talk not to me about the dread of the courts and the supremacy of congress. I feel safe and secure as in a peaceful haven when I am in the courts of my country. The fury of the political elements ceases to rage within their sacred precincts. Here is the shelter of liberty regulated by law.

Now, to the law in regard to jurisdiction. I am content to rest where my learned brother, Mr. Shellabarger, rested the argument—

in the Lord Ellenborough decision in 14 East. In that case Lord Ellenborough did say, as the gentleman here read and reread, that in a case of sheer, naked usurpation by parliament against a party for contempt the courts would interfere. But with pertinacity he clings to the language, "sheer, naked, mere usurpation." What care I for these adjectives, if I can show a plain, palpable violation of the constitution of the United States in this case? It will be "sheer," and "palpable," and "naked" enough to suit the purpose. I do not know what would be a more palpable usurpation than a distinct violation of the constitution we are all sworn to support. Sir, the stress laid by the distinguished gentleman upon the statement that the usurpation must be "sheer," and "palpable," and "naked," amounts to nothing except an attempt to cover up what Lord Ellenborough does decide, and that is, that there is a point where the court must intervene and determine whether the parliament, even of England, certainly the house of representatives, has transcended its powers. I took down a remarkable expression of Mr. Shellabarger's, in which he said that the court would not intervene for one little wrong committed by mistake. If I mistake, you can correct me, but I took it down so.

MR. SHELLABARGER. It was a mistake.

MR. VOORHEES. In pleading for this new power of the house of representatives, Mr. Shellabarger went a great way, and asked us to presume that it would not do wrong, and, as I understood him to say, even if it did a little, the court would not hold it to a very strict account for it.

MR. SHELLABARGER. No. Allow me to correct you.

MR. VOORHEES. I would not misrepresent you. I will accept any corrections you wish to make, cheerfully.

MR. SHELLABARGER. I applied that word "little" to the matter as to whether this inquiry of the committee was to be thrown out as not within the jurisdiction of the house, because it was a little matter; I said no.

MR. VOORHEES. Very well. If the Ellenborough decision is the law—and it is, if it decided anything—you and I know that it did determine that there comes a time, some time or other, in cases

30

of this kind, when the courts are called on to interfere and determine whether the house has transcended its power or not. That is what I am contending for. I am contending that there is something to be inquired into here by this court. They are contending that you have nothing to do. I say, and say it upon the authority of Lord Ellenborough's decision, that if a plain and palpable violation of the powers of the house under the constitution has taken place, then by that decision you are called on to determine that point. When Mr. Shellabarger dwelt upon the sheer, palpable, naked violation, he stopped short of saying that that very thing had to be determined by the court; that nobody else could determine except the court when that state of affairs had taken place. There is where I take my stand—that nobody but the court can determine when the court has the right to intervene and is called on to intervene. Who else can? The proposition in the Ellenborough decision is that sometimes the court is called on to intervene. I say in response to that that nobody but the court can determine when that is. The case is here. It is discussed here. It is returned here. The authorities cited by the gentleman himself say that if there is a plain, palpable violation of the constitution, it is the duty of the court to intervene. Is somebody to come in here and tell this court when the time has come for it to act? Is congress to tell the court? Is some outside power and intelligence to inform the court when that violation has taken place—when you may intervene? The very fact that such a power is conceded carries with it the concession of the right to determine when the point has been reached, when the court is called on to intervene. Can any proposition be plainer than that? Need I stand here to discuss that at any length? There are certain propositions of law and of reason so plain, so direct, that the mere statement of them is all the argument of which they are capable. Let all the rest of his cases go. I stand upon this, his own English case, and he cited none that contradicted the Ellenborough decision. That in the assertion of this great power over life and death by the house; this power to punish for contempt; this power to punish a citizen for an offense which he knew not of and which is written in no law, an offense to be created in the breast of congressmen, which may be created against me for what I am doing, or against you for what you are doing; this omnipotent power to execute a secret law which is nowhere written, nowhere promulgated, unknown by the people; I say that in the exercise of this great power there comes up in the midst of all the decisions this still small voice of the law that some time or other the exercise of such a power comes under judicial review. If it were not so, woe to the land. Our homes might be ravished, private interests destroyed by so-called investigations, business men torn from their desks at the behests of unscrupulous men in and out of congress. There would be no border-line of safety, none whatever; and I proclaim, as far as my voice reaches, such a construction of my government is as alien to my thoughts as the empire of Russia would be.

Again, sir, throwing light upon this question, I find from examination that the states, as far as I have had opportunity to investigate, have not rested their power to punish for contempts on any intangible, unseen, unknown emanation from their constitutions, as is claimed for congress. No state acts on that doctrine. The state legislatures, closer to the people than the federal government, do not rest their power to punish for contempt on any undeclared, secret, hidden law in the breast of the legislator. On the contrary, every state whose action I have had a chance to examine, has passed laws defining their power to punish for contempts. The state of Massachusetts has done it. The state of New York has done it, and, I believe, the state of Ohio. In all of them they have given their people the benefit of a law declaring the power of the legislative body of the commonwealth over this question. They have not left it, as congress has in times past, to sudden construction—to the swift winds and waves of passion. They have defined by law what are contempts, and how they are to be punished, and how great the punishment. Now, sir, will it be contended that where that is the case they have less power than congress, which has no such legislation? That is to say, will it be contended that congress has as a legislative body more power on this question than the legislature of Massachusetts, which has it expressly given by law? And yet, what do we find? Take the celebrated Emery case that has been read in your hearing.

It is a proclamation of liberty. In that case, 107 Massachusetts, the supreme court said: "That any person held in custody of either branch of the legislature is entitled to have the cause of his imprisonment examined by the supreme judicial court upon *habeas corpus*. This doctrine is fully settled by the case of Burnham *vs.* Morrissey, in 14th Gray."

Now, has congress, by implication and by a silent exhalation, as it were, from the constitution, or by an unseen inherent stream from the British parliament, higher powers on this subject than the legislature of the commonwealth of Massachusetts, which has it by express grant? The latter is the legislature of a sovereignty in its sphere as much as congress is the legislature of a sovereignty in its, and yet that high and learned judicial tribunal, the supreme court of the state of Massachusetts, ranking in the day when this case was decided, in learning and intelligence, with the supreme court of the United States itself, holds that any citizen of the state of Massachusetts is entitled to have the cause of his imprisonment examined by the supreme judicial authority upon *habeas corpus*. In the case of Burnham *vs.* Morrissey, 14 Gray, cited in this case, occurs the following language:

> The house of representatives is not the final judge of its powers and privileges in cases in which the rights and liberties of the subjects are concerned.

God forbid it ever should be. Of course it is not the final judge of its powers and privileges in cases in which the rights and liberties of the subject are concerned, "but the illegality of its action may be examined and determined by this court."

> That house is not the legislature, but only a part of it, and is, therefore, subject in its action to the laws, in common with all other bodies, officers and tribunals within the commonwealth. Especially is it competent and proper for this court to consider whether its proceedings are in conformity with the constitution and laws, because, living under a written constitution, no branch or department of this government is supreme.

This is the fundamental proposition I started out with. There is no king in this country. There is nothing supreme here except the law, and what that law is can be determined by but one tribunal, made for that purpose, to avoid forcible collisions. It is the province and duty of the judicial department to determine whether the powers of any branch of the government, and those of the legislature in the enactment of laws, have been exercised in conformity with the constitution; and if they have not, to treat their acts as null and void. This is a case affecting the life and liberty of a citizen. I think, sir, that it will not be contended that the legislature of Massachusetts, the legislature of a sovereign commonwealth within its limited powers, as this is the legislature of a sovereignty within its limited powers and no more—it will not be contended that the legislature of the state has less powers, because they are especially granted, than congress, which has no such express grant. I might stop to consider where this claim of power comes from. The constitution of the United States has a few words upon this subject. I find that when congress is described it is not mentioned as a judicial body. It is not described as a court. It is known in the constitution as follows:

> All legislative powers granted shall be vested in the congress of the United States, which shall consist of a senate and house of representatives.

Now, if the gentleman will find where there is any word granting it judicial powers I would like to know it. It is a legislative body created by the constitution. It is not a court, and to show that it is not, let us run over to another provision of the constitution. The constitution is good reading in these days of uncertainty and confusion:

> The judicial power of the United States shall be vested in one supreme court, and in such inferior courts as the congress from time to time may ordain and establish.

And then goes on to tell us how the judges shall hold their offices.

The legislative powers are given to congress; the judicial powers are given to the courts, and yet the trouble has been, in this country, that every once in a while—not very often, I am glad to say in behalf of the judiciary—once in a while a court tries to legislate, and then it gets into trouble. And once in a while a congress tries to adjudicate, and it gets into trouble. If they could only stand, each on its side of the line of division, we would have no trouble at all, and our beautiful government would move in such harmony as would make music, not clashing and harsh, grating sounds, but sweet music. That is the trouble. Congress once in a while gets in a passionate mood, and is not content with what the constitution gives it in the way of legislative power, but it must assume to be a court; a court of chancery to file bills; as in this case, to try the real estate pool; to determine questions that are already pending in court, and set itself up as having all the jurisdiction, and more than any court I have ever heard of. There is one question on which all lawyers are agreed, that all courts can inquire into each other's jurisdiction to see if there was a case. If there is in this court a judgment, the record signed and sealed, and I take a transcript of it to Indiana, and bring suit on it there, that record is conclusive of all things but one. That is, whether this court had jurisdiction. That is one of the fundamental principles of law. But the house of representatives, without being a court at all, and without having a single judicial power expressly granted to it, gets above and beyond all courts, and says that neither as to the matter itself, nor as to whether they had jurisdiction, shall any court inquire.

And we heard at first, in this case, much talk about courts of inferior jurisdiction inquiring into the powers of congress, as if congress were a court and ranked some other court; as if congress were a court of superior jurisdiction. Such discussion is only calculated to mislead minds unlearned in the law. Congress is never a court, neither is it above or below any court. It is not in the judicial range of the constitution. It is unknown as a court to our policy of government. I listened to the argument of Mr. Shellabarger on this point with that sort of impatience which sometimes comes over me when I doubt my own senses, when I say to myself, "Can a man of high and recognized position, and of such unquestioned intelligence in the law, be advancing something that is utterly preposterous, or is it that I am wrong?" But when I go back to the language of the constitution and find what courts are, and what congress is, I am relieved of all doubt. Away with this discussion as to whether this court is above or below congress. Away with this discussion, as if you were talking between two courts. Congress is simply a legislative body, and in order to exercise successfully its legislative functions devolved on it by the constitution, it may sometimes, and in limited instances, exercise those kinds of power that are akin to, close upon, and perhaps in some instances identical with judicial powers; that is all. They are simply drawn into it *ex necessitate*, and such powers should never be exerted except from necessity; should be avoided always, congress keeping their own plain channel of legislation without trenching upon the judiciary, except where they are compelled to do so for the purposes of legislation. I will show, before I sit down, that there is no more call for the exercise of such power in this case than there is for the exercise of the powers of astronomy, or of the other sciences.

Now, sir, is it clear, or is it not, that some time or other the court is called on to inquire into the exercise of the powers of each house of congress in a matter touching life and liberty? The court having held the power to punish *res adjudicata*, I do not discuss that except as an illustration to show the necessity of inquiring into the jurisdiction of the house. I have only discussed the power of congress to punish for contempt, in order to illustrate the necessity, and the principle laid down in Lord Ellenborough's decision, that, in a case of flagrant usurpation, the court should interfere, for otherwise—as I have stated—the rights and liberties of everybody would be at the mercy of one branch of congress. Then, if I have shown from the authorities cited by the gentlemen themselves—I need not follow book by book, for they are familiar to us all after the four or five days' discussion we have had—but if I have settled that the court has a right to inquire into something, and that being the jurisdiction of the house, let us come a little closer to this exact point before the court. Had the house jurisdiction over Hallet Kilbourn and his private books? The court has the right to inquire, and is called on to inquire, whether the house had such jurisdiction.

The Emery case says that the legislature can not overrule the bill of rights in Massachusetts. That bill of rights exempted a man from furnishing evidence to inculpate himself. The legislature of Massachusetts attempted to compel a citizen to testify in the face of his declaration that his testimony would inculpate him, and declared him in contempt because he would not, and they have the express authority given them by law to judge of contempt, and yet the supreme court says that the legislature could not overrule the bill of rights in Massachusetts; and I do not believe this court will hold that the house of representatives can overrule the bill of rights of the United States. Let us see next what the bill of rights in the federal constitution is, and then examine the attempt to overthrow it. I plant myself upon it. I plant myself upon it, upon the authority of the decision in the Emery case, which comes to us from the Old North Bay State, who, with all her faults, past and present, yet, upon a pure judicial question, has rarely, if ever, given any other than a bright, steady ray in behalf of the liberty of the citizen. I plant myself upon her authority, and I say here that the bill of rights in the constitution, and its amendments, confront these gentlemen at the very threshold. It is so familiar that it is scarcely worth while reading it, but it may sound well, nevertheless. Here is written what I have often read heretofore, when the storm was beating on the land, when the black clouds hung heavy and low, and when power was rampant; when menaced by the outstretched arm of power, when the hurricane beat upon the ship, and the waves lashed around her, still I clung to this rock:

> The right of the people to be secure in their persons, houses, papers, and effects, against unreasonable searches and seizures shall not be violated, and no warrant shall issue, but upon probable cause, supported by oath or affirmation, and particularly describing the place to be searched and the persons or things to be seized.

I do not deny the power of investigation by the house of representatives, or by the senate, or by both branches combined. I proclaim both the power and the duty. It is their duty to investigate corruption; to lay it bare, and to lash naked rascals through the world; but I do not want to see it done at the expense of the constitution of the United States, that protects honest men as well as rascals. I remember once a gentleman asking Governor Crittenden, of Kentucky, then in the house of representatives, whether he was not in favor of doing anything to accomplish a certain very desirable object at that time. "Do anything? Anything?" said he; "Does the gentleman dare to ask me whether I will commit murder, arson, burglary, and all the crimes in the decalogue to accomplish a desirable end?" With regard to investigation, I say let it go on in every proper way; if rascality has taken root in high places, let it be exposed; and that it has so taken root there can be no doubt. Any party in power as long as the party now in the ascendant, will necessarily gather to itself parasites and scoundrels. Not merely your party, but mine will gather the same. Such should be exposed. But if in that hue and cry I am asked to lay my hand upon the pillars of the constitution and tear down the only safety that anybody has, I stop. I would rather rascals should go unpunished than destroy the only safeguard honest men have for their liberties. I confront this claim made by the house of representatives on Hallet Kilbourn by this section of the bill of rights; by article 4 of the first amendment of the constitution. What constitutes the foundation of a legitimate investigation? "Rumor," "say so," "somebody said so," "I reckon so," "it is alleged," "it may be so?" Are these the proper foundations for the exercise of this mighty power, the power to punish for contempt? I do not believe in the power to punish to the extent which has been asserted. But I accept it for this discussion. If it was an open question I would have much to say, and I will show you that wiser minds than mine have discussed the question whether congress has this omnipotent power to punish offenses undeclared and unknown. It is *res adjudicata* though, as the court says, and so it will be for the purposes of this argument, but it is of a monstrous nature, and, although settled, calls with additional force, for that very reason, on this court to look narrowly to the question of jurisdiction in the house.

I repeat, then, what is the proper foundation of an investigation? If there was a specific charge against Hallet Kilbourn, his books would be laid upon the table of the committee. I am authorized to say, as he said over and over again before the committee, and at the bar of the house, which has been read in the hearing of the court, that if anybody will charge him with fraud upon the federal government, or with assisting anybody in fraud to the extent of a single dollar, his books are at their disposal. Nobody has made himself responsible for such a charge. The court has read, and had read in its presence, the resolution on this subject, which I will discuss more fully as I come to it. But I am now dealing with the question as to what is the proper initiatory point of an investigation. Can it be contended that if a man should arise upon the floor of the house of representatives and say that he believes my journal and ledger in my law office at home would disclose something to the interest of the government, that therefore they could subpœna me and make me bring my books and lay them down before them? If so, then those three hundred men on Capitol Hill have power over every man's private concerns in the Union. If one of them has at home a constituent that he does not like, and desires to inquire into his business, all he has to do is to make a vague, insinuating charge. They say they expect to discover something for the benefit of the government by Mr. Kilbourn's books. With the same propriety they could say they expected to discover something for the benefit of the government on the subject of the tariff by examining the books of sale and purchase of every merchant in New York; to see how they bought their goods, how they sold them, and how the tariff was operating, and make that the alleged basis of an investigation. In other words, there must be something specific in the charge. In that connection I find a letter from one who was an apostle of the faith, whose authority, I think, will be taken by some gentlemen who have questioned the course taken by Mr. Kilbourn in this case. It is not exactly legal authority, and yet I do not know why. He was a judge of a federal court in early life; he was a senator of the United States, and if it had not been that his achievements as a hero in the field in defense of the liberties of American citizens eclipsed all the rest of his life, except his presidential terms, he would have been known as a very excellent jurist. I allude to Andrew Jackson. I find a letter of his, dated January 26, 1837, and if the gentlemen will not take it as reading an authority in a closing speech, I will read it. I know that Colonel Christy reveres the name and memory of the author. I can not say about my friend, Mr. Shellabarger, but I have no doubt he does also.

WASHINGTON CITY, January 26, 1837.

SIR: I received on the evening of the 24th instant your letter covering a copy of a certain resolution purporting to have been adopted by a committee of the house of representatives, of which you are chairman, and request that you will lay before that committee this my reply, which I hasten to make.

It appears by the published proceedings of the house of representatives that the committee, of which you are chairman, was appointed on your motion. The resolution offered by you and finally adopted by the house raised a direct issue with the last part of my message, in which I held the following language: "Before concluding this paper I think it due to the various executive departments to bear testimony of their prosperous condition, and to the ability and integrity with which they have performed their duties. It has been my aim to enforce in all of them a vigilant and faithful discharge of the public business; and it is gratifying to me to believe there is no just cause of complaint from any quarter at the manner in which they have fulfilled the object of their creation." Your resolution is in the following words:

"*Resolved*, That so much of the president's message as relates to the condition of the various executive departments, the ability and integrity with which they have been conducted, the vigilant and faithful discharge of the public business in all of them, and the causes of complaint from any quarter at the manner in which they have fulfilled the objects of their creation, be referred to a select committee, to consist of nine members, with power to send for persons and papers, and with instructions to inquire into the condition of the various executive departments, the ability and integrity with which they have been conducted, into the manner in which the public business has been discharged in all of them, and into all causes of complaint from any quarter at the manner in which departments or their bureaus or offices, or any of their officers or agents, of every description whatever, directly or indirectly connected with them in any manner, officially or unofficially, in duties pertaining to the public interest, have fulfilled or failed to accomplish the objects of their creation, or have violated their duties, or have injured and impaired the public service and interest; and the said committee in its inquiries may refer to such periods of time as to them may seem expedient and proper."

What a resolution for an investigating committee! It is a wonder somebody has not re-offered it, so as to take a wide range of everything at once. General Jackson proceeds to comment on it:

It also appears, from the published proceedings of the house, that this resolution was accompanied and supported by a speech of considerable length, in which you preferred many severe but vague charges of corruption and abuse in the executive departments. The resolutions adopted by the committee, as well as that adopted by the house itself, must be taken in connection with your introductory speech, which gives a character to the whole proceeding. When thus regarded, it is obvious that, by the resolution of the house, an issue is made with the president of the United States, as he had alleged, in his annual message, that the heads of the executive departments had performed their official duties with ability and integrity. In your speech you denied this. You charged them with manifold corruptions and abuses of trust, as you had done in former speeches to which you referred, and you demanded an investigation through the medium of a committee. Certain other members of congress, as appears by the published debates, united with you in these accusations, and for the purpose of ascertaining their truth or falsehood, the committee you demanded was ordered to be raised, and you were placed at its head.

Here was a sweeping resolution supported by gentlemen of the high character and distinction of Mr. Wise and others, preferring grave and serious charges of official misconduct on the part of officers of the government, which is not the case here. This is the case of a private citizen. He holds no official relation to the government at all. Nobody has charged him with having abused a single trust, for he has had no trust. Nobody has charged him on the floor, as far as I have seen, even in a vague way, with assisting any public officer in violating a trust, or with assisting a private citizen in committing any fraud; nothing of the kind. So the case made here is much stronger than the case at bar. General Jackson goes on to say:

> The first proceeding of the investigating committee is to pass a series of resolutions which, though amended in their passages, were, as understood, introduced by you, calling on the president, and the heads of the departments, not to answer any specific charge; not to explain any alleged abuse; not to give information as to any particular transaction; but, assuming that they had been guilty of the charges alleged, calls upon them to furnish evidence against themselves.
>
> After the reiterated charges you have made it would have been expected that you would have been prepared to reduce them to specifications, and that the committee would then proceed to investigate the matters alleged. But instead of this you resort to generalities even more vague than your original accusations, and in open violation of the constitution and of that well-established and wise maxim, "that all men are presumed to be innocent until proven guilty according to the established rules of law," you request myself and the heads of the departments to become our own accusers, and to furnish the evidence to convict ourselves; and this call purports to be founded on the authority of that body in which alone, by the constitution, the power of impeaching us is vested.
>
> The heads of departments may answer such requests as they please, provided they do not withhold their own time or that of the officers under their direction from the public business to the injury thereof; to that business I shall direct them to devote themselves in preference to any illegal and unconstitutional call for information, no matter from what source it may come, or however anxious they may be to meet it.

There was an excellent opportunity for this unlimited power of the house to punish "Old Hickory" for contempt. He says he shall direct the heads of the departments to pay no attention to this resolution; no attention to what he terms illegal and unconstitutional calls, coming from whatever source they may. Did the house put him in jail on a dollar a day for food? I do not hear anything of that kind come ringing down the pages of history. This was not merely Mr. Wise's resolution; it was the resolution of the house, and General Jackson told the house of representatives that his heads of departments should not obey. He said he would hold them to the strict consumption of their time, and the discharge of their official duties. He goes on:

> For myself, I shall repel all such attempts as an invasion of the principles of

justice, as well as of the constitution, and I shall esteem it my sacred duty to the people of the United States to resist them as I would the establishment of a Spanish inquisition.

Why? Because there were no specific charges. I am discussing how investigation is properly commenced; what should be its foundation, and I am bringing to my aid one who, then in the evening of his life, was closing a career full of good deeds to his country, and illuminated with the light of glory and of immortality.

If, after all the severe accusations contained in the various speeches of yourself and your associates, you are unwilling, of your own accord, to bring specific charges, then I request your committee to call yourself and your associates, and every other member of congress who has made the general charge of corruption, to testify before God and the country whether you or they know of any specific corruption or abuse of trust in the executive departments; and if so, what it is. If you are able to point to any case where there is the slightest reason to suspect corruption or abuse of trust, no obstacle which I can remove shall be interposed to prevent the fullest scrutiny by all legal means. The offices of all the departments will be opened to you, and every facility furnished for this purpose. I hope, sir, we shall at last have your charges, and that you will proceed to investigate them, not like an inquisition, but in the accustomed mode. If you either will not make specific accusations, or if, when made, you attempt to establish them by making freemen their own accusers, you will not expect me to countenance your proceedings.

It is true that Mr. Kilbourn is not asked to be his own accuser, but he is asked to surrender his private books and papers, which are protected by the bill of rights as much as he is from being his own accuser. The argument is the same.

In the short period which remains of my official duty I shall endeavor, as I have heretofore endeavored, to fulfill the obligations of that oath of office by which I am engaged to the best of my ability to preserve, protect, and defend the constitution of the United States; and for this and other reasons of the most solemn character I shall, on the one hand, cause every possible facility, consistent with law and justice, to be given to the investigation of specific, tangible charges; and, on the other, shall repudiate all attempts to invade the just rights of the executive department, and of the individuals composing the same.

So will we. Specific, tangible charges we will aid to investigate, but we will at the same time repudiate all attempts to invade the just rights of a citizen.

If, after all your clamor, you will make no specific charges, or bring no proof of such as shall be made, you and your associates must be regarded by the good people of the United States as the authors of unfounded calumnies, and the public servants you have assaulted will, in the estimation of all honorable men, stand fully acquitted. In the meantime I can not but express my astonishment that members of congress should call for information as to the names of persons to whom contingent moneys are paid and the object of those payments, when there are six standing committees under the seventy-seventh rule of the house of representatives, whose special duties are to examine annually into all the details of those expenditures in each of the executive departments. The like remark is applicable to some other branches of the information sought by you, ample details in respect to which are to be found in the reports laid before congress, and now on your files, and to which I recommend you to have recourse.

I am, respectfully, etc.,

ANDREW JACKSON.

To the Hon. HENRY A. WISE,
Chairman of the Investigating Committee of the Abuses and Corruptions Charged against the Executive Departments.

I have read this great letter in aid of my own argument in regard to the necessary basis of an investigation. It must be specific charges. Vague generalities, insinuations, can not be respected, and we find one of the most illustrious men at the head of the government going far beyond what we, in our humble capacity, do; for in the face of the resolution passed by congress he told them it should not be obeyed, because it was a violation of the constitution. Now, what the president of the United States could say certainly the judicial power could say. Certainly the executive is not higher than judicial authority; and if Andrew Jackson, as president of the United States, was authorized to determine whether a resolution of investigation was legal or illegal, constitutional or unconstitutional, certainly the courts of the country can do so; and if his decision was acquiesced in by a hostile congress, and respected all over the country, I presume the judiciary of this government will be so respected also in the exercise of its unquestioned functions.

To resume. This investigation is not based upon such charges as warrant the invasion of a person's private papers, house, person. Understand me; I admit that an investigating committee can be clothed by the house of representatives with power to investigate, and for that purpose to send for persons and papers, and to enforce their attendance. But to do that great thing, to exercise that mighty power, to invade houses, and lay hands upon persons, to bring forth secret papers from drawers and safes, to make the bolts of locks turn back, dusty ledger-books come forth from shelves to the inspection of the whole world, to the idle gaze of the curious for sensational purposes, and as news for the news-gatherer —in order to do all this there must be a basis in the shape of specific charges, of a solid and tangible nature, as General Jackson says. No one citizen can invade the home of another, take his papers, open his drawers, and pick his locks, except on oath or indictment, sustaining a warrant for that purpose. No one person can go a step in that direction, except an oath is the basis of the proceeding, and a warrant is the authority. In order to do that very thing the house of representatives certainly should be held to some rules. The constitution says that this shall not be done except upon oath or affirmation, and upon warrant legally issued. It is true the houses of congress can, for purposes of investigation, call for books and papers without this preliminary oath. But can it be done without a specific charge? Is the government so much more powerful over the citizen, than one citizen is over another, that all the safeguards can be dispensed with in its favor? Is it claimed that congress can do its own will, while, as between citizens, such an invasion of private rights would justify a homicide? If there were two parties litigant, and one should attempt to do without oath and without warrant what the house proposes to do, not only without oath and without warrant, but without specific accusation, the life-blood of the invader would pay the penalty, and the courts would say that the man was standing in the defense of his rights—of his home. Was not General Jackson, then, right when he said, "Let us have specific and tangible charges"? Till then he repudiated and would not obey the resolution. A grosser case of contempt, if the house felt it was strong in the right, could not have been made. They should have proceeded against him at once. Now, I undertake to say that there are no such specific charges here. I hardly need to consume time in reading that resolution again.

THE COURT You may read it. I have heard it read, but it will not hurt me any to hear it read again.

Whereas the government of the United States is a creditor of the firm of Jay Cooke & Co., now in bankruptcy, by order and decree of the district court of the United States in and for the eastern district of Pennsylvania, resulting from the improvident deposits made by the secretary of the navy of the United States with the London branch of said house of Jay Cooke & Co. of the public moneys; and whereas a matter known as the real-estate pool was only partially inquired into by the late joint select committee to inquire into the affairs of the District of Columbia, in which Jay Cooke & Co. had a large and valuable interest; and whereas Edwin M. Lewis, trustee of the estate and effects of said firm of Jay

Cooke & Co., has recently made a settlement of the interest of the estate of Jay Cooke & Co. with the associates of said firm of Jay Cooke & Co., to the disadvantage and loss, as it is alleged, of the numerous creditors of said estate, including the government of the United States; and whereas the courts are now powerless, by reason of said settlement, to afford adequate redress to said creditors.

I do not understand that a matter which is legitimately the subject of the judicial power of the government can be made the subject of an investigation, unless 'the court where it is pending is shown, not by a vague statement, but by some specific allegation, either to be corrupt or incompetent to the discharge of its duties. Then there should be not merely an investigation into the subject-matter before such a court, but likewise an impeachment to remove the judge and put another in his place. Again, however, there is an allegation that Jay Cooke & Co. were members of what is called a "real-estate pool," here in the city of Washington. Is Hallet Kilbourn in contempt for refusing to answer on that point? Do not you know, and all of us, that he answered every question on that subject? There is the record. The committee asked him who were members of the real-estate pool. He answered that Jay Cooke & Co. were members. He answered how much money they put in—twenty-five thousand dollars. He answered that his firm had settled with Jay Cooke & Co., and paid them. There was no refusal to answer one word.

I understand Jay Cooke & Co. and Kilbourn & Latta have settled. Kilbourn testifies that he owes them nothing. Nobody asserts the contrary. There is not an assertion in debate, or in committee, in a specific way, or in any other way, that Kilbourn & Latta owe Jay Cooke & Co. a single dollar. Members of the committee simply say—and I looked carefully at the proceedings before the committee—that they could tell better whether Mr. Kilbourn tells the truth if he would show them the books. That is all. They could tell better if they could see his books. No specific charge that he has withheld money belonging to Jay Cooke & Co. Who makes such charge? Where is it? Where is it in that tangible form spoken of by General Jackson when he defied a resolution broader far than this? Nobody makes it. He refuses to answer no questions in regard to them. He says the proceedings of their firm and of Cooke & Co. have been settled. Bear in mind all the time this is a private citizen; bears no other relation to the government than he himself has graphically described in his testimony; that he obeys the laws and pays his taxes. That is all the relation he has to the government.

By that resolution it is shown that this whole matter is in the courts. The resolution itself shows that it is in court, in bankruptcy, and in settlement, with a trustee, Mr. Lewis, making settlement. And now I want to correct a popular error. It is not Jay Cooke & Co. that ever owed the government anything. The popular notion of the country is that Jay Cooke & Co., when they failed, owed the government large amounts, and swindled it enormously. The real fact, however, is that Jay Cooke, McCulloch & Co.,—a firm that never existed in this country, but which exists in London—composed of Jay Cooke, McCulloch and somebody else, owed this government a million and a half.

THE COURT. Does that appear in this resolution in any way?

MR. VOORHEES. I do not believe it does. But it ought to appear there to treat the country fairly. The statement ought to have been as the facts are and as they are known in the courts. Whether your honor will take judicial cognizance of the record in the court on this subject or not I am not advised, but the court will bear with me in a single statement at any rate, inasmuch as it was discussed by Colonel Christy, preceding me. I understand the facts to be that Jay Cooke, McCulloch & Co. are responsible for their debts. I do not understand that Mr. Hugh McCulloch is bankrupt. I do not understand that the London firm of Jay Cooke, McCulloch & Co. is bankrupt. I do not understand that the government is in danger of losing one cent on account of the bankruptcy of their debtors. In the settlement, however, made with the government by Jay Cooke, McCulloch & Co., they turned over some claims which they held against Jay Cooke & Co. in this country, and the government took them for what they were worth. But if the government or any officer took them in full settlement of its debt—bad paper, bad collaterals—then that officer ought to be impeached, whoever he is. I do not know who he is, or that it has been done; but, as I understand, this case is now pending in court, with full jurisdiction over the question.

MR. ELDREDGE. Jurisdiction over the officer?

MR. VOORHEES. Jurisdiction over the officer, the trustee, Mr. Lewis, and if there is a wrong done the court can undo that wrong.

THE COURT. I put the question when Mr. Christy was presenting his argument to call forth intelligence on that subject. Does the district court of Pennsylvania hold supervisory control and jurisdiction over this officer as a trustee of the court?

MR. VOORHEES. I will answer that question by asking my associate counsel, Mr. Davidge, whether the trusteeship is closed.

MR. DAVIDGE. No, sir.

MR. VOORHEES. The trustee has not closed his trust. The trust remains an unsettled trust. It is subject to the court in which he is transacting his business, until the last act is done and the last cent is accounted for.

THE COURT. But I understood Mr. Christy to state that such was the character of the bankrupt law that the act of the creditors transferred the estate from the custody of the court to an agent of the court, and the reason why it impressed my mind was that I thought it was an extraordinary condition of things if the law emancipated the trustee of the court before a final settlement of the estate from the dominion of the tribunal who created the trustee.

MR. VOORHEES. Why, of course that can not be.

MR. DAVIDGE. Under the ordinary machinery of the bankrupt law the assignee, in almost every step that he may take in the settlement of the estate, is bound to apply to the court for directions, or is subject all along to the control of the court. The forty-third section, your honor, undertakes to wind up the estate of the bankrupt by vesting in a body called the "committee" very large discretionary powers; so that the trustee appointed by virtue of that section, while he has the powers of an assignee, at the same time is allowed very frequently, instead of acting under the direction of the court, to seek his committee and get his orders and directions from that body. But yet nobody on this earth, except Colonel Christy, has ever had the temerity to assert that trustee was not like any other trustee—ultimately amenable for all the acts in connection with his trust, both to the district court and to the supreme court, which, under the very letter of the bankrupt law, exercises a supervisory power over the settlement of the estate; and if there be any irregularity in that settlement, any fraud in that settlement, why, the remedy, may it please your honor, is just as plain and simple as it would be in any case of a private trust, where irregularity or fraud are sought to be rectified by a bill in equity filed in this court. That is all there is to it. The machinery of the committee is interposed in lieu of the court, in the ordinary conduct of the court, as a more facile and a more business-like piece of machinery than the court itself, but still the trustee never ceases to be a trustee. Mr. Lewis had to render an account of this settlement. Like any other trustee he is liable to be wrongfully charged; he is liable to have his settlement itself set aside; he is subject to the large supervisory power that all courts of equity entertain and exercise over trustees. That is all there is to it.

MR. CHRISTY. Pardon me, Mr. Voorhees, for one moment. I will not re-open the subject of discussion, but I think it will advantage your honor, and gentlemen, to read the forty-third section, and perhaps before your honor reaches a determination in this matter, I can obtain from Judge Strong his judicial construction of that section while sitting in the circuit court in Philadelphia with the associate justice. I will not re-open what I have said, but I desire your honor to read the forty-third section of the bankrupt law.

THE COURT. You remain of the same conviction you suggested in your argument?

MR. CHRISTY. Yes, sir; I do, undoubtedly; and I think Judge Strong—I may be mistaken about this matter, but I can be very readily corrected by the recollection of Judge Strong himself.

MR. DAVIDGE. That issue, your honor, lay right here. Judge Cadwalader, the judge of the district court, claimed that he had the same authority over the trustee as he would have over an assignee in bankruptcy. In his judgment the committee were a mere advisory body, and not a body substituted in any degree in law in place of the court. In that he was overruled by Judge Strong, who took the broad ground that the purpose of the forty-third section was to have the estate settled on business principles;

but he never asserted, and nobody has ever asserted, that the trustee was not amenable both to the district court, and, on proper proceeding, to the circuit court. I hope Colonel Christy will produce the decision of Judge Strong.

Mr. VOORHEES. If the court please, Mr. Davidge having been counsel in this proceeding in bankruptcy, I am satisfied his knowledge and position in regard to it are correct. It follows, therefore, that the concluding sentence in the preamble to the resolution of the house is necessarily untrue. I read it:

> And whereas the courts are now powerless, by reason of said settlement, to afford adequate redress to said creditors.

That is absurd. Can your mind, in its wide, vigorous, and manly range, assisted by all your reading and learning, imagine a court, having taken rightful jurisdiction of a bankrupt estate, with a trustee yet in existence as a party to its record, over a trust unsettled, powerless to afford adequate redress to creditors? Can you imagine a sudden paralysis of all the constitutional power in a court? This Pennsylvania court has taken jurisdiction rightly everybody admits. The subject-matter is there; the trustee is there; the creditors are all there; and yet this preamble closes with the statement that the courts are powerless, on account of the settlement made by Mr. Lewis as trustee, and he subject to the court! He can not make any settlement unless the court says so. He is a mere creature of the court, and yet we are told that he has made a settlement by which the court has become powerless on the subject. This is too bald and naked an absurdity to admit of prolonged talk. It can not stand a single moment. The government is a creditor, and, as was said by Mr. Davidge the other day, nothing is more perfectly settled than that the government, when it goes into a court as a creditor, goes as an individual. It goes there with the other creditors of Jay Cooke & Co. It goes there to see that this trustee does his duty by it as well as by other creditors. It has taken some collaterals for a debt owed by other parties, and that is the only way the government has any claim on Jay Cooke & Co. It is the only way in which there is any relation made between the government and Jay Cooke & Co. It is by virtue of collaterals taken on them. The government goes to court to look after its interest, whatever it is, against Jay Cooke & Co. The trustee of Jay Cooke & Co., bankrupt, is there, subject to the orders of the court. This resolution shows on its face that this trustee has made a settlement. Will the court say, in the absence of any such allegation in this resolution, that that settlement was unauthorized by the court? It is stated in this resolution that he has made a settlement. It does not say that it was made contrary to the order of the court. He being in that court with the trust, this court will presume that it was done under the authority, sanction, and direction of that court. It can not presume anything else. In the absence of a charge to the contrary, you are bound to presume that the trustee was acting in obedience to the court. He makes a settlement, and I repeat, it was made as trustee; made with the creditors, the government being one, and made, of course, under the jurisdiction, power, and authority of the court, where he was standing and administering this trust. They say it was made to the disadvantage of creditors. Very well. If to the disadvantage of creditors, whom does that impeach? Why does not that resolution set out specifically that the court was corrupt, and allowed a disadvantageous settlement to be made as to the government? Why does it not set out that the court was incompetent, and did not know enough to have a fair settlement made with the government as a creditor? But simply, in a vague way, it says that a settlement was made by a trustee of a bankrupt estate, which was then in course of adjudication in a court of justice, and was to the disadvantage of the government. Therefore, by reason of said settlement, courts are powerless to remedy. Mr. Lewis is still a trustee. Now, sir, I say that a clearer showing that this whole subject is within the judicial grasp of this country was never made beneath the sun. It is there, and there by the showing of the resolution; there as shown by the fact set out, that there was a trustee to this estate, that there was a settlement made. If this is not so, then it must be shown, by specific allegations, either that the court, as I have said already, is corrupt and liable to impeachment, or that it is incompetent. Being neither, and there being no such charge, I wish to know, as the next proposition I shall make, by what power one or both houses of congress propose to invade the courts of the country and settle lawsuits? I have already read the constitution, which tells what congress is. I have already read, showing where judicial power is lodged; and while I admit the incidental judicial power of the house in a limited degree, yet, with regard to this great ocean of judicial authority, which flows from the constitution itself, let us see what the constitution says:

> The judicial power of the United States shall be vested in one supreme court, and in such inferior courts as the congress may from time to time ordain and establish. The judges, both of the supreme and inferior courts, shall hold their offices during good behavior, and shall, at stated times, receive for their services a compensation, which shall not be diminished during their continuance in office.

Does this judicial power, which is expressly given to the courts of the country, extend to the matter set forth in the resolution of the house? I read again from the constitution:

> The judicial power shall extend to all cases in law and equity arising under this constitution, the laws of the United States and treaties made, or which shall be made, under their authority; to all cases affecting embassadors, other public ministers, and consuls; to all cases of admiralty and maritime jurisdiction; to controversies to which the United States may be a party; to controversies between two or more states; between a state and citizens of another state; between citizens of different states; between citizens of the same state claiming lands under grants of different states, and between a state, or the citizens thereof, and foreign states, citizens, or subjects.

There is the grant of power to the federal judiciary. Do you see anything there which says that congress can come in and by virtue of its incidental judicial powers, however obtained, go upon the bench, and crowd the judge out of his seat; depose him, strike down his authority, and say, "I will do all these things"? Where is the power by which congress can invade the express grant of judicial authority? This grant of judicial authority covers the case that we are discussing, probably under a half-dozen heads; covers it under the provision made for the United States as a party. Here she was a party creditor. By this constitutional provision this case is in the courts, and there it has to be.

I have asked the question whether the house of representatives can swell, enlarge, extend, spread broad its limited phylacteries of implied, incidental judicial power, so as to cover the entire judiciary of the country, and try private lawsuits wherever somebody may vaguely insinuate a public interest. Aye, the very question is provided for there. The house says it desires this information because the United States is a party, and there are public interests involved. That very state of things is covered by the clause which I have read, which says that the judicial power shall embrace cases where the United States is a party. There is a vague, loose idea in the minds of some that whenever the United States is interested, congress is omnipotent; can do anything; and if both branches have not a mind to take hold, why one can do, as well as both, anything it pleases. There is an idea of that kind. But when you come to the constitution, read its grants of powers and limitations, you will find that its framers did not leave to congress to determine anything where the United States is a party to a suit; a party to litigation, as here; a party creditor in Pennsylvania, seeking to collect collaterals against a bankrupt estate, her rights still existing against a firm that is not bankrupt. The government is not in danger of losing a dollar. That cry is groundless. But even if it were not so, she is there a party litigant, a party to the suit; and under this clause of the constitution it belongs to the judicial power in the courts to determine what her rights are.

Again, sir, if congress can not usurp this high authority of the courts and crowd the judges off the bench, tell me how this authority can be divided, and how congress can get hold of one edge, one side, or one corner of a lawsuit in a court of justice? Counsel say that investigation is in aid of this litigation. By what clause of the constitution are you allowed to come in and help at all? What clause of the constitution allows congress to assist the courts? You say the court is powerless. In point of fact, I say it is not so, and can not be so. But if it were so, that court can be removed by a process known to the constitution and another court put there that is not powerless. Courts can not be powerless over private rights, and the United States is a private individual when she goes into court as a party litigant. She stands there as one of many creditors, with no higher rights than anybody else. The congress of the United States has just as much power to appear for John Brown or James Smith, one of the creditors, and help him as to help the United States. She stands one creditor among many.

If the courts have not exclusive jurisdiction over this subject, then language is vague, and the provisions of the constitution are a mockery. Judicial power in congress to aid and assist the courts in the discharge of their legal duties! There is not such a thing known.

As I have already said, the house and senate sometimes have to act judicially, and I am sorry to say that they very seldom do it. In fact, as Mr. Shellabarger said, the house provided a law by which elections were to be contested, and has violated it ever since. Of course it has.

MR. SHELLABARGER. Mr. Voorhees, will you permit me to make a single suggestion? I fear, your honor, that I have not been understood in regard to this point that my friend suggests. Very much stress is laid on the idea that congress can not turn itself into a court for the purpose of helping in a chancery case—a case in bankruptcy. Of course no such absurd proposition as this is entertained on our side, and yet I fear, since I was not understood by counsel, that I may not have been understood by the court. I beg your honor to remember that the house has a variety of functions. First, as a branch of the legislature; second, as grand inquest of the nation. Now let us look at this for a single instant, in regard to the materiality of this inquiry on the part of the house as a branch of the legislature. Suppose they can not try that case in a lawsuit, isn't it competent for the house to find out whether this forty-third section of the bankrupt law is working well, and what more pertinent inquiry could be instituted than to see how it has worked in this particular case, with the view of modifying that forty-third section, or blotting it out? That is merely suggestive of the infinite variety of ways in which this information in regard to the operation of that law, and of this transaction, may throw light on the question as to what are the duties of the house in regard to making new laws. Then take the other suggestion, I would suggest to my friend, that I made in my former statement. It may be that an entirely new line of conduct must be adopted by the house in regard to making appropriations, as it shall find out that these particular assets are or are not available. For the purposes of that inquiry, it is competent for the house to go into the matter to find out how this thing stands. Suppose it was $30,000,000 instead of $30,000 that was involved, would gentlemen contend that it would not be an exceedingly important fact for the house to inform itself about before it originates a measure in the way of appropriation, to know whether that asset was available or not? Gentlemen must not reply to me that this thing is too small in magnitude to be looked to in that view. There are no questions of degree in matters of this sort.

Now, then, your honor, furthermore, departing now from that legislative power of the house, and looking to this with regard to the questions of the duties of the house in regard to some public officials, as, for example, some of the members of the court. The gentleman said in one of the last and most excellent sentences he has uttered, that if this court has not acted properly in this case, they ought to provide another court. Why, that contains in itself the *felo de se* of this whole argument and his whole position in this case. The house may find it necessary to impeach somebody, if that somebody has been guilty of a corrupt practice in regard to this alleged settlement. I care not whether it be court, trustee, or who, or what. There may be an impeachment required according as things may have been corrupt or pure. And so his suggestion with regard to providing a new court. That provision may be made by a process resulting in impeachment, or by a process resulting in providing some other instrumentalities in the courts; some commissions; as was done, and is done in a large number of cases. Why, that case decided in the supreme court, inaugurated under Mr. Boutwell's administration; that case where there was a suit brought for the interest upon the United States debt, as held against the Pacific railroad company; that was inaugurated in obedience to a resolution for which, I believe, my friend voted, as I think I did myself. The house had to take responsibilities. That great suit was brought in obedience to an order of the house of representatives alone. For all such purposes, your honor, as a former member of congress, will know and remember, and without being a member of congress will know and remember, how limitless may be the powers of the house—the two houses—in seeing to it that officers and courts and all shall do their duty, or else somebody be provided that will do their duty.

[At this point the court took a brief recess.]

[On the court reconvening, Mr. Voorhees resumed his argument as follows:]

If your honor please, at the rising of the court at recess, Mr. Shellabarger was suggesting the purposes for which investigation of this kind might be prosecuted, and in what it might be useful. This was in response to that part of my argument in which I insist, with high authorities to support me, that investigation, in order to reach these sacred and reserved rights of the citizen, and drag them forth, should be based upon specific charges, and that the fishing process, not knowing what you are going to catch, does not rise to that dignity and gravity which would authorize the invasion of personal rights so sacredly guarded by the bill of rights.

If I understood his proposition, it was that this investigation might reveal something about the courts, and might possibly result in an impeachment. That is the first I have heard of such an insinuation, and the idea that congress can set an investigating committee at work under one guise for another purpose is a very dangerous novelty to my mind. It is a proposition of the same character that I replied to a while ago. Counsel say it might accrue to the benefit of the government—might enable congress to legislate or impeach. In fact, Mr. Shellabarger reiterates that position here, and says they might find out something in reference to the bankrupt act which would enable them to amend it. Therefore, in order to do that, they can seize Hallet Kilbourn, put him in jail, and keep him there; ransack his papers, and may be in that way find out something that will enable them to legislate in regard to the bankrupt act, and may be not. During his imprisonment he may die. That would only be murder.

An illegal imprisonment of that kind, growing out of a mere fishing excursion to find out something not made out as a charge or a specification, in which a man should lose his life in jail, would be the most cruel and cowardly type of murder. These gentlemen on the other side do not seem to be imbued with the horrors

I have of imprisonment, of the deprivation of the liberties of a citizen. I will come to that in a different form before I get through. I utterly repudiate, and shall take but little time in doing it—I utterly repudiate this doctrine that you may go out on a general seining process—a long promiscuous haul to catch something or nothing to aid you in such an indefinite and vague proceeding; put anybody in jail you please, ransack anybody's papers, invade anybody's house. It is an abomination in my sight. Indeed, every proposition in aid of the position assumed by the gentlemen need but be stated in all its length and breadth to reduce it to absolute absurdity. You have to come back to solid ground. You have to come to the wholesome restraints and safeguards of law. You must come to something tangible before you can place the hand of power upon a citizen. You have to stand where Andrew Jackson stood in 1837 on this subject. When they commenced a fishing process for him, on vague charges, he met and defied, spurned and scorned congress. I do not do that. I speak with the utmost respect for congress. But, without Jackson's defiance, I adopt his principle on that subject.

Mr. Shellabarger alluded, just before the court rose, to the Credit Mobilier investigation. That came before the house in the most specific form, involving a half-dozen members, and I believe I never heard any doubt that congress could investigate its own members. It can, and expel them. But it is a singular thing that congress can punish one of its own members only by expelling him, and yet it is claimed that either branch may punish anybody else just as much as it pleases for a contempt. A member of the house guilty of contempt on the floor can only be expelled and told to go away. They say to him, "We relieve ourselves of your indecorous conduct and of your presence." But if a citizen not belonging to congress should be guilty of the same offense, the power of congress is so much greater, where it is not given by any express words, that, according to this argument, they could put him to death, and the court could not inquire into it. That is not in the line of the argument I was going to make upon this point, but it arose as one of the absurdities that spring up at every step.

Now, I take it, if your honor please, it is pretty well understood between us that this matter that the house directs its committee to inquire into is legitimately and fully lodged in a court of competent jurisdiction. That is the point I was dealing with, and was nearly closing when the court rose. It is there. The trustee of the bankrupt estate is there. The power of the court is there, and it will not do to say that that court is powerless, unless you show how and why it is powerless. Is there anything in this resolution to show why that court is powerless? It says that it is powerless because of Lewis's settlement with the creditors. It has power over Lewis to open up any settlement he has made. Will the court entertain—I was going to say with respect; of course the court will entertain with respect any proposition coming from either side—but will the court entertain with any patience the proposition that, under this resolution, the house can pursue an inquiry looking ultimately to a possible impeachment of a court? I apprehend not.

But I approach now another phase of this case. I am clear in my own mind, first, that this court is authorized and required to examine into the question of jurisdiction which the house asserted over this subject. I am clear in my mind that the house has no jurisdiction in so vague a way to institute any investigation, and more especially one on a subject that is in the hands of a tribunal with full and absolute jurisdiction, and that it is not in the power of the house to invade that jurisdiction and push it aside, or to divide it with the courts. But if it ever had jurisdiction over this subject; if it ever had the power to invade a man's house and his office, seize his papers, ransack his drawers, bring him up, punish him to any extent it sees fit, in a moment of heat or party passion, if he should resist such claims of power; I say even if it ever had that power, it has parted with it. Congress has devised a mode and place; a place different from the house of representatives; a tribunal different from its own, and a mode which is in accordance with the spirit of law for the punishment of such an offense, if it be one. As I approach this portion of my argument the statute of 1874 becomes a comfort to me. It is a comfortable thought that at last the American congress has seen fit to abandon this most dangerous claim of power ever set up in any government, dangerous because undefined; the claim of power to punish for unknown offenses; to punish persons for contempt, when they do not know they are committing a contempt; a penal code without any limit to the term of punishment; a penal code carried secretly in the breast of each branch of congress, that may develop itself into a death-penalty, or into imprisonment for life, for that the senate can do—it has endless duration—or the whipping-post, or the cart's tail, or any other mode; a penal code that has no definitions; no edges, no boundaries, no terms, no form; without form, but not void; to be launched, like unexpected lightning out of a clear sky, at the pleasure of congress.

It is, indeed, a comfortable thought to me that we are drifting away from such a horrible doctrine, and that congress, after a sharp experience in the last few years on this subject, has seen the necessity of doing what the wiser founders of this government thought necessary to be done when the constitution was first framed. We did not have much trouble in this government on this subject until about 1858. There never was an actual imprisonment for contempt, I believe, until within the last twenty years. The attention of congress and the country has been attracted since then especially to this subject; and the necessity of designating some tribunal, governed by law, and pointing out distinctly what a contempt is and how great shall be the punishment, has at last been recognized and acted upon.

This law of 1874 I shall now present to the court; and, in doing so, I shall first meet the proposition made by opposing counsel, that if the house has the power to punish for contempt by constitutional grant, it can not give it to anybody else; that legislation can not overrule the constitution. If the power to punish for contempt is derived from the constitution, it matters not whether it is by express or implied grant. If it is an implied grant, it is nevertheless a grant by the constitution. If it is an express grant, it is no stronger than an implied grant. I shall treat it as a grant of power if it exist under the constitution, and, therefore, it is said that it can not be delegated to anybody else. My answer to that is, if that power exists it is within the power of congress to authorize the mode, the place, and the terms on which it may be carried out. Let us see whether I am sustained in that by any respectable authority. I am fortunate in having the founders, the fathers of democratic as well as republican ideas, with me upon this subject. I read from Jefferson's Manual. Mr. Shellabarger made a close, cogent, legal argument, to the effect that if this power was in congress by the constitution, congress could not get it out of itself into this court.

That is to say, that if the house of representatives has the power given to it by the constitution, the whole congress acting together, and the president signing the bill, can not delegate that power and authority any place else. I find in Jefferson's Manual a discussion on this subject, in which Mr. Jefferson states, first, the high prerogatives claimed for congress and for each house. He states the high prerogatives claimed and exercised by congress in times gone by, and then sums up the argument on the other side. He uses this language:

> But if one branch may assume its own privileges without control, if it may do it on the spur of the occasion, conceal the law in its own breast, and, after the fact committed, make its sentence both the law and the judgment on that fact ; if the offense is to be kept undefined, and to be declared only *ex re nata* and according to the passions of the moment, and there be no limitation either in the manner or measure of the punishment, the condition of the citizen will be perilous indeed.

I repeat his powerful words—

> And to be declared only *ex re nata*, and according to the passions of the moment, and there be no limitation either in the manner or measure of the punishment—

Showing that when I discussed this claim of power in my preceding remarks, I was only following Mr. Jefferson. He says if these things are to be, the condition of the citizen will be perilous indeed. Yes; so perilous that it would be a refuge to go back under the British constitution.

Our revolt from King George was a mistake, if we have any department in this government that can act without restraint on the lives and liberties of the people. Mr. Jefferson goes on then to say:

> Which of these doctrines is to prevail time will decide.

That is, the doctrine that he has just stated, or the one that he is now about to state:

> Where there is no fixed law, the judgment on any particular case is the law of that single case only, and dies with it.

So that the sentence and punishment to-day is the law of that case, but to-morrow a different law may prevail. Each house may follow the law unto themselves; the law of passion or prejudice on the spur of the moment; and their action to-day would be no guide to the citizen as to what to do or what to refrain from doing to-morrow.

> Where there is no fixed law the judgment on any particular case is the law of that single case only, and dies with it. When a new and even a similar case arises, the judgment, which is to make and at the same time apply the law, is open to question and consideration, as are all new laws.

We would go stumbling along, one case being no precedent for another. I read in my boyhood days of a tyrant, I think Caligula, who wrote his laws in small characters, and put them on a high pole where no one could read them, and then put to death all who did not obey their inhuman provisions. Those laws high on the pole were just as binding in morals and conscience, by every rule of reasoning, as laws that are hidden in the breast of a member of congress, which may be promulgated to-day on the spur of the moment, as Jefferson says, in a moment of passion, and any of us called upon to suffer punishment for their violation without knowing what they are. I hope nobody will ever ask me to give my assent to principles of government of that kind. Yet they are here, and we are confronting them in all their naked deformity. The tyrant's laws up in the air, where his citizens could not read them, were just as easy of access, and were as complete a guide to point out their duties, as that undefined, secret, hidden law in the breast of congress on the subject of contempt. It may be changed every day without anybody being the wiser until the thunderbolt strikes a man and he is in prison. What does Jefferson say as to the conclusion of such a state of affairs? His was a great philosophic mind. He thought wider, further, grander than any other American in connection with the theory of our government. He forecast this very law which I am going to discuss. I have often heard it said by speakers, addressing the people, that Mr. Jefferson was a prophet. The speaker himself was, perhaps, dealing in declamation, and really did not understand how truly he was speaking. There is scarcely a subject connected with our government in regard to which Mr. Jefferson's writings do not reach to the very hour in which we live. He speaks of this revolting feature of undefined power in the breast of congress and points out the remedy. He says:

> Perhaps congress, in the meantime, in their care for the safety of the citizen, as well as for their own protection, may declare by law what is necessary and proper to enable them to carry into execution the powers vested in them, and thereby hang up a rule for the inspection of all, which may direct the conduct of the citizen, and at the same time test the judgments they shall themselves pronounce in their own case.

The time has been long coming. The action of congress is tardy. The "meantime," spoken of by Mr. Jefferson, has been a long time on its way, but it has come at last. The years have rolled on, and the necessity that he foresaw is here; congress has had to declare by law the method by which to carry into execution its powers, and thereby hang up a rule to tell the citizen what is contempt, how much he shall be punished, and in what manner. The day has come, and the great prophet and statesman of Monticello is vindicated in the wisdom of his views by the law of 1874, which brings this case before you. So, aside from the question of the power of the house to punish for contempt, aside from the question of its jurisdiction, this law comes, by the authority of congress, as a mode whereby the power that is conceded for the purpose of this argument shall be exercised. Could there be anything more magnificent than Mr. Jefferson's commentaries on the constitution, as he describes the monstrous evils flowing from the doctrine for which opposing counsel contend? Well may he speak of the perilous condition of the citizen. Perilous, indeed, would it be. No measure to the punishment. No manner fixed by written law. He says, in the meantime, perhaps congress will see the necessity of pointing out and fixing by law a mode to carry out the powers invested in them, and hang up a rule for the inspection of all. Not hung up so high that the people can not see. Not hidden so deep in the breast of congressmen that the people can not find them out. But in the old-fashioned way; declared, written, and put upon the pages of the statute-book, so that all may know the danger they are in; so that all may know what penalty they incur. If your honor please, however, it is contended, although this statute has thus been passed, defining accurately what is contempt, where the party shall be punished, and how much, that it is only cumulative; that it is in addition to what the house itself may do.

In 1857 a law was enacted making a refusal to answer an investigating committee a misdemeanor. In that law it was provided that in addition to the punishment to be inflicted by the house or senate, the recusant witness might be punished here. Congress in that case attempted to retain for each house the right to inflict pains and penalties for contempt, and make the offense a misdemeanor besides.

THE COURT. I think the language of the statute is, that in addition to existing pains and penalties, the penalty enforced now was added there. I think the recital of the original law is in addition to existing pains and penalties.

MR. VOORHEES. After some years of experience, however, and of legal investigation, it was found that such a law as that could not be enforced; that to punish a man once, inflicting the pains and penalties then existing for contempt, and punish him besides for the same precise action as a misdemeanor, and by the same sovereignty, not by a state in one instance and the government in another, but by the federal government itself, would be a violation of the constitution, and hence this act now before the court was passed, in which the words "in addition to the pains and penalties now existing" were carefully excluded. In construing this statute, therefore, it is to be construed with reference to this act of 1857. which reads:

Be it Enacted by the Senate and House of Representatives of the United States of America in Congress Assembled, That any person summoned as a witness by the authority of either house of congress to give testimony or to produce papers upon any matter before either house, or any committee of either house of congress, who shall willfully make default, or who, appearing, shall refuse to answer any question pertinent to the matter of inquiry in consideration before the house or committee by which he shall be examined, shall, in addition to the pains and penalties now existing, be liable to indictment as and for a misdemeanor in any court of the United States having jurisdiction thereof, and on conviction shall pay a fine not exceeding $1,000 and not less than $100, and suffer imprisonment in the common jail not less than one month nor more than twelve months.

After an experience of seventeen years, congress wisely, and under the advice of her judiciary committee, substituted another act for this. Let us compare them, and see why one statute was made to take the place of the other. We will find the acts almost identical in language, with the exception to which I am calling the attention of the court. I read from the act of 1874:

SEC. 102. Every person who, having been summoned as a witness by the authority of either house of congress to give testimony or to produce papers upon any matter upon inquiry before either house, or any committee of either house of congress, willfully makes default, or who, having appeared, refuses to answer any question pertinent to the question under inquiry, shall be deemed guilty of a misdemeanor, punishable by a fine of not more than $1,000 nor less than $100, and imprisonment in a common jail for not less than one month nor more than twelve months.

All the change is that this language is left out—"in addition to the pains and penalties now existing." Can it be possible that the court, in construing this statute, will be indifferent to the fact that it supplants in the same words a statute of similar import, with that single exception? The statute of '57 was made for the purpose of reserving to either house of congress the rights they already had. This statute that I am now commenting upon was passed, waiving that reservation of the existing pains and penalties for contempts, and sending the party into this court for punishment. It is so palpable to my mind that it is difficult to dwell upon. In the first place, our government goes on without any statute, in the condition pointed out by Mr. Jefferson—waiting for that period which he denominates "in the meantime." At last congress enacted that law in '57. They attempted to make it cumulative and punish the man more severely. They reserved to themselves the right to inflict the pains and penalties, whatever they might be. For they had, according to argument here, unlimited and indefinite power to put a man to death, or to punish him in any manner they pleased. They tried to reserve that, and at the same time make it a misdemeanor. As soon as the question had to be met in a practical form, it was necessarily seen that it could not be done.

And why? I might as well meet that point at this stage as at any other. It is said here that a man may be punished twice for the same identical act. Indeed, it can be done when he has offended against the powers that have a right to punish. A man may offend the state of Indiana by passing counterfeit money in her borders, and be punished there, and he might be punished for passing that same money by the United States government, if it be government currency. But there are in that instance two powers that have the right to punish. In this case, however, has the house of representatives an independent power to punish, aside from the United States? It is a mere creature of the constitution, in no sense of the word a sovereignty; not even a congress; not even a legislative body; only a part of a legislative body. Can one branch set itself up and say that it assumes the authority of this government as another and independent power to punish? Unquestionably not. It is the creature of the constitution, and in this case he can not be punished twice, because his offense is against the United States. It is the same identical act. I regard the act of '74 as an express declaration by legislation of the abandonment of that reservation which was attempted to be made by the law of '57.

THE COURT. Have you any authorities upon that point?

MR. VOORHEES. I read now from Sedgwick on Statutory and Constitutional Law, page 126: "And in the case of a statute revising the common law, the implication is equally strong. So, where an act is an offense at common law, and the whole subject is revised by the legislature, common law is repealed."

Before I pass from that point, if the court will permit me, I desire to show that the rule we are now insisting upon is not a novel one. The case of Irwin has been alluded to here. That was thoroughly debated in the house of representatives. With the leave of the court I wish to read some remarks made at that time by Alexander Stephens, of Georgia. I will incorporate them into my own remarks, giving the authority of his name.

MR. VOORHEES then read as follows:

MR. STEPHENS (Alexander H.). Mr. Speaker, I wish to say but a word. This is, as the chairman of the committee on ways and means (Mr. Dawes) stated in his opening remarks, a very grave question. It involves the rightful power of this house to punish for contempts of this sort. This, sir, is not a new question here. It is as old as the arrest of the editor of *The Aurora* (in 1798, I believe) on the charge of a contempt, or what was styled a libel against the senate. There must be a violation of law before any body or any tribunal can rightfully punish in heaven or on earth. Where there is no violation of law there is no sin against man or God. *This resolution proposes to punish by this house against law.* * * * *When this question arose some years ago, and when the contumacious witnesses were put in jail, congress saw the necessity for passing a law on the subject.* That law has just been read. *It was passed with reference to just such a case as this,* and it provides that a *contumacious witness shall be turned over to the court to have a trial. That is what I say should now be done here.* This house has no right to punish in such a case as this. In my judgment the case is already provided for by law, and should be turned over to the courts.

The concluding section of the act referred to by the gentleman from Iowa, which he did not read, provides what shall be done in this very case. The matter is to be certified to the *proper officer of the proper court*, and the party is to be indicted and tried by a jury, *as all other offenders of a like grade. Real contempts* of this house should be properly punished, *but they can be only properly punished when punished according to law. The great right of all persons charged with high crimes and misdemeanors* (except in cases of impeachment) *is as sacred as any secured by the constitution.* I ask the clerk to read the whole act.

A MEMBER. What is the title of the act?

MR. STEPHENS. The title of this chapter in the "Revised Statutes" is "Congressional Investigations."

Sec. 102. * * * * * * *
Sec. 103. * * * * * * *
Sec. 104. * * * * * * *

MR. STEPHENS. Mr. Speaker, I call particular attention to the last section just read. Upon the report of the committee now before us, as I have said, our power under this law in this case is exhausted if this party has committed a crime. It is not for me to say whether he has or not. I prejudge no man. *He has a right to trial by a jury of his* countrymen; and, *Mr. Speaker, it is your duty under that* act to certify this case to the district attorney that the grand jury may indict him, and that he may have a regular trial like all other persons accused of crime. *We have no rightful power to punish in the way proposed. We are as much bound by law as other people. Our duty is to maintain the law and not to break it.*

MR. KASSON. Will the gentleman from Georgia (Mr. Stephens), before he sits down, state whether, in his opinion, the act which has been read does not only give an additional remedy in the nature of a punishment, but deprives the house of congress of the remedy existing by ordinary law?

MR. BUTLER, of Massachusetts. Where is the "ordinary law"?

MR. KASSON. The law under which we have acted for years. We have in many cases held men for contempt under the provisions of parliamentary law.

MR. STEPHENS. Mr. Speaker, parliamentary common law is not in force in this country. *This house has no inherent power whatever*, and can rightfully exercise no power except that which is conferred upon it by the written constitution. These powers are ample, but they are to be executed according to law. *There is no common law extending to this house.* This body has no right, on its own mere volition, to punish for contempt, except so far as may be necessary *to preserve order in the house*, or for securing a quorum, as provided in the constitution.—*Congressional Record, 2d session, 43d congress, 177. 1874.*

The following was the resolution under discussion:

Ordered, That the speaker issue his warrant, directed to the sergeant-at-arms attending this house, or his deputy, commanding him to take into custody forthwith, wherever to be found, the body of Richard B. Irwin, and him bring to the bar of the house, to show cause why he should not be punished for contempt;

and in the meantime keep the said Irwin in his custody to wait the further order of the house.

I read that as the opinion of one who served twenty years in the house of representatives. He was as good a parliamentary lawyer as was ever in congress, and as familiar with its rules and powers. But, it is said by counsel that there can be no conflict of punishment between what the house does and what is to be done under this law, because what the house inflicts is not punishment, and, therefore, the grant of power to congress by the constitution may be exercised by the house, and at the same time congress may grant to this court a power to punish for the same act. I deny it.

Let us see in the first place whether this is the same offense. It will not be necessary for me to take the time of the court in reading the constitution, which forbids two punishments for the same act. Neither in heaven nor on earth, neither in law, human or divine, is it allowed. The only question is, whether the person is the same, and the offense the same. Let us see whether it is so here or not. In the first place this act of congress, by which the speaker certifies the case into the criminal court of the District, specifies that it shall be an offense punished by fine and imprisonment in court to refuse to answer questions properly within the jurisdiction of congress, or of a committee, to ask; that is what he is to be punished for. Let us suppose Hallet Kilbourn on trial in the criminal court. What would be proven? It would be proven that on a certain day he went before a certain committee, and was asked certain questions. He was asked to produce his books and papers, and he refused to do so. It would then be proved that he was taken before the house of representatives, and the same thing was asked of him there, and he refused again. Then the district attorney would read this law, and would show, conclusively, that that was the identical offense provided for in this statute. There could be no discussion on the subject. Let us, then, go to congress and ask why Hallet Kilbourn is in jail. He is in jail for exactly the same thing. Why, the speaker's certificate that brings the case here sets out just what the committee sets out. The resolution committing him to jail in the District by the house states the precise facts that the speaker of the house does, in certifying him here for punishment. The house of representatives recites his offense there, and says, "Go to jail as a punishment for your contempt." The speaker of the house, under this law, certifies to the district attorney of this District the same precise offense, and says, "This man is guilty under the law of 1874, and, therefore, punish him." The house of representatives authorizes the speaker to certify the case here. He is called on by the statute to do so, and he can not refuse. The speaker of the house would not disobey a plain law. The house find that Hallet Kilbourn committed an offense, and while they punish him in jail for it, the speaker of the house, under his oath to obey the laws of his country, can do no less than certify to the district attorney the same fact; and you may take every paper—the certificate of the speaker bringing the case here, the resolution committing him to the common jail of the District, the report made by the committee to the house of representatives of his contumacy; every step and every paper consists of the same printed slips cut out of the proceedings of congress. The foundation is the same all the way through. There is no variation from beginning to end. That proves a unity. Where is the divisibility of this offense? Where does his offense against the house separate itself from that offense which the court is called on to punish? It is one and the same, and it narrows itself down to the question whether the house can put him in jail for exactly the same thing that the house itself under this law calls on the court to imprison him in jail for. As to the offense, there is no room for arguing; the house certifies to the district attorney, through its speaker, in obedience to a law of congress, to take charge of this man and punish him for his offense; and then they say, through their returning officer here, and through their counsel, that they can hold him and punish him too. As your honor suggested from the bench, in the one instance by statute a limitation is provided for the duration of his punishment. He may be punished by a fine of a thousand dollars here, in the court, and by imprisonment not more than one year. Yet, if this argument is good as to the house, it is good as to the senate, and if he had committed this contempt against the senate, the senate could punish him as long as it pleased; and, indeed, the house could do the same thing, because it is contended nobody can inquire into the powers of the house of representatives, either as to the jurisdiction, or the manner, or the measure, as Jefferson says, of the punishment. There is no reason why a commitment to jail should not last beyond the duration of congress

MR ELDREDGE. The house did that in the case of Pat. Wood.

MR. VOORHEES. Yes; in the case of Pat. Wood, who invaded the person of an honorable member of congress in Richmond; he was arrested and punished by the house of representatives as for a contempt of the house in the streets of Richmond. The house held a grand inquest—I believe that is what Mr Shellabarger and and Colonel Christy call it—a grand inquest of the nation; it held a grand inquest of the nation in the case of Pat. Wood, and put him in jail, and punished him with an imprisonment that extended three months beyond the life of congress itself. That man is in Richmond now, and has brought no suit for damages; but if he ever does, there is no court that would refuse to award him a proper amount.

Let me call attention to the fact that when Joseph B. Stewart sued Mr. Blaine, as speaker, and the sergeant-at-arms for illegal and false imprisonment, the house of representatives, through its officers, then asked the court to decide on the question of the jurisdiction of the house, and it became one of the very questions that decided the case. If the court had held in that case that there was no jurisdiction, these officers would have been at the mercy of a jury to lay damages upon them. This is a double-edged sword. Congress now denies the power to investigate the jurisdiction of the house, but if to-morrow Hallet Kilbourn should sue my friend Mr Thompson, who, of course, would be sustained by the house, and would not suffer a dollar's loss—and I would not want him to—but if he were sued, his instructions from the house would be to raise the question whether the house had jurisdiction and power to imprison Hallet Kilbourn, and then you would be asked, as you are asked now by us, to pass upon that as the fundamental proposition.

But to go back to the line of my argument. When the counsel are forced to abandon the right to punish a man twice for the same offense, they exclaim that the imprisonment of Mr Kilbourn by the house is not punishment at all. It looks to me like punishment to put a man in jail and regulate his diet by the action of the house. I speak in illustration; for if the house of representatives has the right to say that a man shall live on one dollar a day, and nobody has a right to question it, they have a right to say he shall live on twenty-five cents a day. Why not? You say no court shall investigate or inquire into this thing. You say the writ of *habeas corpus* does not confer the power on a court to inquire into it; that if he was starving, and we came here and said congress is starving that man to death, and make proof that he is dying, the argument on the other side would be, " the house is supreme; we are imprisoning him for contempt; our action can not be investigated; courts must not meddle with us, or we will show them the folly of doing so; we are representatives of the people, higher than courts; we are the grand inquest of the nation."

That is the legitimate conclusion of their argument. There is no earthly escape from it, for if they can do the one they can do the other It is only in further illustration of what I have advanced all the way through my argument, that if the right of judicial review over their action is totally denied, they may put him in the damps of a dungeon; put him in a cell and let him rot; and all the answer that we will get will be, as Mr. Shellabarger has said, "we are not to presume that congress will do wrong." Away with such a doctrine. I do presume it will do wrong. I know that any human body on earth, parliament, congress, my party, your party, anybody trusted with irresponsible, lawless power, with no restraint, no bridle, will do, and always have done, wrong It is the old doctrine of the divine right of the king revived here. I spurn it, and trample it under foot; cast it from the presence of the court. It has no place in the hallowed precincts of an American court of justice. Presuming that men will not do wrong, you, therefore, give them unbridled power over their fellow-men; you turn loose the tiger of lawless power, and say that you assume the tiger will do right. I say, chain the tiger.

There is a limit to be put upon all bodies of men. To proclaim a power beyond the reach of judicial inquiry into the commitment and imprisonment of a man, in the face of a law already provided on the same subject, is too monstrous to be characterized in moderate terms. Punish him! They say it is not punishment by the house, and yet they claim a power of punishment that reaches even unto death. If it be not punishment, I should like to know what it is. The power of imprisoning, without any limitation, implies the power to do everything else. The power that can reduce a man's diet to a dollar a day, can cut it down still lower. Sir, all the comfort we have is in the law, on which we can repose our heads as on a pillow. To high and low it says, "Thus far shall power go, and no farther." I say the imprisonment by the house is punishment; punishment of the most boundless kind. Mr. Shellabarger, finally, however, seeing that under the constitution he could not sustain himself, in admitting that congress could punish, and likewise the criminal court here, says the action of the house is "remedial" and "coercive." Men walk the streets also and say, "Why, if a man can refuse to testify, what is the use of investigating committees? There must be some way to make men testify."

Ay, if your honor please, do you know any way? Do you? The ways have been sought through ages of fire and blood, and have made the heavens red with the flames of martyrdom. The coercive method of making men testify to faith and belief has filled the world with bloodshed and horror. "Remedial and coercive!" Toward the last of the argument, Mr. Shellabarger, appreciating that the word "coercive" came up smoking hot from the regions of damnation—regions of history which have been damned by the common consent of mankind—departed from its use; he shrank back from it, and adopted the term "remedial."

They say that Mr. Kilbourn will not testify. He will not bring his books where no charge has been made; no specific accusations. He will not bring his books and lay them down for inspection, and they will make him. Now, can they? I believe in investigations. I believe in them inside of the law, however. And I ask you whether it is in the power of any court, if a citizen, standing securely on his rights, says, "I will not answer your question," to coerce him? Mr. Kilbourn says: "The bill of rights of my country protects me in keeping secret my private business, and the business of my patrons who have trusted their affairs to me, and I will not expose my business to the illegal and unconstitutional inquiry which is proposed." Emery said, in the Massachusetts case, "I will not testify, because it will criminate me." Suppose in that case they had said, "You shall." Remedial and coercive measures will be instituted against you. We will put you in jail first, for the power of remedial and coercive measures exists. It is like this assumed power of the house to punish; it has no limit; it has no bound." If you are thus coercing Hallet Kilbourn to make him testify, why not bring the matter to a short conclusion? The precedents in history are ample, and if Massachusetts had treated Emery as it is said in some of the darker stages of her history she treated some of her citizens accused of witchcraft, we would have had a horrible scene with which to illustrate the argument of opposing counsel. It is said that in one of the persecutions for witchcraft a wealthy man was put on his trial, under a peculiar law of that dark and barbaric period. By the law, if he pleaded "not guilty" and was found guilty, all his property was forfeited to the church. He knew he had to die. He would not plead guilty, whereby he might have saved his property to his wife and children, because such a plea would leave a stain upon his memory. Therefore, when they brought him into court and asked him to plead, he said nothing, not a word. They said he must plead; he did not plead. They urged him to plead like the house is urging Hallet Kilbourn to produce his books, to testify. He would not plead, and he did not plead. They took him out of that temple of Satan and laid him on the ground and commenced piling logs on him in the effort to coerce a plea, as they are trying to coerce the books from Kilbourn, only in a different way, in a malarious jail. They piled logs on the old man, but he would not yield. They piled more on him and more, but he had made his will, he had fixed his property to his satisfaction, and so he felt content. So they piled on the logs until they squeezed the breath out of his body. He died, but he did not plead. Can coercion get a plea? Can coercion get testimony? You may say, "This will defeat investigation." No, it will not. It is only once in a long while that a house of representatives goes beyond its proper limits and a citizen of good repute stands upon his rights. There is a point where courts are powerless and where congress is powerless, unless you are willing to launch yourselves on the avowed doctrine of coercion. James the Second tried it on the people of Scotland. With great pleasure to him he put the knee-boots on to force parties to testify against their accomplices or co-conspirators. He lost his throne, and ought to have lost his head. He fled across the British channel, and from that hour to this no male member of the Stuart family has been allowed to step foot on English soil. Coercive measures against free men; not punishment, but coercion! From the third century down to the thirteenth, this idea of forcing testimony was in the minds of those who then possessed what was called the civilization of the world. The people of southern Europe imbibed the vices of the Asiatic powers, their espionage, their system of spies, their liars, before whose accusations, if an honest man stood upon his rights, he was put to the torture. And from the thirteenth century to the fifteenth the Spanish inquisition was fully established as the best representative of coercive measures the world has ever seen.

The victims of coercion were cast into prison, starved, broken on the rack, burnt by slow fires, their joints wrenched apart, the flesh torn off their bones. They were all the time told that by testifying properly their agonies would cease. Men in the image of their Maker, made in the lofty likeness of Almighty God, are often readier to die than give up their rights under coercive torture. Why, if this doctrine of coercion is to be recognized, let us not stop with a jail. Let us have the whipping-post. Let us have the torn back under the lash. You say we have the right to make him testify. What will investigating committees be worth unless we can make him testify? Let us tie him to a cart-tail, crop his ears off. He can relieve himself of this torture at any time if he will only testify.

If we are to have coercion, let it be coercion. Let it be the full-grown monster, not the mere babe. Aye, if the court please, there is another court in which this doctrine of coercion is more becoming than here. It is the court of the wild western frontier; the court where Judge Lynch presides; where the midnight assassins of private rights assemble and sit upon some man sleeping at home who they think knows something about horse thieves or counterfeiters. They take him out of his bed, they tie him to a tree, and they say to him, "Tell where that horse is, where the counterfeit money is;" and, whether the poor wretch knows or not, they whip him till he tells something to save his life. Valuable testimony, priceless truth, extorted by coercion, whether by the lash in Judge Lynch's court or in the county jail of the District of Columbia!

What right-minded man would judge a dog on testimony thus procured? And cognate to that kind of testimony is another that I may speak of in passing, and for which I have no respect. It is that kind which is procured by a proclamation of amnesty to scoundrels who are steeped in crime. "Come forward all ye that can come, concoct anything, tell any lie, and though your sins be as scarlet, and though you be fit for the gallows and the penitentiary, if you can implicate somebody else, we will let you go."

Titus Oates made London a reeking shambles by such principles, and the reign in which he figured was stained with the most brutal crimes the world ever saw. But there is one satisfaction I have in all those blood-stained pages of English history, and that is, when this same Titus Oates was afterward dragged through the streets of London at the cart's tail, whipped at every step, his ears cut off, and fastened in the pillory.

Coercive measures in this free government to procure testimony! "But," says Mr. Shellabarger, "it is so easy for Mr. Kilbourn to settle this trouble by bringing his books." So spoke the tories and the friends of high prerogative in the reign of the Stuarts, when Hampton and his compeers refused to pay the ship-money. It was not much; only a few shillings; it was very easy for them to pay it, but they would not do it. They were born with certain constitutional rights, and they dared to stand and defend them. "It is a small matter," says the opposing counsel; "let Mr. Kilbourn answer, and all the trouble will be over." The tories said to Hampton, "Pay it and there will be no further trouble." His answer was written in his blood on the field of battle. Some people can not comprehend these instances, and the example of devotion to principle. The matter of principle is never small. It is always a great question. It to-day involves Hallet Kilbourn. I never saw one page of his books; I never had dealings with him; I know nothing about his private affairs; but this I do know—that he is this day making a contest for the dearest principles of American liberty. In our race, in our blood, runs an abhorrence for the doctrine that would procure testimony from any other than an undefiled, pure, voluntary source. The Anglo-Saxon race established the trial by jury and judicial inquiry before the face of the world. Our race will not convict upon testimony procured by lynch law' —the doctrine of coercion. Nor will we convict upon testimony procured from the lips of perjured knaves who are promised free pardon in advance. What has been the result? The races of southern Europe, who have practiced coercion on the one hand and procurement from corrupt and infamous sources on the other, have sunk lower and lower, until a healthy idea of civil liberty does not exist in all their boundaries. Spain has tried her republic, and, after a futile effort, in which was displayed an utter ignorance of all these great safeguards of liberty, she has gone back to the spurious offspring of her profligate queen. France is trying the experiment with little better success.

Do not misunderstand my remarks. I desire to see all transactions of a doubtful nature laid bare. I would aid to the utmost; but when I am called to judge my fellow-men on testimony procured either by imprisonment on bread and water, or by the lash and scourge, or any other mode of coercion; or, on the other hand, by the promise of free grace to knaves, I will have none of it. I am not speaking on this point for the first time. I have spoken before the country in regard to this matter, and that recently. Let man be judged by the law, fairly and impartially, and I shall be content.

I wish to read, if your honor please, a paper submitted by Judge Black, my associate counsel, to the committee, on the power of the house in this matter. I read it because of the great reputation of the author; his high character and the soundness of his views.

I read it as a part of my own argument, but I read it with the proper credit given.

GENTLEMEN: It must be apparent to you that a legislative committee has no power to investigate the private affairs or search the private papers of any citizen unless for the purpose of establishing some fact in which the public has an interest. Even then it can only be done if the fact sought to be established is such as ought to be the foundation of some legislative proceeding.

There are precedents for examinations of this kind prompted by political or personal enmity. In the better days of the republic efforts to make such use of the congressional committees were always unsuccessful. A notable instance of failure was the attempt to expose the private business of General Cass and others, then officers of the government, in the purchase of real estate. No man can doubt that all evidence offered on that subject was rightly rejected. An example of better success was set by a committee of the senate in 1839, which compelled the production of all papers and other evidence relating to the purchase of a newspaper establishment in this city, called the *Constitution*, the object being simply to furnish opposing papers with material for abuse of the editor. And the anti-constitutional party made some capital out of it, which they valued quite highly. A year afterwards a committee of the house of representatives sat here for a long time inquiring into private conversations and getting private letters wherever they could find them, and used them to frame personal scandals and excite ill-blood among men who might otherwise have been friends.

To suppose that this committee is at all inclined to follow the latter precedents would be a want of respect for the character of all its members. While you are no doubt determined to ascertain the true condition of public affairs, to the end that the proper remedy may be applied to every wrong, it is not believed for a moment that you are willing to let your authority be used or abused for the mere purpose of exposing a private transaction which the parties, for reasons of their own, desired to keep secret and which they have a perfect right to keep secret.

I admit that every man is bound to show any paper or to testify to any fact which the purposes of public justice or good government require the legislature or the courts to know. If there be any cause pending (no matter between what parties) in which these papers can be regarded as relevant testimony, the person having them in custody is bound to produce them when legally called for by the tribunal having jurisdiction of the subject. Nor do I deny that a committee of congress investigating the conduct of any officer may lawfully demand the inspection of a paper tending to show that he is guilty or innocent. The refusal of the witness to produce the papers now called for is based upon the ground that they have no kind of connection with any public interest or any private controversy which you have authority to settle or inquire into. The inquisitorial power of congress is large, but it has a limit. It does not extend so far that it can be used for the mere purpose of compelling men to reveal those affairs in which nobody but themselves have any concern. The confidences of business and friendship are sacred, unless their disclosure be rendered necessary to protect the rights or enforce the obligations of other parties. "The real estate pool," which our friends are so anxious to look at, is as completely beyond the scope of your jurisdiction as the history of the witness's marriage or the advancements to his children.

I ought not to make this averment so positively without mentioning more in detail the known facts which prove it.

It is admitted on all hands that divers persons and firms put into the hands of Kilbourn & Latta certain sums of money, making a common fund, which Kilbourn & Latta were to use, and did use, in the purchase of real estate. The property so purchased was conveyed to Kilbourn & Latta, who held the legal title in trust for the use of all the parties in proportion to the amounts by them respectively contributed.

It was on its face a private partnership; a matter of purely private business;

the parties invested their own money in the purchase of property for themselves, intending to hold it in the hope that they could afterward sell it at an advance on the cost price, and thus make gain for themselves. All this was perfectly lawful, honest, and just. No man has ever complained that the trustees or any one of the beneficiaries ever injured or wronged him to the amount of a cent. But they chose to keep secret the terms of the trust, the names of the contributors, and the amounts put in or drawn out by each one. They choose now not to publish their business to the world, for reasons which seem good in their own eyes. The right of keeping it to themselves is so clear and so well protected by the law that if an eavesdropper had found it out by listening at a key-hole or a window, he might be indicted as a criminal offender for blabbing it abroad. If the papers relating to it should accidentally come into the hands of an enemy or a rival, a chancellor would enjoin him against the publication.

But it is contended by those who prompt this investigation that it is not wholly a private affair, and we concede that if any reasonable ground be shown to believe that the information sought for is necessary for a guide to congress in ferreting out public abuses or in framing legislative measures, we are not justified in withholding it.

Two years ago the joint committee on the District government demanded these same papers, believing, apparently, that the real estate pool was part of a conspiracy to defraud the people of the District by taxing them corruptly in such manner as would improve the lands purchased by the trustees.

This suspicion (for it amounts to nothing more) was repelled—the witness stood upon his rights as a citizen, and refused to produce his papers or submit them to a search. I will not say what reasons actuated the committee, but in point of fact no coercive measures were taken against him. Henry D. Cooke, the governor of the District, was called and testified that the firm of Jay Cooke & Co., of which he was a member, had subscribed $25,000 to the pool, but he completely disproved all connection of this business with the District government.

You are now looking after corruptions in the District. The present call for these private papers is based upon another ground altogether. Let me see what it is.

Jay Cooke & Co., who had $25,000 in the pool, have become bankrupt. Mr. Lewis, their trustee, under the forty-third section of the bankrupt law, has made a settlement with Latta & Kilbourn, trustees of the pool, and has received out of the pool all that belongs to Jay Cooke & Co.'s estate. The preamble to the resolution under which you are sitting avers that the settlement for Jay Cooke & Co.'s share was disadvantageous to the creditors of Jay Cooke & Co.; therefore, there must be an examination into this private affair of the other parties. We have several answers to this:

1. The decision of the circuit court of the United States, lately affirmed by the supreme court, shows that the government is not interested in the fund which the trustee of Jay Cooke & Co. may have in his hands; its debts against Jay Cooke, McCulloch & Co. being otherwise secured.

2. It is not even suggested that the settlement between Mr. Lewis and the associates of Jay Cooke & Co. is fraudulent.

Here is the nearest a specific charge contained in this resolution:

And whereas Edwin N. Lewis, trustee of the estate and effects of said firm of Jay Cooke & Co., has recently made a settlement of the interest of the estate of Jay Cooke & Co. with the associates of said firm of Jay Cooke & Co., to the disadvantage and loss, as it is alleged—

By whom? "As it is alleged." Who has alleged it? I want to know. I do not want to follow Judge Black and inquire who stands behind the counsel here to prompt them, but I would like to know, if they dare to say, who is the "allegator" in this case, and what "swamp" he comes from, and where his "pool" is. [Laughter.] "It is alleged!" and yet Mr. Kilbourn said over and over in his testimony before the committee, and again before the house, that if anybody would stand up and specifically charge that either he, himself, was defrauding the government, or was aiding anybody to defraud it, to the value of a dollar, he would lay his books all down. Nobody dare do it. "It is alleged!"

Simply this whole inquiry by which a man's house is to be invaded, his papers ransacked, and himself laid in jail, is based upon "it is said," "they say." You remember the old anecdote of Aaron Burr, when a family acquaintance said to him, "General, they say you did very bad things in your young days." He replied, "My child, 'they say,' 'they say,' is the fountain of all lies. It is the vague repository from which come all anonymous scandals; all anonymous falsehoods; all irresponsible assaults." "It is alleged," "they say." Here the house gravely plants itself on "they say," "it is alleged," "it is said." If they would come forward and give us somebody who says that Mr. Lewis made a fraudulent settlement, or that the court was a party to it, or allowed it to be done, or overlooked its duty, we would know something of the nature of the inquiry we were engaged in.

2. It is not even suggested that the settlement between Mr. Lewis and the associates of Jay Cooke & Co. is fraudulent. It is perfectly just, honest, and fair to all the creditors. You will not proceed upon a mere assumption that the government was cheated by such men as Mr. Lewis and Mr. Bullett without first calling them and making sure of your ground.

3. Assuming that the United States are creditors of Jay Cooke & Co., admitting their interest in the settlement with the trustees, conceding that the creditors (including the United States) have been losers by the settlement, does that make the case a subject of legislative inquiry? Can you set aside the contract by act of congress?

4. It is not true that the courts are powerless to furnish whatever redress may be needed for any conceivable wrong which can have been committed in the adjustment of Jay Cooke & Co.'s interest. The court in which the bankrupt proceedings are pending has ample authority to hear and determine any complaint of that kind against the trustee. No such complaint has been made. Why? Manifestly because there is no ground upon which it can be sustained.

5. This is an unreasonable search of a citizen's papers. I admit that it is not, in form, a warrant for that express purpose. But it is in substance an order that he shall produce about a cart-load of private books and papers, where the witness's enemies may go through them and use them for the injury and annoyance of himself and his customers.

6. The witness's opponents admit that they are not seeking for matter of criminal accusation either against him or against anybody else. They can, therefore,

desire only to get some advantage of him in private business, or to furnish food for personal scandal. Is the gratification of such a wish consistent with your dignity, or that of the great body to which you belong?

7. We have said already, and we repeat it now, that if any gentleman urging this investigation will pledge himself to a statement showing that the transaction in question has any kind of relation to any public interest requiring legislative protection, or that the trust reposed in the witness by his associates is not purely private, we give up all opposition. If they will set forth any fact from which a reasonable inference to that effect can be made, let them have the benefit of all doubts. I have confidence enough in the honor and veracity of these investigators to make me certain that they will use no false pretenses in this case. So long, however, as there is no suggestion of any specific ground for treating this private affair as if it were a public one, I do protest against any attempt to enforce this unreasonable demand for papers with which they have no concern.

I read the latter part of that to show that at every stage, and under all circumstances, the offer has been freely made that if anybody would make a specific accusation it would be met; but until it is, we feel that we are protecting not merely the rights of Hallet Kilbourn, but the rights of every man, black and white, from one ocean to the other. It is the common right of an American citizen that we are defending here; and instead of denunciation, detraction, and abuse, Hallet Kilbourn deserves the thanks of all who desire the foundations of the law to be ascertained and its power to be upheld. If the court please, the analogy which has been attempted to be made between the power of courts and of congress to punish for contempts is still further destroyed from the fact that, looking at my notes, I find that in 1839 a law growing out of the impeachment of Judge Peck was passed, governing the federal courts on the subject of contempts, and defining what a contempt is, and how it shall be punished. So that neither in the state courts nor in the federal courts does this analogy hold, even if congress were a court, which it is not.

I approach, now, the conclusion of this argument. I have spoken longer than I am accustomed to, but after listening four days to the logical and learned discussion on the other side, I feel that, occupy what time I could, I could do no more than justice to the case, and perhaps, a great deal less. It is a question of the gravest moment, and I share with the gentlemen in the earnest desire that there shall be no conflict between the different departments of this government. Mr. Shellabarger and Colonel Christy closed with the patriotic hope, in which I join, that nothing may occur to disturb the harmony and peaceful relations of the various departments of the federal Union. But who has precipitated a collision, if there is one? Is it the court, standing by the time-honored practices of a court, or is it the house of representatives, in an attempt to do what no congress ever did on American soil? Such a thing has not been done by one branch or both—defying the courts on this great question of *habeas corpus*—never since the foundation of the government; not once. No state legislatures ever did it, and it is nearly two hundred years since the parliament of England attempted to do it. Therefore, I say, if congress will act as the constitution tells it to act, as a legislative body; make laws, and let the courts interpret what the laws are, and the president enforce them, we will sail on a smooth sea of prosperity and happiness. But if congress attempts to usurp all the powers of the government, as sometimes I have known it to do—both legislative, judicial, and executive—then we can have nothing but tribulations I need not say to this court that the sound heart of this country, all over the land, believes in the conservatism, the wisdom, and purity of our judiciary over every other department of the government. Presidents come and go, and fall into trouble. Their surroundings betray them; friends prove treacherous, and drag their high names in the dirt. Congress changes with changing years. Sometimes one party is in the ascendency, and sometimes another, desiring to break down the safeguards of law to reach their enemies. And I am tempted, as I look over across the Potomac, to say, that of all the people in this country who ought to cherish most the protecting, saving power of the courts, they are those who have had the horror, first of war, and then the plowshare of reconstruction driven through their homes; where a lieutenant with six men at his back can suspend the writ of *habeas corpus* and throw anybody in prison. I think I can say for that people, that the writ of *habeas corpus* is dear and precious in their sight, and the sanctuary of the court pleasant to them as a shelter from congress. The man who, because his party is in the ascendency for a time, desires to revel in power, setting a precedent for his adversary when he may come in, is short-sighted indeed. There is only one safe rule—determine what the law is and follow it through good and evil report; follow it as the hosts of Israel followed the cloud by day and the pillar of fire by night. If it runs you counter sometimes to an associate, so be it; it will guide you safely at last. It is our only safety. Let this case be determined according to law. The pathway is open to the only higher tribunal than yourself, from which there is no appeal, except to the sword; whichever way it may decide, if parties are not content here, they will have to be content there.

Thanking your honor for your patient attention, I am done.

FIRST TRIAL OF KILBOURN vs. THOMPSON

ADDRESS TO THE JURY

Closing argument for the plaintiff, made in the supreme court of the District of Columbia, April 21, 1882, in the suit of Hallet Kilbourn *v.* John G. Thompson, for $150,000 damages for false imprisonment.

This cause arose out of the arrest and imprisonment of Mr. Kilbourn, by John G. Thompson, then sergeant-at-arms of the house of representatives, and acting in pursuance of its order, for an alleged contempt of the house, in refusing to expose to its scrutiny certain of his private books and papers. Mr. Kilbourn was released by *habeas corpus*, the court holding the arrest and imprisonment unlawful; Mr. Voorhees' argument in which proceeding precedes this address. He then brought this suit.

Mr. Kilbourn was represented in this trial by Mr. Voorhees, Col. Enoch Totten, Gen. Noah L. Jeffries, and Hon. Charles A. Eldredge.

After five hours' deliberation the jury returned a verdict for the plaintiff for $100,000.

It is worthy of note that this enormous verdict was rendered upon a declaration which averred no special damages, for which reason the evidence as to injury to business and health, and loss of time, was very meager.

Justice McArthur sustained a motion to set aside this verdict as excessive, and, in doing so, indulged in the following observations:

I think we can trace the influence upon the minds of the jury largely to the powerful appeal addressed to them in the argument of the counsel who closed the case on the part of the plaintiff. They were evidently moved by his eloquence and inspired by the magnanimity of his sentiments, so that they overlooked the more sober and impassive instructions of the law. While feelings of this description were laudable to the members of the jury as men, the law can make no allowance for susceptibilities of this character in its impartial administration.

The second trial of this cause occurred in the supreme court of the District of Columbia, beginning October 29, 1883, upon an amended declaration, averring special damages and enlarging the prayer for judgment from $150,000 to $350,000.

The counsel for plaintiff were Mr. Voorhees, Col. Enoch Totten, Gen. Noah L. Jeffries and Hon. Charles A. Eldredge, as in the former trial, Mr. Voorhees again making the closing argument to the jury.

The defendant was represented by District Attorney George B. Corkhill, Hon. Jeremiah M. Wilson and Randolph Coyle, Esq.

The second trial resulted in a verdict for $60,000 damages, which was set aside by Justice Cox, as excessive, and a new trial awarded.

The cause was a third time tried in the same court, in March, 1884, by the same counsel, Mr. Voorhees again addressing the jury in the closing argument, and a verdict for $37,500 was secured.

Upon a motion to set aside this verdict, Justice Hagner announced his conclusion that, upon the filing, by the plaintiff, of a remittal for $17,500, the verdict would be permitted to stand for $20,000. Such remittal was filed by Mr. Kilbourn, and he eventually received the sum of $20,000, with interest from March 26, 1884, until payment, amounting in all to $21,000.

May it Please the Court, and You, Gentlemen of the Jury:

SIX years ago, when I was not a member of either branch of congress, a citizen of the United States, whom I first knew as a citizen of my own state, Mr. Kilbourn, was thrown illegally, arbitrarily, into the jail of this District. At that time I was called to his side as one of his counsel, a place I cheerfully and promptly took, because I knew the laws of this country, its constitution, and all that is dear on earth to an American citizen, had, in his person, been stricken down. The result of six years' litigation has proved the correctness of my views. I allude to this fact, however, mainly for the purpose of saying that my connection with this case then, and ever since, compels my attendance here now in its closing stages. My presence here to-day is in the fulfillment of professional obligations to a client, incurred years ago, and continuing from that time to this.

Gentlemen, the wrong and injury complained of in this action were not committed by the government of the United States. The house of representatives is not the government. It is an important branch of the government, but it is only a branch. The injury inflicted upon Mr. Kilbourn was the act of the house alone; the senate took no part in it, in this instance, but both the senate and the house have, almost from the beginning of the government, committed similar violations of the constitution in the arrest and imprisonment of citizens, and the action of the house in 1876, in the case of Kilbourn, was sustained by a long line of bad precedents.

Both branches of congress, under a mistaken idea of their authority, have, up to a recent date, imprisoned citizens at their own unrestrained will and pleasure, for indefinite terms, without sworn accusation, without trial, without due process of law; simply under a vague claim of power to punish for contempt. They had been in the habit of throwing men into prison in this way for years prior to the present case. Down in the lowest basement of the capitol there is what is called a crypt, which has served as a prison; a fact as odious and revolting to my mind as any of the horrid appliances of the inquisition; recalling as it does the ancient methods of extorting testimony in the vaults of dungeons under ground.

But at last this power was asserted against a man who dared resist it, and I rejoice exceedingly that he did. I rejoice that Kilbourn had the courage to confront the arbitrary giant which so long crushed everything before it.

It is no small thing for a private citizen, single-handed and alone, depending on his own resources, to confront either branch of congress, with all of its machinery and its power; with its organized, corporate thunderbolts to hurl upon his head. It is no small thing, and whenever a man does that in the right, and conquers for himself and for you all certain great fundamental principles of liberty, he should be an object of tender and careful regard at your hands; he should not be an object of assault. He becomes a public benefactor; he has fought a battle, not merely for himself, but for each one of you, and for your children when you are dead and gone.

Gentlemen, never in the whole course of my life have I heard such an attempt to belittle the great question of human liberty as has been made by the defense in this trial. Is it, indeed, a small thing for an innocent man to be in prison? A sadder sight can not be witnessed; a sadder thought never entered my mind. Think for a moment. Our sympathies sometimes go out even for the guilty in their deprivation of liberty, but what shall be said of man wholly innocent in slavery, chains, and prison! You are now considering the case of a man who was cast into prison without lawful charge or accusation, and who has been found by the supreme court of the United States, not only innocent of the semblance of wrong, but to have been upholding and defending the constitution of his country from first to last.

Does he stand before you in an attitude to be rated at so much a day for loss of time while in jail; to be sneered at because he tried to console the weary hours of imprisonment by refreshments —by a generous table? Does the man who was asserting that for which armies have been marshaled, for which nations have struggled, for which men have bled on the scaffold; does he seem to be the man who should be assailed in a court of justice when he comes before you to ask that which has already been decided by the highest tribunal in the land to be his right? I place Hallet Kilbourn before you here just as he is. He stands here in the right. That is a great element in a trial of this kind. There is not a flaw in his conduct. When arrested, when brought before the committee, was he contumacious? Did he stand merely upon a stubborn notion of refusing to do what he was required to? Let me show you the just and careful appreciation of his rights, and of yours, which he evinced at the time. He says here in the official proceedings of the house of representatives, which the court has held to be in evidence before you:

> But I will make no conflict with the authority of this house, unless I am driven to it by the stress of sheer necessity for the preservation of my undeniable rights. It is easy to bring this affair to a plain issue. If the committee of the house will find and assert the truth of any fact which connects the real estate pool with our public interests which it is the duty of congress to protect, you shall at once have all the information I can give you about its nature and history.

Point it out. Let it be shown, and he would respond. He proceeds:

> I have asserted on oath that it is purely a private transaction, having no connection, direct or indirect, with any public affair or with the official conduct of any officer. The truth of my statement is made manifest by all the facts which are known, and nothing is even alleged from which a contrary inference can be reasonably drawn. Now let the question be squarely presented. If the committee or the house has any well-grounded reasons to believe that the production of my private papers or the revelation of my private business will promote any public interest or remedy any public wrong, and if either the committee or the house will assert that to be true as matter of fact, the house and all its committees shall have whatever is demanded; or if any private individual will make oath that the papers asked for will lead to the detection of any misgovernment or the exposure of wickedness in high places they shall be open as day to your inspection. On the other hand, I can not acknowledge—

And if he had he would have been bastard-born to the institutions of liberty—

> And, on the other hand, I can not acknowledge the naked arbitrary right of the house to investigate private business in which nobody but I and my customers has any connection.

That statement rests on the principles of the constitution, and the stand which Mr. Kilbourn made then was in the interest of every man's right to the privacy and security of his own personal concerns. "Show me," said he, "where my concerns affect the public interests—show me where a public wrong can be redressed by opening my drawers—and they shall all be opened; but until you show that I stand upon my rights;" and less than that would have made him unworthy of the protection which the courts for six years have given him, and which I know this jury will give him here to-day. Let me go a little further. My brother Smith saw fit to convey in a delicate sort of marginal way—I will not use the word insinuate, for it might not be agreeable, but it was something after that order—that there might have been something wrong; that an investigation was very desirable, and that possibly Mr. Kilbourn was not so entirely in the right. Gentlemen, in this action of tort for damages I intend that my client shall appear before you just as he was, in the right absolutely, not qualifiedly, but everywhere broadly in the right; conceding everything that a citizen should concede to his government to detect wrong, correct wickedness, punish crime, if there was crime. In this connection I wish to read to you an answer in another part of the report of the elaborate investigation that took place. And this was before the committee itself:

> Question. You refuse to produce them before the committee in response to this subpœna?
>
> Answer. Yes, sir. I would like to state the reasons therefor—my personal reasons. My partner and myself are in a private business. We have no connection with the government of the United States, and never had ; are conscious of having violated no law ; are not charged with any fraud. Our business that we do is done with private citizens throughout the country, and I stand upon the right which I think belongs to every private citizen not accused of violating any law of being protected in his papers. Whatever the law decides, however, I am willing to abide by. I sustain but one relation to the government, and that is to pay taxes and obey the law. That is the only transaction I have with the government at all.

You will remember, gentlemen, this investigation was not launched at Mr. Kilbourn for anything alleged to have been done by him. It was launched at him for the purpose of tracing up somebody's else business that was supposed to run in its ramifications through his office. A more generous battle for right no man ever made. Not fighting alone for himself, but for the rights of men who had intrusted their affairs with him. I will now read the answer of Mr. Kilbourn to the committee to show you the starting point. I have, in my life, often talked to juries, and know that it is agreeable to them, as it is to me, in summing up to take a starting point, and see where we are; who is in the right and who is in the wrong, and then step along to a conclusion. Inasmuch as the counsel on the other side have sought to raise a mist upon this question, I shall undertake to clear it away. There is sunlight in these answers here. He continues:

> The Witness. I want you to understand that I do not resist it because I want to shield anything from the government interests. I am only resisting it and protecting my own interests as a citizen who has but one relation to the government, and that is to obey the law and pay taxes. The government has no interest one way or the other in this matter. If it had, through Jay Cooke, or Lewis, trustee of Jay Cooke & Co., it was all settled. We have settled through the courts. If the settlement was not fair the court is open for it, I understand. Instead of resisting anything that affects the government, as I said, I would help to promote the government's interest if it can be shown wherein I can do it.

All that he asked was that the constitution should have some respect paid it in attempting to reach his papers and in the effort to ride over all his private rights. In all this, he has since been fully sustained—but more of that as I go on. I want to fix his status as a law-abiding citizen, shielding nobody in wrong; covering up nothing that the government had a right to inspect; if the house of representatives would point out exactly what they wanted in his books, he would cheerfully furnish such information; but the proceeding was as if the house of representatives had asked some large business firm here on Pennsylvania avenue, some mercantile establishment, to come up and bring all their books and let them be inspected without any specific allegation as to what was sought. It was the most thorough, unqualified, drag-net proceeding ever known. No seine was ever thrown into the Potomac with a wider, more unqualified view to catch everything without any specific purpose to catch any specific thing, than was this proceeding against Kilbourn's office. He resisted on the grounds which I have read, and thereupon the order was made for his arrest and imprisonment. It was then that I came into this case. The house reluctantly at last responded to the writ of *habeas corpus*—that giant writ that pries open prison doors the world over, except in Ireland, I believe, where American citizens are imprisoned as suspects, with exactly the legality that Hallet Kilbourn was imprisoned by his own government, and no more. And I say in this connection that the first duty of a government is to protect its own citizens at home or abroad. No higher duty was ever imposed upon a government than this. The government which is willing to imprison one of its own citizens without law or allow any other government to do it is on the road to ruin. It was said by the wisest man of Greece when the Greek republic flourished highest and strongest that the greatest injury a government could receive was in the injury of one of its citizens, however humble, whether inflicted upon him by his own or by any other government. The first duty of a government is to protect its own citizens. There lies the power of a government. Protect your citizens, and they will love their government; protect your citizens, and you have a loyalty that is not mere lip service, but a loyalty that springs from the heart. Protect your citizens; give them the full shield of the law and ample protection of their rights under the law, and you make good citizens. Leave them to be buffeted, imprisoned without redress, without justice, and you alienate them and create a disloyalty equal to any that ever raged through this or any other country.

Gentlemen of the jury, when this question came before the house of representatives, I wish to show you what views were held there. They were somewhat different from the views of Mr. Smith. They were somewhat different from the views of my friend, Colonel Corkhill, if I gathered what his views of the law were, and I am not certain that I did. When the question came up in the house of representatives, whether Colonel Thompson should be allowed to respond to this writ with the person of this prisoner, a debate arose that will throw light on this question, and I desire to call attention to some utterances that were made at that time. They fall with peculiar force now on this question. I read the words that fell from the lips of James A. Garfield, then a member of the house of representatives. What said he upon this great question? Did he differ from the views that I am pressing here? Did he agree with the gentlemen on the opposite side of this case? No, no. He said:

> But there are some things that courts and congresses and houses of representatives and people everywhere must pay heed to, at least as a matter of good conscience and discretion. Now, I wish to refresh the minds of gentlemen for a moment with a reference to the fourth article of amendments to the constitution, to see what they think it means.

I will read that as he read it on the floor of the house.

> The right of the people to be secure in their persons, houses, papers, and effects, against unreasonable searches and seizures, shall not be violated; and no warrants shall issue, but upon probable cause, supported by oath or affirmation, and particularly describing the place to be searched, and the persons and things to be seized.

No such procedure as this was had in this case. General Garfield proceeded with his argument:

> In our original proceeding in the first step we took, admitting for the sake of argument, our jurisdiction and our right, did we use the proper discretion?

He was speaking then of the arrest and imprisonment of Kilbourn.

> Was probable cause shown why this particular inquiry should be had, and these particular papers be demanded?

Garfield made that inquiry just as I did.

> On the contrary, did not the witness declare his readiness to answer if the committee would say that they had any ground for believing that he had in his possession papers which would disclose, or that a true answer to the question would disclose, a single official personage with whom this house desired to deal? And they did not answer that they had any such ground on which to plant the question. Then, does not this house put itself in the attitude of going to a private citizen and demanding that his private papers, his private business, shall be disclosed to them, only because they hope, yet without probable ground for believing, that the answer will disclose something that may lead to something else? Why, sir, do gentlemen remember that that article of our constitution was put there by our wise fathers to prevent precisely such a consummation as that? Do they remember that the great Algernon Sidney was visited inquisitorily, that his papers were searched, that his library was seized, and as a result of throwing a drag-net over the whole, when no special allegation of any trea-

sonable thing was made as to his papers, there was discovered a manuscript essay on Liberty, which he had written in the seclusion of his own home, and which, being thus fished out by the drag-net of that sort of search and seizure, he was put upon his trial, condemned to death, and publicly executed as a traitor to his country, upon evidence that could never have been disclosed except by unreasonable search and seizure? And it was to prevent such invasions of personal liberties of citizens that our fathers put this clause in the articles of amendment to the constitution.

That is wisely and well said. Gentlemen, these are strong, just words, none the less strong that they come from the man who uttered them. He proceeds:

Now, I must say that the party to which I belong have, in the stormy years of their administration and career here, done many things that I have looked upon as of doubtful propriety and doubtful authority in reference to the rights of private citizens. In the very turbulence of that time I stepped forward to do what I could before the supreme court to prevent the punishment by military commission of persons whom I had never seen, and have never yet seen; of people who had committed an offense most offensive in my sight against the country. But I was unwilling they should be punished unlawfully, and did what I could to prevent such punishment.

That is the language of the late president of the United States; and if he had no other monument over his tomb, while in fact he will have thousands—if he had but this one to speak for him, it would speak through all the universe, and show that he understood the constitution and was faithful to personal liberty. But again, before I pass from this debate, I wish to read just one more brief passage from what he then said. He was at that time the leader of the house. Speaking of this proposition to arrest a man and imprison him under such proceedings as were then pending, and to refuse him the writ of *habeas corpus*, he says:

That is to me a most bold and startling heresy that this house is above the constitution. That is what it tried to be. We brought it down to the level of it when we got into the courts. We have of course the power to expel a member. We have the power to preserve order. We have all those ordinary parliamentary powers. But when we have pushed these rights of the house so far in these modern days, that according to the doctrine of my friend from Ohio [Mr. Hurd], the house may imprison a citizen for two years, and the senate may imprison him for life (because the senate is an immortal body); when we have so far pushed the privileges and powers of this house to make it an uncontrolled and uncontrollable despot, a tyrant that overbears all boundaries, that forces itself into all private closets, and breaks into every man's domicile, that its power knows no limit but its own discretion, that it shall have the right to uncover the secrets of all families within the republic, that there shall be no privity to which it can not penetrate, but, unrestrained by law, unlimited by the constitution, like the despots of the middle ages, shall be lord paramount of all rights within its boundaries, is a doctrine so monstrous, if adopted by us, that it ought to cover us with infamy and bring down upon us the wrath of an outraged people. Let this doctrine be once proclaimed, and you arm every citizen in hostility against the congress of his country. You make the house the natural enemy of every citizen, and every citizen ought to be our enemy. I declare myself the implacable foe of such a tyrant and of the doctrine that makes such tyranny possible. The doctrine asserted to-day on this floor would make this house the most odious tyranny that ever stalked abroad over any land to curse it.

Now, gentlemen, I have thought proper to dwell upon these points surrounding the birth of this case so that you might see it plainly in all its bearings. Instead of there having been any assertion of authority contemplated by the constitution, under oath or affirmation, what do you suppose the language was on which this arbitrary, high-handed proceeding was based? "And whereas Edwin W. Lewis, trustee of the estate and effects of said firm of Jay Cooke & Co., has recently made a settlement of the interest of the estate of Jay Cooke & Co., with the associates of said firm of Jay Cooke & Co., to the disadvantage and loss, as it is alleged "—there is the point " as it is alleged." There is the assertion of power on the part of the house, "to the disadvantage and loss of the government, as it is alleged." Alleged by whom? Alleged where? Under what authority of law? Is there a lawyer here at this bar, is there a court anywhere, is there a jury anywhere, that would not spurn, scorn, and spit upon such a basis as the foundation on which to deprive a citizen of his liberty, cast him into prison, destroy his health, destroy his business, and threaten his life by disease? "It is alleged!" Who alleged it? The constitution pointed out how it should be alleged on oath or affirmation. Those vague words "it is alleged!" Oh, what a common liar they are! "They say," in a newspaper, is the proclamation of an article resting generally upon the statement of liars. "It is alleged!" It is the irresponsible manner in which statements are put forth. It is worse than anonymous; worse than irresponsible. It is the worst form of slander; vague, vile, creeping slander. That is all there was on which to arrest Mr. Kilbourn, whose punishment in jail, and whose sufferings there are made so very light of here. Not a single form of law was complied with. And when we came before this court six years ago—I see, on looking, that it was on the 24th day of April, 1876—I had the honor of addressing this court then on great questions of law. Now I am addressing you on questions of fact. Then the great questions of legal right were outstanding.

They were unsettled. Precedent, authority, usage were quoted against us to remand Kilbourn back to prison. He had the manliness, the high sense of honor, and of duty, to confront all the power which the house of representatives could bring to crush him. It is six years since those questions were submitted. During that time he has pursued his rights as a citizen should. We are coming now to the close, and I intend, before I sit down, to see whether this jury measures cheaply, values lowly, the right of a citizen whose rights are beyond question.

If one single step had been taken by Kilbourn compromising his honor as a man; if one single word had ever fallen from his lips in derogation of his high character, you might mitigate these damages. But as the case stands there is nothing to mitigate them. Not that Mr. Thompson did more or less than his duty. He knows, and we all know, that he is incapable of doing anything else than his duty. I will make but one single passing remark in regard to his responsibility. This is not a claim against the government. If the house of representatives does not stand by one of its own honorable officers, out of its contingent fund, it would be so blighted and disgraced that no man would ever want to occupy a seat in it again. It is their place to do it. It is not a claim—and I mention this because Colonel Corkhill alluded to my position as a senator—that I shall ever vote upon. As a matter of course not. But, gentlemen, to continue my thought. What is there to mitigate these damages? Is there anything in Mr. Kilbourn's conduct? Not so. I have dwelt upon his conduct. I have dwelt upon the beginning of this case to show the attitude in which he comes before you—fighting a great battle for the liberty of the citizen. He has done nothing unbecoming an honorable citizen. I am glad to stand here for him. He has destroyed this despotic claim of power which congress in both branches has exercised so long. What was that claim of power? I am not going to dwell upon it again, as I once did at this bar. But I shrink appalled when I think of it. It was the claim that, without oath, without accusation, without affidavit, without indictment, without presentment, without information, one branch of congress—not both branches, but one, could resolve itself into a court, where, without trial, it could convict and sentence to indefinite imprisonment any citizen of the United States who refused to answer any question they proposed to him—any question, no matter how private, how secret the matter to which it related. The house claimed to be the sole judge of the propriety of the question. The citizen had no right.

The house proposed the question, and proposed to judge of its propriety, and no matter where it reached, whatever might be the domestic relation, it was not for the citizen to say no. If you did, under this claim of power, which is now broken and shattered (and the Kilbourn case will be pointed out in after years as the point of time when it was broken), they had the right, without further trial than your refusal, to arrest you and imprison you for an indefinite length of time. The house, perhaps, might, out of some sort of concession, liberality, courtesy or other grace, determine that their victim might go out of jail when they adjourned, but in the case of the senate there would be no such concession, because there is no term of existence to the senate. And, in fact, in one instance, the house of representatives went off and left Pat. Wood in jail for some weeks afterward when, I believe, some sergeant-at-arms who was more respectful to the constitution than the house was itself, at last turned him out. Do you tell me that that man ought not to have recovered? The statute of limitations bars him now. He went away broken in spirit, as dozens—I might say hundreds—have done before and since. In other instances that I could name they were thrust down in the crypt, kept for imprisonment purposes, and remained there at the will and pleasure of congress. And this was not, as I have said, confined to the house of representatives, for the senate has done it.

It was high time that the constitution should be reasserted; that its great principles should be revived, and further, that the limits of the power of congress should be determined. Those powers should not be allowed to overflow everything; to overflow your hearthstones, to overflow your private drawers, to overflow not merely your papers, but your mind and its secrets—powers which, in their full assertion, as six years ago, could penetrate the recesses of your soul, and drag hence your secret thoughts, or put you in prison without limit as to duration. It was high time for this power to be broken, and I am glad that I stood in this court, mostly relying upon the writings and teachings of that great apostle of human liberty and constitutional government, Thomas Jefferson, for the correction of this great evil. Authorities of courts also were at hand; but his writings on the question were a flood of light, demonstrating that this arbitrary power could not exist.

Gentlemen of the jury, let us take another step in this case. The defense presented here on the question of assessment of damages I hardly know how to treat. I will speak respectfully, of course, of the counsel for the defense, for I feel that way; but it was such a trifling—such a belittling of the great fundamental rights of man; rights for the maintenance of which men have walked unfalteringly to the scaffold; for which nations have drawn the sword, that I was sorry to hear it. They told you that you ought not to give much damages to this man, whose fortune was broken, whose life was jeopardized; that you ought not to give him much damages because he was treated kindly and as a gentleman by Colonel Thompson. Is not Mr. Kilbourn a gentleman? If Hallet Kilbourn is not a gentleman I have yet to hear the fact mentioned, and I have known him a quarter of a century. We were young men together in Indiana. Why should he not be treated as a gentleman? In fact, Mr. Smith was dissatisfied on two points. First, he was dissatisfied with the decision of the supreme court of the United States; and secondly, he was dissatisfied because Kilbourn received kindly treatment from Colonel Thompson. Mr. Hallet Kilbourn was not a burglar. He was not a forger; he was not a thief; he was not a murderer; he had killed nobody. Why should not he be treated kindly? But it seems that such treatment was compensation in the minds of counsel for the defense.

Gentlemen, did you ever reflect on what imprisonment is? Do you think a carpeted floor would make a jail anything but a jail if you were there? Opposing counsel ask you to put yourselves in Thompson's place. I have no complaint to make of John G. Thompson. I know him well, and I know that no truer, better man lives than he is. They ask you to put yourselves in his place. Put yourselves in Hallet Kilbourn's place likewise, and then answer me whether a carpet will make the jail floor any softer to your feet. Put yourselves in his place, and then answer me whether a picture on the walls would make those walls any less the walls of a prison. Put yourselves in his place, and then answer me whether, although you can solace yourselves with a glass of wine with your friends, whether it is not the jail still; and whether, however good the fare may be, it is not still prison fare. It has been said that captives' tears have watered their bread through all the ages, and that is true. The prison is a prison—it matters not how you adorn it. In prison, gentlemen, liberty assumes its dearest form. It is not for you to measure here in your jury-box how Hallet Kilbourn felt for those forty-five days. Liberty is said to be brightest in dungeons, for then its habitation is the human heart. When it has no other habitation than the heart then it grows brighter. That means simply to convey the thought that man dwells on it then; he knows what it means then; he knows its value; he properly estimates the priceless heritage of liberty when he is deprived of it. The slave knew the value of liberty better than you do. The man who is deprived of a blessing feels that blessings brighter grow as they fly away. So the enjoyment of freedom, the right of constitutional protection, when you are deprived of them, assume then their greatest value. Oh, how little (my friends will pardon me for saying so), how beneath the lowest point to which my contempt can descend is a defense based upon the fact that a man was allowed to board himself in jail and that he had the right to purchase some delicacies beyond the prison fare that was allowed him. I can not appreciate such a defense. I was born with a mind incapable of comprehending such an argument.

The jail rises up before me. I breathe its polluted air. I feel its humiliation and shame. I shrink from its degradation. The prison has an awful life of its own. Look at the dark, weird shadows of the evening gather over the lonesome inmate as he longs for home and those he loves. How his heart sinks down in the gloom and hush of night; behold him awaken in the morning after a dream, perhaps of home, to find himself behind bars of iron. For awhile he may wonder in a dazed way where he is, and what it all means; but the reality will soon enough break upon him that he is in jail herded with criminals. Compensate all this if you can; I can not make the figures. Counsel for the defense made some in your hearing. They talked about a *per diem* rate of compensation. Why, gentlemen of the jury, there is not money enough in this world to pay a man who is innocent, and who knows that he is innocent, as Hallet Kilbourn does, and as the supreme court of the United States has decided that he is—I say there is not money enough in the world to pay a man for thoughts such as must have passed through his mind as he saw Mrs. Kilbourn and his children drive away, leaving him in the dungeon. There might be money enough to pay my friends on the other side—no, I will not say that; I will defend them from any such charge. You could not pay Colonel Corkhill money enough to hire him to stand behind the prison bars under an arbitrary commitment, without law, as he knows; without oath, without charge, and without crime, and see his wife and children driving off in the dusk of the evening, leaving him there to solitude and disgrace. Compensatory damages! I will tell you, gentlemen, what the attitude of this government should be. Instead of the government sending her representatives here to defend this case, those in charge of affairs should have come forward and said frankly, "We laid our hands on this man wrongfully; we were mistaken; we are able to be magnanimous; we are able to be liberal, generous, and just; we are not standing here to higgle about a money compensation; he ought to be compensated liberally and broadly because we have been mistaken; we were in error, we arrested a citizen and trampled on his rights under a mistaken view of the law and the constitution, and it is ours to make reparation." That should be the voice of the government. I have no hesitation in saying it, widely, and as far as my voice may reach, that the attitude of this government toward Mr. Kilbourn, or any other citizen it has wronged, whose rights it has trampled upon, should be one of broad, generous reparation, not one of technical, miserable calculation of *per diem* for suffering. There are times in the lifetimes of men when you can not measure an outrage by the day. There comes sometimes a flash of wrong and of outrage that degrades and humiliates a man for which it is impossible to give too great a compensation; but when you find in addition, as in this case, a man contending for his own rights, for the rights of those whose trusts he held, and for your rights just as much, you certainly will lend no ear to this pitiful plea on the part of the defense, that you should mitigate damages because he was not put in irons, or treated more harshly.

In fact, Mr. Smith said that if Mr. Thompson was to be censured at all, it would be because he treated him with too much kindness. Ought he to have treated him with any less? How strangely that sounded to me. As good a lawyer as Mr. Smith is, knows the supreme court of the United States has decided that Mr. Kilbourn ought not to have been there at all, ought not to have been there a moment; that he had no more business to be there than I had, and yet there was an implied censure absolutely of his own client, because he did not treat him with a little more severity; and this when the laws of his own country now say in his ears and in his face that he ought not to have been there at all. It is greatly to Mr. Thompson's credit that his broad heart comprehended the proprieties of the situation as it did. The supreme court of the United States, as I have just said, says broadly to this defense, that you, who are in the wrong, have been in the wrong all the time; you are in the wrong now, and Mr. Kilbourn is in the right, and has been in the right all the time. How does it sound for men who have been condemned as in the wrong trying to belittle the claim of a man who has been decided to have been in the right from first to last? As I have already stated, gentlemen, the saddest sight on earth to my mind is that of an innocent man in prison. No thanks to congress that Mr. Kilbourn was released at all. He would have remained there until the end of that congress, if not longer, but for the courts to which he appealed as a law-abiding citizen.

Gentlemen, I know there is some vague trouble often in jurors' minds to get at a measure of damages. You know that, and I know it. We mutually think on that subject alike at this moment. There is some trouble in reaching a point from which to start a calculation. But let us look and see whether we should have much trouble on this subject in this peculiar case. Mr. Kilbourn lay in that jail for a month and a half at an insalubrious part of the year. He lay there from the middle of March to the latter part of April, during the capricious, changing, damp weather that prevails here in March and in April. I shall not stop to dwell upon the unsightly things that were surrounding that jail. There is nothing that can surround a jail looking worse than the jail itself. The blue sky is outside, and the free air, and that is of right his. His home is outside, and there he should go, and anything short of that is no compensation or alleviation. He was there during these six weeks. Its effect upon his health is undenied, except in so far as my medical friends on the other side say differently. I do not know whether they speak from practice in the profession or experience in their own lives. At any rate, they suggest that high living is a bad thing. I will agree with them on that, but we are not left to the high medical attainments of the counsel on the other side on this point. We have evidence on this subject. Fortunately we are not left to any conjecture or appeal to you. I appeal to Dr. Bulkley, his physician, and who has been his physician most of his life in Washington. What does he say? He tells you that he contracted malarial fever. Those were the exact words. That Kilbourn contracted malarial fever in that jail. Now I never heard that a glass of champagne would give a man malarial fever. [Laughter.] It may do so. It may give the counsel for the defense malarial fever, but it never did me. [Laughter.] It is said that troops of friends went out there to see him, and my brother Corkhill says that imprisonment under such circumstances can not call for any compensation. Why, gentlemen of the jury, I have read of prisons turned into palaces by the devotion of friends; devotion to a man who was asserting human rights and had fallen under the power of a despotic government. They say his friends flocked to see him. Why should they not? They say there were members of congress and senators went to see him. I am glad to hear it. I was in neither the one nor the other branch of congress at that time. I certainly would have gone if I had been here. He had done nothing to be ashamed of. On the contrary, he had done that of which any man had a right to be proud. He had asserted the constitution of his country in all its purity, its strength and glory, as has since been decided. Why should not men go to see him? But could that compensate him for loss of his liberty? Could the fact that Algernon Sidney, or Russell, or any other martyr to human freedom, received the calls of sympathizing friends, compensate their wives and children after their heads had rolled upon the block? Now I put a square question to the counsel for the defense; Hallet Kilbourn might have died there; he might have died there of disease contracted in that jail. He might have died there of the malarial fever that Dr. Bulkley speaks of. Would it have been a compensation to Mrs. Kilbourn and the children after his death, or tended to allay grief in the private circle, to have been told that friends called to see him? I say his life was endangered there. The medical testimony shows it. It might have gone; it might have been lost. It is a wonder that it was not, for there was a great pressure upon him.

There are different types of men who go to jail; on different types of men imprisonment tells differently. Take a man with an active brain like Mr. Kilbourn's, a fine temperament, proud of his standing, engaged in a large business that was being destroyed, and his credit broken down, and imprisonment to such a man is more than the imprisonment of the body. The iron was entering his very soul. His mind was racked and tortured, and to my personal knowledge he was not the same man again for two years afterward. Suppose he had died under this pressure. Pressure—I have not half described it; pressure and loss upon the one hand; separation from his family, pride of character, a man widely known, a man with patrons who had trusted him in his business—all these things weighing on his mind; and then, what was even possibly more than all, the determination of a brave man to confront an outrage and to fight it out. He was employing counsel. I was but one. I was associated in the case with Jeremiah Black, with Matthew H. Carpenter, whose bright spirit has now passed from earth, and others living, who are around me—all these were called to his rescue. What for? In vindication of the right of an American citizen; in vindication of the right, under the constitution, of each one of you from a similar outrage. Such a load was hardly ever upon a man's mind. Public and private cares were all surrounding and crushing him. No wonder he marched from that jail a broken man. No wonder he came forth with malarial fever. No wonder that his medical attendant told him to take a trip far away; to go away from these scenes; to go away from this atmosphere; to go where he could obtain rest. No wonder that a good friend (Mr. Hutchinson) had to go with him to California, where, in that cooling atmosphere and climate he could bathe his fevered frame. That is the condition in which he came out of this prison. And yet these gentlemen say all that does not call for compensatory damages. Compensation covers a great many things. Compensation covers much more than the mere destruction of property.

They will say, however, in the next place, in estimating this question of damages, that it was impossible for his business to be hurt by it. And the solicitor of the treasury, with infinite shrewdness— I do not know whether he was born in New England or not— wherever he was born he does credit to his birthplace—with infinite shrewdness tells the jury that Mr. Kilbourn was well advertised, and that therefore his business could not have suffered. He was well advertised! Good Lord deliver you and me from such advertisement! [Laughter.] He was well advertised; advertised, they said, as a man who was faithful to his clients, and would not divulge their secrets. Very well; he was advertised that way perhaps once, and then he was advertised 1,750 to that once as a rascal, who had great frauds covered up, that this real estate pool was a cesspool, and that he had the top lid on it and would not take it off. [Laughter.] His credit and standing all over the country was thus impaired, and everybody knows it. Discredit, calumny, and accusation followed him everywhere, and although one might say, "he stood it pretty well, he has good pluck, and will not go back on his clients;" still he would not want to get into such a concern where another investigation might take place and Kilbourn might break down, or there might have been something wrong. There was nothing wrong, no more than in my bare hand, for I say here to the gentlemen on the other side that after we made the house of representatives know the law and Chief-Justice Cartter released Mr. Kilbourn under the writ of *habeas corpus*, Mr. Kilbourn sat down and wrote a letter (which I have here), respectful in tone, to the speaker of the house, saying in substance: "Now, having asserted a great principle and vindicated the fact before the courts that I was right and you were wrong, you can send a committee and look through my whole establishment if you wish." They did not do it. That is the history of this case. Advertised was his business! Why, you must go by the testimony here. Mr. Kilbourn swears—and I am dwelling on these points to enable you to come to a verdict—Mr. Kilbourn swears that it destroyed his business; that it broke up his firm. This occurred in April, and the firm dissolved in December; and he remained in that business only a year afterward. This imprisonment destroyed his business as a real estate operator here; as a buyer and seller of real estate it destroyed him, drove him out and broke him up. It is proved that he was doing a large and lucrative business before that. How large we were not permitted to tell, and the exact extent of the loss we were not allowed to give, but it will not be difficult for you to arrive at a just conclusion. He was doing business upon a large scale. I say here, in the light of this testimony, and of my own knowledge, this proceeding broke him down to the ground, destroyed his firm, destroyed his business and ruined him financially.

Now, gentlemen, this is a case calling for mighty redress; not small, but large. Mr. Olmstead swears to the same thing. He was one of the partners. It does not depend upon Mr. Kilbourn's oath alone. Mr. Olmstead swears that this proceeding ruined the firm; broke it up, and broke up their business. This treatment of Mr. Kilbourn caused a scandal to surround them that no firm could withstand. As I said a while ago, the man who confronts either branch of congress, with all its power, takes a great risk and encounters a great danger; he braves the power of the house and senate, the power of the press, the power of human imagination, and that power which is worse than all, the disposition to hunt down a man whenever anything befalls him. All this Kilbourn had to contend with. Are you to say that with a few thousand dollars you are going to compensate this man? I hope not. He has undergone degradation, humiliation in a common jail, when guilty of no crime. If there had been no loss of health or property such treatment would call for a heavy verdict under the circumstances, because he was in the right and his antagonists in the wrong. Of course there was no malice on the part of Mr. Thompson. It is not for me to charge malice on any branch of the government. But that there was a harsh spirit of pursuit in this case I do know. It was from the 11th to the 18th of the month before an answer could be had to a writ of *habeas corpus*—that writ which goes with a power that no other writ possesses. Is this a case for light damages? I repeat that if, under the circumstances, no harm had been done to health, no harm to property, no harm to reputation, still it would be an action such as is not to be answered lightly with a few thousand dollars. This is a great question. It is as vast in its magnitude and assertions of human rights by peaceful methods as can be conceived of. It is the assertion of a principle in the face of the precedents of the government for nearly one hundred years. It came in the centennial year, in 1876, and in that same year, through the bravery of this man, came the downfall of an arbitrary power in congress which was as dangerous to liberty as the inquisition of Rome or as the knee-boots of James the Second.

Gentlemen of the jury, there are great landmarks in human history. You hear men speak of them as though they were built to mark the progress of man on the land. Jacob built a landmark of the stones he had rested his head upon at night, when he dreamed he saw the angels ascending and descending. He built it the next day with the stones he had used for his pillow and called it Bethel. And so this imprisonment of Kilbourn shall be as a landmark of freedom, a landmark in the assertion of right and justice. Gentlemen, not for the sake of the money, not for the sake of the dollars and cents, but for the sake of the dignity of this issue, its relation to human progress and right, its relation to constitutional law and justice, I ask you not to belittle it at this late stage. It was great at the beginning; let it be great at the close. It was a great revolution achieved by Kilbourn in setting right the principles of this government, and having them declared from the supreme court of the United States, in accordance with the constitution. Now, in its closing stage, we come before you and ask that twelve men of the District of Columbia may announce to the world that they appreciate its dignity and value. Whether we ever collect a dollar or not is not your affair—not mine—but whether you return a verdict that shows you cheapen liberty, cheapen your own rights, trifle with those fundamental principles which have made battle-fields red with blood, or whether you arise to the dignity of the occasion, and assert in a manly, broad, strong way the approval which you have in your hearts at this moment of this brave man for doing what he has done, is another question, and one of vast importance. I will leave this case with you, gentlemen, with the parting injunction that as you measure these rights that are your own so they will be measured unto you; as you measure the great rights involved in Kilbourn's case at some time you or your children will have them measured back to you. No man errs on the side of a high appreciation of the constitutional rights of the citizen. When spoken to about the argument of this case, and the question was submitted to me whether I would go into it now, with my connection with the congress of the United States, I resolved the doubt in my mind by saying: "No man can make a mistake on the side of constitutional liberty. The supreme court of the United States has decided that Hallet Kilbourn was right from the beginning to the end in asserting his freedom from the jail." And as I stood with him in the beginning I have no hesitation in standing with him in the end. I can not err in upholding what has been declared by the highest judicial tribunal of my country as the citizen's rights. Nor can you err unless you cheapen those rights. You can not err by letting it go forth that here in this great capital the spirit of constitutional government has not died out in your hearts, and that you do not hold the life or the liberty of one of your fellow-citizens cheaply. It might have been the loss of his life as well as his liberty. If they had a right to take his liberty they had a right to take his life. Life is not dearer than liberty. Liberty is the dearest in my estimation. As to the loss of one or the other, as a choice, I would say, take my life, for without my liberty life is of no value, none whatever; not the slightest. The iron hand of power laid on Hallet Kilbourn was not more merciful than the hand of the executioner would have been on his throat. It might have been his life, for it was imperiled. It might have been lost. With these views in your minds, gentlemen of the jury, you can not go astray. I submit this case to you in confidence that it will not grow less by reason of your treatment of it.

DEFENSE OF CAPTAIN EDWARD T. JOHNSON

"HOME, HOME! SWEET, SWEET HOME!"

For the invasion and destruction of his home, Edward T. Johnson killed Edwin Henry with a double-barreled shot-gun, near Greeneville, Tennessee, September 23, 1884.

He was indicted in the circuit court of Tennessee for the first circuit, and was tried in said court, Judge Newton Hacker presiding, by the following jurors:

J. J. White, A. H. Pierce, E. L. Harrold, William McMakin, John L. Bartley, James Woolsey, R. C. Jones, Allen Jeffers, William Harmon, H. Thompson, B. G. Johnson and W. A. Pierce.

He was defended by Mr. Voorhees, Hon. Henry H. Ingersoll and A. N. Shoun, Esq., of Tennessee.

The commonwealth was represented by Hon. John Fain, state's attorney, and Captain James H. Robinson.

The opening argument to the jury for the defense was made by Mr. Ingersoll, and Mr. Voorhees made the closing argument June 23, 1885, speaking nearly four hours.

The closing argument for the prosecution, was made by Captain Robinson.

The case was then given to the jury, who, after an absence of twenty-four hours, returned a verdict of "not guilty." It has been asserted by one of the jurors that, within ten minutes after retiring and upon the first ballot, a verdict of acquittal was reached, but that it was agreed that because of the great influence and importance of the cause, the verdict thus reached should be withheld until the next day.

May it Please the Court, and You, Gentlemen of the Jury:

THAT deep and painful sense of responsibility which has weighed so heavily upon me in this case is lighter this morning than heretofore. It has been lightened by the remarkable speech to which we all listened with such intense interest and delight throughout yesterday while my eloquent and able associate, Judge Ingersoll, elucidated the law and unfolded the widespread details of this

most sorrowful chapter in human experience. I know that I might with perfect safety leave his great work with you without a word of addition or supplement from me. This may not be, however, and I proceed to the discharge of my duty.

The reason for my presence here has been asked and answered in certain quarters. The attorney-general, in his opening argument, suggested to you that I would mislead you as to the law and the facts of this case. I have no power to do so, if I desired; and I have no desire, if I had the power. Why should I mislead you? Why should I mislead any of my countrymen as to the due administration of the law? My life has been passed in upholding law; in laboring to extend its equal and just protection to the American people, one and all. I love my countrymen and their institutions; I love the people of all sections alike, and I come to the state of Tennessee to do what I have tried to do elsewhere—bear aloft the law, see that it is enforced and obeyed, and to aid in its just administration. We are not under the slightest necessity of asking one thing in behalf of this unfortunate defendant beyond the strict letter of the law as it will be laid down by his honor. We ask not the abatement of a single jot or tittle in the most rigorous administration of justice. His safety lies between the lids of the written and adjudicated laws of his country. On them he relies with absolute confidence for his life and liberty, and for that which is dearer to him than both—the vindication of his name and fame as an upright man and a law-abiding citizen.

When, if ever, did such a defendant appear before you for trial? In many of its leading features, and taken as a whole, this case is without a parallel. You are not trying a member of the criminal classes. You are not trying one steeped in crime or familiar with the ways of vice. His heart never went out to evil, nor have his purposes been prone to wickedness. His whole life is open before you. His forty-three years of existence is now an open book. You see it all. In the searching sunlight of the voluminous evidence wherein do you find an ignoble thought, word, or act on his part? You hear the cries and groans, and witness the streaming tears, and more than mortal anguish, of a heart-broken man; but I challenge the most unsparing scrutiny to find a taint or a trace of dishonor in his whole checkered career. How are you called upon to deal with such a character? I will point out your duty from the pages of one of the greatest American law writers. I read from Bishop:

> On the one hand, no man is to be punished unless he deserves punishment in pure retributive justice.

Retribution is for conscious crime; retribution is punishment for evil in heart, as well as in conduct; the act and the intent must combine to make a criminal. He must have the impure and evil heart accompanying the act in order to make him liable to punishment. He is then a fit subject for retributive justice, but not until then. If, however, the defendant's life has always been, and still is, pure and noble, without dishonorable flaw or blemish, a jury will pause long, and consider with the utmost care every fact and circumstance, every line and thread of proof submitted in explanation of his conduct, before they will find that without sufficient and legal cause he committed an act having even the appearance of a violation of law.

I read again:

> On the one hand, no man is to be punished unless he deserves punishment in pure retributive justice, aside from all extraneous considerations; while on the other hand, though a penalty is merited, it will not be inflicted by the governing powers, that do not assume the full creative functions of the Deity, unless a public good thereby be done.

Even when retributive justice is merited, yet it is not to be inflicted unless a public good thereby be done.

The attorney-general asked you to be the instrument of a verdict not called for by retributive justice, not called for on account of any public good, and suggested that in the event of a conviction the governor might exercise the pardoning power. Mr. Bishop says this is not the proper administration of the law; that it is not the function of the court and jury to inflict a penalty for some one else to remit.

You have full control of this case; if it appeals to you for punishment, let the fatal blow fall; if, on the other hand, it appeals to you in tones of the deepest and most convincing proof for an acquittal, you will gladly make that joyful record. When was such an argument as the attorney-general's ever made to you before? When before were you told it was your duty to take the life of your fellow-man, when you are told in the same breath that it ought not to be taken, and that the governor would save what you are called on to destroy. To no worse use was a jury ever sought to be put than this. No worse proposition was ever stated to a jury. Will you condemn to death a man whom the state has admitted ought not to die?

There is no manslaughter here; there is no penitentiary punishment in this case. It is murder in the first degree or it is nothing; it is the gallows-tree or liberty. There is no imprisonment nor convict stripes for this defendant. Bear that in mind to the last moment and at every step of his trial. You have no compromises to make. If sane, if responsible, if, having the power to control his actions as to the deceased, the defendant in cold blood committed the deed with which he is charged, then he is guilty of murder in the first degree, and you can not evade that verdict. If, on the other hand, his mind was goaded to frenzy by a ghastly and unbearable combination of horrors; if his mind was diseased by brooding over wrongs far more intolerable than the executioner's scourge and more deadly than the scorpion's sting; if his will was led captive by his overmastering emotions on the subject of his brutal wrongs and persecutions, as described so well by Dr. Boyd, then he is not guilty, and you will not require him to depend on the governor for his life through executive clemency. I shrink with horror from the attorney-general's proposition that you should blight a man with a verdict of guilt whose conduct calls for no punishment, either as retributive justice or on account of the public welfare.

Mr. Robinson. He did not say that. He said the place for mercy——

Mr. Voorhees. I do not think the attorney-general knows now what he did say when his kind heart mounted the throne of reason and swayed his thoughts. I marked his words, and so did this jury. There were occasions when he gave his whole case away—when, moved with the feelings of a husband and father, he said, with fire and force, that Captain Johnson's feelings were most natural; that no man could have felt otherwise; that he himself sympathized with him in these feelings, and pitied him in his awful calamity. I watched his face, and saw then the man, the gentleman, the husband of a wife and the father of children, who would not touch a hair of this defendant's head save in kindness, if left to him. When he asked you to convict him and let the governor wipe out your verdict with the gentle qualities of mercy, then I saw again the commonwealth's attorney. I do not complain; far from it. One was the natural man speaking; the other was a strained, artificial, and distorted sense of official duty. Again and again the attorney-general spoke in the natural tones of the human heart, and each time he gave you the burning reasons why you should acquit, while each time asking for a technical conviction! He could not, he would not, he did not, and he dared not ask for a conviction that was to stand. The conviction he asked for was to be rendered null and void without delay.

Do you think this is dealing fairly with a jury? I am here to say no hard or unkind word. I have been treated with kindness by the people of Tennessee, and my reply to the attorney-general he must know has no personal harshness in it; but his position is not warranted by reason, law, sound morality, or public policy. The responsibility is yours, and you may not shift it to another. The issue of life or death is in your hands, and you can not push it from you. It is not an issue that stops short of life itself. This wan, pale-faced, sorely stricken man is in your hands to live or to die.

And now, who is Captain Edward T. Johnson; and why is he here environed by the terrors of the law? He was born on the 7th of June, 1842, at Lexington, Kentucky, and there is no better blood in that proud, historic state than flows in his veins. At an early age he came to Indiana. I have known him seventeen years. No keener, more vigorous, or industrious intellect; no purer, more upright, or attractive young man has entered upon life's journey in Indiana in the last quarter of a century. I speak in the hearing of the people of that state. I am here, knowing exactly what I am doing. I did not wish to go into this case. I knew its burdens and its labors. I would gladly have evaded it. I have done much hard work in the courts, and much of this kind. I knew beforehand what it meant; but when the question became one of duty I settled it at once, knowing as I did then, and as I do now from the evidence, that the record of his life is clean; that no stain or foul aspersion can remain upon it; that his enemies would be met and overthrown as they have been at every point.

This defendant is somewhat known,here, but not as he is known at home; not known as I know him; and I say here now to this prosecution, measuring every word, that I will stake whatever of repute or standing I have in Indiana upon the truth and honor of Edward T. Johnson. I make no reservation whatever. I have no desire for conflict; I have no desire to encounter men who have seen fit to make themselves his enemies; but I have no wish to avoid them in this contest. I have known but one path in life; I have known but one rule of action; it has been to determine for myself what is right and then do it. It has carried me through every trial, and it will carry me through this.

But, I repeat, who is Edward T. Johnson? I have spoken of my own personal knowledge of him as a lawyer, as a political speaker and writer, always a gentleman, fighting his battles gallantly and well, never meanly or basely. Searching the whole record with a glance of my mind, from the hour when I first saw him, handsome and in health, buoyant, and brilliant, I can discover not one speck or flaw in his uprightness, or his moral conduct, or his manliness. But other and further answer than mine has been made; and who are they in these piles of proof who tell you who Edward T. Johnson is? We have placed him under a calcium light, uncovering and revealing everything. Who can better stand such a test than he has?

After all the storms have beaten upon him, his home in ruins, self-murder in its once happy chambers, darkness over the grave of the loved and the lost, torrents of calumny poured on his naked head, his hour of deepest woe and weakness seized by malignant enmity for his total destruction, every poisoned shaft which malice could invent hurled against him; yet I stand here holding the depositions of twenty-six of the foremost people of Indianapolis, and twenty-six hundred might have been obtained, telling you who

Edward T. Johnson is, and what manner of life he has lived. I know all these people. You may pray to the great Father, when you, six hundred miles from home, fall into trouble by the arts of a scoundrel, that such people as these may send after you such a volume of good words and healing comfort as we have here for this defendant. There are some things that can not be taken from him in his deep distress. You may take his life, but you can never take from him this towering testimony to a good life which follows him like a blessing from his old home, over the mountains and over rivers, down into this valley of the mountains of East Tennessee. Who are these witnesses? I have told you I know them. They comprise the leading men of both political parties. We have hard political battles in Indiana, but we have manly ones. We contest the field closely; but when the battle is over, and the bugle sounds truce as the night cloud lowers, we meet in peace, and the strife is ended. We fight like men and we have peace like brethren. Colonel John C. New—his name is here—who is he? The chairman of the state central committee of the republican party of Indiana; the proprietor of the Indianapolis *Journal*, the leading republican organ of the state; the treasurer of the United States at Washington under General Grant; the assistant secretary of the treasury under Arthur; for years the clerk of the circuit court of Marion county, in which Indianapolis is situated; the political friend of Albert G. Porter, governor of the state. What says John C. New within the last three months? He says, speaking of Captain Johnson: "He has ever borne in this community the character of a moral, upright, peaceable citizen, and has commanded and held the respect and confidence of this community as such."

I read that as a key-note to all the other depositions read in your hearing as to reputation, not intending to go over them again, nor long to dwell on them. They are all in harmony, and equally conclusive.

The judges of the supreme court of Indiana have not been silent. Byron K. Elliott of that court has known the defendant ever since he went to Indianapolis to live. Judge Elliott's voice from that high tribunal follows this sad, broken man into this court and says to you that "his character in every respect has always been, and is, excellent."

Whose name do I see next? Joseph E. McDonald, a name known and honored in every state in this Union; fit and qualified by nature and by acquirements to fill with dignity and honor the loftiest position within the gift of the American people; a broad, commanding man, warm in heart and clear in head; for nearly thirty years one of the great leaders of the bar at Indianapolis and throughout the state. Would such a man prostitute his word in behalf of the unworthy and the dishonored? He endorses the estimate of Colonel New, and concurs with Judge Elliott as to the standing of Captain Johnson.

Who else are here? William R. Holloway, the brother-in-law of Oliver P. Morton, and proprietor of the Indianapolis *Times;* A. P. Stanton, a lawyer of distinction; William Sullivan, eighty-one years of age, whose signature we showed to his honor upon the bench, to show how well a man who has lived in Indiana eighty-one years can write at that period of life; Mr. Haughey, for twenty years the president of the Indianapolis National Bank; Mr. A. D. Lynch, a bank examiner and receiver of years' standing; Mr. Malott, the manager of railroads and president of the Indiana National Bank; Colonel Holstein, United States district attorney, representing the federal government in Indiana as against criminals. He says this man on trial here for his life is the peer of anybody in character, purity of morals, and obedience to law. General R. S. Foster, United States marshal, not supposed to be in love with bad characters, gives the defendant the same introduction to you the others have; Colonel Wildman, the postmaster at Indianapolis; Hon. Stanton J. Peelle, ex-member of congress; W. T. Brown, the prosecuting attorney of the county. Where vile calumniators said he had murdered his wife, or driven her to suicide, we dared to call the prosecuting attorney as to his reputation, the officer whose duty it is to bring criminals to justice—he who stands against all evil-doers. Mr. Brown did not say that Captain Johnson ought to be convicted of murder and then take his chances of a pardon. On the contrary, he says he is a man of the loftiest character, never suspected of crime. Judge Julian, himself on the bench; John M. Butler, the partner of Joseph E. McDonald, and a man of high position and ability; these and other honored names I might dwell upon; they introduce and vouch for Edward T. Johnson; and I ask you, in view of that introduction, whether he is a fit subject for retributive justice? Does he belong to those criminal classes that call for punishment in order to promote the public good?

But, gentlemen, allow me another thought in this connection. Captain Johnson came into your midst as a government officer. Did Indiana, did the government at Washington, send a scoundrel into your midst? Did we treat East Tennessee with discourtesy when we sent him here? No. We sent a splendid lawyer; a gentleman; a man of integrity; we sent one beloved and respected by all who knew him. Colonel Dudley, an Indiana man, who at that time presided over the pension bureau, knew he was sending one adapted to and qualified for the position. A soldier himself, when a mere boy, honorably discharging his duty in the field, he knew how to sympathize with his fellow-soldiers.

I have been utterly amazed since I came here at some statistical facts. How little is it known, except here in these mountains and valleys, that thirty thousand men in East Tennessee took up arms for the Union. With the return of peace came the duty of the government to its wounded and broken-down soldiers and to the widows and children of the heroic dead, and it is a historical fact that when Captain Johnson came here in January, 1883, the soldiers of East Tennessee, their widows and orphans, entitled to pensions, were further behind in their rightful allowances than the pension claimants in any other part of the Union. It is also a historical fact that during the fifteen months he was here as a supervising examiner of pensions he, with his assistants, caused more than $1,500,000 of money to be paid out of the public treasury to the people of East Tennessee, not only doing justice to claimants, but promoting the prosperity and happiness of all.

Pension money is a general blessing, not a drain upon the treasury. I have aimed to be liberal on the subject of pensions, sometimes accused of being too liberal; but I know no better use for money than to put it in honest circulation, first, in the hands of those who merit most the support and sympathy of their government, then from them passing into the general business of the country, helping everybody, the Confederate here in the South as well as the federal soldier. A good volume of circulation makes good prices, stimulates industry, and helps every interest of the country.

So we not only sent you an honorable man, not only a clean man, but he came here as a benefactor of this whole people. He was the first supervising examiner appointed in the United States. He organized the system, and was selected by Colonel Dudley for that purpose by reason of his high integrity and his organizing ability. He came here as a blessing; he came to help your people, not to hurt them; and now, in the hour of his wretchedness and despair, in the depths of his woe and anguish, he appeals to you twelve men, and to all the men and women throughout all the counties of East Tennessee and Western North Carolina, wherever his jurisdiction extended, to know whether he ever harmed you or yours, or brought anything but sunshine into your homes and lives. Tell me where he has wrought evil to anybody. Show me the law, human or divine, broken by him in his intercourse and dealings with your people. He was faithful, just, and pure.

Another man came to East Tennessee. He was here long before Captain Johnson came. He was likewise from a distant state. This man now sleeps in a dishonored grave, far away from the soil of Tennessee, not allowed to be buried here where homes are held sacred. These two men, in some sense, are here before you. Judge ye between them! Can you recall the frightful and far-reaching destruction of soul and body wrought by Major Henry without uttering maledictions on his name?

While Captain Johnson, eager, earnest, with unsparing industry, toiled day and night in his office in behalf of the soldiers of East Tennessee, their wives, their children, and their mothers; while he labored far beyond his physical strength to do the duty which the government had too long neglected, bringing money, hope, and comfort to thousands of homes, the other sojourner in your midst was a noxious reptile, baser far and more loathsome than the snake that, with undulating form and lifted and baleful crest, in the Garden of Eden allured the trusting woman to the tree of knowledge and accomplished the first seduction. Look upon the two pictures. Look upon the conscientious, faithful public official, burning the midnight oil to discharge his duties; then look at the other, a sweltering, venomous monster; an agent of pollution, tracking every step of the absent man's wife, and hounding her with persistent lust to her downfall and death.

These are the two pictures for Tennesseans to look upon. Pause a moment and dwell upon them. I ask the counsel for the prosecution which is the brighter picture of the two. Whose presence will you encourage in your midst—the man who does his duty, works hard, accomplishes good, and blesses every one with whom he comes in contact, or the slimy wretch, besotted with lust, the hoary lecher, the practiced seducer, the aged debauchee, the common enemy of social purity, the outlaw from Christian civilization? Shall retributive justice be invoked in the name of the outlaw, reeking with infamy, against one whose life is blameless? I challenge again the contrast. I rejoice that I can stand before a court of high intelligence and high appreciation of moral purity, and before a jury of Christian gentlemen, and make the challenge I now make. There is the one, your benefactor and your friend; there is the other, a curse to the human race, so vile that language falters in painting him.

While this most unhappy defendant stood faithfully at his post of duty, Henry incessantly haunted his wife's presence and preyed upon her weakness. With what arts, or hellish wiles, or deep-laid craft in vice her ruin was accomplished, the infinite God only knows. The one inexplicable mystery to me is that Mrs. Johnson fell. I want to say this in the hearing of all, and in justice to her memory. The evidence which makes her fall so great a mystery is here before me, and has been read. It establishes the fact, beyond the shadow of a question, that her reputation, her moral standing as a lady, and her social position, were second to none in Indianapolis, nor in all this broad land. Her associations were with the purest and most refined; her life was absolutely modest and domestic; she moved in none but the very best ranks of society; no social circle was above her—the loftiest were open to her, and sought her presence. All this the evidence discloses.

Her husband came here, according to the proof, in January, 1883; she joined him in April, and in four months she crouched away from here a ruined woman, a fallen angel. She was the angel of her household at home, of her husband's love, and of her son's idolatry. She went away from this town polluted and defiled. How it came the omniscient Deity only knows. Before his throne I honestly declare my belief that she did not fall in the ordinary way; she did not fall from an ordinary lust. Her temperament was not ardent; she had never betrayed special fondness for gentlemen's society. There was not a principle of her nature to invite the advance of even the most daring libertine. Cool, unimpassioned, she did not fall in that short time from an evil heart.

I believe, as occurred in another celebrated case, that the first breach in the citadel of her honor was made by wine or drug, by mesmerism, or some diabolical art. Her destroyer spoke, as the proof shows, of his mesmeric power, and she confesses to an influence exerted by him which was a mystery to her. How it was I know not; but, supported by the splendid reputation she bore in Indiana, I declare again my belief that her first step in the pathway of dishonor was not taken from a sense of depraved desire. On what followed in her frailty let the curtain fall. Once embarked on the maddening stream she was borne swift and far, a helpless victim in the remorseless grasp of a deadly monster. As I look upon her life and conduct while here in Tennessee, she appears so transformed, so far removed from her real self, as her family and friends had so long known and loved her, that nothing but a potent and unnatural spell which paralyzed her reason and chained her will for the time being can account for the awful change. Yes, this must be so; for when the home she had left so recently, pure and radiant in the robes of domestic love and peace, once more opened its doors to receive her, she returned at once to her original convictions of truth and virtue. You may say that the letter from Knoxville, in which she suggested her stay for several days at Louisville, was an invitation to him to join her there. It may be so; perhaps it was.

MR. ROBINSON. I do not know that I shall claim that.

Mr. Voorhees. Even if it was, it only shows that she was not yet far enough away from her destroyer to reassert herself, as she did when once more under the sacred influences of her beautiful home at Indianapolis. She was still at Knoxville; the horrid spell was yet upon her, and it may be she thought of meeting him again at Louisville; but when the demon of her downfall pursued her to Indianapolis he found that the sorcerer's satanic enchantment had no longer its power over her soul. She spurned him, and refused to look upon his face. There had been no quarrel between them, but she had escaped; she was free, she was restored, and in her right mind, and the tempter and pursuer slunk away. There is some balm to the bruised hearts of the living in this fact. The darling wife and mother was once more placing her wayward feet on the Rock of Ages, and preparing for that peace and mercy which the penitent soul is promised in that high world beyond the stars.

But there was one other dreadful ordeal for this most unhappy victim in her struggle to retrace her steps, and to repair, as far as might be, the incurable wrongs inflicted on her faithful, trusting, and devoted husband. I pause before this pile of penitential grief, her letters of confession. They have, alas! been read; I will read them no more. I could not if I tried. Their story is more pitiful and full of sorrow than the wail of the heart-broken over the dead. They seem vocal with sobs and wet with tears. No duress, threats, conditions, or promises extorted them. Her stricken husband was not within five hundred miles of her when they were written. She was alone in her home; he was at Knoxville. She was in Indiana, he in Tennessee. It is sometimes said, and it sometimes happens, doubtless, that an injured husband, in immediate contact with his penitent, humbled, and crushed wife, brings coercive influences to bear upon her, based upon conditions of the future, or even based upon terror. Nothing of that kind could have happened here. The husband wrote from Knoxville, and his letters were received at Indianapolis. The wife had her own time in which to answer; she was surrounded by her friends; her father was there; if any advantage was sought by her husband she could have consulted tried friends on every hand; she could have proclaimed her husband insane with jealousy; that he was seeking from her a confession of guilt which was not true. All this she had the opportunity to do from September to November, for more than sixty days, while he remained in Knoxville and she at Indianapolis. Bear this in mind. Never were letters written more free from every earthly consideration, except the desire on her part to relieve her tortured breast of its horrible secret, and to seek forgiveness by her repentance. Nor did one word ever fall from his lips or pen that he would cast her off, or that he would put her away by divorce; on the contrary, the proof is ample that he declared his purpose to always care and provide for her, and to support her aged father. What more could he do? As to a future domestic life, it could never be; but he did not terrify her even by making known that decision. The substance of his language to her was that the future could not be fathomed, but that for the present he would shelter and protect her from harm and exposure, and that the world should never know her shame and degradation. She had no earthly inducement to make confession except the promptings of a naturally pure heart, overcome and burdened with a guilty secret which it could not retain, and which finally made confession still more absolute by suicide.

But to proceed. We will examine another link in this chain of circumstances, which has been to this defendant's brain and heart like a blazing chain of molten metal to the shrinking flesh. The first of these dreadful letters came to him in November, at Knoxville. His son—this boy here, with a face that Raphael would have loved to paint—simply saw by the writing that the letter was from his mother, and tells you so. Captain Johnson read it. The world grew dark. He sought to rise from his chair. He staggered and fell on his face as if a blow had crushed his brain. While we pause a few moments over his prostrate form, still as if in death, you must remember that this is a sick man, weak in physical strength, without the powers of health to uphold him in sudden and appalling calamity. He has chronic diseases unto death. With consumption clutching at his throat and lungs, and aggravated chronic dyspepsia depressing the mind, darkening the spirit, and casting the soul into gloomy depths, he tottered, reeled, and fell. You strong men in this jury-box; you men with perfect digestion, who eat three hearty meals each day, remember you are dealing with your brother who is in no such condition. You are dealing with the shadow of what he once was, reduced by physical disease, so that, as Dr. Boyd says, he could not resist the causes which overwhelm the mind as one in robust health might do. Come, now, put yourselves in his place. One of the greatest works ever written in the wide field of splendid fiction is that of Charles Reade, "Put Yourself in His Place." (Addressing counsel for state:) Suppose you and I, who are both strong men, with sound lungs and with good stomachs, should put ourselves in the place of this nervous, suffering shadow we see passing to and fro, and who is not able to remain in this court-room now.

CAPTAIN ROBINSON. I have been in as bad a physical condition myself, and—

MR. VOORHEES. Then suppose you extend him your sympathy.

(To the jury:) Let us put ourselves in his place, if we can, and then deal with him as we would ask to be dealt by. Broken in health, and wrecked by physical disease, when he realized that the love of his life was blighted; that the peace and honor of home were forever gone; that his wife had fallen from his arms far worse than dead; when he realized all this, and, with a swift insight into the future, heard her cherished name bandied about, hawked from tongue to tongue as a by-word of scorn, is it to be wondered, when he arose from the floor, and hours afterwards from his bed of pain and fever, where in agony and tears he had been laid, that henceforth his brain was seared by one perpetual and burning thought, and that the iron had entered his soul, never to be withdrawn?

I have heard the doctrine of "cooling time" invoked in this case. Cooling time! That scene at Knoxville occurred nearly a year before Henry paid the penalty of his crimes. I care not if it had occurred a hundred years before, could the parties have lived so long. You may become cool after an insult, or even a blow in passion; but when the form of the wife has once been seen by the mind's eye writhing in the arms of the seducer; when once the husband has pictured to himself, looking through walls and across rivers, beyond the deep valleys and over mountains, it may be, the fair, loved form that has rested on his loving breast in happy repose surrendered to the desires of a besotted and lustful wretch, a cooling time will never come to him, and how well you know it! As well might you visit a lost soul who had lain upon the burning marl of hell a thousand years and say: "You have been here long enough to become cool; there has been cooling time since you took up your abode in eternal torment." He would answer that it had been perpetual hell; that it had been burning time, and burning time alone. Suppose years pass by, and the husband thinks at all of his wife lost in shame, will his thoughts be temperate and his blood cool? The whole horrible subject comes up again. He can never think of her, whether living or dead, after defilement, without involuntarily recalling those revolting particulars that have crazed the brain in all the ages of the past, and will continue to do so in all the ages to come. I do not want to know a man who can grow cool under such circumstances. I wish no man for my friend whose heart can be temperate and calm with something so much worse than murder, so much worse than death in his home. Cooling time! From the moment Edward T. Johnson fell forward on his face, with the fatal letter of confession in his hand, from that moment, instead of the fires of suffering, grief, bereavement, bitterness, hate, revenge, if you please, dying away by the lapse of time, they grew stronger, hotter and fiercer. What further element of wretchedness, what additional pang of woe and desolation could he experience? Every deadly ingredient of human misery which the blackest malice could invent or find was in the accursed cup which he has drained to the dregs.

What greater crime do you know than that which prostrated Edward T. Johnson in the Hattie House at Knoxville? Is it murder? Had the villain cut his victim's throat, had he poisoned her to death, she would still have been a precious memory, mourned by husband, son, and loving friends "till pity's self be dead," while the sweet June roses would have bloomed over her honored grave with no taint of impurity in their perfume. Had he burned the defendant's home, it could have been built again. Had he robbed him and taken all his worldly possessions, he would still have had honor left. Human history makes but one answer. The darkest crime, the one without pardon or mercy from God or man, is the invasion of a home and its destruction by lust and pollution. With the downfall of the wife and mother the home crumbles to ashes. The divinity which presided and filled it with light and joy is no more. This defendant is homeless. The walls are standing, but they are barren of rest or peace to him. He could not dwell in such a ruin, nor survive where his past joys and hopes all now lie withered and dead. The altar of home has been desecrated, the hearthstone has been defiled, and the name of him who did it is here invoked to sanction this prosecution. Edwin Henry died as he ought to have died. He who commits this worst and most pervading, far-reaching, and destructive crime ought to die, and I have the highest authority for my words.

Why did the world witness that wonderful and beautiful spectacle a short time since on the northern coast of Africa? More than thirty years ago the American consul at Tunis died at that distant place, and there was buried. He was not great as statesman, jurist, or warrior. He had never led in council, court, or field. Why was it that one whose own name will never perish as the benefactor of the present and of future generations, and as the munificent patron of literature, the arts and sciences, called back the bones and dust that had lain so long on the far-off shores of the Mediterranean? William W. Corcoran, the most eminent citizen of the republic, in the love and esteem of his countrymen, simply asked his government's permission to bring, at his own expense, the remains of John Howard Payne home to rest in his native land. And then, on the 5th day of January, 1883, there gathered around his grave in the little cemetery at Tunis the representatives of the most powerful nations of the earth. The Christian and the Mohammedan stood together and bent with reverence over the hallowed spot where the American had slept so long on a foreign shore. They carefully raised his crumbling coffin and tenderly preserved every atom of his precious dust; and then in a triple casket all his mortal remains were covered with flowers, and to the music of an immortal song he started on his final voyage home. As the ship that bore him rode into the harbor of New York the authorities of that great metropolis rose up to do him honor, as if one of the mighty dead had returned to earth. The city hall was opened, and there his remains, although invisible, were laid in state, while thousands and tens of thousands of people crowded by to catch a glimpse of even the outside coffin in which they reposed. At Washington City, the capital of a government of more than fifty-five millions of people, the wanderer's return was hailed with an ovation never to be forgotten while American history endures. Statesmen and heroes were his pall-bearers; distinction, culture, and refinement felt honored with a place at his funeral. Eloquence paid its lofty tribute, and music, with its sweetest, richest, and most imposing strains, welcomed John Howard Payne to his final abode in the city of the dead. And why, now, were all these honors, without a parallel in human history, paid to his memory? Ah! how well you know the answer, how quickly your swelling hearts respond! He wrote one song in which he embodied and unbosomed the most precious desire and the most undying emotion of the universal heart of man, woman, and child. He wrote " Home, Sweet Home." There are but fourteen lines in this blessed song, including the chorus, but it will live as long as these blue mountains stand, " Home, Home! Sweet, Sweet Home!" Its strains have visited all lands and encircled the globe; they have ravished the listening ear in the palaces of royalty and wealth and in the peasant's lonely hut. John Howard Payne sung the song of home; he interpreted the human heart. "There is no place like home," the poet cries; and the whole world cries in unison, " Be it ever so humble, there is no place like home." Can this be true, can this song live, if the defiler's step may cross the threshold of home with impunity? The habitation may be built of boards, or its walls may be constructed of unhewn logs; it may be a sheeling on the mountain side or a hovel in the valley below; the bleak winds of autumn and winter may blow through it; the rains may descend through its frail roof, and a leather string may be its latch-key by day and by night; but it is home, the home where the wife and mother loves and nurses, where children are born and bloom in strength and beauty, where joy and smiles greet their coming, and groans and tears their departure; it is home where the ordinances of God are fulfilled for the progress and ultimate destiny of the human race. Each one of these homes is a beacon-light of civilization. In the lands of Christian civilization woman is most loved and reverenced. There womanhood is most refined and exalted, and there men fight for the purity of their homes. Here in East Tennessee you fought on both sides in the war for the Union, and you fought from high convictions of duty. When a man is willing to die for his opinions they are honest opinions. I appeal to you to permit my client to make one honest fight for the purity of home. In his early youth he fought under the beautiful, the starry flag, emblem of united power and of glory, and with eager enthusiasm offered his young life in the cause of his country as he saw the right. On the 23d day of September, 1884, this sad and lonely man, bereaved and stricken beyond cure in this world, made one battle, down in yonder mountain gorge, twelve miles away, not merely to punish the destroyer of his own dear home, but in vindication of the principle which makes all homes secure from the intrusion of the lustful outlaw. He fought for "Home, Home! Sweet, Sweet Home!" and when the reports of his double-barreled gun echoed on that autumn morning throughout these mountains of Greene county, and throughout the state of Tennessee, and all over the Union, they were welcomed by all except lechers, libertines, and adulterers as a fit accompaniment to the spirit, letter, and melody of the immortal song. In barbaric countries home, depending on woman's virtue and domestic purity, is without conception or appreciation and is without value. In the interior of the dark continent the African prince, as the first and most pleasant duty of hospitality, invites the honored guest to make a selection from among his wives, and to share with her the pleasures of his sojourn. In the deep, dark recesses of Africa and other benighted lands the principles which inspire this prosecution would be better authority than here.

Yesterday my eloquent associate, in glorious and thrilling words, cited the law of God, written in the old and hallowed ages of the past, in defense of the homes of his people. May I not also be allowed to comment a moment on the theme, and to point out the actual relation in which Major Henry stood toward Captain Johnson from the time he accomplished the ruin of the defendant's wife until he died at "The Furnace" with thirty-two buckshot through heart and brain? Here is the high old law, and in the light of human experience how closely and cogently it comes into your counsels:

> The man that committeth adultery with another man's wife, even he that committeth adultery with his neighbor's wife, the adulterer and the adulteress shall surely be put to death.

I know how this is met in modern schools of thought. The law reads harshly as to the woman, and the question is interposed whether she should die as well as the man; whether our civilization and our times will admit of the full application of that law. Pause a moment; I will answer. There came after this Mosaic edict a new dispensation. He who walked the waters of Galilee, and bade the winds be still; he at whose touch the lame and crippled rose and ran; he at whose command the blind saw; he who spoke at the grave of Lazarus and the dead came forth from the grim embrace of the tomb, brought a new and gentler administration of the divine law into practice. He modified the law I have read. It sentenced both the offenders, the man and the woman, to death. The merciful Redeemer, during his three years' ministration on earth, granted a remission to the woman of her share in the death penalty, but never as to the man. You all know the record by heart. I have it here:

> And early in the morning he came again into the temple, and all the people came unto him, and he sat down and taught them. And the Scribes and Pharisees brought unto him a woman taken in adultery, and, when they had set her in the midst, they said unto him, "Master, this woman was taken in adultery—in the very act. Now, Moses, in the law, commanded us that such should be stoned; but what sayest thou?"

There was a square question: "Moses, in the law, commanded us that such should be stoned; but what sayest thou?" You remember all the rest:

> Go, and sin no more.

She was not stoned; she was not put to death. Her accusers slunk away, and the penalty of the Mosaic law as to the woman was remitted by the Saviour. Where was it ever remitted or repealed as to the man? Tell me. Search these evangelists; search this blessed book—guide in life and comforter in death. Let doubters scoff; but it is the power that regulates life and fills the last hour with peace. Where, between its holy lids, do you find any remission of the penalty of death against the man who committeth adultery with his neighbor's wife? Christ softened the Mosaic law in respect to the woman. By his decision she was not put to death; but no decision was ever made by the Almighty Father nor by his Son that the adulterer should not die. And I stand here in the presence of the highest intelligence of this great state, and in the hearing of the ministers of the gospels of our blessed faith, and challenge a denial from any one, or from all, that the adulterer, "the man that committeth adultery with another man's wife, even he that committeth adultery with his neighbor's wife," is, by the law of God, under present, continuing, and eternal sentence of death. There is no point of time where this sentence stops. There is no instance in the book of books where it has been remitted. As to the woman, it has been; as to the man, never! And from the moment that Major Henry, this vile monster of mesmeric power or some other satanic agency, defiled the wife of his friend, committed adultery with the wife of his neighbor—from that moment he walked by day and by night under a perpetual and unending sentence of death pronounced by Almighty God. Answer this who can! Answer it who may!

Let us come back to first principles, let us have an elementary review, let us understand one another. I assert that the home of man is under the especial care and guardianship of God, and that he who defiles a home has already been tried in higher courts than those of earth and sentenced to death as an odious malefactor and common enemy of social peace and morality. After Johnson fell on his face—fell in the dust and in the ashes of domestic ruin, shame, and humiliation—he arose, in the light of God's word, as the instrument of judgment and of the execution of judgment against one who bore the curse of divine condemnation on his brow henceforth and forever. The able and accomplished gentlemen managing the prosecution seem to be amazed at the assertion by Captain Johnson that he considered himself an agent in the hands of the Almighty to inflict divine punishment on Henry. Well, let us look closer. When God pronounced the penalty of death against the adulterer he declared he should be stoned to death. That looks as if anybody could kill him. There is no trial provided for, no court-house designated wherein to arraign him; there is no attorney-general to prosecute, and there are no funds provided with which to hire able counsel, as here, to assist. It is all left to the people, and he is at their mercy; and to whose mercy and justice should he be surrendered rather than to the man he has wronged? Indeed, this position has been sanctioned and approved in the most emphatic manner by your own great state of Tennessee. For, inasmuch as she has enacted no law for the punishment of the adulterer, she has thereby expressly recognized the binding force of the law of holy writ, and has left the seducer to the vengeance of the injured husband.

It was once said by a brilliant and distinguished lawyer of Indiana that while he fully yielded to the divine claim, "Vengeance is mine, saith the Lord, and I will repay," yet he as fully and sincerely believed and claimed that the Lord, omniscient and omnipotent, chose his own instruments and his own time and place for the execution of his will. What matters it who kills the adulterer? God gave him up to the people, to the multitude. It is true that the dishonored and outraged husband is likely to be first in stoning the wretch, or in any other mode of putting him to death, and he ought to be. Will I be answered here, "Thou shalt not kill?" But God says the adulterer shall be killed. He has no shelter under the great commandment, which was meant for the innocent and the blameless. Am I answered again, "You shall do no murder?" God says, however, this is not murder; it is justifiable homicide for the criminal who saps and poisons the fountains of life to be exterminated.

In this old, historic town you have a glorious spring of wonderful size, beauty, and purity. I have stood upon its brink and gazed with delight into its sparkling depths. I have wondered what would have been the destiny of Egypt, and how different history might have been, if such a fountain of living waters had cooled and fructified the parched plains of the Soudan. To you it comes a laughing, joyous blessing, bestowing health in your households, causing the sward, like a velvet-green carpet, to vegetate down to its very edge, your gardens to be rich with their productions for the table, and these beautiful groves on which I now look from yonder window to grow dark, and strong, and majestic. Suppose you now knew that last night that fountain was poisoned, and the miscreant was clearly identified; that day after day and night after night he had been there systematically poisoning its clear, sweet waters, and disseminating disease and death into all your households. I doubt whether you would be content that such a man should live an hour. I think the people, the multitude, as in the case of the adulterer, would stone him to death without trial. But the adulterer is far worse; he poisons the springs of eternal life, and kills the soul as well as the body of his victim.

In the case you are now trying, was adultery the only crime for which Henry had forfeited his life? On the contrary, the blood of murder was on his hands. Had he let his neighbor's wife alone; had he not pursued her like the sleuth-hound after his prey, she would this day have been the proud and honored wife and mother, loving and beloved in her home in Indianapolis, the air redolent of happiness around her, and the future stretching away before her as pure and as bright as the flowers of spring. Why is this not so now? Because Edwin Henry murdered her. You are prosecuting this defendant for murder. I will tell you who the murderer is— the man who corrupted the woman and drove her in remorse to robe herself for the grave and put a ball through her heart; and wherever he is in the world beyond he is this hour answering not only for adultery, but for murder. The blood of that self-slain woman is on Edwin Henry's soul. He, and he alone, was the cause that started the current of her misery, widening into a whirling gulf of fantasy and flame, and bringing her into a mental condition wherein death was her only refuge. In the act of suicide committed by the despairing victim, Edwin Henry committed the crime of murder as certainly and with as much guilt as if he had fired the pistol with his own hand. Had he never lived, had she never seen him, or had he not lusted after her, she would not thus have died. I charge here that by the law of Almighty God, as the destroyer of a home, he was under sentence of death and ought to have died, and that he died justly. I charge further that he was directly guilty of her murder, and that he was morally as guilty as if he had held the pistol. It is some satisfaction to know that remorse haunted him; that when he returned to this community, when all his wickedness was known and his victim was in her grave, the men averted their faces, and the women drew aside their skirts as if they said: "Room for the leper; room for the leper." Thus loathed and hated, avoided by all, he passed on to his doom.

In approaching, as I do now, the personal condition of this defendant, and the influence which "unmerciful disaster" has had upon him, my heart shudders, and I shrink from the task.

As he says, in one of his heart-broken wails: "It seems that the depths of human misery were never fathomed before." It may be said that Captain Johnson made a mistake, which increased his sufferings, when, after his wife's death, he attempted to conceal her dishonor. If that be so, it is the only mistake in conduct which he has made from the beginning to the end of this tragedy, and the motive on which he acted exalts him in the estimation of all honorable minds. We all have a clearer vision of things as we look back upon them from a cool, safe distance, than when in the midst of exciting and heart-rending scenes requiring immediate decision. Looking backward now, after nearly two years' experience, to that dreadful morning when he saw his poor wife in the cold but pure embrace of death, it would have been wiser, in the ways of the world, for him to have given up at once the awful secret which had caused her, "rashly importunate," to seek the silence and the refuge of the tomb. We can all see that now, but we can also understand the deep, undying love which controlled him. He determined that her name should not be sullied; he believed he could carry her guilty secret to the grave, and hide her disgrace forever from the world. In answer to Mr. Dooley, his loved and trusted friend, he only said that in the distant future, when they were old men, if they lived that long, he might tell him all, but not sooner. He said his wife was insane, as the reason why she died by her own hand. Perhaps she was. Who shall determine? The medical opinion of the world is divided, and it is an unsettled question whether a sane person ever commits suicide. In this case I have the gravest possible doubts. I can not conceive Mrs. Johnson to have been entirely sane while here in Greeneville. Viewed in the light of all her previous life, conduct, and reputation, she was an insane woman in her relations with Major Henry. Be that as it may, however, Captain Johnson gave a natural, manly, and humane answer—the answer of a man who loved her devotedly in life and cherished her memory in death. He laid her tenderly in her grave, fondly hoping and believing that shame would never mildew the flowers that would grow over her. Then, reeling from mental anguish and physical weakness, broken in heart and broken in health, he found his way back to his post of duty at Knoxville.

But there were those who were unwilling for the dead wife and mother to sleep in peace, who questioned the reason of her death as given by her husband, and, when it was ascertained that certain arrangements of property had taken place on the evening she died, it was natural that interest and inquiry should be aroused. It was most unnatural, however, that personal enmity should seize such an opportunity as this to wreak vengeance for personal and political offenses on one already afflicted by the direst misfortunes known to the fate of man.

His wife's downfall and suicide by the arts of the brutal seducer were now to be followed by the publication of her shame to the world through the malevolence of heartless enemies. An action was brought in the superior court at Indianapolis, in the name of old Dr. Griffith, against this defendant, ostensibly to annul the deed executed by Dr. Griffith to Dr. Wakefield, but in reality solely for the purpose of compelling the surrender and publication of the letters of the poor dead woman to her husband, revealing the awful story of her fall. Under a peculiar provision of our statute, enacting that either party in a pending suit may be examined on oath by the other party, Captain Johnson was brought before an officer and subjected to a sworn examination. He employed able counsel and resorted to every legal expedient to avoid the threatened exposure. He offered to compromise the case by giving to Dr. Griffith, not only his original half, but the whole of the homestead property, if thereby the publication of his wife's letters could be averted. He humiliated himself before Governor Porter, begging him, as a friend of his dead wife, and in the name of purity and truth, to interpose, knowing that one word from him would avert the impending calamity. It was all in vain. His overtures were all rejected. Porter responded to his appeal with jeers and taunts; and the cruel case went on. All else failing, he at last resorted to silence. He appeared, when summoned by the officer, but sternly closed his mouth. Question after question was hurled at him in vain. Defying counsel and court alike, he refused to answer. And it was only when he had driven the court to the last method of enforcing its authority, and only when over his head impended the majesty of the law, menacing fine and imprisonment for contempt, that he finally yielded. It was in this way that the sad, piteous letters of his wife were wrested from him and given to the world.

He said to Mr. Dooley:

> I would rather have died a hundred times than that the letters should have been published. But for my noble boy I would never have given them up. I would have burned them all and taken my own life.

If the fight he made to save his wife's fame was injudicious, it was for that reason not the less manly and heroic. But what are we to say of his pursuers? Their crime is well described by Captain Johnson in his letter to Mr. Self, where he says:

> Oh, most pitiful of all catastrophes! They caused a poor demented old man to consign the name of his own daughter to eternal infamy.

God pity him and pity them! This day I would rather endure Captain Johnson's ill fortune than their responsibility. I need hardly say that among all the defendant's terrible wounds this ruin of his wife's fame was one of the most murderous hurts he received.

The charges made against him at Indianapolis are all here before you, and they are each and every one as false as if coined and minted in hell. I desire to make no personal assault on any one. Those who have brought themselves into this case by their own hostility to Captain Johnson can not and will not complain if I deal candidly with the evidence as I find it. This I shall do; no more and no less. I have no personal hostility either toward Governor Porter or Major Gordon. I have no reason to have any. We have fought our battles, political and professional, and I have no reason to be dissatisfied with the results. I mention their names simply and solely as they have brought themselves into this case, and as they have borne down upon this broken man. I speak of them simply to show what influence their bitter warfare had on his mind; how much they contributed to his mental troubles; what results sprang from their most unnatural interference. Here is a man who passionately loved his wife, idolized her, who craved death as a blessing when she was lost to him, whose entire wedded life with her had been a poem of love and exquisite happiness. What would be the effect on his mind, in his morbid and feeble condition, of an accusation that he had murdered her?

Before his wife was buried, and while she still lay a corpse in his house, these men deliberately, and without the slightest evidence upon which to base their assertions, made this hideous charge of murder. The deposition of Mr. Woodard, the well-known correspondent of the Cincinnati *Enquirer*, is before you. They first attempted through him to give publicity to the charge. He wrote the letter to the *Enquirer*, as they desired, but it was suppressed. Next, old Dr. Griffith was sought and induced to publish the charge, though the reporter of the Indianapolis *Journal*, who wrote the terrible publication, testifies here that Dr. Griffith had no agency in it, and that it came entire from J. W. Gordon. To Mr. Fortune, to Judge Hill, to Mr. Van Vorhis, to Mr. Brown, the prosecuting attorney, and to many others, Gordon repeated the imputation in strong and positive terms. It was again repeated in letters purporting to have been written by Dr. Griffith, though certainly composed by others, to the southern press, and cruelest, most fiendish of all, in letters to the defendant's son. These men well knew that this awful charge would not be believed unless it was shown that there was some motive actuating Captain Johnson to the commission of such a crime. Accordingly, two audacious fictions were invented and promulgated through Dr. Griffith along with the charge of murder. One was that he had killed his wife for her jewelry, alleged to be worth $13,000; the other was that he had killed her that he might marry a rich woman of New Albany. God of heaven, what lying! The testimony of expert jewelers is before you who carefully examined every article of that jewelry, and they place its full value at $100.53. As to the New Albany lady, it is shown that at the time of Mrs. Johnson's death this lady was, and for six years had been, a married woman, the mother of two little children, and that Captain Johnson had not seen her for eight years. Thus two subordinate calumnies, both as groundless as the first, were invented and published in support of the horrible calumny of murder. It is hard to realize that human nature is capable of such depravity.

On the other hand, I have shown you who was responsible for Mrs. Johnson's death; I have shown you who was her murderer. It was the man whose dead body was carried last September out of Tennessee for burial. He was the murderer. Why have I spoken on this point? The prosecution raises no question as to the manner of Mrs. Johnson's death, but I am determined that you shall know by the evidence the manner of man you are judging. I have told you there is no stain upon him, and the proof will make good my words. His reputation was so strong in Indianapolis, he stood such a pillar of moral strength, that, with all Governor Porter could say, and all Major Gordon could do, they could not deprive him of the best reputation ever proven for a citizen of Indiana on trial for his life, at home or abroad; they could not hinder you from knowing that there is no blot on his name, that every aspersion against him is false, and all this is established by the testimony of the foremost citizens of Indiana, taken since every accusation has been made by his enemies, and since his indictment for murder in this court. But we do not stop even with all this; we have in evidence before you every movement he made the melancholy night of her death. When he went to his home that night he had with him a venerable Episcopal minister, Dr. Wakefield, who had married them, had baptized their babies, and officiated and wept with them at the funeral of little Eddie. What an excellent accomplice for hideous, cowardly wife-murder! A well-chosen companion for the guilty scoundrel who was then creeping and stealing into his wife's chamber to send a bullet through her heart! Gentlemen, it is hard for me to talk about this phase of the case, knowing Captain Johnson as I do. It is so thoroughly and damnably infamous that it chokes me, it stifles me, it humiliates me that he had to meet such a charge; but has he not met it? Has it not been met by Dr. Wakefield, by the evidence of the hack driver, of the chambermaid, of the porter, of the elevator boy, and of the clerk and the telegraph operator of the Denison House, who all testify that on the night of his wife's death he was in that hotel all night after returning to it early in the evening?

Away with this infamous calumny, horrible, execrable in the extreme. Murdered! How could she have died by any hand save her own? She was prepared, with a refined lady's taste, for the tomb. Knowing her poor body would be handled by her friends, she prepared it herself; she bathed and perfumed for the sepulcher; she made her own toilet in which to enter the royal court of death; she left off her underclothing as not pertaining to grave clothes: she robed herself in immaculate linen, fresh and white, put on her stockings of purest white silk, and her slippers, adjusted her dress around her limbs and person with that taste and grace which only belongs to a refined and cultivated woman; and then, with the picture of her husband placed where her last look on earth would be on his face and her last thought be his, showing the devoted wife, true and pure of heart at the last, she placed the pistol over her heart and died mercifully without a pang. The physicians say death was instantaneous; she did not move; not a muscle shook with pain or convulsion. How strained, forced, and malicious seems the suggestion of murder! Never within your knowledge or reading, nor within mine, has there been so systematic and, if I may use the word, so artistic a suicide as this. In that household there lived an old man more than fourscore, the father of Mrs. Johnson, who did not believe, and did not intend to believe, and does not now, although she has written it all out herself, that his daughter had sinned or fallen or wronged her husband. Well, spare the old man; let him believe what he will. The men, however, who have taken advantage of the dotage and the childishness of old age and used his name unjustly and falsely to crush this defendant will have to answer for it, not to me, but to the public opinion of Indiana and to Almighty God. Let them look to it. They made this charge of murder. I appeal to this enlightened prosecution, to the court, and to the jury to say whether it has been answered.

It is hard to think with patience of that other scurrilous and loathsome charge—that this defendant, born and bred a gentleman, cultivated, educated, and widely read in literature, the arts, history, and science, was a poor, miserable sneak-thief of jewelry stolen from the trunks and drawers of his dead wife. Is it not a shame and a scandal that this man, who has proven by Joseph E. McDonald, John C. New, and the most prominent and honored men in Indiana by the score that no other man in the state, and I care not who the other is, has a higher, purer, more attractive reputation than he enjoys, should be subjected to the necessity of meeting such a degraded lie as that? The liars and dealers in calumny asserted the jewelry to be worth $13,000, and he proves that the articles he took away after his wife's burial were a few trinkets placed in his trunk by Mrs. Talbott and worth $100.53.

But here is the other abomination: Captain Johnson, in his hour of deepest trial, has had hurled at him with the sanction of Governor Porter's name, never recalled or denied by him, that nine or ten years ago this defendant wanted a divorce from his wife; that at French Lick Springs, in Indiana, he had fallen in love with the rich lady of New Albany and desired to marry her, although then a married man. And how has this slander been met? Do you remember the testimony of Mary R. Lewis, his faithful and devoted old servant? She came into his family on the day of his marriage and is there yet. Let me read a passage from her deposition:

Q. Have you heard the charge that Mr. Johnson met and fell in love with some lady at the springs on the occasion mentioned, and after returning home sought a divorce from his wife? If so, what do you know about it?
Ans. I never heard of such a thing until after Mrs. Johnson's death. I know that the charge that he tried to divorce his wife is not true, because there never

was an estrangement between them, and there was no period in their married life when they were happier and more devoted to each other than the time following his absence at the springs. * * * Right after that visit, in the fall of 1874, he went to great expense improving and beautifying their house. He took the old mantel out of the front parlor and put in its place a fine marble mantel and grate that cost about $100. He furnished new and costly brussels carpets for the parlors, and one, at least, of the chambers. He put a new carved center table in the back parlor that cost $45, and a bronze drop-light on it that cost $16. He bought a large and beautiful French-plate mirror for the front parlor which cost $50. And he made his wife a present of a bed-room set of three pieces, bedstead, dressing-case, and wash-stand, which cost $175. It was, and is, a magnificent set. He also put rich and costly lambrequins over the front parlor windows. I think they cost $40 to each window. He also had the house repainted inside and out, and the parlors newly papered with very costly and elegant silver-leaf paper. The same season he gave her a fine horse and buggy worth $500, a splendid piano which cost $750, and a policy of insurance on his own life for $5,000.

It was during these very days of happiness, and at the very time when these many tokens of his love and devotion to his wife were being bestowed, that these calumniators assert he was seeking a divorce. That horrible calumny came to his ears when he was mourning the death of his wife, when he was weeping over her new-made grave. Again he shrieked with pain, as if a bruised and wounded place on his body, commencing to heal, had been made to bleed afresh from the blows of an iron hammer. But the accursed lie could not live. You have heard the depositions of the two brothers of the young lady and of the venerable Justice Sullivan and others. The defendant never wrote her a letter in his life. She was a good girl, perhaps indiscreet and impulsive at that time, but now the honored wife of a gentleman of the highest character. No one but a fiend from the depths of hell would have dragged that lame, inconsequential, trifling circumstance from its grave and started it on its rounds to reach eventually, I fear, the woman and her husband. It has also been charged that Captain Johnson offered Governor Porter a thousand dollars to obtain for him a divorce. If that is true, why is not Albert G. Porter here? We have met the charge, and ground it to the earth under our heels. He knows the charge has been made; and, if it were true, he would have been here. No more abominable and atrocious lie was ever hissed from the lips of man or fiend. It has gone its rounds and done its vile work, but at last it has been met and silenced forever. Captain Johnson, speaking the voice of manhood's highest morality, as well as nobility, exclaimed in the hour of his wife's overthrow, "When I was tempted I took you and my babies in my arms and met the temptress, and she went away."

How dares this infamous suggestion of divorce to be made? What kind of a home at Indianapolis was disclosed by the evidence? Did you see a picture of discord in which there was strife, bitterness, or coldness, and want of connubial love? On the contrary, we stand here on the proof, meeting every malicious slander. I am now speaking to the shocking accusations hurled at him from Indianapolis, when he was crying out in his extremity: "Oh, if they would only let me alone!" Who are the people who testified to us about his home? There are here the names of nineteen persons, embracing those of social prominence, and also embracing every servant they ever had, and the old servant, Mary R. Lewis, who has been in the service of the defendant's family since their wedding day to the present hour, and is at their old home now. I wish her to speak in her own person:

> Mr. Johnson and his wife were always to me a model couple. I never knew any other couple so completely devoted to each other or so happy and contented with each other as they were. From their marriage to the end, their devotion and affection seemed to increase and become stronger as they grew older. They treated each other always with great kindness and tenderness of manner and speech. There was never a time, when in the house, that I did not witness acts of love and affection. I have seen them in each other's arms a thousand times. His knee was her favorite perch when he was at home. Sitting together in the family, evenings and other times, they were always near each other, and never satisfied except when together. They loved their children devotedly, and were all perfectly united. They had for years and years a kind of little baby speech which they used to one another in conversation, when nobody but ourselves was present. I have often heard Mrs. Johnson say that she was careful never to ask her husband for anything that he could not readily afford, because if he found there was anything she wanted he would know no rest until he had procured it for her, and he would furnish it, if she asked for it, whether he could afford it or not. This was true. So far as I could judge, his greatest happiness consisted in making his family, and especially his wife, happy and contented. There were no quarrels, no bickerings, and no ill-feeling between them at any time, so far as I knew or could observe. I never heard, or heard of, an unkind word or act between them. My intimacy with them was so close that if there had been difficulty or unhappiness I certainly would have known it. I never saw a cloud or a shadow in their home until after Mrs. Johnson's return from Tennessee late in September, 1883.

Another old domestic, Maria Jones, says:

> A. Their relations were very kind and affectionate. They were all devotedly attached to one another. Mr. Johnson was extremely fond of his children, and his wife said he was too good to them and not strict enough. He believed in governing them altogether by love and affection, and such a thing as striking one of them, he often said, was not to be thought of. He considered it barbarous. I

have heard it said in the family that little Eddie lived and died without ever hearing from his father a harsh word, and I have heard Mr. Johnson say that for Eddie he never had in his heart one ill or harsh feeling. When in health, he devoted much of his time to the children, amusing and playing with them; often down on the floor with them tousling and tumbling over him, and often romping about the house and yard with Eddie on his back and Griffith hanging to his coat-tail. When Eddie died it almost broke his heart. All their friends spoke of his great sorrow at the loss.

Mr. Johnson and his wife always treated each other with kind regard and affection. He was more affectionate than she was, and always showed a great deal more feeling. He always kissed her good-by when going down town and again, when he could find her, on returning; and when he came in, if she was out of sight, the first thing was to ask for or call her. He always had pet names for her and they often prattled to each other like little children. I have seen a great many demonstrations of fondness between them, and I can truly say that I never knew or heard of anything but love and affection between them.

Here is another domestic, Lena Wachstetter. Listen to her strong language:

> I was a servant in the family for years. I never saw nor heard of a single harsh or unkind word or act between them. It was the happiest family I ever knew.

I could stand here and read by the hour voluminous testimony of the same import. Mary Bordley, a cousin of Mrs. Johnson, testifies to the unbroken kindness and affection between them. A. P. Stanton does the same. So does Mr. White, Mrs. Robbins, and all the rest.

Colonel Thomas Hunt, who knew them, perhaps, better than anybody else, tells the whole story of their life together. His home was their home; they came, they went, they loved him and his, and all his household loved them. Their baby, Eddie, died in his hospitable mansion. His heart is like the blue-grass acres of Wayne county—broad and generous. We have heard him mentioned by the attorney-general as "the man of the name of Hunt." Yes; he is well known in Eastern Indiana by that name, and he has traveled long miles to be here, as he is now, close to his friend in the hour of peril. To this defendant and his family, though not of kin, he is known as Uncle Tom. I love such a man. He leaves his business and the large interests which are in his hands to come and see whether Tennesseeans have the same hearts we have in Indiana. I am satisfied he will find they have.

Suppose we turn to this community; what kind of relations did this family seem to bear toward each other during their sojourn here?

Were this husband and wife on such terms of coldness and indifference as to lay her open to and invite the approaches of the seducer? Sometimes such cases occur and the wife is exposed to temptation. I have one such instance in my mind now where the husband was a millionaire. His palatial home was invaded and defiled; but he had been so neglectful of wife and home, so absorbed in money-making, such a constant worshiper at the shrine of Mammon, so seldom a worshiper at the altar of domestic peace and felicity, that the world did not much sympathize with him, while the world was unusually tolerant towards her. But the adulterer fled the country to escape death. There was neither toleration, nor sympathy, nor safety for him, though people divided as to the husband and wife. But was there any such opening for the tempter presented here? Was there any such invitation for the persistent, pertinacious, remorseless pursuit which was made of Mrs. Johnson?

Dr. Taylor testified that while Captain Johnson was here he was sick, and the wife came and joined him; and you all remember his testimony as to her kindness to her invalid husband. In that connection the doctor used a word I was glad to hear. As the doctor described the tenderness and assiduity of the wife, he said in return Captain Johnson was very grateful. It is the good heart that is grateful for kindness. Some natures receive the kind offices of the wife as mere duties and without thanks, while others brighten her pathway and sweeten her life by gentle and loving words of appreciation and affection. Dr. Boyd, who also attended the defendant, says there was "the utmost kindness and affection between them that could prevail between husband and wife." Mrs. Godfrey, the landlady where they lived, testifies the same. She says they never came to a meal without the son on one side of his mother and the father on the other, with their arms around her, making common cause in their admiration for the wife and mother, both much in love with her. Martha Garrison, the colored woman, describes the same thing.

You have this picture of domestic happiness and peace, of harmony and love, as you first see it at Indianapolis, and then brought down here, to refute the abominable and atrocious falsehood that there had been bitterness, coldness and want of affection between them. We have traced them from their wedding day, when Dr. Wakefield pronounced them man and wife, and in the name of God announced that no man should put them asunder. In the light of the most critical and trying evidence which ever searched a household we have traced them from that time to the day of her death, and I defy the production of one word of proof that a single unkind word ever passed between them, or a frowning look was ever given by one to the other. We have examined their neighbors and intimate friends. We have examined all their household servants—one who has been with them from the morning she helped dress her mistress as a bride until she helped to lay her in her untimely coffin. We have revealed all the inside of the house. Society sees the surface; social callers see the parlor, where politeness and courtesy reign. The servants see the dining-room; they see the kitchen; they see the bed-rooms; they know all the family secrets; they unlock the closets of the house; and if there is a skeleton there, do not deceive yourselves—they will know it. We have passed through this most searching ordeal; no domestic skeleton is found, not a word of discord is heard; and yet we have thrust into our faces, even during this trial, not from the counsel for the prosecution, but from one source and one alone, that only a few years ago Captain Johnson loved another woman, and offered a large fee to a distinguished lawyer to secure him a divorce from his wife. I put my foot on this calumny here, now and forever; and the man who hereafter repeats it, whether in Indiana or elsewhere, will be marked and branded as an outlaw from every sense of truth or decency.

Their next charge was that he had robbed her of her home; that he had extorted a deed from her and taken the roof from over her head. Now, men and brethren, once again I ask you, put yourselves in his place. Here was a home that stood, half of it in her name and half of it in old Dr. Griffith's name—thus held for convenience, Dr. Griffith not having a dollar invested in the property. Dr. Griffith, at the age of eighty-two or eighty-three, as he was then, was liable shortly to die. Captain Johnson knew then, as he knows now, that his own lease of life can not be a long one; that the candle will go out at no very distant day. Suppose that he and Dr. Griffith had both died, as the title then stood. This is a very easy and not at all a violent supposition. The one was a very old man and the other a very sick man; one on the brink of the grave, having passed fourscore years, having far outlived the allotted time of life, and the other with no secure hold upon life from day to day. In the event of the death of both, Mrs. Johnson became the owner of the entire property. Suppose, then, again, that this infatuation, which Captain Johnson had only discovered a few weeks before, for this wretch from New York had continued. I speak of him as a wretch from New York. Pardon for a moment the digression. I have here and there heard Major Henry spoken of as a Tennesseean. No, no; he was not a Tennesseean. He was a bastard. He was not legitimate. He tried to run for the legislature here and he voted here; but he was a bastard—not a legitimate growth of your state. I know the people of Tennessee. One of the greatest men of Indiana was Tighlman A. Howard, born in Tennessee, and here in East Tennessee. Your people are brave, generous, and love pure homes and domestic bliss. Do not tell me that this crawling, besotted old beast belongs here at all. He was worse and baser than the kite in the eagle's nest. Your nests here in these mountains were made for eagles, and not for filthy carrion crows. But to return: Suppose her infatuation had lasted for him, and suppose there had been a legal divorce between Henry and the woman who makes formal advertisement that she is now his widow, which I presume is true, whether she lived with him or not during the last eighteen or nineteen years; what then? I am now following the workings of Captain Johnson's mind on the subject of the homestead property.

He felt, and said to himself, and was entitled to say, "If I should die and if Dr. Griffith should die, both likely events in the near future, my wife would hold the legal title to the entire property, and, being already torn from the anchorage of virtue, she might very readily be again thrown into the clutches of this beast, again subjected to his will and power, and be drawn into a marriage with him, and he thus become the possessor and control everything."

Captain Johnson reasoned that with himself and Dr. Griffith in the grave, and the slight tie that bound Henry to Flushing, Long

Island, broken, a marriage would take place, stripping his son of every dollar and making him dependent on a combination founded in crime the most detestable. This is all in evidence. I am not saying a word outside the record; I am not manufacturing a syllable; it is all in the proof. To preserve the property to the boy, to whom it rightfully belonged, and to save him from the fate of becoming stepson to this wretch, who might crawl into his father's place, Captain Johnson thought it best that old Dr. Griffith, for his part, and his wife, Mariette, for her part, should join in a trust-deed for the whole property, and to whom? Who did he select for a trustee to rob his wife, as it is charged, of the roof that sheltered her? Who? I again rejoice and feel well in showing you how his truth and honor shines out at every step. He selected Dr. Wakefield as the trustee. Was he to rob the wife? No. He was to so handle the property, in the fear of God, as to take care of her and her aged father, and save it eventually for the son. Captain Johnson at the same time gave an obligation for the support of the demented old man who has been used to pursue him, and is now paying interest on $3,000 to provide food and raiment for the man whose name is invoked to send him to the gallows. This old man, Dr. Edward Griffith, whose letters have been read, whose communications to the newspapers, dictated or written by other men, are being used to crush Captain Johnson, is to-day eating his bread; the interest on the $3,000 is giving him all the support he has.

Captain Johnson says, "I told Mariette that night that so long as I lived her father should be comfortably and respectably supported." And he has faithfully kept his word. He selected Dr. Wakefield as trustee to take and hold this property in a condition of safety, not for himself, but as trustee for his and Mariette's son. Did he do right or wrong? It is not a question that bears upon his life or death, but I want to feel that I have left my duties at Washington and my loved ones there and come here to appear for a man who can answer on every point in his whole life, every one. We ask no grace or quarter. We answer on everything. Did he vilely rob or attempt to rob his wife, according to this evidence? On the contrary, he put the property in the hands of an Episcopal minister of forty years' standing, with a reputation and character as good as that of any man in Indiana, to hold for the benefit of that boy, and to care for his mother and grandfather. Death was closely trailing Dr. Griffith and Captain Johnson, and lust might be on her trail again. Villainy and lust had been there, and Captain Johnson did wisely and well in preparing for what might most probably occur in the future.

But at this point I shudder to hear another charge, which reached this defendant as he wandered in sickness of the soul and in midnight despair, so hideous and revolting that human nature recoils and cries out in maledictions against its author, whoever he may be. It is in proof in this case that a report was put in circulation, and came to the knowledge of this defendant, to the effect that he had connived at the ruin of his wife, and that his son was in the conspiracy for the pollution of his mother! And upon this charge this innocent boy has been disinherited by his grandfather's will. O God! I can not talk of this; I can not discuss it. If the gates of the bottomless pit were opened, and the great dragon unchained on the earth for a thousand years, with all his malice and guile, in all those years he could not invent a calumny so atrocious, so heart-breaking, so villainous as that. Is it any wonder that at times reason tottered on her throne, and ungovernable emotions swept like waves of madness over the suffering and tumultuous soul of the defendant?

In January the defendant returned again to the South. From Knoxville he went to New Orleans. Early in February he was assigned to North Georgia. Everywhere his pursuers are on his track.

Letter after letter was written to his son, filled with poisonous falsehoods, to alienate him from his father, to destroy the last hope, to break the last link which bound Captain Johnson to life. Once the rose tree bore its fullest bloom for him; once it was loaded with promises of happiness and of honor; but "leaf by leaf the roses have fallen," until Griffith, the darling son, was the last on the stem; and then, as Judge Ingersoll said yesterday, with more than the hate of fiends, persistent and repeated attempts were made to poison his young mind against his own father. Malice could go no farther; and do you wonder, oh, do you wonder that there is insanity in this case? I wonder there is not more. What with the sickness of the body and the sickness of the mind and heart, I wonder he lives. I do not wonder that he has shrieked and raved and wailed and wept and wearied the hours from night to morn and from morn to night again with the wish that he was dead; but I wonder he is not dead.

Early in June he resigned his office and settled at Marietta. And now the bolts fall thick and fast. The galling persecutions had done their deadly work also upon the mind of his noble son. The cruel, heartless letters of the crazy old grandfather had driven the boy to desperation. His mind, as well as that of his father, had become filled with tragic purposes. To kill the destroyer of his mother had become the one absorbing, all-consuming purpose of his soul. In presence of this terrible thought all the better and gentler impulses of his nature were perishing. Captain Johnson says he tried to weed this deadly thought from his son's mind, but to no purpose. The bloodhounds kept howling on his father's track, and the boy was bent on revenge. He lost his spirits. He became gloomy, morose, and exclusive. His father says, "I could not bear the thought of seeing his fair young hand stained with blood." To see his brave boy kill Major Henry, or to do it himself—that was the terrible alternative to which he was driven by his persecutors.

Just before leaving Georgia, late in July, he received from his faithful friend, Mr. Self, editor of the Greeneville *Herald*, that dreadful letter, written for publication in his paper. It contains an elaborate defense of Edwin Henry, and a labored argument to prove that this defendant had murdered his wife. It went farther still, and declared that he was "a surpassing liar," a swindler, a thief, and an adulterer, and closed with the challenge:

Whosoever wishes to learn his infamous character has only to inquire at Indianapolis, where he is well known and is universally detested.

Well, we have accepted that challenge. We have inquired at Indianapolis; and in that heap of depositions you have the answer to that inquiry, and also the answer to these reckless and appalling slanders. But who wrote that letter? It bears the signature of Dr. Griffith; but Colonel Hunt, who has known him for thirty years, tells you it is perfectly absurd to suppose that he was the author of any part of it. He says that he is so old and senile that he can scarcely speak two coherent sentences together on any subject, and that he is almost illiterate. This letter is written in clear, logical, lawyer-like style, and Colonel Hunt is right in saying that—

> Dr. Griffith could not have written it. He could neither compose its sentences nor spell its words.

Can you conceive anything better calculated than that letter to goad this defendant to utter desperation, to absolute insanity?

Early in August, utterly broken in health, he went with his friend, Colonel Hunt, to Tate Springs, Tennessee. Hardly had he arrived there when he received the letter written by Dr. Griffith to his son, and by him transmitted to his father, asserting that he had been dismissed in disgrace from the government service for infamous crimes. The son knew better, as you know better; but to this defendant the slander, uttered to his faithful son, was bitterer than the stab of a dagger dipped in poison.

It was one week later, at Galbraith Springs, that in the same manner he received another letter, written also by Dr. Griffith to his son, in which occurs this shocking passage:

> Here public opinion is universally against him. He is utterly infamous. There is not a respectable house in the city that would open its doors to him. Yesterday I heard a gentleman say that if he ever returned to Indianapolis he would be tarred and feathered and burnt alive.

And that to his idolized young son! Those words—that awful falsehood written by Mariette's father to his only grandchild, her only son! How quickly and with what exquisite sense of torture did Captain Johnson perceive that the "gentleman" by whom those words had been put into the mouth of that old madman was no other than one of his own arch tormentors.

Reeling onward from Galbraith, it was the last of August when he reached Greeneville. It was here, and only a few days before the great tragedy, that he learned of the last and most inhuman act of all. In his own words, their malice had pursued him, or rather preceded him, even into the grave. In his burial lot at Crown Hill cemetery, in the grave which he had reserved for himself, they buried the body of an old woman who had died at St. Vincent charity hospital. The graves in his lot, six in number, corresponding with the number of members in his family, had all been designated on a plat, and each grave marked with the name of the individual destined to inhabit it. Mrs. Griffith, Mrs. Johnson, and Eddie are all in their graves. On Mrs. Johnson's right lies her aged mother, to whom she fled in death. On her left, in the grave reserved for her husband, lies the body of the involuntary intruder. She lies in his grave, by the side of his wife, and between poor Mariette and her little Eddie. No place is left in that lot for him to rest, and he must seek a grave elsewhere, banished, even in death, from his own family. No wonder he wrote to his friend, Mr. Condit:

> It is the most painful thing I ever heard of. I drop the pen in the utmost perplexity and grief.

Who was the author of that sickening outrage? That it was perpetrated by Dr. Griffith's direction is certain; but it is impossible to believe him, sunken as he is in senility, capable of conceiving anything so horrid. It must have been, it was, instigated by others. Of them we can only say:

> They are neither man nor woman,
> They are neither brute nor human—
> They are ghouls!

A brave man will never strike another who is in misfortune. In his utter desolation, in his total downfall, with his high hopes of professional success gone; his ambition in the political world destroyed; his home taken away; his wife in the grave, and dishonor grinning and gibbering over her memory—it was at such a time as this that two or three people, and no more, sought to annihilate his feeble remains from the face of the earth. You heard the lamentations of Captain Johnson over the loss of his reputation. You have heard read his letters to Lamb & Hill, his counsel at Indianapolis. He believed he had been rendered odious at Indianapolis; that no decent house would open its doors to him. He felt like one who had stood on the mountain top, in the sunlight of hope and glory, suddenly hurled into an abyss a thousand feet below, among hissing serpents and crawling reptiles. What change or transition could have been more terrible than this impression that he had fallen from the high estate of his splendid reputation under the calumnious reproaches and vile accusations of his enemies? He was morbid; disease was preying on both mind and body; he overestimated the injury to his reputation. Aspiring with eager ambition for the good opinion of all honorable people, he felt that he had fallen in their estimation never to hope again.

When he wandered forth the last time from Indianapolis and fresh calumnies followed him while he sojourned amongst strangers in Georgia, he felt he was utterly and entirely lost at his old home. He conceived that his traducers had the power to blacken him beyond the recognition of his old friends. In that he was laboring under a delusion. Else why this all-powerful pile of depositions as to character and reputation? It was the morbid exaggeration of a mind partially insane. Everything he heard he magnified. The whisper of the wind was the shriek of the hurricane in his ear. There are inmates in the asylums to whom the chirping of a cricket, or the running of a mouse across the floor, is a startling event. They hear in the one the premonitions of the storm, and in the other they see the lion leaping in his strength. These are the exaggerations of a diseased mind. Captain Johnson exaggerated upon this one subject. You have heard his letters to Lamb, to Hill, to Dooley, to Stanton, and to Condit. Whose eyes have been dry while listening to them? Every heart throbbed, every lip quivered, and every eye moistened as they were read by my gifted colleague. Their one great burden, their one sad refrain, is the incessant wail, "I am lost, lost in the estimation of my friends."

He says, in one of these letters:

> You know that no one has lived more for the good opinion of honorable men than I have. No one has cherished the regard of virtuous people more than I, and now I shall lose them all. My enemies are painting me as the murderer of my wife. What can we do?

He was like one chained to a post, and he suffered more than man ever did, in my reading, to live. Men have died at the stake, in flames. Lattimer and Ridley, when chained to the stake in England for religious opinions, smiled to each other and said:

> We will light a fire this day in England that will never be extinguished.

And so they died, upheld by the joyous consciousness that there was a future for their doctrines and a future for their souls.

It has not been long since, passing through Pennsylvania, there was pointed out to me the old home of Colonel Crawford, who was burned at the stake by the Indians at Lower Sandusky. I have read the horrible details of his cruel death, of his walking steadily around and around the stake to which he was chained, in the midst of the flames, while the merciless savages thrust blazing fagots into his writhing flesh at every step. He was long in dying, and he appealed to his enemy, the infamous Simon Girty, to end his torture by shooting him. His appeal was in vain, and at last he fell upon his face and expired on a bed of live coals. Dreadful as are these details of human pain and dissolution, I can read them with more composure than I can recall here in your hearing the scenes of misery which this defendant experienced during the last six dismal months before he started in August, as if impelled by a higher power than his own, in the direction of Greeneville, the original seat of all his woe. Day after day his shriek of sorrow told of his utter wretchedness. It may be said he ought to have controlled himself. Put yourself in his place! He was sick; he was lonely, bereaved, and perishing away from home. His will power was gone in the presence of his burning and intense emotions. He could not, if he tried, stop thinking on the one subject, where his heart and brain concentrated all their power. He could not stop; his malignant foes would not let him. Goaded to desperation, moody to the confines of madness, he did nothing, and he could do nothing, except look incessantly into the face of his dead wife, and into his home as it once was, but is now no more, and listen to the false, unjust and brutal railings of those who chose the hour of his helplessness in which to thrust their blazing fagots, not into his flesh, but into his soul. But one thing, and only one, upheld him on the shores of time.

> No more shall bloom the thunder-blasted tree,
> Nor the stricken eagle soar.

But by the side of this defendant, riven and blighted as he is, there grows in beauty, grace, and strength the production of all that is noblest and best in father and mother, and for this son and for him alone Captain Johnson has lived. You have heard the evidence. "I would not," he says repeatedly, "live an hour but for my boy; I want to die every day." I want to die every day! I have heard the Christian, in joyous ecstasy, sing:

> I would not live alway, I ask not to stay.

But where in the regions of mental health and sanity was there ever found one sitting among the tombs, as it were, surrounded by the ruins of every hope in life, crying with every tearful sob:

> Fly swift, O spirit of death! I await to welcome thee.

Not an hour would he have staid, but with uplifted hand of self-destruction he would have followed the loved and lost one, had not the glorious child of their sacred love given him pause. He was the link, the only link, and the link of more than gold, that bound his life to the earth, and kept him from joining his wife by the same road she had traveled. We see him moving round and round, like the tortured prisoner at the stake, being burned to death in unhallowed fires, shrieking in his misery. Might all this be simulated? No, no! You remember how often he said, in every form, in the evidence, "If they would only let me alone, I would try to live through this for the sake of my boy." Did they let him alone? It is a most sad and melancholy truth that they did not.

I know not why these calamities came. I am a believer in the providence of God. I believe there is an overruling power directing men and nations. We may not question the Deity; his ways are past finding out; but why unbearable affliction should fall with such merciless force on this man, who has never done you nor me nor any man evil, is a mystery not to be solved on the shores of time. If he has sinned, we do not know wherein. Judge Ingersoll alluded yesterday to Job. Whether history, or a teaching by fable, God gave the man of Uz to be touched and hurt by Satan himself. He had seven thousand sheep, five thousand camels, three thousand she asses, five hundred yoke of oxen and other property in proportion. All was taken from him. His harvests were burned in the fields; his children died. He bore all this, and cried: God's will be done! Then power was given to the arch enemy of mankind to smite his person, only sparing his life. In sackcloth and ashes Job bewailed, in tones that have lived in all languages and through all ages, his overthrow and desolation; but the utmost humiliation of man he was spared. Almighty God did not permit his home to be defiled. He had decreed the death of the adulterer, and the wife of Job was not debauched by some libertine inspired by Satan. She was untouched and unpolluted in order that home could be rebuilt. Home was rebuilt. It never could have been if the wife had been corrupted, defiled, and worse than slain. The wife, the key to the domestic arch, remained pure and strong; and that fact alone enabled every blessing to be restored.

Had Job's home been laid desolate by the impurity of his wife, could he never have had a hope of happiness in the future, perhaps he too would have had emotional insanity and irresistible impulses; possibly he would have cursed God and died. Who knows? I only know that the wife in her purity was left, and, after the test was over, Job had fourteen thousand sheep, ten thousand camels; all his property was restored twofold; children came again, seven sons and three daughters, and he lived one hundred and forty years. The elders, all the people, did him honor; no shame was on his name. He had suffered, but was not disgraced. Anything can be borne but dishonor; anything but to hear our names, and the names of our loved ones, associated with shame and mocked at with scorn. We can follow the pure and honored wife or daughter to the grave, and time, after awhile, with its healing influences, will bring calmness and consolation to our hearts and enable us to control our grief. Death is no calamity, if we die with a good name; but let dishonor once come to follow us over the world like a hissing serpent, and neither in life nor in death is there peace or rest.

Gentlemen, I am now approaching a phase of this case which I have often heard discussed with great ability; I wish I could discuss it myself to-day with more. After a life, not now very short and never inactive, I am deeply impressed that there is far more insanity darkening the minds of men and women in this world than is generally understood or admitted. People stare and wonder, with incredulous looks, when the plea of insanity is raised in court, and sometimes fools are heard to deride and jeer, as if such a thing as insanity did not exist. Let us glance for a moment at statistics. According to the census of 1880, the splendid state of Tennessee had a population of 1,542,359, and her insane numbered 2,404, the ratio being one insane person to seven hundred and twenty-four sane persons throughout the state. You have an insane asylum at Nashville which accommodates about 500 people; I am informed you are finishing another and a larger one at Knoxville; and then you will fall far short of sufficient room. Indiana, with her population of two millions, has more than thirty-five hundred insane, showing an insane man or woman in the midst of every five hundred and sixty inhabitants of the state. We have an asylum at Indianapolis sheltering with its beneficent care about thirteen hundred of these children of misfortune, and we are building three other extensive institutions of a similar kind in different parts of the noble commonwealth. The ratio of the insane to the entire population of the United States is about one to five hundred and sixty-six, or almost identical with Indiana. I mention these instructive facts in order to ask whether insanity is of such rare occurrence that its plea should fall under your suspicion or displeasure. It is around you and on every hand; and I appeal to you, on your consciences, to answer whether, in all your observation, experience, or reading, you ever knew causes of insanity more bitter, more impelling, more infernal than those which have tortured the man you are now trying for his life? And yet men may have said that our plea in this case is merely the lawyer's plea. It is not. I say here, in the fear of my Maker, that I know our plea to be true. I have had that experience among men—

Mr. Robinson. I object, if your honor please, to the course which this argument is taking. I know counsel does not intentionally violate our rules of practice, but one-third of his speech has been in direct violation—

Mr. Voorhees. I have tried cases in many states of this Union, and I was never before arraigned for such an extensive violation of the rules of court. I only wish to know the rules, your honor, and I will obey them.

The Court. The rule will not allow—

Mr. Voorhees. Perhaps my statement is too broad. But have I not a right to believe this evidence? I think I will venture to do so. If I did not, I would take my seat. I repeat, with the permission of the court, that the plea of insanity in this case comes before you not under any bar of adverse opinion, not under any supposition that it is manufactured, or that mental disease is so unusual that you ought not to credit the plea. In the light of human experience in states and in nations, and with this evidence before us, I am warranted in asking, as I did a little while ago, whether in all your lives you ever knew as many and as powerful impelling causes to mental unsoundness as have been shown in this case?

There are one or two features as to the defendant's mental condition upon which I wish to dwell. While these fearful and baneful accusations were being hurled after him day after day, in his letters to Condit, Dooley, Hill, Lamb, Stanton, and others, we discover, by his agonized utterances, the condition of his mind, as well as the physician would know his physical health by holding his finger on his pulse.

The mind has been likened to a stringed instrument, and when in health it gives forth a perfect tune, a strain of harmony on all subjects; but let a string be relaxed or broken, and there will be harsh discord. On one subject there was a broken string in Captain Johnson's mind; the harp of reason was jangled and out of tune. There was one string that gave forth a strange, unnatural, weird, unearthly sound. It was the chord in the instrument which responded to a horrible memory, which threw him on his face, as one dead, at Knoxville. It was the broken chord in the great harmonium of his mind which caused him to cry out to John Condit: "Oh, tell me how it now is! Last night I was almost lost. My God! What is it all for? Mariette, my wife; oh, my precious wife, where are you? For months I have not seen you or heard your voice. Sweet, sweet wife, come back. It must be all a dream; she is not dead; she will return. Oh, where, where is she?" That is his lamentation; it is everywhere in his writings. It is the perpetual refrain of his mourning heart—"Mariette, oh, my precious wife, where are you?" Is this the natural call of a sane mind? Do men in their right minds see unreal visions? Do they read in blood on the window-panes the names of those who have hurt and wounded them? No one ever charged this intense and candid man with feigning anything. He is the least of a sham I ever knew. God help him! I wish things could be at times less awfully real to his earnest, truthful nature. "Oh, I am so heartsick!" What cry is that? The stomach is sick, the lungs are sick, and the other portions of the human frame are sick; but when one of manly spirit exclaims, "Oh, I am so heartsick!" you know the soul is shrouded in gloom, depressed, walking in the shadows of present death and in the horrors of the past.

> Oh, I am so heartsick, so weary! The oblivion of the grave would be a thousand times preferable to this existence of agony and torture.

Is that the voice of one fit for retributive punishment? Again, this man of pallid lip and blazing eye shrieks forth: "My wife appeared to me last night;" not that he *thought* she did, not that she *seemed* to be there; but, "My wife *appeared* to me last night, dressed in a robe of white, with a spot of blood just over her heart. She said: 'Eddie, rely on yourself.'"

Gentlemen, lay not your hands on this man. Beware! God's hand has been heavy enough. Take yours off. He saw sights and beheld visions. The horrors of his persecutions, his bereavements, the death of his wife, haunted him everlastingly. There was not for him a moment's surcease of sorrow. If a drop of water falls incessantly on one spot it will wear away your hard blue limestone; and a great grief, pressing intensely and perpetually on the mind, with nothing to mitigate its tortures, will at last drive the strongest intellect shrieking to the cells of a mad-house. I have been through the greatest benevolent institutions in this country. I know by my own experience and by the evidence in this case that a man may be entirely sane on all subjects but one, just as Dr. Boyd, that rare ornament to his profession here in your midst, has testified. I listened to Dr. Boyd's testimony with more surprise than I have experienced for years in a court of justice. It was a stream of light from the beginning to the end. He should have a place in one of the foremost institutions for the treatment of the insane. He tells you, under the sanction of an oath—and all the great authors sustain him—that a person may think, and talk, and write, and play music, and attend to business, and trade with rationality, and yet, on one subject, be insane, and, when acting on matters pertaining to that one subject, be not responsible. That is the history of the world, and that is the proof in this case. Dr. Boyd has given testimony here that this defendant was rational on all subjects but one; that he would talk on any other subject but this one in a normal tone; but strike that one bruised and always bleeding place in his heart, and the response that came was emotional and beyond the power of his will. He says: "I saw certain names written in blood across my window." This is an insane emotion, distortion, and delusion. "My wife appeared last night," he says, "dressed in white, stained with blood," and, I may say, murdered by Henry, driven to suicide by her seducer. "I saw her," he raves, "and she said, 'Eddie, rely on yourself.'" Thus his mind wandered and dreamed dreams that were not all a dream. When we attempt to analyze the mind of man tortured to insanity by one burning, searing thought, it is most difficult to trace every diseased fiber, every detail of aberration, every involved and unnatural motive, and every indication of unhealthy and illogical evolution. All I ask is that you do not think of the defendant as you do now of yourselves—you, who are healthy, strong, and robust in body and in mind. Think of him as he was when he poured forth his disordered conceptions to Colonel Hunt, and wrote in the following strain to the beloved Condit:

But the principal trouble, of course, is my great mental and nervous depression. My agony is unutterable and inconceivable. I would not like to have you know what a night of horrors last night was. *Every hour I wish myself dead.* Duty to others is the only remaining tie that binds me to life. I must educate my son, and I must repay the debts of gratitude I owe my friends. First of all these is yourself. The obligation is far stronger and far more sacred now that its discharge would be so great a benefit to you. *Yes; I must live. But oh, what a sad, broken, ruined life!* I search my own heart daily to find, if possible, some ground for self-reproach. Of course, my life has been full of minor errors—all lives are; but I want to convince myself of the true state of my own conscience. All my introspection ends always in substantial self-satisfaction. I believe that all my main purposes have been right; that all my chief motives have been good; and that I have been all through life actuated by a sincere desire to do right and do good. Therefore my conscience is clear. If I were called to die to-night, I am sure I should respond without the least fear as to the great hereafter. I feel deeply, and oh! so painfully, that I am a helpless victim of misfortune.

And again, a little later:

MY DEAR OLD FRIEND: I am sorry, indeed, that I wrote you a letter that gave you so much pain, for your suffering on your own account is enough for you to bear. But since the beginning is made you may be relieved by a few additional lines. I wish I had your faith, your charity, your patience, your noble magnanimity. But alas! I have not. Yet, who can wonder that I am less than a perfect man—less than you? Have you ever known a young man to start in life with brighter prospects, higher motives, or better purposes than I possessed? Have you ever witnessed such a pitiless succession of calamities, ending in so complete and hopeless a shipwreck of life? Have you ever known a life, in itself so high and serene, rendered by outward influences so troubled, so turbulent, so tragic? I recall so often the piteous wail in one of poor Mariette's letters: "Oh, Eddie, what is it all for? Why has it been permitted?" God knows, poor lost wife; I can not tell. St. Pierre says: "There are in life such terrible, such unmerited evils that even the hope of the wisest is sometimes shaken." Is it, then, to be wondered at that the entire nature of one like me, who was never wise, should be wholly subverted by calamities like mine? Faith is dead. Hope is extinct. Ambition is a forgotten dream. My home is a paradise lost. *Ashes! Ashes! Ashes!* But *courage* remains, and *revenge,* like a consuming thirst, burns and rages throughout my being. I have strange illusions. My bed often rises and falls, as if I were riding waves higher than hill-tops. I frequently clutch my chair to save myself from falling when the floor seems giving way. I fall sometimes twenty or fifty feet perpendicularly down with a force that is terrific.

In this condition of mind he started from North Georgia. You and I have been with him, in this evidence, through the dismal hours he spent with Colonel Hunt, and in writing on the one corroding, cankering theme to others; we have listened to his long talks, in which, with the simplicity of a sobbing child, he said he did not know but these things would drive him insane; we have heard this true and conscientious man, Colonel Hunt, say he was absolutely insane on the subject of his wife's ruin and death. Colonel Hunt strains nothing in testifying; he does not herd with C. H. Thomas; he would not swear a lie. Captain Johnson went from North

Georgia first to Tate Springs, and there Dr. McAllister, a competent and an eminent physician, was called to attend him. You have already heard his deposition, and heard it commented on by my learned associate with infinitely more eloquence and power than I possess. I will ask you, however, to allow me to submit some portions of this cogent and conclusive testimony:

> He was suffering from indigestion, and his color and appearance indicated a bilious condition.
> But his principal trouble, as I soon perceived, was mental and nervous. His nervous system was seriously disordered and he was in great mental distress. I did not inquire into the cause of this condition, but was convinced that he was suffering from some great grief or other trouble, which was exerting a powerful influence over his mental and nervous condition. He was in a state of most serious mental and nervous depression. To this cause I ascribe, in large degree, his mere physical derangement.
> Q. 15. What, if anything, of unusual or peculiar character, did you observe in his conduct?
> A. One thing was that he was always alone. He had no associates. The first time I saw him he asked me not to introduce him to any one as he wanted no acquaintances.
> Though feeble in strength, he seemed to seek relief from his nervous agitation and restlessness in walking. He moved slowly, but walked about the grounds a great deal. He often stopped to rest, and would sit or lie down on the benches or the grass. All the time he seemed abstracted, gloomy, and sad. Sometimes when thus alone he would for a time seem to be in deep thought; then suddenly he would smile or weep. I saw him several times with the tears streaming down his face. His manner generally indicated deep abstraction. He seemed absorbed in gloomy thought, and totally unconscious of his surroundings.
> Q. 16. What did this conduct suggest to your mind as to his mental state?
> A. Overwhelming grief or sadness and deep mental disturbance.
> Q. 18. What were usually the subjects of your conversations?
> A. So far as I could control them they generally related to commonplace topics; for our method I used was to divert his thoughts, as much as possible, from the secret trouble, whatever it was, that I saw was preying so terribly upon his mind. But he would frequently break away and commence talking about his son, who seemed to occupy a large space in his mind, and who, in some mysterious way, seemed to be closely connected with the sources of his mental trouble.
> Q. 19. What did he say on that subject?
> A. He described his son as a very beautiful boy, and spoke of his great courage and fortitude and his devotion to him. I remember expressions of this kind: "He has stood by me through everything, and has all the time been the braver, stronger, better man of the two. I could not have survived what I have without his aid. He walks the streets with his arm around me. He is absolutely devoted to me, and is now ready at the shortest notice to fly to his papa." He frequently spoke of him as his brave, beautiful, noble boy, and he talked of him a great deal.
> Q. 20. If you can recall any other of his conversations, please state as fully as you can what was said.
> A. One I remember very distinctly. He came into my office and was talking to me about mesmerism. The same evening he had created great consternation among the guests of the hotel by rushing excitedly into the parlor and interfering with some exhibitions of mesmeric power which were being given by a gentleman there; and that was the occasion of his speaking of the subject to me. He talked with great excitement. He said he knew by terrible experience

the danger of that mysterious power of mesmerism. He took from his pocket a picture and handed it to me. It was the portrait of a beautiful lady. While I was looking at it his breathing became heavy, and when I looked at him he was weeping, and the tears were streaming from his eyes. He said: " There was one of the loveliest and purest beings that ever lived. She is dead. She was the victim of a scoundrel who overcame her by mesmerism."

Q. 21. While in conversation generally what was his manner?

A. He impressed me as a gentleman of high culture and thorough good breeding. His manner was always gentlemanly, but always sad and never cheerful. In talking of commonplace matters he was affable and agreeable. But this was never long at a time. Very soon he would suddenly become dejected; his whole expression would change to sadness; and then he would break off and become silent, or leave, or else abruptly change the subject. While talking about his son he always exhibited much emotion, and frequently cried, and talked in a way that seemed to indicate that he regarded the boy as the innocent victim of some great misfortune. At the time when he showed me the picture, his manner was of the greatest mental anguish. I think I never witnessed a more painful exhibition of mental distress.

Q. 22. What did his manner suggest to your mind as to his mental condition?

A. That his nervous system was completely disordered, and his mind thoroughly morbid on the one subject of his troubles.

Q. 23. Did he tell you who the lady was whose picture he showed you?

A. He did not.

Q. 24. What, if anything, did he ever say to you about his wife?

A. Nothing directly; but I inferred that the lady whose picture he showed me had been his wife and was the mother of his boy. And this was the only clew I had to his trouble. And this was confirmed by subsequent developments.

Q. 25. From what you observed and knew of his condition, what is your opinion as to whether he was sane or insane?

A. On the one subject of his grief or trouble *he was undoubtedly insane. He was governed entirely by his emotions, and his emotions were all morbid and unnatural. My judgment, therefore, is that he was the victim of emotional insanity.*

Behold that scene, when, for mere amusement, mesmeric influences were invoked. He was alone, amongst strangers, with not a single acquaintance, save his physician of two or three days' standing. A few young persons had gathered in the parlor, and, in a most harmless, social way, were going through the forms of mesmerism, when, with a step and look of fury, the defendant strode in and broke up the performance and the gathering. Immediately afterward his physician found him in a paroxysm of agony and excitement, and drawing from his pocket the picture of a beautiful woman, with tears streaming down his face he exclaimed: " This was once as good a woman as ever lived, a virtuous wife and mother, and she was ruined by that accursed craft called mesmerism." He said he would not allow it to be practiced in his presence. Was that a sane act? And then the testimony shows that he wandered over the grounds alone, weeping, and in great sorrow. As Judge Ingersoll said yesterday, a sane man may be overcome by sudden grief; but you do not see a man in his right mind walking about and indulging in silent, solitary paroxysms of tears in the grounds of a public resort? Dr. McAllister makes your duty clear and easy by testifying that Captain Johnson at that time was undoubtedly insane. This was in the first week of August, 1884; and from there, as if under a spell, he moved on to Galbraith Springs. He seemed to have to move on. Perhaps he heard a voice we can not hear which said he could not stay; perhaps he saw a hand we do not see which beckoned him away; perhaps he followed a phantom of the mind—such things have been.

At Galbraith Springs the testimony of Dr. Leighton and his wife shows that he was a frenzied man. Their united voices are those of a Christian minister of forty-four years' standing and of his wife.

But it is said that as he left Galbraith Springs and came in the direction of Greeneville he declared he had a mission in East Tennessee. I care not for that. Perhaps he said it. How would it differ from the declaration we all know he did make, that he considered himself an instrument in the hands of God for the punishment of the malefactor who had ruined his home and murdered his wife? The best books on insanity lay it down that one of the most frequent forms of mental alienation is for one to conceive himself chosen by divine authority to execute some great purpose. Suppose he did say he had a mission. It was only expressing the idea in another form that he was in the hands of God for a purpose. Be it so. I am not talking now of a sane man, but of a man proven by medical testimony to have been insane on one subject, at every step, for more than four months before the commission of the homicide, in Georgia, at Tate Springs, at Galbraith Springs, and here.

And who are they on whom we rely for this proof? Who is Dr. Boyd, that his testimony is to be overthrown by non-professional men who have been called? He is a hard student, a faithful, conscientious man, who surprised me with the clearness of his ideas and his language and the extent of his learning, as he doubtless did you; a man whose acquaintance I have not made, except in a passing introduction, but one who would adorn any position connected with the subject of mental disease. Who is he, that he should be cross-examined, and questioned and caviled with, when he renders his impartial opinion? Dr. Boyd has been Captain Johnson's physician ever since the latter came to East Tennessee. He said in substance and effect, that Captain Johnson was insane on one point; that his will had lost its power over his emotions on one subject; that he was irresponsible in his relations to Major Henry, the seducer and murderer of his wife, because he sincerely, intensely, and without any doubt or hesitation at all, believed it his first duty, in the sight of God and man, to slay the man who had wantonly inflicted such ruin and misery on him and on everything he prized and loved.

It is not intellectual insanity of which I am speaking; nor do I place this defense at all upon that ground. Temporary emotional insanity upon one given subject is our defense, and is as well recognized by the highest authorities as any other form of human infirmity. I might cite many names of the highest standing in support of this position. It was recognized by Chief Justice Shaw of the supreme court of Massachusetts as early as the year 1844, in the case of the Commonwealth against Rodgers; and it was again presented, in his charge to the jury, by Chief Justice Gibson, of the supreme court of Pennsylvania, then holding an oyer and terminer in Philadelphia, in 1846. He there speaks of—

> An unseen ligament pressing on the mind, drawing it to consequences *which it sees but can not avoid*, and placing it under a coercion which, while its results are *clearly perceived*, is incapable of resistance.

Dr. Ray, in his celebrated Medical Jurisprudence, quoting Hoffbauer with approval, says:

> It is clear that mania may exist uncomplicated with mental delusion; it is, in fact, only a kind of moral exaltation, a state in which the reason has lost its empire over the passions and the actions by which they are manifested to such a degree that the individual can neither repress the former nor abstain from the latter. It does not follow that he may not be in possession of his senses, and even his usual intelligence, since, in order to resist the impulses of the passions, it is not sufficient that the reason should impart its counsels; we must have the necessary power to obey them.

Dr. William A. Hammond, an eminent living author on this subject, says:

The knowledge of right and wrong is not a test of the mental condition of an individual except in a very limited degree. * * * A person manifestly insane will reason logically in regard to conduct which he knows has been contrary to law and at variance with the principles instilled into him from childhood, but which he was not able to prevent or control. * * * The emotions are at all times difficult to control; but they may acquire such undue prominence as to dominate over the intellect and the will, and assume entire mastery of the actions in one or more respects. * * * The emotions are also subject to insane exaggeration through the influence of motives which act slowly, but with constantly increasing force. * * * The brain may be so disordered that insanity is manifested *only* as regards the will. * * * There is a form of insanity which in its culminating act is extremely temporary in its character, and which in all its manifestations, from beginning to end, is of that duration. This species of mental aberration is well known to all physicians and medical jurists who have studied the subject of insanity.

Where now is the weight of evidence on the question of emotional and partial insanity in this case? We do not have to convince you that Captain Johnson was insane; we do not have to show a general impairment of his intellect. He may have been as clear, acute, analytical, and exhaustive in his mental processes as ever in his life; but if it appears there was an uncertainty as to his mental soundness on the subject of his domestic misfortunes and the author of them, then you will stay your judgment and tell him to go free. If you doubt whether the defendant was sane, you doubt whether a guilty act has been committed—nobody but a sane and responsible person can commit crime—if you doubt whether Captain Johnson was sane, you doubt whether the crime named in this indictment ever took place, and you must acquit.

The supreme court of Tennessee has decided that if there is any uncertainty in your minds whether the defendant was sane on that subject at the time of the homicide, it is the same to you, in the discharge of your duty, as if it was uncertain whether Major Henry was killed. If there is a doubt as to sanity, the benefit of that doubt must go to the prisoner, and he is to be acquitted. But have we put in evidence enough to raise this doubt? We have followed this unhappy man through all his life, as it lies open now before you, until he came again to this, to him, most fatal and unhappy town, on the last day of last August. We have seen him at Knoxville, at Indianapolis, at New Orleans, in North Georgia; we have seen him at the different springs—at Tate and at Galbraith; and, finally, we see him here. Here his family physician and his friend, Dr. Boyd, took him in charge, and he tells you, from his learning, his experience, and his knowledge of this defendant, that he was emotionally insane; that his emotions, in connection with the tragic fate of his wife, the brutality of her destroyer, and the unparalleled, unprovoked, and seemingly diabolical persecutions he had experienced from Governor Porter and Major Gordon, had unbalanced his reasoning faculties, and left him a helpless prey to ungovernable impulses. Dr. Boyd spoke of the defendant's eager, morbid, and uncontrollable desire for revenge, and I observed the prosecution make a note. Very well; those maddened by the desecration of home most thirst for revenge. This is true of the inmates of asylums, placed there by the disgrace, shame, and death of their best beloved, as well as of those who walk the streets and are rational on a hundred subjects, while irresponsible and dangerous on one. A man may be emotionally insane on the subject of religion. He may also be insane on all the other emotions; that, as I understand it, is Dr. Boyd's position, so clearly laid before you.

The defendant was here three weeks, from the last of August to the 23d of September, before the homicide, and every hour under the observation of Dr. Boyd, Dr. Taylor and others. The evidence shows he came here a wreck, bleeding at the lungs and staggering from physical weakness, while his mind was lurid and inflamed. The ugly and hateful memory of his former stay and experience in Greeneville rose up to greet and clutch him and to suck his life away, like the octopus, the devil-fish first described to the world by Victor Hugo. He had learned that Major Henry was keeping and carrying about with him a letter from his dead wife and a portrait of his beloved son. Were his relations to Mrs. Johnson, and her consequent death, a pleasant subject for the seducer to dwell upon; did he pass his nights in looking at that letter and at the face of this boy? Was the man under the influence of a spell, a species of madness, on this subject? Would not any man, except one with a mind imbruted with passion, have burned every scrap of paper and destroyed every memento that reminded him of this dismal and guilty chapter of his life, and then slunk away from these pure hills and scenes, never to have shown his face again? But no; and when the defendant heard he was defiling her memory by carrying that letter, and also outraging his son by keeping his picture as a memento of his mother's ruin and death, the effect on his mind, as described here, was something never to be forgotten. As Major Pettibone expressed it, his mind flamed up. Yes! It is in proof from various sources that he saw flames of fire at times, burning down forests and devastating cities. He saw the earth open and felt himself falling into its depths, and then at other times he seemed to be rocked and tempest-tossed on the bosom of the sea. All these things he had often suffered; and when, therefore, he dwelt upon the thought that the letter and the picture were treasured up in the possession of the man who had first destroyed his wife's soul and then had driven her to kill the body, it is no wonder he saw flashes of fire, bright and red as blood.

In the spirit of kindness, and aiming to be peace-makers, Major Pettibone and Mr. McWilliams undertook to get them and return them to the defendant. On Sunday, two days preceding the death of Major Henry, they were returned. You will never forget the effect upon him, the agonizing, burning grief and pain, as he looked that letter over; and then that baleful, deadly look of murderous insanity gleaming from his eyes when McWilliams told him, "Why Henry says your wife seduced him; that he did not seduce her." McWilliams was a man of deadly dangers in these mountains during the war, and has iron nerves in the face of peril; but he says when that look came into Johnson's face he watched him. When asked on the witness stand, "Why did you watch him?" he answered: "I watched him closely on my own account; I did not know what he might do. I never want to look into a face like that again." That was his condition Sunday afternoon. To many millions that day was one of blessed peace and rest; to him it was one of inexpressible torment. The last drop of degradation had been poured into his cup, and he had drained it.

The juggling fiend who had wrecked his home and life now leered in his face and mocked him with the horrible taunt: "The woman tempted me, and I did eat"—"she seduced me; I did not seduce her." With these false and accursed words scorching brain and heart, the sun went down on him, the most miserable being in all the broad confines of the state of Tennessee. He went to his room, but not to sleep or repose. An accomplished and intelligent lady occupied a room adjoining. We all listened to the clear and graphic testimony of Miss Virginia Davis. She says he walked the floor of his room all night; that it was daylight Monday morning before he was still; that he was alone, but talked incessantly to himself, and often called some one, whose name the witness could not distinguish. This was less than thirty-six hours from his final and fatal meeting with Henry at the furnace. All night he walked: his wounds had been made to gape and bleed afresh. A blow with an iron hammer on flesh already bruised, inflamed, and swollen will cause shrieks of pain and new streams of blood; but such an infliction would be merciful compared to that which fell upon the bleeding, bruised heart of this defendant when he heard Henry's last brutal calumny, making his wife utterly shameless, proclaiming her a prostitute, a free, forward harlot; that she had come to this community from Indianapolis, where she stood a good woman with the best, and had turned to an openly soliciting harlot, plying her vocation, luring men to her wanton embrace. This was more than a sane man could have borne; but, falling upon the defendant in his condition, do you wonder he walked all night and talked to himself, calling somebody all the time? Who do you think he was calling? Doubtless, his cry was the same as it was to Condit—"My God! What is it all for? Mariette, my wife! Where is my precious wife? Oh, where are you?" Yes; he was calling somebody. "Where are you, Mariette? Where are you? I have not seen you for months nor heard your voice. Come back, sweet wife; come back. It must all be a dream. She is not dead. She will return. Come back. Oh, where, where is she?"

Do you recall the painful description of a similar occasion by Colonel Hunt? It was on the fearful night at Cleveland, when they were on their way to Tate Springs. Let me read it to you again:

> He begged me to do something for him. I got him into his own bed and held him there. I smoothed his temples and held his wrists, and tried every way I could to quiet him. He kept up his wild incoherent talk a long time, and until

his strength was gone. After an hour or so I got him quieted down and he went to sleep. But it was a restless, troubled sleep, and for a long time he lay tossing and grinding his teeth, and now and then muttering oaths, and at times crying and calling for his wife. It seems to me that nearly all night he kept, at intervals, calling his wife, as if he expected her to answer, and crying and wailing because there was no response.

Oh, no! In the light of that testimony there can be no doubt who it was he was calling when heard by Miss Davis. Poor sufferer! Uncle Tom was not there on that occasion to soothe and quiet him. He was alone in his terrible agony.

All that long Sunday night he called and paced the floor. His wretched heart one melancholy burden bore, and it was always the same. Miss Davis heard him hour after hour totter wearily along, talking and calling, calling the loved, the lost, the beautiful dead. Who else did he ever call? Who else ever heard him and came back to him? She came once, he says. He saw her once, and his cry is now, and ever will be: "Come back again, my poor, lost wife!" Thus he spent the last night in Greeneville while this man, Henry, lived to curse the earth. The next day he seemed bewildered, and, at times, frantic, as has been described by Harrell and others; at last evening came again, and with it the strangest, most unnatural scene of all. You say there was a plan that night, and method. Yes. I know a reported case where a lunatic, a patient in an asylum, incensed at his keeper, lay in wait for him months with a gun and finally shot him dead. There was method and planning; but, at the same time, he was insane and an inmate of a hospital for the cure of mental diseases. But were Captain Johnson's plans that night and the next morning the indications of a healthy mind in its normal condition? I will not pause to comment on the little one-horse wagon without springs in which a man in his condition jolted over these rough mountain roads in midnight darkness, driven by a negro he never knew before, and who knew not where he was driving or the object of the mysterious expedition. Perhaps it will be urged that these were preparations for assassination. But he did not assassinate Major Henry when he could have done so. When he was in the barn Tuesday morning, what had he to do but to remain there until Henry came out on the steps of the store and then shoot him down? If he had gone there with a sane idea of assassination it would have happened in that way. But he reached the vicinity of the furnace some time in the night. In the morning he went into the barn, and waited there until 10 o'clock. Then he crossed the road in full view of the store, walked slowly to the door, spoke to the hunch-backed boy, Lamb, and entered the store. From that moment he was exposed to instant death. The office in which Major Henry sat was divided from the main store-room by a partition, the lower portion, perhaps three feet in height, being of wood, and all above was composed of common panes of thin window glass. Captain Johnson walked a distance of twelve feet by the side of this thin glass partition while Henry was on the other side, and looking at him, with his pistol on his person. The defendant exposed himself as absolutely as if he had met Henry in the road and told him to get ready, that he would give him a chance. He did give him his chance by walking into that store as he did. A braver deed was never performed. The moment he was inside Henry saw him; and yet he walked the whole of that distance in order to get to the door where he could turn, look him in the eyes, and fire. The defendant could have fired through that glass; he could have shot Henry the moment he entered the door; but he would not. There was no thought of assassination in his suffering mind. When he fired they were standing face to face. Henry died with his pistol half drawn from his pocket. It was far more like a duel than an assassination.

Why should the prosecuting attorney complain that "Johnson gave Henry no chance?" He gave him an equal chance with himself. But in point of justice and right, what chance for his life did Major Henry merit at the hands of this defendant? Did he give Johnson any chance when toiling day and night over his pension books and over soldiers' claims here in East Tennessee? Did this old, hoary scoundrel give Captain Johnson any chance, when, in pursuit of his wife, he lay about the hotel, hour after hour, persistently, day and night, whether Johnson was in town or out, and, when out of town, in his room all the time? Did he give him any chance then to defend honor, home, peace, purity, love, and hope, and all the other domestic blessings, each one of which is a thousandfold dearer than life itself. Will you tell me what chance was due by merit to Henry? None at all. Johnson gave him far more than was his due. The attorney-general said, to use his own language, that "Johnson followed up Henry." Yes, and Henry followed up Mrs. Johnson, and drove her to shame, horror, and death. It is true, and it could not be otherwise, that the bereaved husband followed up the adulterer; but he gave him an equal chance to fight for his life at the last hour. Henry professed to be the defendant's friend, his bosom friend, and wrote him touching letters when he was turning his home into a hell upon earth. He followed his friend's wife like a sleuth-hound; he followed her to her undefiled home at Indianapolis. Not content with his work of destruction here, he thought to resume his illicit love and beastly passion in Captain Johnson's bed, in his own home. That was the mission of the scoundrel at Indianapolis. He sought to see her at the hotel, as a preliminary step, but in his friend's house he designed to resume his lecherous conduct of Greeneville. When the counsel for the state say that Captain Johnson followed Henry, I say he did right. Let me, in return, ask: Why did Henry follow his friend's wife? Why did he desolate his home? Why did he bring himself under the eternal and unrepealable condemnation of Almighty God as an adulterer? Why did he become a convicted felon, sentenced to death by the written law of Jehovah? Why did he make it right for Captain Johnson to follow and kill him? It was all with himself. He might have left a happy home unsullied, and been alive to-day, if he had obeyed the laws of God and man. But he did not. He went on, and died as the fool dieth; and by your verdict you will say that the man who follows your wife shall not complain if you turn and follow him. What license has a man to follow our loved ones and invade our homes? If he is punished with death, shall his voice come back from the grave whining in the courts because he has not been permitted to remain and pollute other households? As far as my voice can extend, I declare, supported as I am by the word of God and by the laws of all civilized lands, that the seducer who falls has nobody to blame but himself. He takes his life in his hands; and if he plays a losing game, good morals and pure society win by his death.

On Monday night, just before starting on his strange and fatal journey, the defendant wrote his bosom friend Condit this touching adieu:

GREENEVILLE, Sept. 22, '84.

MY DEAR FRIEND: It is 11 o'clock at night. I am just starting to the mountains, bleeding at the lungs, and weary, weary of life. I may never again grasp your kind, friendly hand. There is danger among the gorges where the wild beast hides. The last line I write is to you. God avenge my wrongs! Farewell, my dearest friend, farewell! E. T. JOHNSON.

Gentlemen, I have sometimes thought, when this thin, pale, wan, ghost-like apparition left Greeneville in the direction of the Furnace that Monday night he was the somnambulist of a horrid dream. That dream was of a once happy home, now desolate and black, as if the fires of hell had scorched it. That dream was of a once happy wife, radiant with beauty, loving, smiling in her welcome home, now dead in her dishonored grave. Perchance it was the dream as he last saw her, robed in white, with a bloodspot on her breast, saying to him, "Eddie, rely upon yourself." Again it changed, and it was the dream of one who had taken a fiend to his fireside, had introduced him to his wife as a gentleman, who turned to a serpent and stung him in the heart, and who still lived to hiss and mock at him: "The woman tempted me." It has seemed to me that all these things and more were in his dream that night, as he jolted along, lying prostrate upon the straw, in the negro's little old board wagon, coughing and bleeding at the lungs, a prey to physical and to mental misery. The night before he had walked and groaned, and cried, and called; and all this night he jolted on the road in the darkness, and at times talked like a man in his sleep, no more responsible for what he was doing, or was going to do, than the mariner for the course of his ship with rudder broken, compass gone, the north star blotted out, and an irresistible storm walking the waters of the great deep.

I make this statement in no vein of fancy, but supported by the proof. Shall I array this testimony before you? Who are they who say the defendant's mind was broken down on the one subject of his domestic ruin? Shall we sum them up? At Indianapolis lives a gentleman by the name of Dooley, an experienced newspaper man and an able editorial writer. On this point he says:

He was under a great mental strain.

Mr. Stanton's testimony I will recall to you:

He was not capable of forming a rational judgment on any subject connected with his wife's dishonor and death.

John D. Condit, the best beloved, perhaps, of all, devoted to Captain Johnson, having loaned him thousands upon thousands of dollars, and indorsed for him for many thousands more, when asked,

From your knowledge of him, and from the letters and card made a part of this deposition, what, in your opinion, was the defendant's mental condition in the latter part of September, 1884?

Answered:

He was undoubtedly insane.

The deposition of Colonel Thomas Hunt has been read to you. He says:

On the subject of his great loss, owing to his abuse and ill-treatment by enemies, and ill-health, I think he was morbidly insane.

This is sworn evidence, upon which you are to try this case. You will remember that I have read the names of a large number of witnesses who have sworn to his mental condition, and there is something in the number when they are respectable. Now, these gentlemen whose names I have read have every one sworn that he was in a condition of irresponsibility. Nearly all use the word "insane"; one or two use the word "frenzy"; but all state that he was beyond the control of his will. Hon. A. H. Pettibone, of Greeneville, while not saying in words that he was insane, stated that his excitement was terrible and his emotions beyond his own control; that he was beside himself. Miss Virginia Davis, who testified as to the walking scene of that dismal night, discloses a condition no one can misunderstand. Dr. M. B. Taylor, Dr. J. R. Boyd, Dr. M. M. Alexander, Dr. McAllister—there are, in fact, thirteen persons, of respectability and high intelligence, four of them practicing physicians of eminence, and nine others who knew the defendant well, all testifying that he was insane on one point at the time of the homicide. All we have to do is to raise a doubt in your minds whether he was sane on that point and at that time or not. Are you going to say, or is anybody going to ask you to say, with these thirteen men, four of them leading physicians, swearing to his insanity at that time on the subject of his overwhelming grief, that we have raised no doubt in your minds that he was an entirely sane man? Are you going to say that he was not insane, because Mr. Starnes and Mr. Snapp, and perhaps two or three others, all good men, no doubt, but almost total strangers to the defendant, and without the slightest pretentions to educated knowledge on this subject, say they saw nothing unnatural in his conduct immediately after the homicide except, perhaps, that he repeatedly kissed his gun? I will not discuss such testimony as a contradiction to such proof as we have made. People in a normal condition do not kiss cold steel nor sticks nor stones. In his distorted emotions he invested that gun with a living power and a sentient being for which he was grateful. These few unlearned witnesses for the prosecution, called in rebuttal, think but little of such a startling paroxysm as the highest manifestation of human love bestowed on an inanimate object, and pronounce the defendant an exceedingly cool man just after he had avenged his home and fulfilled the law of God. He may possibly have been. If so, however, it was because he believed he was upheld by a higher power than earth affords. But, after all, this is a practical question; and whom will you accept as competent to guide you to a correct verdict on the subject of mental disease? You must find beyond a reasonable doubt that the defendant was without mental disease and under self-control as to Major Henry, or you must acquit him. If we have put in enough proof to raise a doubt in your minds whether he was sane or not, not whether he could distinguish between right and wrong, but whether he could control himself and his emotions with reference to the deceased; whether he thought he was an instrument in the hands of God for punishment—if we have raised a doubt in your minds on these points, he is entitled to an acquittal, and the court will so instruct you.

Gentlemen, when you render your verdict, as you soon will, it will ring joyously through the world. I have not a doubt what it will be. For the last two hundred years, since the dissolute and debauched reign of Charles the Second of England, no man free born and invested with all the rights of citizenship has ever been punished in an English-speaking nation for slaying, in good faith, the seducer of his wife, daughter, or sister. After the Restoration, in 1660, and during the reign which followed, it is a matter of history that female virtue was a mockery and a jest. The wife, the sister, the daughter were open to the approach and solicitation of the adulterer and the seducer. A carnival of immorality, a banquet of lust succeeded, during which the injured husband was the sport of sarcasm, the jest of the clown, while the successful seducer and the lady of licentious pleasure constituted the hero and the heroine of public and private life, of the parlor, the ball-room, and the stage. The courts followed their king and the fashion he made for the times. If a manly husband slew a privileged and presumptuous scoundrel for dishonoring the bed made sacred by marriage vows he was punished. But since that degraded, bawdy reign, both in England and in America, the husband who fights an honest battle for the purity of home has been sheltered in safety, not only by the common law of England, as molded by custom, but by the common law of mankind, as written in the verdicts of juries, and derived from the inspiration of the Most High. Home is of divine sanction and origin, and he who kills the destroyer of a home has an especial protection, both human and divine. There is not a verdict of an American jury, in our one hundred years as an organized people, wherein or whereby a husband who, in good faith, slew the man who had defiled his wife, has been punished. The father who slays the seducer of his daughter has the same protection. The brother who kills the seducer of his sister can never be punished. The voice that comes down from the ancient days of Israel is ringing now just as freshly over the world as when Jacob rebuked his hotheaded sons, Simeon and Levi, for slaying the abductor and seducer of their sister, Dinah. Jacob was old, and in his fear he said: "Ye have troubled me, to make me stink among the inhabitants of the land, among the Canaanites and the Perizzites;

and I, being few in number, they shall gather themselves together against me and slay me; and I shall be destroyed, I and my house." Nothwithstanding, however, the alarming picture he drew before his sons, fresh and bloody from the slaughter of the seducer of their sister, they answered, doubtless with their hands on their swords: "Should he deal with our sister as with a harlot?" Then, as if God was pleased with what had happened, Jacob journeyed from that country in safety to another, and the fear of God fell on all his warlike enemies; not one lifted his finger against him or his. The sons of Jacob smote the adulterer, the seducer of their sister and the daughter of their aged father, and then went in safety, God's power and influence falling upon the surrounding troops, all ready for assault, and holding them while Israel went their way. "Shall he deal with our sister as with a harlot?" How just and powerful comes that expression! It has survived the chasm of the ages, and stirs your hearts this moment as it did the hearts of men in the remote and illimitable past. It embodies an eternal truth, that the home shall be pure and protected; it contains the primary and vital element of civilization; it was the key-note utterance in behalf of human happiness, elevation, culture, refinement, and Christian purification. It was this same old cry, with the antiquity and authority of God upon it, on which Captain Johnson spoke and acted. The one burning, throbbing, incessant, unappeasable cry of his heart was, " Shall he treat my wife in life and in death as a harlot?" I have known the father to bathe the upturned face of his daughter, still in death, with his tears, plant evergreens over her grave, and then call her betrayer and murderer to deadly account with the stern and awful question: "Shall he deal with my daughter as with a harlot?" This question comes down from the days when Jehovah dwelt face to face with his people; when he declared the adulterer should die; that the sentence was eternal, and there was no reversal. The blood-stained earth, from the plains of Judea, where Jacob fed his cattle, down to the county of Greene, in East Tennessee, all speaks the same voice; and God is here, the same yesterday, to-day, and forever.

You can but render one of two verdicts in this case. If

Captain Johnson is guilty of anything, he is guilty of murder in the first degree, and should suffer death. If you should reach that conclusion, I pray you, when you go home, tell your wives and children, as they cluster around you in love and happiness and ask you all about the great trial, what was said and what was done; what the truth was, and what it was all about—tell them this defendant was feeble and sick, hardly able to appear in court, and could not hear much of what was said if he was here; that his wife, whom he loved with tender, deep devotion, had been ruined and defiled by his pretended friend; his whole life had been laid waste, his idolized son put to shame; and in all this he was without fault, and had done no unmanly thing; yet you have decided he shall die on the gibbet. Tell them all, and they will be filled with wonder and horror at such a verdict.

But I turn away from such a hideous thought and picture. There is no such fate in store in your minds and hearts for this manly man, this kind husband, this loving father, this good citizen, with a life record free from stain or blemish. Soon you will perform a far different duty. You will not render this fair-faced boy fatherless as well as motherless. In one of his letters to his wife the defendant said: "I can not forget that you are the mother of a hero and an angel." One boy on earth and one in heaven. The hero is here in court looking on with rigid lines in his young face, sustaining his feeble father as he has from the beginning, and waiting to lead him forth once more to liberty and to a life, perhaps, beyond the region or the reach of the whips and scorns by which he has been so cruelly scourged. How often a father pleads for a son. The scene is here reversed; the son of only sixteen pleads for his father of only forty-three. They are both young, and they are all the world to each other. By your verdict they will be reunited and walk the world together.

My task is done. I drop this sorrowful theme, knowing by the universal law of the human heart that there is light just ahead. With my earnest thanks for your interest and attention, I surrender this great issue of life or death into your hands. May he who marks the sparrow's fall have you in his keeping, and direct all your thoughts aright.

DEFENSE OF HARRY CRAWFORD BLACK

On the morning of October 17, 1870, Harry Crawford Black killed Col. W. W. McKaig, Jr., on Baltimore street, the principal thoroughfare of the city of Cumberland, Maryland, for the betrayal of his sister. For such killing he was indicted at the October term of the circuit court of the sixth judicial circuit of Maryland.

On April 11, 1871, the trial began before the Honorable W. P. Maulsby, chief justice, and the Honorables John A. Lynch and J. Veirs Bowie, associate justices.

The prosecution was conducted by Milton Whitney, Esq., of Baltimore, Isaac D. Jones, attorney-general of Maryland, and Francis Brengle, Esq., state's attorney of Frederick county. The defense was maintained by Mr. Voorhees, and by the following Maryland lawyers: A. K. Syster, Esq., of Hagerstown, Fred. J. Nelson, Esq., of Frederick, and Lloyd Lowndes and William M. Price, Esq's, of Cumberland.

The following jurors were sworn to try the cause: William M. Feaga, Joseph W. Etzler, Ephraim Stoner, George W. Foreman, Henry T. Deaver, Robert Lease, Pottinger Dorsey, Benjamin P. Crampton, Jonathan Biser, George H. Fox, Michael Zimmerman, and Daniel T. Whip.

Mr. Voorhees, on April 21, spoke three hours and thirty minutes in making the closing argument for the defense, and was followed by Milton Whitney, Esq., who occupied two hours in making the closing argument for the state.

The case was given to the jury a few minutes before 3 o'clock, and at eight minutes after 4 o'clock a verdict of "not guilty" was returned into court.

Gentlemen of the Jury:

WE have now reached that point where it becomes my duty to address you. In doing so, I have but one thought and but one purpose. I believe, with fixed and solemn convictions, in the innocence of the young prisoner who is here by my side, and I shall try, while I stand before you, to make manifest the grounds of my belief, and, to the utmost extent of my humble powers, to obtain for them the consent of your minds.

Allusion has been made to my position as counsel here. It is true that I live in a distant state, but I can not feel that I am a stranger to you. We are allied to each other by many ties. We are husbands, fathers, and brothers. We have wives, sisters, and daughters. These vital and precious domestic relations form all mankind into a universal holy alliance. By them you and I are acquainted. We understand each other by their promptings. Let us come close to each other in this discussion. I can have no purposes that ought not to be yours. As a citizen of this great country, desirous of the welfare of the people, desirous of the supremacy of the laws, I can not invoke any results that you ought not also to desire. We are all wedded to the public good. We do not want to destroy the peace and good order of human society. None of us are interested in such a baleful issue. Good or evil to you and yours is the same to me and mine. A blow at your peace and homes is a blow at all the homes in the land, and an assault upon the humblest family circle puts in peril everything that we all hold dear. We meet, therefore, upon a common level, and in a plain and simple manner I expect to speak to you in this spirit.

There is one consolation that I have in rising to address you that presents itself to my mind at once. I have stood before juries quite often, but never before, in the whole range of my experience, have I known a man arraigned for murder who produced such a record of character as has been produced here. All the powerful presumptions of a virtuous and well-spent life arise at the very opening of your deliberations in favor of the defendant. By the light of the proof let us see who it is that we are trying. You have your fingers on his pulse. You are measuring his life, and the manner of that life is all before you. He is young—but twenty-four years of age. How much of usefulness and manly life he has crowded into that brief space! If one of your sons at that age was arraigned for a high crime, how proud you would justly feel if you could call, as has been done in this case, from every quarter and from every class everybody who had ever met him, everybody who had ever done business with him, and receive from them all one unbroken strain of commendation and eulogy!

The aged and gray, who have known Harry Crawford Black from

his infancy, have here, in your presence, praised his pure and blameless life. His young comrades have spoken of him as an example far beyond his years. His fellow-prisoners during the war describe him as a model amidst the hard and demoralizing scenes of prison life. The dusty miners from Piedmont, as well as members and senators in congress, come here to bear their voluntary and affectionate testimony in his favor. He does not pass this ordeal alone; he has the sweet reward of virtue in the presence and consolation of those whom his good conduct has attached to his fortunes; and the voice of reason, as well as law, proclaims that such a man is not a criminal. He is not familiar with the walks of vice, where criminals are made. His hand and his heart are free from the guile and the practice of crime, and yet the learned gentlemen for the prosecution insist that he stands now at the foot of the scaffold, soon to ascend its desperate heights for the commission of a crime without a parallel in the eye of the law. Pure, innocent, and virtuous up to this time! Do men of that kind, without just provocation, enact deeds of bloodshed? If they commit what seem to be violations of law, are they not always upon the most dreadful and imperative causes? It is this presumption which gives to character its priceless value when the motives and conduct of a human being are under investigation. But such a reputation as the defendant here produces is usually the growth of a long lifetime, and is seldom the accompaniment of early youth. Recall in your minds at this moment the friends and neighbors by whom you are surrounded at home. The best and most reliable are those of longest standing. Some you have known for more than a quarter of a century. You have seen their heads whiten as the winters and summers have come and gone. Their characters are good and solid. Little by little, day by day, week by week, month by month, they have built them up as firmly as your beautiful mountains; but it has been the labor of long years. How much more should your hearts lean to a mere boy, who has not had much time, and yet comes into court with a character that the old men of the country might be proud to produce. He has had but few years, but in them he has been so prone to virtue, so free from vice, so free from evil associations, that he has not a spot or stain or blemish.

Show me another boy in these bright valleys who went from home at seventeen years of age, had an army experience—always terrible—tasted the horrors of the prison-house, came out untainted in soul and body, went to the far West into the employ as chief clerk of a heavy mercantile house, returns with their warmest testimonials, becomes at twenty-two the superintendent of one of the foremost mining companies of the Alleghanies, winning at all times and places and under all circumstances golden opinions, and nothing but golden opinions, from all sorts of people; show me, I say, another boy like this beside me within the range of your acquaintance who has borne or can bear the mighty tests to which the prisoner has been subjected, and you will find him the cherished object of universal regard, beloved by the fathers, and welcomed by the mothers into every domestic circle as a model for their sons and an associate for their daughters. Can the mark of Cain rest upon the brow of such a one? Can the ineffaceable brand of bloody guilt be there? Such an assertion is a perversion of all the laws of human nature. The tree shall be known by its fruits; the thorn and the thistle do not bear delicious figs, and a life of innocence and peace does not bloom and ripen of a sudden into a harvest of atrocious crime.

If we were defending, indeed, a criminal, one whose character we did not dare put in issue, with blotches and stains upon him, how different would be our feelings and our positions. But now we come with all our hearts clinging closely to the defendant in his peril, believing, earnestly believing, in him and in his innocence from the very depths of our souls; and we have no fear. The weight of a good name is recognized in the books of law, but over and above all it is recognized in your own hearts. When the Hebrew children were cast into the furnace, with its sevenfold heat, there appeared to the astonished gaze of the Babylonish king another form, of celestial aspect, walking with them in the midst of the flames, and comforting them under their fiery afflictions. So is Crawford Black's good name this moment hovering near him, like a beneficent angel, to guard, to bless, and to protect; and, when he emerges from this trial, his raiment will not be scorched nor have the smell of fire.

Gentlemen, mention has been made of the change of venue in this case. I have something also to say on that subject. The McKaigs are a powerful, able, intellectual, and wealthy family. That family, with its numerous connections, represent, I am told, more wealth than any other five families in Alleghany county. The prisoner has no means of his own, and no kindred nearer than cousins who have. He is poor, and so is his father, and, except through distant kindred, he has not a dollar to aid him; yet he was so strong in the community where the deed was done, and his defense sprang up so powerfully in the hearts of all, that the influence of the McKaigs melted like a mountain mist before the opening dawn. They dared not meet this stripling youth at their own homes. They fled from their native heaths. There these two young men were born; there they were raised; there one was slain, and the other awaited his trial. Upon the side of one is numerous kindred, strong, accomplished, intellectual, and full of life and power. On the other is merely a good cause and a good name; nothing more. And yet what a scene I witnessed in January last in the county of Alleghany! I never beheld the like before, and hope never to again. I saw an American state seeking to convict a man of crime, though afraid to put him upon his trial where the alleged crime was committed. It was his right there to be tried. My associate counsel has read to you the constitution of Maryland, with its bill of rights. It is there declared that one of the principal rights of the citizen is to be tried where the facts arise. When our forefathers alleged the causes on which they fought King George seven bloody years, they laid down as a marked grievance that he transported American citizens beyond the seas to be tried for offenses committed here. It was one of the prominent causes for which our fathers bled, for which Smallwood's Maryland regiment charged on the battle-fields of the Revolution. They fought for the right of trial where the offense was committed; the right to be tried by their peers and neighbors; the right to be tried where witnesses are known. The counsel for the prosecution in this case seek to invalidate the testimony for the defense. How dare they assail men in this community whom they were unwilling to confront in Cumberland, where they are fully known? Gentlemen, they ask you to do what an Alleghany county jury would not do. They come away from that county and ask you to do a deed of horror that no jury there would commit. How stands this case? The state of Maryland says: "Alleghany county acquits the prisoner, but we ask Frederick county to convict him." He has already one verdict of not guilty in his favor. The state said Alleghany county would not convict him; thereupon a change of venue was taken. It amounts to one verdict of not guilty. It is a confession on the part of the prosecution that the county where he was born, where he was raised, and where McKaig was born, where he was raised, and where he fell, will not convict the defendant.

The attorney-general spoke of the scenes of Colonel McKaig's funeral in Cumberland; that the stores were closed, and mourners went about the streets as if a great public calamity had befallen the city. If this dramatic picture is true, if there was a deep sense of wrong and outrage in the breasts of the people against Black, why is he here for trial? If stores were closed, if there was burning indignation, if there was grief over the loss of an unoffending citizen, why are we not all in Cumberland, rather than in Frederick? What did this prosecution flee from? Why did it flee at all? It fled, hoping to hide from a jury the true causes of this disaster. The public mind was too full of knowledge where all the facts were known. The very air was filled with the wrongs committed by the deceased upon the defendant and his family. It was too well known by the entire people that there was one desolate home, one ruined daughter, one frantic father, one broken-hearted mother, and one outraged, insulted, and menaced brother and son in their midst. The witnesses by whom we have proven McKaig's assault upon Black on that fatal morning were also too well-known in that community to suit the purposes of the prosecution.

This prosecution fled from another fact. A jury in Cumberland could inspect the premises and examine the ground where the collision took place. They could see the exact position these parties bore toward each other; they could determine where McKaig came from, where he was, how he crossed the street, whether there was a natural crossing there, and that Black did not seek him by crossing the street, but that McKaig sought him. All that could be seen by the jury there, and all that we lose by being brought here. This course upon the part of the prosecution is virtually a *nolle prosequi*. It amounts to a dismissal, so far as the county of Alleghany, where the trial properly belongs, is concerned. In my judgment, this law that allows the state to drag a prisoner from his home for trial, to transport him from the location of his conduct, is unconstitutional, is not in accordance with the constitution of the United States, nor the constitution of Maryland. I believe, whenever this question is raised and the law tested, it will be so decided.

But we come now to a close and patient examination of the facts in detail of this sad and dreadful tragedy. I will ask you to start with me on Saturday evening at Piedmont, next preceding the fatal Monday morning. There, to my mind, the curtain first rises bringing the prisoner into mental cognizance of the deceased on the subject which has wrought such wide-spread ruin. Black and his friend Henshaw were together. Henshaw, not liking to intrude upon such a subject, yet ventured to ask whether the father of the prisoner had yet been indicted. The answer was that he had not. "I thought he would have been," said Henshaw. "Why so?" inquired the prisoner. "Because," said Henshaw, "of what occurred on the fair ground." "Well," says the prisoner, "what did occur at the fair ground? I have never been able to get the truth of that. Father was not in a condition to remember, and mother will not talk to me about it." Henshaw then informed him that the deceased, Colonel W. W. McKaig, had publicly denounced the sister of the prisoner as a strumpet on that occasion. These were the burning, awful words for a brother's ear to hear and heart to feel. They wrung from his pale lips one brief exclamation of agony; he changed color rapidly, and his breast heaved with strong excitment. He grew silent, and with an ashen face invited no further conversation, and Henshaw attempted no more.

He disappears from our view for that night. His tortures are not for us to fathom. In hours of darkness and deepest woe the heart has no confidant this side of Omniscience. How that wretched night was spent there is no proof to show, for it passed in solitary despair.

The next day dawns on him in Cumberland, now intent on solving the painful mystery connected with his sister. We find him immediately in conversation with Mr. Lowndes, a relative by marriage, and a gentleman of the highest character, and a member of the legal profession. Was he not a most proper person of whom to make inquiry, and with whom to advise? Mr. Lowndes not only confirms the statement of Henshaw in regard to the language used at the fair ground, but also informs the prisoner that Colonel McKaig is the seducer of his sister. This is his first information as to the author of his sister's shame and ruin. It is true that he suspected she was in trouble— she was absent from home—but who was to tell this young and hopeful spirit that the idol of his childhood was worse than dead to him? His parents were silent on the dreadful theme in his presence. You heard the stricken and sobbing mother on the witness-stand. With tearful eyes and voice she told you that the wrongs of the sister were never mentioned to her brother; that it was a forbidden subject in the little circle of home upon the occasions of the prisoner's brief visits from the mines in the mountains. It was kept, as far as possible, a sealed book to him; nor is this any new phase in domestic life, or in family histories. How often do we read of one portrait with its face to the wall and its name never mentioned? It is, perhaps, the image of one who, though deeply loved, has planted sorrow and shame in the hearts of the household. The name is to be spoken no more forever. We can speak with a saddened pleasure of the dead who sleep in purity and honor. The memory of their virtues fills our hearts with love and peace, and we train white roses to bloom on their graves. But for one on whom a blight has fallen, beside which the touch of death is merciful, we invoke a deeper silence than the tomb. There is a gallery in Venice where the faces of the Doges of ancient days adorn the walls, but the eye suddenly rests upon one vacant panel—

no portrait is there. He who should have filled it is blotted from the walls of memory. He fell in an hour of temptation from his high estate, and an oblivion was extended to him by his own and succeeding ages. And so, when the poor, deluded girl in this case fell into the snares of the spoiler, and the knowledge of her wayward steps came partially to her suffering parents, they strove to draw an impenetrable curtain around the horrible event; and most of all did they wish to conceal the humiliating and harrowing truth from their son, their only remaining child—their staff and hope in the gloomy and desolate future. His life was dawning with auspicious omens; he was rising rapidly in business; his prospects were brilliant, and well might the father and mother be reluctant to mar them with a grief that always ranges in noble natures close upon the confines of madness. They were journeying toward the sunset of life, and wished to bear their burden alone. They sought to spare the prisoner in the bright morning of his existence this bitter cup of which they drank in solitude, and whose wretched dregs they are now draining in public. It was the sublime struggle of deep parental affection and fortitude under the darkest calamity that ever blasts the peace of a home. Their conduct was true to the loftiest instincts that ever adorned the annals of human nature.

And so it was that the prisoner, on Sunday, for the first time, and from the lips of Mr. Lowndes, learned of the awful abyss into which his sister had fallen; who had led her trusting footsteps to the brink, and hurled her into its frightful and remorseless depths. The letter in evidence was at the same time shown him, and he was reliably assured that it was written to his sister by the deceased. It conclusively proves criminal intercourse. The writer speaks with an easy and familiar sense of power over his victim. She was plainly the subordinate of his wishes. All this penetrated the heart and brain of the prisoner at a glance. The facts were accumulating upon him with startling rapidity. The night before he learned of the defilement of his sister's name on the public fair grounds; on this day he was informed that the very man who had hawked her name as a harlot in the midst of gaping and wondering multitudes was himself the author of the ruin aud dishonor which had befallen her, and which he thus proclaimed. The written proof was placed in his hands.

He went next with Mr. Lowndes to his mother. If he hoped for comfort there, for once, at least, he did not find it; rather he found the revolting climax of his misery, shame, and horror. It was disclosed to him that a child, four months old, was then in his sister's arms, at her distant place of retreat, as the result of the treacherous embraces of the deceased. Oh, gentlemen, no tongue can paint the force of this last blow upon a heart already bruised, swollen, and bleeding! The pride of the prisoner's young life—his pride in an honored and unsullied name, in the ties of home and kindred, in the friends he had won, in the career opening before him, was overthrown and trampled in the dust by the haughty and insolent tread of his sister's seducer. At the prisoner's time of life, and with such a nature and reputation as his, how sensitive is the human mind to dishonor! And the fame and good name of mother and sister are then more precious than all this world contains and than life itself. In after years, wife and children may divide the bounties of love, but to the pure and upright son and brother who has not yet left the hearthstone of his childhood, the mother that bore him, and the sister who has grown up by his side, are the tender and cherished objects of all his earthly devotion. It was so with Crawford Black. He felt in a moment all the agony of a whole life suddenly wrecked and covered with disaster. Everything crumbled to pieces in an instant. Hope died, and despair took its place in his breast; his bright dreams of the future disappeared, and a wall of darkness rose up around him. The sky, so clear before, grew black over his head; he felt, too, that all the world knew the story which was consuming his heart with bitterness and grief. It had been proclaimed by him who best knew its fearful truth. The finger of scorn is a more dreadful instrument of torture than the cruel ingenuity of man ever devised, and the prisoner now knew, for the first time, that it was upon him; that he was pointed at as one on whom the brand of a sister's degradation had been placed by the successful arts of triumphant villainy.

In this mood of mind he witnessed the close of that eventful

Sabbath day. To others it had been a day of rest; not so to him. To others it had been a day of grace and of blessings; to him it was full of curses and of evil—the darkest day in all the calendar of time. And when night came with its healing influences for the weary and sore-hearted, it brought no oblivious antidotes to pain for this unfortunate prisoner. Who shall tell of the scorpion stings and lashes of that miserable and sleepless night? You have caught glimpses here and there from the mother's testimony of the dismal hours as they slowly passed away. They were laden with the baleful ingredients which kindle a frenzy in the soul and a madness in the brain. Gentlemen, have you ever passed through the deep floods of sorrow? Have you ever walked the floor through the silent watches of the night, praying for the day to dawn, and feeling that the wings of time were loaded with lead? Have grief and woe ever affrighted sleep from your eye-lids and rest from your hearts? But yours, perhaps, has been the sorrow which comes of death and ordinary bereavement. Here was the blister of shame burning like a hot iron on the prisoner's brow, and a sense of disgrace, like a corroding, cankering poison, inflaming his brain with a fever which no medicinal drug can allay or cool. The art of the healer stops at the threshold of the diseased mind, and sinks down baffled and helpless in the presence of the delirium of woe.

Toward day, when all the world was dark and lost to him, when the precious providences of God themselves seemed blotted out like stars in the midst of clouds and storm, he turned his weary steps toward that love which never falters or grows dim, which triumphs over dishonor and death, and shines brightest amidst the wailings of broken hearts and the ghastly ruins of domestic peace and joy. He threw himself by his mother's side to comfort and be comforted in their mutual misery. He laid his bright and manly head where he had slept the placid sleep of infancy. There, sobbing and oppressed, he sought a shelter. The pitiless and merciless storm was pelting him, and "other refuge had he none." Mother and son wept together over the erring and the lost. There is often a mercy in tears, but not in such as are shed over a loved one ruined in soul and body. Then the unsealed fountains are scalding and bitter as the waters of Marah. While the parent and child thus lament together, we will turn from this scene of holy pathos and tenderness, and consider an important question which here arises in the order of my argument.

You have been asked, with earnest emphasis, by the counsel for the prosecution, why the prisoner was so crushed and appalled with grief and frenzy against the deceased. You are reminded that we were not allowed by the court to prove the direct fact of the sister's seduction by McKaig. You will remember our urgent offer to do so, and the determined opposition to such proof on the part of the learned gentleman for the state. The court held in your hearing that the information which the prisoner received on that subject was competent evidence, but that the fact itself of the seduction was not an issue before you. Was he informed upon competent authority? Had he a right, as a reasonable and prudent man, to believe that Colonel McKaig had seduced Myra Black, and that she had borne a child as the result of their sinful intercourse? Did the facts, as communicated to him, justify such a belief, and did he entertain it with the deep convictions of an honest sincerity? If so, then his sister's ruin by the deceased became a proven, fixed, and absolute reality in his mind, as much so as if his eyes had beheld or his ears heard the secret deeds of shame over which the deep spell of silence reigns forever. If he believed, then his mind was wrought upon by the power of a sincere faith. His emotions and his conduct were under its omnipotent influence; and in this respect he simply conformed to the great laws which have governed all the races and tribes of mankind since the birthday of human history.

You and I believe in the great and merciful Father in heaven, the creator of the boundless universe, yet we have not seen him, nor hath any man and lived. We believe that the blessed Saviour walked the hills and plains of Judea, and died to redeem the souls of men, but our eyes did not behold the majesty of his face, nor our ears drink in the deep and melancholy music of his voice. We believe because we have faith in the sources of our information. We have been told, that is all. The testimony of the ages is ours. Nature, throughout her illimitable realms, proclaims a God, and the Bible, the book of books, reveals him; while the existence and the divine mission of the Messiah are established by witnesses whose evidence we read and accept as true. Upon these sources of faith Christian men and women found their hopes of immortal happiness. They make heaven an immediate reality, and uphold the martyr as he smiles joyfully amidst the blazing faggots at the stake.

Nor is the power of human belief over the actions of men lessened because it may be founded in error. The untamed Indian has his faith as we have ours. He has not seen the Manito; but his trust in the happy hunting-grounds, the sparkling rivers, and the fadeless verdure of an eternal world, is as unfaltering as that of the bravest disciples that ever died for the cause of the Cross. He sings his death-song under slow tortures, recounts his earthly deeds of merit, and anticipates his blissful rewards hereafter with all the calmness and confidence of a Christian philosopher. The eastern Mussulman worships with sincere devotion at the shrine of Mahomet, and, giving full credit to the testimony of his fathers, follows the crescent, and rejoices in the prospect of a sensual paradise at the end of life. The Chinaman, the countryman of Confucius, has a faith in his system equally firm and unrelenting. The history of the whole human race forces us to exclaim, "How little is known and how much is believed!" The world of faith is wide, the world of knowledge is narrow.

What we think we know best depends mainly upon the credibility of those who have narrated to us the facts. How few of you have crossed the mountains and beheld the valley of the Mississippi! Yet you know that there it lies, stretching from the regions of perpetual snow to the land of unending summer, an empire of present and future wealth and populations. What one of this jury has ever beheld the great father of waters as he rolls onward to the gulf of Mexico? Yet you all know that the ceaseless and resistless current is forever there. You have listened to the tales of travelers; you have read their letters and their books, and you are convinced as fully as you could be through the medium of your own senses. I only ask for the prisoner that these universal rules of faith be extended to him in this dark hour of his peril. I do not ask you to shield him if his belief was irrational and unnatural—if he accepted information from unworthy and unreliable persons. Put yourselves in his place; could he doubt the truth and candor of his faithful and tried friend, Henshaw? Could he distrust his kinsman and adviser, Lowndes? But, above all, were not the words of his idolized mother sacred and holy with him? No better, surer foundations of human belief ever challenged the consent of the human mind. Crawford Black as much knew, by the time the sun set on Sunday evening, that McKaig had destroyed his sister as it is given to mortals to know the affairs of this life. No doubt or misgiving for a moment mitigated his anguish. The awful fact stared him in the face with painful and maddening intensity. It confronted him incessantly. It would not down at his bidding. It taunted and mocked him in his sleepless desolation and despair. It tempted his imagination with the appalling details of the victim's surrender and debasement, and the destroyer's triumph and insolence. And if he arose and acted upon this fact and slew the man who put out the light and joy of an innocent and unoffending household, would his conduct have been without precedent, novel and strange in the history of mankind?

There is a very old case and of very high authority on this point. It is the earliest on record. The daughter of Jacob was seduced by a prince of one of the neighboring tribes. Her brothers, Simeon and Levi, were in the fields at their usual avocations, when they were told by others what had befallen their sister. They believed the story of their disgrace, and with their swords, in due time, they acted upon it to the total destruction, not merely of the seducer, but of the whole tribe who supported him in his conduct. And when their father, who was old and apprehensive of trouble growing out of their terrible vengeance, deplored their fierce and sanguinary measures, they gave that memorable answer which has sprung to the lips of manly brothers in every age and clime from that hour to this, "Shall he deal with our sister as a harlot?" Human nature is the same to-day as it was then, and Crawford Black simply exclaimed with Simeon and Levi of old. You would cry out in the same indignant words under the same circumstances.

You are now asked to punish this young brother in Maryland. Were the brothers in Israel punished? God ruled immediately and directly in the house of Jacob. Are you wiser and more just than your Maker? Will you sit in judgment upon the Almighty and condemn his ways? Should you not rather find out his rulings in a case so similar to the one you are trying and then implicitly and humbly adopt them for your guidance? The patriarch and his family, including the defenders of their sister's honor, were led by Jehovah out from their enemies, up into Bethel, a place of safety. "And they journeyed; and the terror of God was upon the cities that were round about them, and they did not pursue after the sons of Jacob." They were thus protected, not prosecuted. I may cite other cases hereafter, but with the approval of God upon the conduct of the prisoner, I know that I might safely leave this branch of his defense where it now rests.

Gentlemen of the jury, the light of Monday morning at last broke over the hills of Cumberland and brought that dreadful night to a close. The sun of the morning comes with life in its beams to all. It illuminates the hovel and the palace, the home of the heart-broken and the circles of gayety and pleasure. In all its kindly visitations of human abodes, however, on that morning, it lit up no lonelier, sadder, drearier hearthstone than that around which once shone the pure and innocent face of the beloved daughter and sister, to be seen there with the angel light of virtue no more forever. The prisoner went forth from that blighted home, and the hour of retributive justice drew nigh; not by his artifice or device, but by the spirit of the avenging Nemesis who sooner or later overtakes the violators of domestic sanctity. His provocation was already sufficient in the estimation of all the ages of the past to justify the death of McKaig.

While he stands, however, on the brow of the hill, and before he descends, weary and heavy laden, into the town, let us examine still more closely into the relations which the deceased and the accused bore to each other. What were the purposes and feelings which McKaig had deliberately and repeatedly evinced toward Black? One of the oldest and basest principles of human nature was at work in the heart of the deceased. He had wronged the prisoner beyond the reach of forgiveness, and he therefore hated him. The scandal, too, of his conduct, had become public, and he thought to browbeat all complaining voices into silence. His own domestic peace was doubtless in peril, and it was necessary to overawe the injured family into abject submission. He had met the insane and frantic father, and received an assault vaguely mentioned here in the evidence. No danger or menace, however, threatened him any longer in that quarter. The forbearance of the distracted father was secured by indictment and heavy bonds. There was but one other who held the honor of the name and the household in his keeping. It was the brave, generous, dauntless being here before you, and it was for him that McKaig wore his daily belt of loaded fire-arms. Conscience told the deceased that he had forfeited his life to the prisoner. He would have slain the seducer of his own sister like a dog in the highways, and the guilt in his breast bade him beware of the brother of his victim. Perhaps friendly tongues had also warned him of his danger if the accused ever made a full discovery. Thus steeped in crime I shall demonstrate from the evidence that he sought a collision with Black under circumstances of his own choosing, and with the advantages all in favor of himself. He could not retrace his steps and undo the wrongs he had inflicted. He therefore prepared to go forward and wade in blood to a place of safety—a place of security, as he supposed, against the consequences of his own evil deeds. He believed the issue would come, and he became restless and aggressive in order to have it no longer pending. Why else did he rudely jostle the prisoner in Ferguson's saloon? Between friends such an act might pass without significance; but when men are deadly foes, when their hostility is open and proclaimed, when unpardonable wrongs have been given and received, when their blood is full of wrath, when the insulter is armed with weapons of death, then the intentional touch in passing is a threat and a challenge of the deepest and most sinister import. What Lawrence Wilson saw has that meaning and none other. It was McKaig's palpable purpose to provoke Black into a fight at a time and place of his own selection, and with his preparations doubtless fully made. Wilson is not contradicted. He located the place and fixed the time, and mentioned the presence of others on the occasion. The bar-keeper was especially identified. If this evidence was untrue, if the deceased and the prisoner were not there at the time named, if the circumstances of insolence and assault did not take place as described, the means were amply furnished by the witness himself for his detection and contradiction. If it was a fabrication, it would have been demolished long ere now. There is power and wealth and the thirst for revenge in this prosecution, and no great fact like this would be left standing if it could have been overthrown. It occurred but two weeks before the fall of the deceased, and throws a full flood of light upon his movements and motives at the final and deadly encounter. Its importance in this case can not be magnified. It is uncontradicted, and therefore conceded, that when these two young men are first brought to your view together, the deceased was the hostile aggressor, seeking to degrade or slay the brother as he had worse than slain the sister. How much longer was Crawford Black to endure? How much more of the proud man's contumely was he to bear? But the hour had not yet come; he knew not yet the full story of infamy which afterward filled his soul with horror.

But there is yet stronger and more striking evidence of McKaig's deadly purposes toward the accused. John Long, born and reared in Cumberland, well known by all, detailed a scene upon the witness-stand that will never be forgotten by those who heard it. It is said that the deceased was a brave man. It may be so. I have no doubt he acted with courage in battle. Many have done so, surrounded by admiring comrades, inspired by hopes of distinction, who have faltered in the face of a personal conflict—especially so when not upheld by the consciousness of right. He who hath his quarrel just has a contempt for danger which the heart oppressed with guilt never knows. A troubled conscience makes many strange and devious steps. Many actions that are mysterious to the world would be thus explained if the secrets of all hearts could be laid bare. When John Long saw McKaig watching the prisoner at that street corner with his hand on his pistol, he was but acting in obedience to the hard necessities of his criminal position. The consequences of his evil career were developed in his own character. His own nature was depraved and perverted until we see him, by the light of this evidence, lying in wait, meditating what measure of destruction he should next adopt against this unoffending family. It gives me no pleasure to speak these words. The truth is painful to me when it reproaches the dead, but the claims of the living here in this court-room can not be denied. What the immediate intentions of the deceased were while he was waylaying the prisoner, you and I may not fully determine. He may not have entirely comprehended them himself. To my mind he appears on that occasion irresolute, undecided, wavering and halting between the conflicting purposes of his own disturbed and agitated breast—at one moment strongly impelled to confront and assault the prisoner, and the next hesitating and doubting, until the opportunity for decisive action went by. But an effort has been made to discredit Long. In what way? He is a native of Cumberland, and there grew up to manhood; and, though his face wears a darker color than yours or mine, yet no man dares to say in your presence that he has not borne as good a character for truth and veracity as the loftiest and proudest in that community. Although hundreds of citizens of Alleghany county have attended this protracted trial, and hundreds more could have been obtained in a few hours, yet no impeachment of the reputation of this well-known and vitally important witness was attempted in the remotest manner. This is equivalent to the affirmative support of his credibility by the entire community in which he lives. But, at the last moment, two zealous co-laborers in this prosecution rushed into court and lifted up their hands and voices to contradict John Long—Dr. Dougherty and Smith Johnson. Both admit that they are partisans in feeling against this unfortunate young man, who has never harmed them by word or deed. They tell you that, two nights ago, in the dim still hours between midnight and day, when the evil and prowling spirits of the known and the unknown world usually commit their nocturnal freaks against the peace of mankind, they inspected and surveyed the localities described by Long, decided there in the dark that he could not have seen McKaig where he swore he did see him, took the cars in haste for this city, and arrived just in time to detail their astounding discovery before the testimony in the case was finally closed. Long was examined more than a week ago. There is a line of telegraph and a railroad from here to Cumberland, and there is a venomous energy and power in this prosecution unparalleled in my experience. If Long was false, and the locality itself, as given by him, would expose his perjury, would his contradiction have been left to the finishing details of the case and to the ridiculous testimony of Dougherty and Johnson? No! Scores of men would have been promptly produced, having made careful daylight examinations of the points in dispute, and ready to tell you that this great, gigantic fact established by Long was impossible from physical causes. Gross and Ferguson, the proprietors of the saloon, and familiar with the corner where McKaig was seen, with the spot where Long stood, and with the positions of the lamps that have been mentioned, would have been the most competent and proper witnesses on this point. Why were they not called instead of these hasty, prejudiced, midnight surveyors? John Long might and would have been contradicted if his statement had been untrue, but he stands here now uncontradicted and unimpeached. Let the doctor, therefore, assuage his feelings in the use of his scalpel and pills upon his patients, and let him and Johnson both hereafter abandon the business of willing and anxious witnesses against an innocent man on trial for his life. If they are satisfied with their appearance in this sad drama, I will now drop the curtain, while the audience hoots and hisses them out of sight and out of mind.

But again: Long was faithful to his early playmate and friend. On the distressful Sunday, when the fearful truth was rapidly breaking upon the distracted mind of the prisoner, John Long met him, as he told you, on the bridge in Cumberland for the first time since he had witnessed McKaig's secret menaces a few days before against his life. His inquiry of him was most natural—"When did you see Colonel McKaig last?" Crawford Black's heart was bitter and sore at that moment. The sound of that name maddened him. His reply to the faithful boy that loved him was stern and angry: "What is that to you?" Grief and humiliation have their right to solitude and exclusion, and the prisoner repelled what he took to be an attempt to invade his confidence and look upon the bleeding wounds of his miserable heart. Long corrected his mistake, and narrated to him the recent strange and threatening behavior of McKaig. He put him in possession of every detail. The prisoner listened and left in silence. He now knew not only that his sister had fallen, but that his own life was hunted. Dishonor had already come, and death was pending. His sister led to her ruin, and then advertised to the public by her destroyer as a common bawd; his aged father reviled, and denounced and prosecuted as a felon for his feeble and vain attempt at redress; and now thoroughly convinced that he himself was to be watched, threatened, glared at, bullied, waylaid, and eventually subjected to deadly assault! What more of outrage and provocation can man submit to unless, like a hound, he receives the kick and the lash of his master? Bear in mind that meeting on the bridge and Long's statement. Do not for a moment forget it. Invoke it into your presence when you retire, for, with such a notice as he then received, the prisoner had the right to kill the deceased whenever he approached him with the slightest evidences of hostility in his movements. No retreat, no delay was after this required of him. Henceforth, if he slew McKaig, he had a double defense—each one as sure and firm as the everlasting hills. His sister's cause and his own united in their appeal, and the spirit of his noble manhood responded; a volcano justly raged within his breast, and Providence dictated the moment of its eruption and the result which followed. The burden of the prisoner was more than he could bear, and he moved and acted as an instrument in the hands of a just God. You are to judge of his conduct as if you had been in his situation. That is your duty to-day. I state it in the hearing of the court, and in the presence of my professional brethren. You are not to estimate his guilt or innocence by the appearance of the circumstances to a cool, indifferent, and disinterested observer. You are to put yourselves in his place, assume his relations to others, imbibe his affections, and survey everything from his point of view; stand with him on the brow of the hill, near the old homestead, where I left him some time ago; recall to your minds all that he then knew of McKaig's conduct in the past, and of his purposes against himself in the future, and answer in your hearts whether the wealth and honors of the whole earth would have tempted you to embrace the prospect that lay before him as your own. You can not desire to take this young life, to cut the briefly spun thread of his existence; you can not wish to rear a gibbet against your sky with that elegant and accomplished form upon it, and that handsome and intelligent face shrouded for the grave. Such a doom can not be a welcome thought to you. Identify yourselves, then, with him as the waves of sorrow and of peril rolled over his head, and you will reach forth your hands, your all-powerful hands, to bless and to save him.

And, gentlemen, now as Harry Crawford Black descends into the town, the other party to this tragedy of blood, of broken hearts and ruined lives, came forth from his home at the other extremity of the place. It is claimed by the able attorney-general that he was slain contrary to the peace of the state of Maryland. If so, then he must have been at peace himself with her citizens, and in obedience to her laws. The picture of his peaceful departure from home has been vividly drawn. As a pure work of fancy it has high merits. The reality, however, was speedily shown when he met the prisoner. When he arose that morning he made a toilet of death, and clothed himself with the implements of destruction. Three loaded revolvers, as the proof establishes, constituted his supply—one in the prepared pistol-pocket on his hip, and two in their leather holsters belted around his waist. He sallied forth more heavily armed than any man who had walked the streets of Cumberland since the close of the sanguinary strife between the North and the South. Instead of being a follower of peace, he was a moving machine of war. Instead of being a law-abiding citizen, his preparations were those of the desperate and deadly outlaw. And as he thus prepared himself, I ask you to look at him in the light of his previous conduct toward the prisoner; in the light of his conduct as described by Long at the corner of the street, and of his menacing insult at Ferguson's saloon. You can not mistake his fatal meaning. He was bent on bloody mischief. Black had uttered no threats against him — not one has been proven or attempted to be proven; he did not arm, therefore, for self-defense. He had not been apprised of any danger from the prisoner, except by the suggestions of his own guilty conscience. . They told him, perhaps, of the necessity of prompt, determined, and aggressive action. We can only judge, however, by his acts, and they speak in clear and certain tones. When you once saw armies in these now smiling and happy valleys equip themselves with the cannon, the rifle, and the bayonet, and move forward toward the enemy, you knew that the sorrowful heaps of the slain and the wounded would soon cumber the ground and appeal piteously to heaven So, too, when you behold a citizen in time of peace invade your streets with the most extensive and extraordinary preparations for taking human life, you at once fear and expect scenes of violence and calamity.

Am I answered that Black, too, was armed? Who ever had so much reason to be? May not a threatened life defend itself? He had one pistol; was not one-third as powerful in conflict as his enemy; he had five balls ready for action. It is admitted by the prosecution that McKaig had twelve, and the testimony shows conclusively that he had eighteen. I have thus traced these parties, described their relations to each other, and their disposition in regard to a collision, until I have reached the time and place when and where they met. And here I again deplore your absence from the spot where a personal inspection would give you a more accurate knowledge of the transaction than any description at this distance. But, concerning the leading facts, there can be no doubt. Black was on the south side of the street, going west; McKaig was on the north side of the street, going east. Thus they were on the same street, but meeting with its whole width between them. Through Cumberland runs Will's creek, and over it, on this street, is an elevated bridge. The evidence first disclosed the deceased as he was crossing that bridge, with the prisoner in full view diagonally to his right, on the other side of the street. There they first beheld each other that morning. Every step now assumes the most terrible importance, and is charged with the responsibility of life and death. Who sought the banquet of blood? Who turned from his own pathway to interfere with the course of the other? Not an object was between them to obscure the view. The instant McKaig saw Black, he left his own sidewalk, immediately at the east end of the bridge, where there was no crossing for pedestrians, as at the intersections of streets, diverged obliquely to his right, on a line that would bring him to the sidewalk on which the prisoner stood, about thirty feet in front of him. He walked rapidly in that direction. Why did he thus leave the even tenor of his way, and bear suddenly down on Black? Why did he not pass on, and let the prisoner do the same? Was that Providence, whose moral laws he had mocked and spurned, hovering over the scene, and guiding him to his swift and awful doom? Did the fair and open opportunity tempt him to his own destruction in seeking the destruction of another? He could have let the prisoner alone; but a belief in the efficiency of his arsenal, and a blind and fatal infatuation, carried him with defiant confidence into a presence most dangerous to him on that morning—the presence of one who had just emerged from a night of sleepless frenzy over the injuries, the incurable and burning injuries, he had received from the man who now sought and approached him.

Is it pretended that this sudden movement by McKaig had no hostile meaning? Consider all that had passed between them before; consider all the provocations, the insults, and the threats, for actions often utter louder and deadlier threats than words; consider all the past, and consider the warlike preparation of the deceased, and then determine whether he crossed that street without a purpose. But you are not left to the uncertain field of conjecture. The evidence makes his motives as plain as the light of the sun. The sinister movements of his hands make a perfect revelation of his designs. The cane was in his right hand as he passed over the bridge. Conner, a witness for the state, saw it, as well as Davis, a witness for the defense. Conner turned away and saw no more; Davis saw it shifted from the right to the left hand by the deceased, as he approached the prisoner. He saw that right hand, thus relieved of the cane, go back to the hip-pocket, and come in contact with a shining object, the polished handle to one of his pistols. Do I misstate the testimony? Would I dare do so, even if restrained by no higher motive than the success of my cause? Nothing is more dangerous than to attempt a fraud upon a jury. You have heard every word here uttered, and you quickly resent the effort of counsel to mislead you. No attempt was made to contradict Davis; this you know. Others profess to have seen the deceased while crossing the street, who were called by the prosecution. Why was not one of them asked in regard to the change of the cane? Because it was known to be true. There was no hope of contradicting this crushing fact. And the motion of the hand for the pistol is equally proven. Is there anything unreasonable in all this? He had betrayed active hostility on former occasions. Why not now? He was fixed for the affray; he never could be readier; he did not know the condition of the prisoner's mind; he did not know that in the prisoner's breast had been boiling a fierce cauldron for the last thirty-six intolerable hours; he did not know that he was himself at that moment the one supremely horrible thought in Black's feverish brain. He thought to confront him unawares, perhaps to browbeat, degrade, and trample him under foot; perhaps to slay him where he stood. Colonel McKaig was a full man in years, large, commanding, and powerful in person. Crawford Black is slight, almost a boy in size, as in age. There was the contemptuous confidence of Goliath on the one hand, and the just cause and unquailing heart of David on the other.

Gentlemen, I need not read from books to inform you what the prisoner's rights were when he saw his mortal foe approach him, preparing with hasty strides to become his instant executioner. The law of self-defense is written in the heart of man more plainly and powerfully than in the pages of libraries. We here place our feet on its solid and eternal foundations. We build upon it a house of refuge for the prisoner, which will withstand the fury of the storm and the malice of his enemies. He was not called upon to retreat. I spurn the doctrine of being driven to the wall or the ditch, that odious doctrine of degradation, danger, and death to the assaulted party. Every inch of ground on which he stood was his own. Who had the right to command him to yield it? The free air around him was his wall, and he who sought to drive him further embraced the peril of his own lawlessness. Nor was the prisoner required to wait for the development of McKaig's designs upon him; he already had full notice. No shot or blow was necessary to make them clearer. He had the right to presume the bloody intentions of McKaig from his previous as well as his present movements, and to act with promptitude. This is the law of the courts, and is sustained by the authority of reason. In it lies all the safety bestowed by the great principles of self-defense. The whole panorama of the past flashed upon the mind of the prisoner at a glance, and called upon him to defend life, honor, sister, and home, without the delay of an instant. There was the destroyer, the insulter, and now the threatening assailant.

After carefully examining and comparing the testimony, I think any candid mind will agree that as the deceased stepped upon the sidewalk in front of the prisoner, they simultaneously drew their pistols. There are six witnesses who prove that McKaig had drawn when Black fired, and two of them were brought here, though not sworn, by the prosecution. The same number or more saw the pistol fall from his hand as the prisoner's first shot took effect. The cane fell from the other hand at the same time. As the evidence shows, the ball had taken effect in the side and had ranged near the spine, producing a shock to the nervous and muscular systems. The prisoner had been able to fire quicker than his antagonist from the fact that his pistol, as you have seen here, is self-cocking.

It is contended, however, that the deceased had not drawn, because Dr. Smith and some others did not see the weapon in his hand, nor see it fall to the ground. This is no proof at all; it is of a character which is always scouted from the presence of positive, affirmative evidence. What one man did not see is often seen by many others. Instances of this rule are very familiar in all the books. In this case, however, those witnesses who did not see the pistol in McKaig's hand were also blind to his cane. Yet no one disputes that he had the cane. That is conceded by all. They say they did not see the pistol drop at the curbstone when the first shot was fired; but they admit also that they did not see the cane fall, and yet it is not denied by the prosecution that the cane fell there. If this negative testimony disproves the pistol, it likewise disproves the existence of the cane, although the cane and its fall from the hand of the deceased, the moment he received the prisoner's fire, are accepted facts in this case. But in this connection, why was Dr. Hummelshine not called by the prosecution? A strange and most lamentable feature in a criminal trial is here developed; it oppresses me with sorrow and apprehension. The suppression of evidence more extensive, systematic, and deliberate than I have ever known, here commences. Dr. Hummelshine's name is on the back of the indictment as the witness on whose testimony, and on whose testimony alone, before the grand jury, it was found. He has been here in obedience to the process of the state from the opening day of this court to the present hour. Yet the prosecution did not place him on the stand. The learned prosecutors closed their case without submitting to you the evidence on which the indictment was procured. Such an unnatural proceeding of course fixed our attention on this witness. We placed him on the witness-stand before you, and then it was discovered why he had been kept back. He saw the pistol fall from the hand of McKaig at the curbstone, into the gutter, when Black first fired; thus proving conclusively that it was already drawn for action. These are the words of the original witness for the state. Was it not the clear, plain duty of the prosecutors to call him? Do they wish to obtain a verdict against this young man by hiding the truth from you? Do they wish to shed his blood by fraud? Would they encompass his destruction by low artifice? What explanation is possible here? Have they not denied him the evidence in their own hands which demonstrates his innocence? What is the object of a trial like this? Is it the mere display of skill on the part of counsel in obtaining a verdict from you without scruple as to the means? The stake here played for is a human life; does the state of Maryland demand its sacrifice with only a partial knowledge on your part of the circumstances that have put it in jeopardy? I appeal to you; you represent this noble commonwealth to-day; you have been mocked and trifled with; you wanted the whole truth, and you had not received it when the prosecution closed and rested. They kept back a vital part and hoped we would never find it. Have you a favorable regard for such a prosecution? Does it commend itself to you? Those who ask and demand a verdict against the life of a fellow-mortal should do so with clean hands and pure hearts. I aim to say nothing unkind of counsel, but not for all the land that lies between the swelling waves of the two oceans would I strive for the conviction of a human being, concealing at the same time within my own mind a fact which would justly acquit him if made known to the jury. Where, also, was young Clark, the boy brought here with so much pains by those who inspire the private branch of the prosecution? You did not hear him testify until we put him, another state's witness, on the stand. He saw McKaig's second pistol drop from the relaxed muscles of his hand when he fell. Out of the mouths of its own chosen supporters this prosecution stands condemned, and Crawford Black stands justified. But more than all this, you were not allowed by the state to know that the deceased was armed at all, that he had a single weapon upon him. The learned counsel for the state ceased their examination without suffering a word or a hint of the truth on that point to reach your ears. Yet they were possessed of all knowledge in relation to it. They not only knew the evidence of Hummelshine as to the pistol at the curbstone of the south sidewalk, but that another was also found by his side when he was raised up in the middle of the street, and the third was yet remaining in the holster of his belt. He was carried into Dr. Smith's office, where his heavily armed condition was disclosed; yet the doctor was not called in chief—only in rebutting, when we had proven all the facts that were within his knowledge by others. Then the brother of the deceased, Mervin McKaig, appears next in this wholesale suppression of proof. He took his brother's belt and pistols and disappeared. Turney picked up one in the street; a man, whose name was unknown to the witness Hall, picked up the other, and the holster yet contained the third. Why was Mervin McKaig made to remain silent in your presence from day to day throughout this entire trial?

This is without a parallel in the annals of criminal jurisprudence. I candidly and firmly believe that it is utterly without precedent in English or American history. The man who became the keeper of those weapons of death, and who alone can tell their exact condition when the deceased fell, sits before you for two weeks, and opens not his mouth. The presumptions are all against a proceeding like this. Evidence that is suppressed is presumed to be injurious to those who suppress it. This is an ancient maxim of the law as well as a proverb of wisdom. You have a right to know the condition of those pistols immediately after the fatal affray. Were they all loaded, or had one barrel been discharged from the first or second one in the street? Is that the reason that Mervin McKaig made no explanation here? The defendant has the right to that presumption. The law gives it to him and you will not strive to withhold it. It is said that four shots were fired, and that the prisoner fired them all. Possibly it is so, but it would have been much easier to decide if the arms of the deceased had undergone the proper inspection and the result been detailed to you. There is a dark and cloudy spot here; all is not plain and fair; there is something to conceal and it is done. Two pistols have been produced here in the rebutting testimony as those of McKaig. How are they identified? Dr. Smith simply says they look like those he saw. Mervin McKaig, then, as now, present, could have removed all doubt by a word, but that word he did not speak. This strange and astounding plan for the conviction of a man by the suppression of facts, however, does not stop even here. Will some one tell me why Turney has remained dumb in this case? He has been here all the time, subpœnaed by the state, and doubtless ready to do his duty if permitted by those who brought him here. Several persons have testified that he was seen to take a pistol from the street after the deceased was removed. His name has been repeated over and over again in your hearing, and the fact that he himself was not brought forward to explain his own conduct, and to inform you of the condition in which he found that fire-arm, is damning and overwhelming to this prosecution. You should not move a single step toward a conviction. You should not even consider the testimony produced for that purpose. You should stop at the very threshold, and say to the state: "You have withheld vital and important facts that were under your control; you have not dealt fairly with us or with the prisoner at the bar, and yet you ask us to imbrue our hands in his blood. We decline and utterly refuse to join in such practice, and we dismiss your proposition as an insult to our intelligence and sense of justice."

But it has been urged, and will be again, that after the first shot the prisoner might with safety have ceased firing before he did. The perforated coat will be displayed in your sight, and a tongue of vengeance made to speak from every rent. But if Black had reason to believe that McKaig was seeking his life, and was amply prepared to take it, at what point of the conflict was he to pause, and say that the future was secure? He had seen the deceased come to meet him. He witnessed the shifting of the cane, the right hand in deadly preparation upon the pistol, and the act of drawing, all before he commenced his defense. Was anything more needed to convince him that the awful moment had arrived when one or the other must fall—when the fight was to be to the death? And with such bloody hostility proclaimed by the deceased, the prisoner was not required to cease the strife that had been forced upon him until he knew that his adversary was disabled and rendered incapable of further attack. Such is the written law of the land as administered in its courts of justice. I announce this in the hearing of their honors on the bench as one of the great cardinal doctrines of self-defense. Without it, indeed, there would be no self-defense. It would be a delusion and a snare. When, therefore, McKaig, as described by George Garner, sprang into the street after the first fire, and put his hand behind as if to draw another weapon, Black had no reason to believe that his life was yet safe. He could not know that the deceased was hit at all. He still stood and endeavored to continue the fight with the abundant means that were upon him. There was no security or peace for the prisoner until McKaig fell. If McKaig moved from Black, the evidence shows that it was only for the purpose of obtaining time and opportunity to draw a second pistol. Under these circumstances, was the prisoner to cease firing and allow the deceased to turn and fire upon him when he got ready? The deceased, in fact, did turn, and fell with his face toward the prisoner and with the pistol, afterward found by his side, in his hand. His arm had become nerveless, and it was too late for him to execute the last purpose of his life. And as he fell, the last scene in a long drama of secret sin and open shame, of private grief and public ruin, was closed by the sudden pall of death. But as that stalwart form lay there under the early sun of that morning, and as the liberated spirit ascended to the great fountain of life on high, what accusing word of guilt could it bear to the dread presence of a righteous God against Crawford Black? Wherein is his offense against the laws of man or the majesty of heaven? Would you have him avoid the encounter that was sought, abandon his right to the highway, and turn and flee from the face of his enemy? The laws, human and divine, make no such demand, nor does the history of your state. The fame of Maryland is glorious and full of honor in peace and in war. She is a child of the Revolution, and its baptism of fire and blood rested upon her head. Her sons are reputed brave, and her daughters beautiful and virtuous, wherever her name is spoken. The Maryland line met the scarlet uniform and the glittering steel of England, from the darker hours of Bunker Hill to the triumphant glory of Yorktown, in behalf of personal as well as national independence. With what pride you can point to that long and brilliant, though bloody, record; it has extorted terms of eulogy from the pens of even reluctant historians and commanded the admiration of posterity. Nor has her soil in modern times bred the spirit of cowardice. She has not infused it into the veins of her children, and no dastard's example is in her escutcheon to tempt the prisoner to flight and dishonor. He but stood his ground, as his fathers did before him, against the armed destroyer of life and the ravager of peaceful homes.

At this stage, however, of this dark and melancholy affair, the bitter cry, wrung at last from the prisoner's heart, is caught up by the prosecution and urged against him. Yes, when he saw McKaig fall, his lips broke forth for one brief utterance as if touched by the spirit of retributive justice. He thought no more of his own danger; he was unconscious of the peril of his own life, as the image of his poor sister, torn from her high estate of virtue, and then spurned and trampled upon, rose before his inflamed vision. It is said that the dying have a swift and far-reaching glance of the realms and records of time, but not more so than this prisoner at that supreme instant had of the pure-faced playmate of his childhood, now the prey, the sport, and the scorn of human perfidy— once wandering by his side in the early dawn of their lives; then expanding into womanhood like a "flower in flushing, when blighting was nearest;" then plucked by the ruthless hand of the seducer from the garden of honor, and flung away in a little while withered and dead. He beheld, too, the sweet, bright home of other days, when his loving mother smiled in her narrow, but happy and untainted, domestic circle; when her days and nights were not filled with weeping, and her face was not furrowed with tears; when her voice was not lifted up with lamentations more bitter than "the wail above the dead;" when his father's brow was not bent before the gaze of men because the deceased had covered it with the mildew of shame; when he himself looked forth upon the enticing career of manhood with a proud, high heart and an unblemished name. All this came as a flash upon memory, illuminating all the dear objects of his existence, and then giving way as suddenly to the worse than midnight darkness of the present hour. In the twinkling of an eye all was changed, and home, and sister, and father, and mother, and his own youthful hopes and pride, all lay together before his eyes in a heap of ruin and misery. The imprisoned pangs of his soul burst forth, and he spoke the fulfillment of human and divine justice. He announced the execution of the decrees of God and man; he proclaimed the fate of the man who had ruined his sister and pursued her father as a felon because he resented her destruction. Though his own life had been assailed, though he had justly stood upon his defense, yet his tongue gave the true interpretation of the reason that his adversary had fallen. "The wages of sin is death," and they had been earned, and were now paid.

Am I told that there is no law by which he who rifles a home of its most precious treasures shall be slain? Am I told that the prisoner announced a sentiment for which he should die, when he declared his sister's ruin to be the cause of that bloody scene? With magnanimity he waived all considerations of himself, and thought only of those dearer to him than life. For this shall he sup the horrors of a conviction at your hands? What more did he do, even if no principle of self-defense shielded him, than others have done in every age and in every clime? The Christian and the pagan tribes of men alike give him their examples and their support. Examine all that is left, all that can be found in every distinctive period of history since the great flood of mankind commenced to flow from a single family in the morning of time, and, with the exception of now and then a licentious reign like that of Charles the Second of England, where the object was to cheapen female virtue and license the unbridled lust of the court and its infamous favorites, you can find no precedent for the punishment of the prisoner, no authority to lay your hands upon the defender of your firesides and the protector of your homes against the common enemy of the human race. And I here, in this solemn presence, with the dread issues of life and death intrusted to my care, declare, as far as my voice will reach, that he who invades the sanctuary of a home, imposes the impurity of his debased and brutal desires upon the presence of innocence, breaks the charm and halo of virtue, and defiles the altar of domestic life, forfeits his right of abode in the midst of human society, and deserves to die. The husband's hand is thrice armed for his destruction, the father rises against him in paternal majesty, and the brother may scourge him from the face of the earth wherever he is found. His offense is beyond the reach of pardon, and appeals to heaven and earth combined for redress. It is rank with crime, and invites the lash of chastisement from every virtuous quarter. Nor is this doctrine without that same powerful sanction of which the mighty common law of England was born. That vast and splendid structure is simply the offspring of the customs and usages of the people of the British empire. Its broad and enduring foundations rest upon the long-continued habits and practices of an enlightened race and nation. It springs from the consent and approval of centuries. Has not the principle for which I contend the same great support? Is it not a common law within itself, the eldest born of all laws, antedating the days of Edward the Confessor and Alfred the Law-giver, as widespread as the light of history, and as universal as the nations of the earth? Has it not the sanction of Jehovah himself in the case I cited from the pages of sacred history? Did it not blaze forth from the heights of Sinai to the uttermost boundaries of space and time? The death of the seducer and the adulterer was decreed in the high courts of heaven when the ages were in their infancy, and the decision has been followed wherever the marriage couch has been spread and the family tie has been woven. The usages of civilization; the uniform conduct of men at the same moment of time, and in different and distant parts of the globe; the rulings of judicial tribunals, and, above all, the unvarying, unbroken chain of verdicts rendered by juries since the beginning of human jurisprudence, have all combined to establish and consolidate the fatal but just decree. Modern ages have lent their sanction to the customs of antiquity. The span of our own lives in these latter days is crowded with illustrations of the great truth which I lay before you. American history has its faithful story to tell, as well as the annals of the family in Israel, and of every civilized coast and tribe from that hour until the present day.

A quarter of a century ago, there occurred in Philadelphia, the city of meek and peaceful antecedents, a full and perfect test of this common law of homicide where a seducer is slain. The Singleton-Mercer case rang out upon the ear of the world as a note of safety to the young and confiding members of virtuous homes, and of warning to those polluted and polluting wretches who look upon woman in the same debasing spirit with which Satan, prowling amidst the splendors and the innocence of paradise, looked and leered with lustful eyes upon the unsuspicious and angelic movements of Eve. No ingredient of self-defense was there. The bald and naked issue was presented. The arm of the brother was made naked, and his right hand red in the defense of his sister's honor, and a jury of the vicinage and a jury of the world acquitted him with universal acclaim. The District of Columbia has the case of Jarboe, with the same unerring and philosophic result. California spoke within the last two years; and the great central state of Ohio makes her recent contribution in the case of McQuigg and his sister. I might multiply until I would degenerate into the simple narrator of a catalogue of events and names well known to you all.

And when we mount up to the unclouded regions of impartial reason and natural right, why should. not this rule against vice and on the side of virtue prevail? What mitigation can be offered for the conduct of the most evil monster produced from the lowest and most depraved elements of our fallen humanity? Can his crime be lessened or brightened by comparison with any other that darkens our brief pilgrimage beneath the stars? If the door or window of your house is broken, for an article of the meanest value, you may take the life of the burglar. It is only your house and its material contents that are in danger, but so tender is the regard of the written law for property that you may arise and slay to defend it. Do your dwellings contain nothing more valuable and sacred than silver and gold? Are there not gems this moment in the circle of your households, whose luster you would not have tarnished or their presence torn away for all the glittering treasures of the Golcondas, the Californias, and the Perus? Wives and daughters and sisters are there, and the loss of one to the embrace of dishonor would rend your hearts in twain, and plant a poison in the cup of life which would never cease to rankle until the grave gave you peace. Yet it is contended that for the criminal monster who might thus destroy all for which you live, and make life itself one long-continued and unbearable anguish, there is no personal punishment, no pain for him to suffer; that he may walk your streets in peace and security, and spend his days in ease and comfort, while his victim, pale and wasted with sorrow, is sinking into an untimely grave in some lonesome and secluded spot where she lies hidden from the unpitying eyes and unfeeling scoffs of the world. His crime is a thousandfold blacker than murder, yet there are no prisons or scaffolds for him. For the betrayed and ruined woman there is nothing left of life except the pain of living. The joy of existence never comes again. When we see the autumn leaf falling to the ground, and the white shroud of winter spread over the face of the fields, we are blest with the certain hope that the soft air of spring will, after a little while, come back to us and renew in our midst the splendors of this beautiful world; that the fresh greensward, adorned with flowers, will again spread at our feet, and the deep foliage of the forest will weave its bright canopy over our heads. But to the soul that has loved, trusted and lost, there comes no second spring. The solemn sky of autumn and the chilling winds of winter alone remain to her. No glad and golden summer awaits her in the future. A scorched and barren desert without verdure, without tree, or plant, or blossom, or shrub, or one single cooling fountain at which to rest in all the desolate pilgrimage, lies before her tired and faltering footsteps. She makes the rest of her journey, too, alone. The leper's taint is upon her in the eyes of the world, and friends fall off and avert their faces. And, with such a spectacle as this before you, are you willing to say that the man who thus curses the entire existence of one whose sole offense has been her blind, unreasoning devotion to him should pass unscathed and unwhipped of justice? Such a decision would spurn and trample under your feet the holiest and tenderest interests, affections, and loves of humanity, and would blaspheme all the attributes of a just and righteous God.

Does some one, however, who is careful of the life of the destroyer, profane this subject with a suggestion of damages as a measure of legal redress? The bare thought stifles an elevated nature with feelings of loathing and disgust. Who can estimate the value of family honor? Who shall lay a price on domestic happiness? Who shall remunerate you for the stolen and defiled members of your household? As well might you attempt to fix the value of a lost and ruined soul in hell. "What will a man not give for his own soul?" and will he not give the same, or even a higher ransom, if need be, for the salvation of wife, mother, daughter, and sister? Without them, in their purity, the regions of time and earth would be filled with fiery tortures, and the condition of the fallen spirits in eternity could be no worse. Can you pay the husband for his wife, the son for his mother, the brother for his sister, and the father for his daughter? Can you make atonement to the heart-broken woman herself for violated vows and wanton perfidy? Can she or any of those that love her be redeemed to their original estate by the assessment of damages? A division of property between the social outlaw and his prey may be just, but, as a mode of punishment, it is vain and void of meaning. Who, also, would have such gain? If a judgment was taken in favor of the husband or father, in whose behalf an action lies, what a revolting acquisition to his fortune it would be? In what way would he expend it? If the husband invests it in "ships that go down to the sea," he makes his ventures into foreign lands and distant waters upon the wages rendered him by a jury for his wife's infamy. He traffics upon the honor of her whose dear and precious head once laid in its sweet sleep of fidelity upon his confiding heart. If his argosies come home from successful voyages, they are freighted with gains founded upon the dishonor of his bed, the debasement of his name, and the overthrow of all his fireside gods. His bills of lading stare at him as the reward of his submission to the lowest depths of degradation ever fathomed by the most abject spirits of the human race. The articles of merchandise, which he unpacks and offers in exchange at his counter, would salute him with the taint of moral death and remind him perpetually of his hideous bereavement. The ghost of his murdered peace would arise and confront him wherever he turned.

If the father accepted a pecuniary award for the shame of his daughter, it would bitterly mock him in all the after years. In what channel of trade would he embark with the proceeds? If he bartered them for lands, his growing meadows, his waving corn, his ripening wheat, and flocks and herds upon his hills would seem to be flourishing over the dishonored tomb of his lost and undone child. His soul would sicken at the sight of his own prosperity springing from such a source. He would turn away, and, though filled with the peaceful precepts of our holy religion, he would invoke the death of the seducer and pray for the blessings of heaven to rest upon the hand that smites him in his career of wickedness. This is the universal law of the human heart, and the prisoner at the bar simply proclaimed it when he slew the deceased. Such is the meaning of his exclamation when tried by all the experience, instincts, and reason of mankind.

And now, gentlemen, my labors are drawing to a close. I have endeavored to treat plainly and fairly all the material aspects of this painful and most important case. If there is guilt in the conduct of the prisoner, I have not found it. Soon you will discharge the most momentous duty of your lives. In a few hours more you will determine whether Crawford Black shall live or die. There is no intermediate point for one like him. If he is guilty at all, he tells me to say to you that he anxiously and earnestly desires the extreme and fatal penalty of the law. I join in that solemn and awful request. That untainted and unsullied spirit must not herd with hardened felons, or taste the fearful degradation of the penitentiary. The odious garb of the prison was not made for such a form as his. Far rather would I bid him farewell forever on the scaffold than to know that he lived with the stain of infamy upon him. But I will not indulge in such gloomy forebodings. I believe that you approach a cheerful and pleasing task. I believe that your faces will be radiant with happiness as you restore the prisoner to life, liberty, and the embrace of his weeping parents. They reach forth their eager arms to carry him home. They have been lonely, very lonely there for many months. This mother has wept like Rachel for her children because they were not. One has been taken—the spoiler's prey; you will not take the other also. As the aged father in Israel clung to Benjamin when Joseph was gone, so do these afflicted parents yearn for their good and dutiful son, and long to clasp him, free and unharmed, to their bereaved breasts. In full confidence that by your verdict you will grant this blessed privilege, reunite this broken family, and solace their wounded hearts, as far as it may be done by human power, I surrender all, all into your hands. Accept my thanks, each one of you, for your kind and patient attention; and allow me to tender you my best wishes for your future welfare and happiness.

MISCELLANY

DANIEL W. VOORHEES

THE INFLUENCE OF THE PHYSICAL SCIENCES ON THE PROGRESS OF CIVILIZATION

An address delivered before the Athenian and Union Literary Societies of the University of Missouri, June 22, 1874.

THE relations which exist between the human mind and the works of physical creation, involve the entire problem of human progress. When man first arose from the dust, he was proclaimed the master of this planet. He received from the divine hand a grant of power, infinite in its scope and value. It was determined that he had a right to dominion over the fruits of the fields and the beasts of the plains, the bosoms of the oceans and the dwellers in the deep, the winged inhabitants of the air, and even the swift winds themselves, and the subtle and burning contents of the angry clouds. This decree was not in consequence of his physical ability to sustain his supremacy over nature by force, but because of the intellect with which he alone, of all created beings, was endowed, and with which it was possible for him to accomplish the task before him. He was placed in such relations to the other works of creation that, by the proper development and exercise of his own powers, he could find out their principles and subjugate them to his uses, and to the happiness and the glory of the human race.

The dominion to which he thus became heir in the beginning, it will be observed, however, was a right announced and not a possession bestowed. The inheritance was spread out before him to entice him forward to obtain it. Its wealth and splendor were in view to stimulate him to action. Its luxuries appeared to tempt his desires; its honors to awaken his ambition, and its obstacles and dangers to arouse and excite his courage. In proportion to the response which man has given to these powerful inducements, so has been his progress and useful achievements in every period of the world's history. And yet how indifferently, for unnumbered centuries, he looked upon the material universe, wherein he all the time had the vested title of a conqueror, whenever he should penetrate its mysteries and discover the science of its various elements! How limited his range of vision and of knowledge!

The earlier tribes of humanity saw the fields immediately about them filled with corn and wine; they saw the flocks and herds on the hills that were to feed and clothe them; but beyond the control of these things, they did not seek to advance their standard of dominion. Their power over the forces and gifts of nature was feeble and limited. Their period was the infancy of the human race, during which its simple wants alone aroused it to action. The conditions on which the children of men were to climb the heights of civilization, and reduce the earth and its fullness to a state of vassalage, were unheeded in the primitive ages. There was no struggle then to enter into possession of the inheritance by the appointed gateways. If there was labor, it was without understanding; and hence there are thousands of years of human existence engulfed in almost total oblivion, leaving but here and there a dim, uncertain page of history, without a single achievement worthy of record or memory.

The one vital condition on which depends the progress of man is a knowledge of the objects, the elements, and the scenes which on all sides salute his senses. Long and dreary ages rolled away, whose pathway is barren and cheerless, before we find the human intellect even considering this great question. It is often claimed that labor is the primary agent of human advancement. It is but secondary. Knowledge must be its forerunner. It must be guided by eyes that see and ears that hear the truths and harmonies of the material world.

The realms of history are filled with the melancholy monuments of toil, directed by ignorance, superstition, and despotism. The massive walls and gorgeous palaces of Babylon, the hundred brazen gates of Thebes, the aspiring and impious tower of Babel, the pyramids of Egypt—those gigantic relics of pride, folly, oppression, and mental darkness—all tell their sad stories of unenlightened and unrequited labor. They brought not a single blessing to mankind. They arose in obedience to no requirement of beneficent nature. On the contrary, they originated in the vain conceits of an ignorant tyranny, and were reared and cemented in the blood and tears of benighted millions. They stand as the shame and not as the glory of labor.

It is true that the student of antiquity often dwells with veneration and enthusiasm on the achievements of Asiatic and Egyptian civilizations. We have the traditions of their success in certain pursuits, but they have left no permanent additions to the sum of human knowledge or human happiness. They did not conquer the elements of nature or find out her now familiar principles. Agriculture, the foundation of all national greatness, was a degraded profession. The farmer, in those periods and countries, was a serf, and knew but little more of the qualities and capacities of the soil than the inferior animals that assisted him to till it. Commerce was confined to a limited coasting trade, because the expansive regions of the oceans and seas were filled with imaginary terrors to ignorant minds.

The laws of navagation, the needle and compass, the shape of the earth and the steadfastness of the north star were all unknown. Instead of the merchantman spreading her prosperous sails from port to port, or the steamship under intelligent guidance traversing the waters of the Mediterranean, the Indian Ocean, the Arabian Sea, the Persian Gulf, the Bay of Bengal, the Red Sea and the Caspian, trains of weary-footed and heavily laden camels toiled slowly over the sands between Cairo and Damascus, Babylon and Bagdad. Nature held out her gifts and powers then as now. There is an absolute eternity in the laws of the material universe. It was blind, undeveloped man, with wealth, and dominion, and glory on all sides, and under his feet, and over his head, without the knowledge to reach forth his hand and possess them. He had no just conception of the relations which he bore to the Creator, or to the creation. He confounded the works which he daily saw with that Author whom no eye hath seen.

The most learned Egyptian knew not enough of science to satisfy him that a loathsome reptile, or a helpless brute, was not the God of the heavens and the earth, and entitled to his humble and abject worship. He saw the crocodile live and die and rot in the sun, and yet cherished his faith in its wisdom, omnipotence, and immortality. His race dwelt for more than two thousand years along the banks of the Nile, in a valley not averaging twenty miles wide, without ascertaining that the rains in the mountains, and not a river god, caused the waters to swell and inundate their fields with rich and fertilizing deposits. No explorer ascended the life-sustaining stream. The centuries came and went; the generations arose and followed each other, like waves, to the viewless shore of eternity; ages upon ages were added to Egypt's hoary history, and yet no Egyptian Speke or Livingstone ever went up the Nile, over the mountains and beyond the equator, to find its deep and everlasting fountains. Fear, the child of superstition and ignorance, chained him to the little valley of his ancestors. The order of things proclaimed by God was totally reversed. Man was not the master, but the slave of nature. He did not control her; she controlled him; and his submission was absolute and degraded. No genuine civilization can spring from this unnatural basis. No healthy products can accrue to mankind from such an apathy and perversion of the mental powers. By virtue of her location, Egypt was simply the foremost power of Africa. This was not much, but it was all.

If we cross over that narrow space, however, between the approaching extremities of the Mediterranean and the Red Sea, which separates Africa from Asia, and penetrate north and eastward into the most ancient and renowned seats and habitations of the human family, the same ignorance of the laws of the universe meet us at every step. Who in all those vast realms, where the innumerable millions of the Oriental races have swarmed throughout all the ages of the past, has given his name to history as an inventor, a discoverer, or an explorer of the natural sciences?

On the plains of Asia, more of human history has been enacted than in all the other four quarters of the globe combined. I speak not now of that limited race, with its narrow possessions, which was set apart and isolated for a special and divine purpose. It is true that it might be done with safety; for while the Jehovah revealed himself to the Jews, there is no evidence that they were wiser in the laws which govern the earth and its productions, the seasons and their influences, than the other far more numerous and powerful nations of Asia. But the manner of their existence was an exception to the general order of the world, and philosophy will reject them when seeking to establish general principles upon the concurrent testimony of mankind.

The various and wide-spread peoples, coming and going with the moving centuries, as countless as the leaves of the forest, or as the falling rain-drops, and from whose teeming ranks were drawn such armies as that which followed Xerxes to "sea-born Salamis"—as that which Cyrus led to the conquest of Babylon, and Alexander overthrew under Darius—must make answer for the achievements of the ancient East and her systems of thought and industry. Where are their practical and useful philosophers? Who will point out their monuments of learning? We have the remains of their poetry as florid and as fervid as the sunbeams of the meridian. Broken fragments of their fables and their fictions have also descended to us. They tell of imaginations riotous and luxuriant; but where are the traces of a mind in Oriental literature which labored to acquire that scientific knowledge of the physical creation, which alone constitutes man's power and supremacy over it? The attempt even was never made. There are traditions, it is true, that the Chaldeans knew something of the plainer rudiments of astronomy; but the most careful researches into the writings of that and subsequent periods will fail to show them more learned in that science than the experienced woodsman or herdsman, who has spent his days and nights beneath the open and instructive sky. The now ascertained and measured movements of the heavenly bodies were to them sealed mysteries. They beheld the stars blazing from the bended firmament, and invested them with strange and weird influences over the births, the lives, the deaths, and the final destinies of the people. They halted amidst the delusive snares and dreams of astrology, and there remained forever.

Nor were the ancient eastern founders of religious faith in a great First Cause ever aided in their inquiries by a knowledge of the properties and laws of those objects of creation with which they were in perpetual intercourse. They walked upon the earth from their cradles to their graves, but they never challenged for inspection its eternal records of dates and formations. It bore no testimony to them of the time and the ages whence it came. The voices of the rocks and the stratas were silent to their ears. The truths of geology lay buried and hidden in the unexplored recesses of matter. No spirit of investigation called them forth to number the years of this planet, or to reveal and mark the changes and convulsions which have taken place in its seasons, its structure, and the myriad forms of animal life with which it has abounded. And in the absence of all this knowledge the imagination sported in unrestrained license with those vast questions which concern the attributes of Deity, and the truth and harmony of his works.

The Hindoo, arbitrarily and without a gleam of science or reference to a single fact, allots to his own nation a period of over two thousand million of years, and to the earth itself much more. In disregard of the plainest principles of our physical existence, he assigns to his earlier ancestors an average lifetime of eighty thousand years; and as if to show the extent to which the imagination can carry a people wholly surrendered to ignorance and superstition, it is a recorded fact in Hindoo history that the first king, anchorite, and saint of that nation, lived until he was eight million and four hundred thousand years old, during which time he reigned over his people for more than six million of years. Such stupendous errors in regard to the works of creation were necessarily accompanied by a total ignorance of the character and purposes of the Creator. As an evidence of this, the Hindoos of antiquity worshiped a triad of malignant beings, the principal of whom was a monster in human shape, clothed in the skin of a tiger, "encircled with a girdle of snakes, with a human skull in his hand, and wearing a necklace composed of human bones," while "over his left shoulder the deadly cobra de capello rears its head," as if to strike. With this revolting being was supposed to roam his wife, as sanguinary and as horrible as himself. If knowledge is power, what indescribable weakness does such mental darkness as this disclose! If such were the ideas of those who wrote histories, made literature, and lived in the front lines of their race, what tongue or pen can portray the deplorable condition of the inferior ranks in their rear—of the laboring masses, on whose intelligent industry the prosperity and civilization of all nations must depend? They came forth into being, and then passed away like the frail and aimless insect tribes of the air, leaving no trace of a useful existence. They left not a single sign in the direction of progress.

But the foremost and most conspicuous place in national antiquity, while the regions of the Orient yet embraced the discovered portions of the human family, was always held by the empire of Persia. The names of her warriors and heroes, her once renowned cities, and her famous battle-plains are all familiar in the pages of modern books. She has been the theme of the sweetest song and most fascinating romance; and the author and the orator have often pointed to her as the theater of human progress and human glory. A resolute look, however, at her systems of thought and action, stripped of that alluring enchantment which distance lends to the view, will speedily demonstrate how meager are her claims to this distinction. The true dominion of man over the forces and the elements of nature was nowhere asserted, much less accomplished, in all her far-reaching boundaries. The laborer was a slave, who toiled to pay tribute in time of peace, and followed his master to a nameless grave in time of war. His position in the social scale and in political consideration was no higher than that assigned to a beast of burden. His calling, as he wrought in the fields, was a badge of the lowest inferiority. Nor did he possess a particle of that information in his pursuits that always enforces respect and confers dignity. The rudest and simplest contrivances of wood sufficed to extort his scanty returns from the spot of his temporary culture and sojourn. His chief reliance was upon the spontaneous bounties of nature. His flocks and herds grew in the green pastures that lined the water-courses, and afforded him a subsistence without mental or physical exertion. His manner of life was no higher than that of the semi-civilized American Indian who plants and rudely cultivates his few acres of corn on the outskirts of the white man's settlements, and depends for his meat on the wild cattle, the elk, and the deer of the neighboring plains.

There was no effort made to spread light and knowledge in

his darkened sphere. The school-house, the college, and the seminary for the masses were unknown. And, indeed, amongst the titled few, who aspired to be thought learned, no such institutions were heard of. In their places were vain and speculative sects, styling themselves philosophers, reasoning from premises of superstition and ignorance, leading themselves and their followers in wild and visionary paths, and reaching conclusions exactly opposed to a just conception of the duties of mankind and the real purposes involved in the existence of the human race. Take their ideas of divine worship. In the absence of the natural sciences to inform them of the qualities and rules of the material universe, they seized upon its more commanding and brilliant parts, and deified them with their unenlightened devotions. They saw the sun in the firmament, and knew not whence it came or whither it went, of what it was composed, or the mighty functions which the omnipotent hand of God had appointed it to perform. They knew not that it was a stationary center, around which moved innumerable worlds, each in its given pathway, without deviation or weariness, since the morning stars sung creation's hymn, and each receiving its allotment of light and heat from the inexhaustible fountain of both. This was a mystery which awaited a higher type of man and a nobler development of his powers for its solution. The Persian mind worshiped what it could not comprehend, and built altars and burned incense to the sun as the supreme Deity.

Fire was thought and felt to be an emanation from the sun, and hence it, too, became an object of ignorant reverence and devotion. It may perhaps be justly conceded that of all the systems of pagan mythology, that of the fire-worshipers was the most elevated, and had more visible reasons, to an uninstructed mind, in its support than any other. They constantly witnessed the wonderful and benignant influences of the heat and the light of the sun. They beheld all nature revive and live and grow under its warmth. The tender blade of grass put forth; the meadows were mantled in green; the stripling corn became stalwart and strong; the gay colors of flowers delighted the eye, and their perfumes enriched the air; the leaves of the forest spread their more than royal canopies overhead; the fields ripened for the harvest, and

brought forth their welcome returns; the orchards and the vineyards produced their treasures of purple and of gold; and the cattle on the hills fattened for the use of man on the bountiful repast of nature. And when winter came and the heat of the sun was withdrawn, the fire on their hearthstones was its representative, and kept them alive and administered to their comfort. They saw, too, the awakening power of light, which came from the presence of the great luminary, and the death-like influence of darkness, which fell upon the world in its absence. With the fresh breaking day, came the sounds and movements of busy life, and with the descending curtains of nightfall, came sleep—the counterfeit resemblance, the twin brother of death. It is not, therefore, a matter of wonder, though it may be of regret, that an untutored mind, with these striking phenomena, and many more than can be here enumerated, forever attendant upon heat and light, and constantly present for its contemplation, should be led to a belief in the supernatural attributes and powers of the source whence they come. But can such an awful misunderstanding of the relations between man and his Maker, and between man and the works of creation, be accompanied by a vigorous and healthy civilization? Can a people be successful in their systems of agriculture, commerce, navigation, and general enterprise, who know not why or whence the seasons come—what natural laws cause the balmy breath of spring, the ripening heat of summer, or the cool and drying atmosphere of autumn; who can not comprehend the source of the dews, or why the rains will fall at their appointed times for the growth of vegetation?

Can a prosperous and abundant husbandry be built up and established by those who are ignorant of the principles by which the seeding-time and the harvest are governed? History gives no uncertain answer to these questions. The moldering ruins and blighted plains of antiquity are all filled with voices proclaiming the shortcomings and the failures of man in the absence of scientific discoveries. And if we follow the migrations of the human family, as it sent forth its branches from the regions of the Euphrates and the Tigris, and from all the eastward realms beyond, we will find this great truth still further illustrated and established. In this connection let us look at the map of the world.

An intelligent look at its instructive face reveals the natural pathways of emigration and of empire. They have forever led from the east to the west, when not diverted temporarily aside by the lust of conquest. The first great movement which we can now discern commenced in the dim twilight of history, by the discovery of that far eastern point of the Mediterranean Sea which penetrates so near to the abode of our first parents. The tribes of men, whether civilized or savage, follow streams and bodies of water, and they soon found their way from the mainland of Asia Minor to the Island of Cypress, and in due time to the Archipelago, in the midst of which the jutting peninsula of Greece pushes out into the waves. There, for indefinite centuries, the human race halted in its westward march, and put forth a strength and glory until then unknown. That veneration which is prone to hallow everything ancient, and covered with the dust and mold of ages, here usually delights to dwell, and revel in the alleged superiority of the past over the present. All, perhaps, have felt and indulged to some extent in this sentiment, and yet who can successfully defend it? The imagination always feels itself at liberty to adorn remote periods and distant objects with pleasing and attractive illusions; but how often they vanish at the touch of reason and of fact!

There is much, it is true, in Grecian history to admire, and a few things for mankind to imitate. A noble and majestic language was there formed and spoken, and became the channel of a powerful eloquence, and resounding and melodious poetry. A wonderful conception of the human face and form remains in marble for the instruction and enthusiasm of the modern sculptor; and the painter and the architect likewise gave immortality to their works. They remain as the evidences of lofty genius and refined cultivation in those pursuits; but in all the more solid and useful branches of knowledge, which underlie the foundations of human greatness and permanent progress, the conscientious student will find the Greeks—the polished Greeks in comparison with the ruder barbarians around them—occupying merely the vestibule, and not the inner courts of the temple of science and learning. Their climate and locality favored a superior physical development, both of form and feature; and with high health and strong vitality, came daring spirits and bold fancies. Their soil and their sea were prolific of their offerings; but in what way did they seek to assert their supremacy over them? Was knowledge their guide to that proud dominion which has been bequeathed as a heritage to man? What were their ideas of the world in which they lived and ambitiously aspired? An eminent author has given an answer which I quote and adopt. He says:

> The Greeks believed the earth to be flat and circular, their own country occupying the middle of it, the central point being either Mount Olympus, the abode of the gods, or Delphi, so famous for its oracle. The circular disk of the earth was crossed from west to east, and divided into two equal parts by the sea, as they called the Mediterranean and its continuation, the Euxine—the only seas with which they were acquainted. Around the earth flowed the river Ocean, its course being from south to north on the western side of the earth, and in a contrary direction on the eastern side. It flowed in a steady, equable current, unvexed by storm or tempest. The sea and all the rivers on earth received their waters from it. The northern portion of the earth was supposed to be inhabited by a happy race named the Hyperboreans, dwelling in everlasting bliss and spring, beyond the lofty mountains whose caverns were supposed to send forth the piercing blasts of the north wind, which chilled the people of Greece. Their country was inaccessible by land or sea. They lived exempt from disease or old age, from toils or warfare.
> On the south side of the earth, close to the stream of Ocean, dwelt a people happy and virtuous as the Hyperboreans. They were named the Ethiopians. The gods favored them so highly that they were wont to leave at times their Olympian abodes, and go to share their sacrifices and banquets. On the western margin of the earth, by the stream of Ocean, lay a happy place named the Elysian plain, whither mortals favored by the gods were transported, without tasting of death, to enjoy an immortality of bliss. This happy region was also called the "Fortunate Fields" and the "Isles of the Blessed."
> The dawn, the sun, and the moon were supposed to rise out of the Ocean on the eastern side, and to drive through the air, giving light to gods and men. The stars also, except those forming the Wain or Bear, and others near them, rose out of and sank into the stream of Ocean. There the sun-god embarked in a winged boat, which conveyed him round by the northern part of the earth back to his place of rising in the east.

After this dark picture of ignorance in relation to the visible works of the material universe, we are not so much amazed at the following portrayal of a miserable faith in the beings of the invisible world:

> The abode of the gods was on the summit of Mount Olympus in Thessaly. A gate of clouds, kept by the goddesses, named the Seasons, opened to permit the passage of the celestials to earth, and to receive them on their return. The gods had their separate dwellings; but all, when summoned, repaired to the palace of Jupiter, as did also those deities whose usual abode was the earth, the

waters, or the under world. It was also in the great hall of the palace of the Olympian king that the gods feasted each day on ambrosia and nectar—their food and drink—the latter being handed around by the lovely goddess Hebe. Here they conversed of the affairs of heaven and earth; and, as they quaffed their nectar, Apollo, the god of music, delighted them with the tones of the lyre, to which the muses sang in responsive strains. When the sun was set, the gods retired to sleep in their respective dwellings.

Can we wonder any longer that a people so bereft of light, so immersed in the darkest superstitions, should have left but little, if anything, for this wise and practical age to adopt, or that their institutions and civilizations should have fallen and passed away forever? Truth alone contains the elements of perpetuity, and the Greeks built upon errors as stupendous and flagrant as have ever blinded the actions of men or disfigured the pages of history.

If I am reminded that Plato reasoned well on the immortality of the soul, my answer is that the red man of the American forests, when first found, untamed in his solitudes, reasoned better, and reached loftier, firmer and more sublime conclusions. Unaided and solitary in the woods and in communion with the aspects of nature alone, he found one supreme, spiritual Deity who rewarded virtues and punished vices, and to whom immortality returned when it put off the mortality of time. The accomplished Athenian rambled in his wavering faith through a Pantheon of many gods, while the untutored Indian was as unshaken as the rocks in his beautiful belief in one. And if Socrates died like a philosopher, calmly disregarding the terrors of death and speculating on a future state of existence, so have unlettered heathens accepted martyrdom with equal fortitude and far greater cruelty, and triumphed in the absolute assurances of an eternal life. If the swift-footed hunter and the painted warrior have asked that the dog and the horse be slain upon their graves to accompany them in another world, so the Grecian sage, after drinking the hemlock, directed the sacrifice of a cock to propitiate a purely fabulous and imaginary deity. In regard, therefore, to an understanding of the attributes of the Supreme Being through the observation and study of his works, there has been but little difference between the most cultivated and the most savage nations of the pagan world. We find the same absence of scientific truth in both, and consequently neither have ever risen to a durable condition of progress and prosperity.

But still farther to the west, and on another and larger peninsula penetrating the waters of the Mediterranean, arose another form of human society and human government, which swallowed up Greece and all her arts, her ideas, and her possessions, and soon became a vast reservoir into which were thrown the systems and nations of antiquity, in confusion, subjection, and almost in oblivion. The extent and magnificence of Roman power has dazzled every succeeding age, and may well fill the greatest minds with wonder, if not with awe. The majesty of Rome, which fills our schools with declamation, was indeed more than a mere sounding title. For seven centuries, the name, the form, and many of the principles of a free government were preserved and enjoyed by her citizens. Under the banner of the republic, all her unparalleled conquests were made, except Britain, Dacia, and the eastern provinces that submitted to the sword of Trajan. Her sway was absolute from the Straits of Gilbraltar on the west to the Euphrates and the Persian Gulf on the east; from the Rhine and from beyond the Danube on the north, to the torrid sands of the interior of Africa on the south—embracing an extent of country far greater than that over which the American flag flies to-day. Through these gigantic possessions, for twenty-six hundred miles, stretched the calm and glorious Mediterranean Sea, so named because it was supposed to be in the middle of the earth. Every foot of its fertile shores, and all the islands of magical loveliness and wealth which adorned its bosom, were owned and held by the republic, and then by the empire. The Romans sat down by this beautiful sea, in the midst of the teeming bounties of all the elements, overspread by the serenest skies, and invigorated by the kindliest climate, and reaching forth their powerful hands, seized upon and rendered tributary the richest and most productive portions of the then known regions of the globe. Their ancient boundaries, explained by the modern map, reveal the startling magnitude of their dominion. The greatest kingdoms and empires of the present day were their obedient provinces, and toiled, not for themselves, but for their masters at the eternal city of the hills. Spain, Portugal, France, England, Belgium, Switzerland, Turkey, Greece, and large portions of Austria and Prussia, comprised the European possessions of Rome outside of Italy, her legitimate home.

In Africa, she was mistress of Morocco, Algeria, Tunis, Tripoli, and Egypt—the five states of Barbary—constituting a productive belt nearly three thousand miles long, with an average of one hundred miles wide, lying in the temperate zone, and between the destructive sands of Sahara on the south and the sea on the north. In the other great division of the eastern hemisphere, her arms embraced all now held within the confines of Asiatic Turkey, together with extensive regions of Persia and Arabia. A territory so expansive, comprising such a variety of climates, soils, rivers, oceans, and inland seas, was never before or since ruled by a single government. Those admitted to the citizenship of Rome, together with their wives and children, numbered twenty million of souls; the inhabitants of her provinces forty million, and her slaves sixty million; making the enormous aggregate population of one hundred and twenty million—more than three times the present population of the United States. It thus appears, however, that twenty million of people held one hundred million in military subjection and in personal servitude; a fact which of itself goes far to explain the final overthrow of this colossal power.

But there were other and even more inevitable causes at work upon the vitality of Roman civilization. The inferiority of the nations and tribes by whom Rome was then surrounded contributed more to her comparative elevation and greatness than her own useful achievements, if tried by the present standard of knowledge and utility. No enlightened historian pretends that her principal concern was for the development of the great industrial pursuits, or for the advancement of those practical and beneficial sciences which have given modern humanity its splendid dominion over the fields of nature. On the contrary, it is admitted by the most eminent authors that the tillage of the earth was pursued mainly for the support of her great and numerous armies; and commerce was encouraged for the purpose of ministering, with the silks, the perfumes, the precious stones, and diamonds of distant countries, to the demands of the opulent and effeminate classes.

That wonderful, though now common article of wealth and food, designated in general as corn, was then wholly unknown, and Gibbon, the warm eulogist of ancient Rome, in touching on her principal products, condescends to make no mention of any great staple of breadstuff as a substitute. This eloquent, though partial historian, makes but a feeble exhibition in behalf of the industrial classes. He enumerates the apple, the apricot, the peach, the pomegranate, the citron, and the orange as fruits cultivated by the Roman people. He mentions their flowers, and dwells with delight on the generous vintage of their bounteous and unfailing vines. The olive also attracts his attention; and he closes his notice of the agricultural products of Rome with the brief statement that the cultivation of flax was transported from Egypt to Gaul, and that the farmers of Italy and the provinces were familiar with artificial grasses, which supplied their cattle with food during the winter.

His mention of Roman commerce is equally significant. After describing the periodical voyages down the Red Sea, and across to the coast of Malabar and to the island of Ceylon, he says:

> The objects of Oriental traffic were splendid and trifling: Silk, a pound of which was esteemed not inferior in value to a pound of gold; precious stones, among which the pearl claimed the first rank after the diamond; and a variety of aromatics that were consumed in religious worship and the pomp of funerals. The labor and risk of the voyage were rewarded with almost incredible profit; but the profit was made upon Roman subjects, and a few individuals were enriched at the expense of the public.

Here is the graphic picture of a civilization which oppressed and enslaved the laborer, and corrupted and enervated the rich and the indolent. To be impressed with the grandeur of Rome, we must leave the furrow of the plowman, the fields of peace and industry, and follow the march of her mailed legions.

War was her element, and helpless nations were her prey. The plowshare and the pruning-hook were not the emblems of her pride and glory. She bowed before no prince of peace, but lavished her devotions on Mars and on Terminus, the god of slaughter and the god of boundaries. Her vast history, expanding over the events of eleven hundred and sixty-three years—from the founding of the city until it was sacked by Alaric and his Goths—surrenders almost every page as a catalogue of armies, conflicts, marches, sieges, battle-fields, pillages, robberies, accounts of the number slain, and the still more miserable captives spared alive.

The mind becomes jaded and sated with the endless repetitions of sanguinary and revolting scenes; the heart shrinks back stifled and appalled, and pants for a purer, higher, and better atmosphere. All the knowledge possessed by the Romans in regard to the earth, the seas, the rivers, the heavenly bodies, the recurrence and the influences of the seasons, and the division of the year into days, weeks and months, was incidental and subservient to their genius and love for war. Geography, that splendid and fascinating study, was unknown beyond the countries that were conquered. They were compelled to survey contiguous regions in order to penetrate and subdue them. The establishment of a boundary, or an outpost, was the signal for exploring parties to advance and mark for conquest the realms immediately beyond. Routes for military movements were required to be laid down on maps with accuracy and care—not merely marking the distances from place to place, but also describing the character of the roads, the rivers that were to be crossed, and the mountains whose summits were to be scaled, or whose gaps and defiles were to be passed and guarded. And after the battles were over, and a country was subdued, among other ample preparations to hold it, none were more necessary and efficient than the construction of those solid and durable highways leading to the capital, the remains of which are yet to be seen. They were links in the powerful chain which bound the provinces to the center. "They united the subjects of the most distant provinces by an easy and familiar intercourse; but their primary object had been to facilitate the marches of the legions; nor was any country considered as completely subdued till it had been rendered, in all its parts, pervious to the arms and authority of the conqueror." Such were the ferocious purposes for which the most useful monuments of Roman industry were erected!

But her warlike spirit, as well as her desire for the gaudy wares of the East, impelled Rome to attempt the art of navigation. All

Europe, Asia, and Africa were open to her by land; and the whole world, then as now, invited men of science to sail whither they listed on the waters, and establish the peaceful triumphs of knowledge over the secrets of space and matter.

The lust of conquest, the love of riches, and the natural thirst for information, however, all combined, produced not one single correct conception of the material universe in the minds of the Roman people, or their wisest philosophers and explorers. The wildest and most fanciful conjectures prevail in all their writings on subjects that are now the most familiar and practical. Mela, Pliny, and Strabo, after Herodotus, were the great geographers of antiquity. Their opportunities for the discovery of truth have never been surpassed; yet their theories are vague and absurd, and their facts limited to a few of the plainest. Herodotus, styled sometimes the father of geography, visited Persia, Assyria, Egypt, Thrace, Scythia, and other distant countries; but he did not even attempt to combine them into a general system of creation, or apply to them the principles of mathematics or astronomical calculation. The globular form of the earth and its rotary motion were treated with scoff and jest by him. He judged it simply as far as he saw it; and science, which, by unerring rules, finds out unknown things from those that are already known, was not called to his assistance. He speedily becomes mystical and fabulous; and this eminent authority of the ancients gravely assures us that he found in his journeyings a race of men with the heads of horses, and others with no heads at all. His successors, five hundred years afterward, were scarcely more intelligent. They knew no more of the physical sciences than he did; and the still unconquered dangers of the ocean prevented them from discovering the nature and shape of the earth by actual observation. Galleys pulled by oars were not to be trusted far from familiar coasts.

Thus the dominion of man over the earth and the fullness thereof, declared to be his birthright in the beginning of time, was not accomplished by the most powerful and most gifted nation of the past. It failed from a want of knowledge. It passed away without the slightest conception of the true mission and destiny of the human race, or of the extent and character of the sphere which we inhabit. It fell, too, from the force of its own example—the example of violence and bloodshed—the sure accompaniments of national ignorance. It had sought not that peaceful supremacy over the natural elements which constitutes permanent progress and glory, but rather the dominion of man over his fellow-man. And for a thousand years after the downfall of Rome—from the fifth century of the Christian era to the fifteenth—the human race gave all its faculties and energies to fields of strife and carnage, and none to the higher and nobler fields of useful industry and intellectual pursuits. In all that barbaric love of war which marks the absence of a high civilization, the dark ages, however, were but a continuation of the spirit and the practices of the nations that had gone before, and that boasted of superior light. Man still perverted all his powers, and strove to dominate over and destroy his species, rather than advance himself along the shining and celestial ways of scientific truth. The highest honors and the proudest distinctions were still awarded to him who had achieved the greatest slaughter of his kind. It was so in all the nations of antiquity—in Persia, in Egypt, in Greece, and in Rome—and the dismal centuries which followed their decline and fall only imitated, in that respect, the habits and customs of those for whom even yet an exalted civilization is so often claimed.

But the fullness of time came at last, when the human mind commenced awakening to its destiny of discovery and dominion. The impulse toward scientific researches was first felt in the fifteenth century, and aroused the intellectual world like the dawn of a divine revelation. Whence or why it came at that time more than any other can no more be told than whence the winds come or whither they blow. We only know that man's empire over the physical world was ordained from the first, and that sooner or later the judgments of God must be fulfilled. In the year 1435, at the city of Genoa, the son of a humble laborer—a wool-carder—was born, whose presence in the world has produced greater revolutions and grander results than ever before attended the efforts of mere man born of woman. Christopher Columbus was the John the Baptist of the sciences which now so brilliantly illuminate the universe. He literally proclaimed their truths in the wilderness—in the wilderness, dark and dangerous with ignorance and ferocious superstition. The power of his intellect and the greatness of his soul almost defy comprehension, when we consider the age in which he lived, and the circumstances by which he was surrounded.

The age was one in which aspiring thought was restrained and enslaved by religious intolerance. To think on any subject contrary to the dogmas of the church was to incur its destructive thunderbolts. The ignorance, too, of the public mind was equally appalling to the spirit of science. The city of Thinea, in Asia, was the eastern limit, and the Cape de Verd Islands the western terminus of the then known world. That portion of the human race which has established letters and made history knew no more at that time. Even the coasts of those continents whereon the empires of antiquity had arisen and fallen were less known to the people with whom Columbus associated than the coasts of the Arctic regions are at the present day to us. Ptolemy was a standard authority on the physical sciences in the fifteenth century, and yet his followers "still thought that the earth, at the equator, was girdled by a torrid zone, over which the sun held its vertical and fiery course, separating the hemispheres by a region of impassive heat." They fancied Cape Bojador the utmost boundary of secure enterprise, and had a superstitious belief that whoever doubled it would never return. They looked with dismay upon the rapid currents of its neighborhood, and the furious surf which beats upon its arid coast. They imagined that beyond it lay the frightful region of the torrid zone—a region of fire, where the very waves which beat upon the shores boiled under the intolerable fervor of the heavens.

It was in the face of such towering mountains of ignorance as this that Columbus struggled, and dreamed, and speculated in the midst of penury and want, from the time when he went to sea on his kinsman's vessel, at fourteen years of age, until he sailed on his immortal voyage at fifty-seven. But when his three little ships left the bar of Saltes early in the morning of the 3d of August, 1492, the spell of the past was broken forever. Old ideas, which had held the human understanding in bondage, passed away. As they sailed on where the winds had never before fanned a fluttering shroud, and where the waves had never kissed a prow, the secrets of nature were overtaken, and gave themselves up to the dominion of man. All the vast fabrics, built by all the blind ages since creation, tottered and fell to rise no more. A new era had indeed dawned, illumined by a sun that was never to set, but rather to continue to grow in brilliancy and power until all the boundaries of the universe were filled with light. But even the bold Genoese adventurer, who had spent nearly his three-score years in developing a knowledge of the natural sciences, did not, with his far-reaching mental vision, behold the full glory that lay before him. He had satisfied himself that the earth was a spherical globe, and he had speculated on the necessity, in the proper order of nature, of a hemisphere in the West to balance the one that was known in the East. He tells the objects and expectations of his voyage, however, himself in his diary, kept "very punctually from day to day," and addressed to his patron sovereigns, Ferdinand and Isabella. After recounting the downfall of the Moors at Grenada, where he had fought under the royal banners of Spain, he says:

> And immediately, in that same month, in consequence of the information which I had given to your highnesses of the lands of India, and of a prince who is called the Grand Khan, which is to say, in our language, king of kings; how that many times he and his predecessors had sent to Rome to entreat for doctors of our holy faith to instruct him in the same; and that the holy father had never provided him with them, and thus so many people were lost, believing in idolatries, and imbibing doctrines of perdition. Therefore, your highnesses, as Catholic Christians and princes, lovers and promoters of the holy Christian faith, and enemies of the sect of Mahomet, and of all idolatries and heresies, determined to send me, Christopher Columbus, to the said parts of India to see the said princes and the people and lands, and discover the nature and disposition of them all, and the means to be taken for the conversion of them to our holy faith; and ordered that I should not go by land to the east, by which it is the custom to go, but by a voyage to the west, by which course unto the present time we do not know for certain that any one hath passed.

It is thus seen that he sought the East by the way of the West, in the sublime faith that he could circumnavigate the globe—a thought even then deemed blasphemous by the theologians and schoolmen. It is true, Columbus expected to encounter islands in his voyage where he might rest his crews and replenish his vessels; but the mighty hemisphere which lay impassable in his course, and put an end forever to his missionary views in the East Indies, was a discovery too vast, too tremendous to be realized by the human mind in theory. Experience alone could comprehend and solve it.

If we should pause for a moment at this point, and transport ourselves in imagination back to the period I am considering, how hard it would be to realize the nature of the prize that lay before the great admiral, the condition in which he would first behold it, and the events which would so swiftly follow! The wildest fables, the most fanciful dreams, the most brilliant scenes ever wrought by the incantations of magic, the most flaming inspirations ever uttered by the frenzied poet, all wither and fade away into nothingness in comparison with the reality which the human mind was now about to encounter, possess, and conquer in the physical world. And how brief is the period since this occurred. Only three hundred and eighty-one years ago—a mere span, the sweep of a pendulum, a throb of the pulse, the flight of a second in the lifetime of this universe of matter—and this gigantic hemisphere on which we stand this hour, lay utterly hidden from every intellectual and civilized portion of the earth. From the beginning, whenever that was; from the time light was commanded, and there was light; from the creative period, when chaos assumed form, on down through incalculable millions of years, the American continents, as well as the others that constitute the globe, had existed. The sciences demonstrate this now as plainly as the problem is proven on the blackboard. Yet no history gives us a glimpse of what occurred here during those illimitable and solitary ages. What man did beyond a few simple arts of savage life, if anything, will remain forever unknown. The slight vestiges of buried towns, which have been discovered in Central and South America, are not sufficient on which to construct a theory of far remote civilization. We only know that nature was here, and man, too, in his natural state. We only know that all the wealth, gifts, forces, and principles of nature were here then as now, ready to submit to the human intellect, and to enrich, ennoble, and glorify the human race. The valleys slept their long sleep with the elements of future teeming harvests in their bosoms undisturbed; the mountains reared themselves up their gradual slopes from the plains, and hoarded their secret treasures of gold and of silver, of coal and of iron; the rivers ran to the oceans awaiting the enterprise of intellect; while the bays and harbors of the coasts invited the commerce of mankind, and invited it in vain. All was here as it left the Creator's hand. The sun lit up these solitudes, and the stars looked down upon them in the deep watches of the night, but the light of thought and of history had never penetrated them. Adam had founded the human race; Noah had preserved it from extinction by the flood; Jesus of Nazareth had died on the cross in the midst of darkened heavens, a trembling earth, and opening graves to redeem it from eternal punishment; and yet, until less than four hundred years ago, not one of these stupendous facts was known, or a name connected with them heard, in all the regions that lie between Behring Strait and Cape Horn, now the abode of more than a hundred million of people.

When the veil of darkness, however, that had hung so long between the Old and the New World was lifted, floods of strange light poured in upon both. Knowledge on all subjects came like a sunburst in the morning of a new day. But first in the bright train after the discovery of America came the science of astronomy. When it was once known that the earth was a spherical body and suspended in space, other facts connected with the planetary system of the universe necessarily followed. Until then the physical sciences could not proceed. They were at a dead halt, and could not take another step until the form and nature of this planet were known as Columbus revealed them. But when a correct map of the earth was finished, a map of the heavens had to follow in the order of logical thought. When a map of this world was marked and measured, a map of the other worlds which move in harmony with this was an imperative sequence to the problem that had just been solved. In this fact lies the reason why the ancients bore such blind relation to scientific truth. They were ignorant of the shape and properties of their own planet, and lacking this key of knowledge, the doors of all the other realms of the material universe were locked against them. With this key furnished, however, though, it seems to us, at a late day in the duration of the ages, the portals which concealed the priceless gifts of the natural world have one after another been rapidly and widely opened.

Copernicus, Galileo, and Newton followed Columbus, and entered into the untrodden realms of the universe, forcing the great secrets of the unknown by virtue of the facts already known.

A knowledge of the laws of gravitation was among the first fruits that were gathered from the rich discoveries of the fifteenth century; a knowledge of those wonderful principles which govern and hold in their proper spheres and pathways, without discord or collision, the worlds, and the systems of worlds, which inhabit space, and revolve and fly through its trackless depths with the speed of thought. They were found to move on a time-table, devised and kept by that Almighty mind under whose regulations all has been safety and harmony for unnumbered centuries among those swift, rushing bodies of blind matter. How awful appears the wisdom of that mind, when we contemplate the design of the universe and the absolute obedience to law impressed upon every part! How sublime its conceptions and how infallible its results! Is there a fool who hath said in his heart there is no God? Let him study the plan of physical creation; let him understand this earth, and then explore the other planets; let him comprehend the laws which govern them in their movements around the great center of light and heat, as the hand of the pilot guides the ship on the ocean, and he must either conclude that matter itself is instinct with thought and has established its own rules with a wisdom that is infinite, or else that, far beyond and higher than all, there exists a Supreme Author, who has fashioned everything, and to whom his works render obedience.

For about two centuries and a half after the discovery of America, the minds of scientific men were engaged in completing the circle of knowledge around the earth and through the planetary systems of the heavens, and in brushing away the musty fables, and the venerable and stubborn follies of the ancients. Then came another era in the relations between the human mind and the physical world, which has extended to the present hour, and which has filled the nations with the marvels and glories of human progress. It is the era of analysis, of analytical investigation, of chemical solution, and of mechanical invention. It is the era in which the mind, having acquired the general principles of nature, proceeded to inquire into her minutest details. The shapes and relations of the great bodies of matter being once fully understood, the aroused spirit of science next found out the substances that composed them. The soil of the plains, the ore of the mines, the stones of the mountains, the waters of the rivers and the oceans, the air that we breathe, the light of the sun, the bursting blaze of the clouds, have all been thrown into an inexorable crucible. They have been dissected, particle by particle, and all their mighty hidden forces discovered and appropriated to the use and advancement of modern civilization. Every step taken in the gigantic progress of the eighteenth and nineteenth centuries has been due to these wonderful developments of the physical sciences. And in connection with the increase of scientific knowledge, there arose in the minds of men new purposes for which to live and to labor; new objects to be attained for the welfare of the human family, and new systems of practical philosophy to supersede the vain and useless theories of the ancients. When it became fully known that man could establish his supremacy over this earth and subjugate all that it contained to his comfort, wealth and happiness, the thinking world bent all its powers to obtain that result. The struggle then commenced to make everything useful. Lord Bacon was the author of this great departure from the rules of antiquity. His philosophy was the simplest and most beautiful that ever dawned upon mankind. Macaulay, in speaking of it, says:

> Two words form the key of the Baconian doctrine—utility and progress. The ancient philosophy disdained to be useful, and was content to be stationary. It dealt largely in theories of moral perfection, which were so sublime that they could never be more than theories; in attempts to solve insoluble enigmas, in exhortations to the attainment of unattainable frames of mind. It could not condescend to the humble office of ministering to the comfort of human beings.
>
> All the schools regarded that office as degrading; some censured it as immoral. Once, indeed, Posidonius, a distinguished writer of the age of Cicero and Cæsar, so far forgot himself as to enumerate, among the humbler blessings which mankind owed to philosophy, the discovery of the principle of the arch, and the introduction of the use of metals. This eulogy was considered as an affront, and was taken up with proper spirit. Seneca vehemently disclaims these insulting compliments. Philosophy, according to him, has nothing to do with teaching men to rear arched roofs over their heads. The true philosopher of the ancients does not care whether he has an arched roof or any roof. Philosophy has nothing to do with teaching men the use of metals. She teaches us to be independent of all material substances, of all mechanical contrivances. The wise man, according to this absurd creed, lives according to nature. Instead of attempting to add to the physical comforts of his species, he regrets that his lot was not cast in that golden age when the human race had no protection against

FRANCIS BACON.

cold but the skins of wild beasts, no screen from the sun but a cavern. To impute to such a man any share in the invention or improvement of a plow, a ship, or a mill, is an insult.

Seneca pronounces the inventing of such things to be drudgery, only fit for the lowest slaves; and he finally expresses his indignant fears that he shall next be told "that the first shoemaker was a philosopher."

Bacon, on the other hand, held nothing unworthy of his attention or labors which promoted the health and physical well-being of mankind. He established that school of thought and action in which practical utility transcends all abstractions. The age in which we live is the offspring of his system of ideas. The inventor of the plow which turns the deep soil of these fields, of the drill which plants them with grain at seeding time, and of the reaper and mower which glean their bountiful harvests, is more honored to-day than all the founders of all the most famous sects of antiquity. The humblest millwright has done more to endear himself to the human race than those who built the walls of Babylon or wrought the columns of the Coliseum at Rome. The names of Arkwright, Hargreaves, Crompton, and Cartwright, for their inventions in the manufacture of cotton, rank as benefactors far above and beyond all the dazzling and blood-stained heroes of history. Far better and brighter, too, is the fame of Robert Fulton, whose genius walks the waters of the world, than that of Alexander the Great. Franklin and Morse will live and shine as deathless as the eternal stars in the heavens, when the shades of a gloomy oblivion have gathered around the memories of Cæsar and Napoleon. Even that humble companion of the fireside, the family sewing-machine, is entitled to more veneration and respect than the pyramid of Cheops; and its inventor has done more to advance the happiness of the human race than all the kings that lie embalmed in the catacombs of Egypt. The engineer and architect of the bridge over the Mississippi river, at St. Louis, will live in fresh and vigorous immortality in the minds of distant generations, when the very names of victor and vanquished at Pharsalia shall have been forgotten. Professor Maury, the great geographer of the sea, now sleeps in his lonely Virginia grave, with no monument towering over his honored dust, and with but slight memory or mention of his useful life in the minds or on the tongues of his own generation, but the practical good he has wrought for mankind has given him a sure and safe place among the few, the immortal names that were not born to die. He explored the bottom of the great deep; made a map of its channels, its volcanic upheavals, its dangerous reefs; marked the undeviating currents which sweep over them in obedience to physical laws, and pointed out secure highways for the commerce and travel of the human race. The enlightened nations of the earth will hold his name in grateful memory, and around it will gather, as the centuries move on, a halo brighter, and more to be coveted, than ever encircled the brow of sea-king or naval conqueror. And in the same shining list will appear the name of another American, who now, from day to day, signals the coming storm, tells in advance where the hurricane will strike, and gives notice of the approaching fury of the elements. The probabilities of the winds and the rains, and of the pathway of the swift-rushing tempest, have been ascertained and reduced to a science for the benefit of this practical and utilitarian age.

It is the blessed fortune of the inventor, the practical discoverer of useful improvements, that his achievements are permanent. His additions to the sum of human knowledge remain. They supply the wants of mankind, and become the property of the world in common. Governments have reared their proud heads, and proclaimed the principles of their existence eternal. But kingdoms, empires, and republics have alike been torn and scattered by the storms of revolution. Their wrecks and remnants incumber all the pages of history. Their brief duration is the scoff and jest of the ages. Creeds of faith, systems of religion, schools of morality, have also come and gone, as shifting and changing with the waves of time as the sands in the bed of the ever-flowing river. The vain speculations of a thousand philosophic sects have perished; the founders of as many religions are forgotten; the learned wranglers of the schools pass away, leaving no useful monument of their existence. "The discoveries of genius alone remain; it is to them we owe all that we now have; they are for all ages and for all times; never young and never old, they bear the seeds of their own life; they flow on in a perennial and undying stream; they are essentially cumulative, and, giving birth to the additions which they subsequently receive, they thus influence the most distant posterity, and after the lapse of centuries produce more effect than they were able to do even at the moment of their promulgation."

Gentlemen of the Athenian and Union Literary Societies: I have endeavored to-night to establish the fact that the civilization of the present era is superior to any other heretofore known, and also to point out the reasons for such superiority. I have aimed to show the sublime harmony which exists between the original purposes of the Creator and the swelling results of these modern days. We are drawing nearer to the great design of man's power and supremacy over all other works and elements of creation than the human race ever approached before. The doctrine of utility has been emblazoned on the banners of progress, and mankind has marched forward beneath its folds for the last four centuries into new and illimitable fields of discovery, invention, conquest, and imperishable glory. The mechanical contrivance of printing was of humble and obscure origin, but it was useful, and became at once the herald and the torch of advancement from the darkness of the night to the light of the morning. The ancients stand afar off from us both in time and achievements. They had a grandeur of their own, but it was glittering, specious, and useless, and consequently not enduring. Modern civilization has been built upon the rock of scientific truth, and it can not fall. It is sustained and fed by knowledge—knowledge which, at its pleasure, ranges the heavens above or dives into the sea and earth below. Speaking, however, in this presence, I would not discourage the study of the literature, the languages, the habits, customs, and histories of antiquity. No man can properly understand and appreciate the present without correct information of the past. Combine, therefore, as far as possible, the practical and useful ideas of your brilliant age with a full knowledge of the various developments of the human race in other ages and under different circumstances.

But let not the alluring voices of the classics cause you to linger on old and barren fields expecting to gather fresh fruit. Seek not to dwell in tents that were struck and abandoned more than two thousand years ago. Go not to the rear in quest of victory. The honors and the spoils of mental conflict and triumph are not there. Turn your faces to the front and strive for the laurels of the present and the future. If you would be leaders in this great and active period, you must equip yourselves with its vital and progressive philosophy, rather than with the rusty and broken armor of the decayed systems of the pagan world. It may not perhaps be given to you to scale the heights where Humboldt stood, or to sound all the depths and shoals of science where Agassiz walked with familiar tread; but it may be yours to enrich your minds with their sublime discoveries, and then, upon leaving these walls, you will go forth heralds of light, assisting to illuminate the world in all its parts. In order to do this and to crown your lives with usefulness, you must learn now, in the days of your youth, the priceless and inestimable value of time. He who inscribes this truth on his heart and brain, and counts the moments of time as more precious than pure-washed grains of gold, and the hours devoted to mental labor as more to be prized than the diamond fields of Southern Africa, holds the key by which the gateways of glory are lifted up, the broad avenues to immortal fame are opened, and the high plains of an unbounded success assured. Be therefore industrious and vigilant disciples of a progressive faith, and the future will place its proudest honors at your disposal.

Mr. President: I find it impossible to close my connection with the duties of this hour, without giving utterance to some of the thoughts which crowd upon me as I stand in your presence. I come from a theater of your former labors. The mental growth and material development of the state of Indiana are forever associated with your name and fame. As an educator and a lawgiver on the subject of education, your influence will there endure for ages, and your name be spoken with gratitude and veneration by generations now unborn. He who gives progressive action to a people, ingrafts the principles of culture and development on their

---

* Daniel Read, D. D., LL. D.

organic laws, and devises a system for the general dissemination of knowledge in their midst, merits their highest honors and richest rewards while living, and their costliest marble and brass should protect his dust after his work is over. Sir, this much Indiana owes to you, and as one of her citizens, I tender you her grateful recollections and appreciation of your great services. I salute you, too, with congratulations on your noble career of progress and utility since you left our borders. I find you in the midst of brilliant triumphs. After fifty years of continuous and unbroken services as a college officer, now the oldest in commission in the United States, you still stand forth with eye undimmed and natural force unabated, ready for all the toils and duties of your exalted sphere.

It is most gratifying, also, to reflect that your labors here have borne rich and abundant fruit; that the foundations of this noble institution of learning have grown wider and stronger, and its towers loftier and brighter in the sight of the world, under your wise and conservative administration; that a fully equipped university has arisen within a few years from a state of almost complete exhaustion, and, with every department of university education in prosperous operation, is now shedding luster on the state of Missouri, at home and abroad. When Wolsey, the great cardinal, lost the favor of his king, and was hurled from his eminence, and stripped of his honors, the honest chronicler of his good deeds, anxious to place his fame on a secure basis, exclaimed:

> Ever witness for him
> Those twins of learning that he raised in you,
> Ipswich and Oxford! One of which fell with him,
> Unwilling to outlive the good that did it;
> The other, though unfinished, yet so famous,
> So excellent in art, and still so rising,
> That Christendom shall ever speak his virtue.

So will the great states of Ohio, Indiana, Wisconsin, and Missouri, with their flourishing institutions of learning, which you aided to establish, be called to witness for you in the diffusion of useful knowledge. And as the past has been full of honorable achievements, so will your future be rich with your mental enjoyments. You have been a leader in the progressive school of thought.

You have held familiar converse with the sciences which have developed modern civilization. They contain eternal truths, and furnish an unending banquet to the philosophic mind. You can truthfully adopt, with reference to them, the language of Cicero, in his defense of the poet Archias:

> *Nam ceterae neque temporum sunt, neque aetatum omnium, neque locorum; haec studia adolescentiam agunt, senectutem oblectant, secundas res ornant, adversis perfugium ac solatium praebent, delectant domi, non impediunt foris, pernoctant nobiscum, peregrinantur, rusticantur.*

Ladies and Gentlemen, Patrons of the University of the State of Missouri: No nobler theater for the onward march of progress, the triumphs of a grand civilization, and the development of the physical sciences, can be found on the maps of ancient or modern history, than your own great state. In extent of territory, in the fertility of its soil, in the richness and boundless variety of its mineral resources, in its mighty water lines of cheap transportation, and in its central geographical position, Missouri is an empire of material wealth within itself. The great intermediate city between the two oceans is also yours. St. Louis lifts up her proud head, the unrivaled queen of the valley of the Mississippi. Standing midway between the sources and the mouth of the longest river in the world, and commanding a trade by its channel as far north as perpetual snow, and as far south as perpetual flowers, she also rises up in the great pathway of commerce and travel that the hand of nature has drawn between the East and the West. Like the city of the desert on the plains of Asia, she is the mart of exchange for the commodities of all sections, and the halting place for the mighty caravans of trade that now float upon the waters, or fly across the country on tracks of iron.

Your state, too, is in the infancy of its development. Only fifty years ago it was admitted into the Union, and, though a giant at its birth, it has still a growth to attain which will place it among the foremost political commonwealths in the world. In this development of your state, and in its future glory, no agency will be so potent, no instrumentality so direct and effective, as the light which has already gone forth, and which will continue to flow from this institution, if you affectionately uphold it by your love, your prayers, and your labors.

TRIBUTE TO VICE-PRESIDENT HENDRICKS

An address on the death of Thomas A. Hendricks, vice-president of the United States, delivered in the senate of the United States, January 26, 1886.

R. PRESIDENT—For the eminent citizen of the republic who lately fell from his high place among living men, and who sleeps now in peace and honor in the bosom of the state he loved and served, we can do no more than has already been done by tongue and pen, and by every method which human affection can inspire. The heavy drapery of woe has darkened alike the public building, the stately mansion, and the doorway of the humble home; the proud colors of the Union have drooped at half-mast throughout the United States and in all civilized lands beneath the sun; eloquence in the forum and at the sacred desk has paid its richest tributes to his exalted abilities and to his stainless character; the tolling bell, the mournful dirge, the booming solemn minute-gun, the mighty multitude of mourners, have all attended the funeral of Thomas A. Hendricks, and borne witness to the deep love and grief with which he was lowered into his last earthly abode. All the honors due to the most illustrious dead have been paid by the chief magistrate of the government, by the authority of states, and by the unrestrained affection of the people.

In the senate, however, we may not be silent, even though the cup of honor to his memory is full and overflowing. In this exalted theater of action, here on this brilliantly lighted stage, he fulfilled his last official engagement and closed his long and commanding public career. When this body adjourned in April last he went out from these walls to return to them no more forever. The chair to which he had been called by the American people was vacant when senators gathered here again, and now we briefly halt in our weary march to do honor to ourselves, and to benefit the living, by pointing out the attractive virtues of the dead.

Thomas A. Hendricks was a native of the Mississippi valley, born in Muskingum county, Ohio, on the 7th day of September, 1819. He had the good fortune to be born on a farm, so often the nursery of mental and physical development and power. His earliest associations were with people who earned their bread by the honest labor of their own hands, and the impressions thus made on his mind were with him always. They inspired his sympathies, and to a great extent governed his ideas of public duty at every stage of his long official life.

Early in the spring of 1820, when the late vice-president was six months old, his father, Major John Hendricks, with his young family, moved to the state of Indiana, then indeed an infant state, but three years older than the strong man-child then in his mother's arms, and destined to control the gravest affairs of the commonwealth and to wear her highest civic laurels. After a brief sojourn at Madison, the well-known historic residence in the interior of the state at Shelbyville, Shelby county, was assumed by Major Hendricks, and maintained with dignity, hospitality, and great practical usefulness until he slept with his fathers.

> In the heart of the dense forest, upon the gentle eminence overlooking the beautiful valley, he built the sightly and commodious brick house which yet stands in good preservation in open view of the thriving city and richly cultivated country around. It soon became known as a center of learning and social delight, and was the favorite resort of men of distinction and worth. It was in particular the seat of hospitality to the orthodox ministry, Mr. Hendricks being the principal founder and support of the Presbyterian church in that community. The presiding genius of that home was the gentle wife and mother, who tempered the atmosphere of learning and zeal with the sweet influences of charity and love. Essentially clever and persistent, she was possessed of a rare quality of patience, which stood her in better stead than a more aggressive spirit.

It was at such a home as this, on one of the outer lines of advancing civilization, shedding its rays of beneficent Christian light over the waste places and lighting up the wilderness, that the future lawyer and statesman began his growth in knowledge, grace, and power, and rose to the full stature of his splendid manhood.

What a swift unfolding panoramic view of the march of empire and of human progress was given him to behold in his own lifetime of less than three-score years and ten! Indiana was admitted into the Union only sixty-nine years ago with but thirteen organized counties, 12,112 voters, and a total population of 63,897. The first impressions of men and things made on the mind of Governor Hendricks in his childhood outside of his own home were of a sparsely settled country, neighborhoods composed of a few families, making here and there an opening in the wilderness, and separated from each other by long miles of towering unbroken forests. He was made familiar with accounts of pioneer privation, self-sacrifice and heroism. Indians were still abundant in Indiana, and, though not on the war-path, were uncomfortable neighbors, and he sometimes listened to the hunter with buckskin shirt and unerring rifle who had fought the red man at Fort Harrison, Tippecanoe, the River Raisin, and the Thames but a few years before. He knew at one time what it was to go six miles from home for the privileges of a very ordinary and uncertain school. The highway of his early youth was the trail through the woods from one settlement to another, surveyed and laid out, not with rod and chain, but with the ax of the frontiersman blazing the trees to give the traveler or the lost wanderer his points of compass and his way onward. His memory dwelt on the mill by the flowing stream, where, with primitive methods, the bread of the pioneer and those beneath his generous roof was provided for.

In after years, when all these things had passed away like a dream, and when he was decorated with almost every official distinction, he would on rare occasions charm his listeners with pleasing pictures which had been indelibly painted on his youthful mind. I vividly recall one such instance only a little more than seven years ago. The Millers' National Association met at Indianapolis in May, 1878, and Governor Hendricks was chosen to welcome them to a public dinner. In the course of his remarks, and after dwelling upon the association before him as one of the most potent factors in the world in providing an increased amount and an improved quality of food, his mind reverted to the scenes of his boyhood, and, with the touch of a master and to the delight of his audience of advanced millers, he produced from memory the following gem of portrait painting:

> As a boy I was acquainted with the miller, and I thought him a great man. When he raised the gate with such composure and confidence, and the tumbling waters drove the machinery ahead, I admired his power. And then he talked strongly upon all questions. He was very positive upon politics, religion, law, and mechanics. Any one bold enough to dispute a point was very likely to have a personal argument thrown in his face, for he knew all the gossip among his customers. He was cheerful. I thought it was because he was always in the music of the running waters and the whirling wheels. He was kind and clever, indeed so much so that he would promise the grists before they could be ready, and so the boys had to go two or three times. He was a chancellor and prescribed the law, every one in his turn. That miller, standing in the door of his mill, all white with dust, is a picture even upon the memory of this generation. It is the picture of a manly figure. I wonder if you gentlemen, the lords of many runs and bolts, are ashamed to own him as your predecessor. It was a small mill, sometimes upon a willowy brook and sometimes upon a larger stream, but stood upon the advance line of the settlements. With its one wheel to grind Indian corn and one for wheat, and in the fall and winter season one day in the week set apart for grinding buckwheat, it did the work for the neighborhood.
>
> Plain and unpretentious as compared with your stately structures, yet I would not say it contributed less toward the development of the country and the permanent establishment of society. So great a favorite was it, and so important to the public welfare, that the authorities in that day invoked in its favor the highest power of the state, that of eminent domain. That mill and miller had to go before you and yours, and I am happy to revive the memory of the miller at the custom mill, who with equal care adjusted the sack upon the horse for the boy to ride on, and his logic in support of his theory in policies or his dogma in religion.

But while Governor Hendricks would thus at times recall the early days of Indiana and her small beginnings, on the other hand his joy and pride, everywhere and under all circumstances, at her unparalleled progress in every channel of thought and action were boundless and unrestrained. His enthusiasm over the development, strength, resources, cultivation, and honor of the state whose infancy he had shared and to whose greatness he had contributed, was of a character not to be fully understood nor appreciated except by those to whom the nature and attributes of his mind were revealed by long and intimate association. Indiana was the one theme, whether in public or private speech, on which his voice would fill with emotion and his eyes flash with unwonted fires or grow moist with affection and gratified pride. He saw her meager population swell to over two millions, her primitive highways give place to more than six thousand miles of railroad, her farms teeming with more wheat and corn than any other state of equal size, her coal beds and manufactories filling the world with their productions and their fame; he saw accumulated the largest school fund per capita of any commonwealth on the globe, and he exulted in the free schools, the high schools, the normal schools, the seminaries, the colleges, and the universities which adorn and illuminate the state.

We have heard and read much in our day and generation on the subject of state pride and the duty a citizen owes to his state government. Governor Hendricks loved the American Union, and gave it his warm, unstinted, and unwavering allegiance, and held that no duty to his state could interfere with his duty to the federal government. And yet his love for Indiana, and his pride in her position before the world, was never less ardent and sincere than that of the most devoted disciple of that school of state rights which existed before the war, but which exists now no more. The people of Indiana well understood this fact, and repaid his affection with their own faithful attachment.

But Governor Hendricks had another and earlier reason for his devotion to the state besides his own connection with her affairs. It will be seen from the records of the territory and of the state that no other name has had so long, so permanent, and so conspicuous a place in the history of Indiana as that of his family. When the delegate convention met at Corydon on the 10th of June, 1816, under the authority of the enabling act of congress, to frame a constitution for the new state, William Hendricks was the secretary of that small but able and historic body. He was an elder brother of Major John Hendricks, and consequently an uncle of the late vice-president. He was large and commanding in person, with marked intellectual ability. In August, 1816, he was elected a member of congress under the new constitution, and thus became the first representative of the state of Indiana at the federal capital. In this position he won such distinction that in 1822 he was elected governor of the new commonwealth.

There is nothing more trying to a young man's reputation and to his future success than to be charged with the duties of executive of a frontier state, with all its bitter necessities; its just expectations, so long deferred as to make the heart sick; its oppressive burdens, which might be lightened by promptitude and justice on the part of the federal government; its keen and constant struggles for full recognition as a member of the Union, with equal rights and dignity in the company of its sister states. This ordeal was passed, however, so successfully, that in 1825 William Hendricks was elected a senator in congress from Indiana and re-elected for a second term, giving him twelve years of service in the senate of the United States at a most important period in the history of the state and nation. A fertile and wealthy county in the central portion of Indiana bears his honored name and stands as an enduring monument to the memory of an able and faithful public servant. In 1837 his public life closed, and it was but eleven years later when another official career began which was destined to be longer and more brilliant and to render the same name still more illustrious. Thomas A. Hendricks came upon the theater of professional and public life better equipped for the duties before him than young men generally were at that early period in the West. While his youth had been surrounded by the privations of the frontier, he experienced but few of them in his own person.

His father was a prosperous man for his day, and, with the commendable family pride of an intelligent, well-read gentleman, he spared no pains or expense in preparing his sons, as far as existing opportunities then permitted, to enter with credit and success upon the duties of manhood. In the village and neighborhood schools, and at South Hanover College, Abram, the eldest son, pursued his studies to become a Presbyterian minister, and his brother, next younger, laid the foundations of his future greatness in the councils of men. Governor Hendricks was a lover of books, and from his youth up his mind was fashioned to industry, study, and research. In making choice of a profession he followed his earliest inclinations and eagerly embraced the law. When a mere boy he loved the court room, and listened with intense interest and delight to the mental conflicts of strong men. Upon his return from college he entered at once on his legal studies in the office of Judge Major, at Shelbyville. He subsequently went to Chambersburg, Pa., and further pursued his studies under the tuition of his kinsman, Judge Thomson. When he was admitted to the bar on his return home he had a student's well-trained mind, and a knowledge of the great principles of the common law, which increased and expanded with his advancing years, and on which he never relied in vain in the conflicts of after life.

The opening years of his professional career were not marked by sensational success, but rather by a steady growth in the confidence of the courts and of the people as a diligent, capable and rising man. In the meager practice of the village lawyer great amounts were not at stake, but in the preparation and trial of small cases the principles of the law laid down by Blackstone, Chitty, and other great masters of jurisprudence were often more clearly and ably presented than in controversies in the highest courts involving millions.

To one imbued with zeal and ambition for legal eminence, no trial in court is unimportant when it presents an issue of law or of equity. In this spirit and with this conception of his profession Governor Hendricks pursued his labors from the beginning. In 1848 he was elected to the legislature; and at that point began that double line of duties, one in the courts and one in the political arena, lasting thirty-seven years, and only closing when his active but weary brain ceased to throb. He became an eminent leader on both lines of action, and so evenly and well-balanced were his powers that it would be difficult to decide on which he was most conspicuous and commanding. To his own mind and heart, as his intimate friends well know, his labors and his triumphs in the courts were the dearest and most satisfactory. The keen, high zest with which he often enjoyed the conflicts of the bar and their results was something, when once witnessed, not readily forgotten. If the law, as the old writers have it, is indeed a jealous mistress, yet she had no cause to complain of his want of love or devotion, or of his absence from her chambers, except when driven to other fields of duty by the highest order that can be issued to a citizen in state or nation. He lived to realize that his fidelity to his profession had met its just reward.

The history of Indiana is luminous with the names of able lawyers and profound jurists from the days of Isaac Blackford down to the present time; and among the brightest and the strongest of that great galaxy the name of Thomas A. Hendricks long since took its permanent place. If to some this may seem merely the voice of personal friendship, perhaps insensible to careful discrimination and close analysis, I would recall to them the imposing meeting of his brothers in the law, held at Indianapolis, and gathered from every part of the state by the dread summons of his death. Into that federal court room, where he had won and worn many of his brightest laurels, there came on that sad day the oldest, the ablest, and the most learned of the Indiana bar. Within its hallowed precincts every thought and recollection of political warfare died away, every memory of party strife was hushed, and men of every creed and faith pressed forward to bear testimony in eloquent and burning words to their admiration for the great lawyer, then cold and motionless forever. Judge Gresham, now of the United States circuit court, and so long and honorably connected with the federal judiciary and recently with the administration of the general government, on assuming the chair by the call of the meeting, said:

> We are assembled to pay our tribute of respect to an eminent member of our profession. Although Mr. Hendricks occupied many high stations in the state and nation, finally the second highest in the gift of the people, all of which he filled with distinguished ability, he never lost his fondness for his chosen profession. His triumphs at the bar were, perhaps, fully as satisfactory as his triumphs in the conflicts of politics. * * * In capacity for rapid absorption of a case, arrangement of facts in their proper relation, and in the application of principles to facts, Mr. Hendricks greatly excelled. While he justly stood in the front rank of the profession, perhaps his real sphere was that of the advocate. In this line he had no superiors, perhaps no equals. As a trial lawyer he was self-reliant and courageous, and when a case took a sudden and unexpected turn, and defeat seemed almost inevitable, he exhibited rare skill and great reserve power. It was on such occasions that he appeared to the best advantage.

In the memorial prepared and presented by the bar committee is the following:

> Mr. Hendricks was throughout the whole period of his active life a lawyer, even in his last days concerned in the conduct of causes. His entrance upon and employments in public life were episodes, excursions, useful to himself and others, but did not divert him from the beaten path of forensic labor. On the floor of the senate, in the halls of legislation, he sojourned—at the bar, in the courts, he dwelt. He was engaged in very much of the important litigation at the capital of his state. His practice was by no means local. He attended in the discharge of professional duties nearly every circuit in our own and many of the higher courts of adjoining states and the supreme court at Washington.

The chairman of that committee, David Turpie, once a distinguished member of this body, drew the following eloquent analysis of the late vice-president as a lawyer, all of which might with equal fidelity to truth be said of himself:

> His legal abilities were so various and diversified that it is difficult to say in what branch of the profession he most excelled; still harder to determine in what, if any, he was deficient.
> As a pleader, that is, in making the statement of a claim or defense upon paper, he was careful, diligent, exact. * * *
> He gave great attention to the preparation of litigated causes for trial. * * *
> Rightly deeming that proof, like glass, should be handled with care, and might be much affected by the manner of its utterance and the time of its introduction, his verb "prepare" had a mood, a tense in it often overlooked by others.
> He had the capacity to grasp a case, and, having grasped, to hold it in all its details; before development, from the oath in chief of the jury to their retirement. He seemed, so to speak, to stand seized of it, *per mi et per tout*, in entireties; so that if it failed upon one hypothesis, it should yet survive and succeed upon another.
> Called upon to name in briefest phrase the most prominent trait in his mental character, aside from those splendid qualities which attracted public notice, I should say it was his power of discernment.
> * * * He saw the relation in which one thing stands to another, their corelative bearings, what these relations would be or might become at any stage, mesne or final, of the proceedings.
> And this did not seem to be so much an acquirement or an accomplishment as a faculty, a faculty of introspection, of prevision, a sort of subsidiary sense or sensibility.
> In this he was exceptionally great. It was a quiet power—calm, tranquil, noiseless in its operation, but strange as wisdom, certain as inspiration, and in its effects unavoidable as the decree of fate itself.
> His powers of analysis were large, yet fully equaled by those of combination and construction. His mind in this respect had a dual capacity seldom found in the same person.

Joseph E. McDonald, so well known and so honored here, held the following language:

> The national flag at half-mast, the city draped in mourning, and the many sad faces that throng our streets, all attest the fact that one who had enshrined himself in the hearts of the people of this state and had inscribed his name high up in the roll of the distinguished men of our country has closed his earthly career; and while we, his brothers of the bar, have met to pay to his memory that honor to which it is entitled, on account of the high rank he held in our profession, a nation bows its head in sorrow. Monuments may be erected to perpetuate his name, but none will be more enduring than the memorial you will this day enroll upon the records of the courts. It is the lawyers' monument, and will remain when monuments of brass or stone have crumbled, and fallen, and mingled with the dust. The memorial and resolutions you are about to adopt speak of him, his character and career, and render it unnecessary for me to more than briefly allude to them.

Others in glowing periods and with stately phrase paid tribute to their departed forensic leader, each one contributing to the establishment of "the lawyers' monument" in the judicial records of the country, "which will remain when monuments of brass or stone have crumbled, and fallen, and mingled with the dust."

Turning our attention at this point from his legal to his political line of duties, we find a circumstance at the start which may be taken as the key to his whole career. In 1850 Indiana had outgrown the methods and the apparel of her childhood, and stood in need of certain fundamental changes in her organic law, better adapted to her stalwart and rapidly developing proportions. The legislature authorized a constitutional convention to be called. To frame the constitution of a state has always been esteemed the proper work of the fathers and the elders, of those ripe in years and full of experience. Here and there exceptions have been wisely made to this general rule, and the people of Shelby county made such an exception in the choice of their delegate. Governor Hendricks had put his foot on the first round in the ladder of his political life when he went to the legislature in 1848, and now he was called to go higher.

Thus it was at every step of his remarkable history. He inspired such confidence in every position he held that he not only never lost an inch of ground once attained, but the constant and confident demand of those who knew him best throughout his entire career was for his promotion from height to height as long as there was a position of honor and duty above him. He rose with steady, unfaltering steps, and never disappointed the expectations of those who gave him their faith. It mattered not in what situation he was placed, he met its requirements with ability, with dignity, with courage, and with clean-hearted and clean-handed integrity. In this one great fact, shining out like a star over the pathway of his life, his friends and followers had their abundant pride and joy.

In the constitutional convention, though but thirty-one years of age, he so bore himself in company, and sometimes in contact, with the oldest and ablest leaders of both political parties then in the state that in the following year, 1851, he received his indorsement and promotion by being elected to congress. This was followed by a re-election, and then by defeat at the polls in 1854, that weird, anomalous year in American politics. Within a few months, however, after his return home to his law office, he was, without solicitation and very unexpectedly, appointed commissioner of the general land office by President Pierce. His conduct in the house and the discharge of his duties there had marked him as an able, safe, industrious, and honest public official. The general land office was then, as it is now, all things considered, the most important bureau in the government.

The interest of the American people in the public lands reaches all classes, and the cupidity of land speculators and the plundering instincts of timber pirates were tempted thirty years ago in the same way and almost to the same degree as at the present juncture. Governor Hendricks was slow to accept the position, and only did so after careful consultation with friends, and especially with his father, on whose judgment he greatly relied. His administration of the office proved the wisdom of the selection, and he continued to hold it under Mr. Buchanan until 1859, when he resigned, returned to Indiana, and once more resumed his profession at Shelbyville. He had but little respite. In 1860, in the very shadow of the thick-coming events so soon to follow, he obeyed the call of his party in convention, and ran a failing race for governor of the state, weighted down from the start by the ominous collision between Douglas and Breckinridge. A high promotion, however, awaited him soon.

The legislature of Indiana chosen in 1862 elected him a senator in congress, and he took his seat as such on the 4th of March, 1863. Here, in this, the most exalted legislative body in the world, or in the history of the world, he gave himself up for six years, with absolute devotion, to public duty, and established that strong and enduring national reputation which ever afterwards attended him. For vigilant attention to the business of the senate, for a knowledge of its principles and its details, and for earnest, candid labor in its transactions, both in committee and discussion on this floor, it is doubtful whether any senator ever surpassed him. The pages of the *Congressional Globe* from day to day attest this fact, and are rich with treasures of his thought and eloquence. He was the ever-present leader of a small minority in this body, and never relaxed his hold upon the laboring oar.

While the war lasted he favored its earnest prosecution, and voted for all supplies to sustain the army. When the war closed, he held that the states whose people had been in rebellion had never been out of the Union, and were consequently entitled to representation in both branches of congress and to the control of their respective state governments. He antagonized the doctrine of reconstruction, maintaining that congress had no power to reconstruct the governments of states which had never ceased to be members of the American Union. I recall his position on this great subject, not for the purpose of reviving even a debatable thought in the minds of senators, but to convey some idea of the character and magnitude of his labors while a member of this body.

In the debates which ensued, every principle vital to the structure and existence of the government of the United States as a republic was involved and its value tested by argument. Every day, and at times almost every hour, witnessed keen and strong encounters between such leaders as Fessenden, Grimes, Sumner and Trumbull on the one hand, and Hendricks on the other. He won the respect and esteem of his opponents here as he did elsewhere. He looked back on his service in the senate with pleasure, but with no desire to again enter this chamber as a member. He often said he had done a faithful work, which would never be needed again, to restore a helpless and broken people to peace and safety and self-control under the constitution, and that he was willing the book of his labors in the senate should be considered finished, and remain as he left it on the 4th of March, 1869.

In the midst of his heavy labors, and the severe mental strain upon him as a senator, surrounded by such peculiar circumstances, another burden of the first magnitude was imposed upon his shoulders. In 1868 his party demanded him again as a candidate for governor, and while he yielded with reluctance and with a full appreciation of the odds at that time against him, yet he entered upon the memorable campaign and conducted it to the close with an ability, courteous bearing, and perfect courage never to be forgotten in the history of Indiana. General Grant carried the state by nearly 10,000 majority, while it will never be absolutely certain whether Governor Hendricks or Governor Baker, his competitor, received the most votes. The count at last dediced in favor of Baker by about 1,100 majority.

From March, 1869, when his duties terminated in the senate, until the summer of 1872, Governor Hendricks diligently and with great enjoyment to himself practiced his profession, being the head of the well-known firm of Hendricks, Hord & Hendricks, at Indianapolis. But the tenacious devotion of his party was not willing to leave the close and unsatisfactory result of 1868 without another appeal to the people on the same issue.

His resistance to the appeals of a unanimous convention for him to run again for governor in 1872 was extreme, and for a long time unyielding. When at last borne down by a sense of duty to a great and devoted party he yielded up his own desires and took the race, he wore a look of patient fortitude and heroic self-sacrifice, well remembered by those who saw him on that occasion. In that year of democratic defeat and disaster, more or less deserved, when Grant beat Greeley in Indiana over 22,000, Hendricks was elected governor by about 1,200 majority, all the remainder of the democratic state ticket being defeated except the candidate for superintendent of public instruction.

From January, 1873, to January, 1877, a period of four years, he made a record as governor of Indiana full of honor, usefulness to the people, dignity, grace, and refinement. It is without blemish, stain, or fault. There is nothing he could have wished to change, amend, or recall; nothing for his most ardent friends to deplore or to cause them to blush or apologize. The people of Indiana know him but little, if at all, by any other title than that of their governor, for in that capacity he was in their midst and in personal contact with them more than in any other. They knew him best, and it followed that they loved him most, as Governor Hendricks.

But in what rapid succession public honors sought him at every stage of his life! While yet governor of Indiana in 1876, he was nominated at St. Louis for the vice-presidency, and I am sure I will not offend the most delicate susceptibility by saying that, as in his contest for governor in 1868, so in that of 1876, it will always be a matter of honest doubt in many minds whether he was defeated by one vote or elected by a considerable majority. When in 1884 he was in fact elected vice-president, but by a very slender majority, it did indeed seem as if the very genius of close contests and narrow margins in the ballot had presided over his political fortunes, but that at last the account was invariably settled in his favor. His victories were the results of hard-fought and doubtful battles, and his defeats the same.

Governor Hendricks has been charged with inordinate ambition. It is true that he was ambitious for an honorable fame, but for place and position he cared far less in his own behalf than his friends did for him. They believed him fit to be president, and they followed his fortunes as his Scotch ancestors followed the Bruce, whatever fate awaited them. That he would have made a wise, prudent, and able administration of the government as its chief magistrate will not be questioned by those most familiar with his public services and private worth.

In the spirit of accusation and reproach it has been charged, and more especially in these later days, that he was a partisan in his political ideas and methods. If by this is meant that he sincerely believed in the principles and purposes of the party to which he belonged, and sought by all honorable methods to promote what he conceived to be the public good by placing its measures and its men in control of the government, then the accusation is true, and the term intended as a reproach becomes simply a just tribute to an honest man. If, however, it is intended to convey the impression that he was ever during all the years of his political life violent, factious, unreasonable, or proscriptive toward his opponents, whoever or whatever they might be, nothing could possibly be more erroneous.

There were no neutral tints in his own political colors, but his tolerance for opposing opinions was so gentle, his manner of meeting them in discussion so free from bitterness, so sparing of assault, and so full of respect for their candor that prejudice melted away in his presence and left his hearers with unbiased minds to weigh his clear and forcible arguments. It has been the partisan with deep, honest convictions, dealing justly with opposing views, who, in all ages of the world and in every field of human progress, has led the way. Wherever the lists of free controversy have been opened, wherever conflicts of opinion have determined the thought and action of mankind, there the well-equipped partisan, his zeal tempered with respect and magnanimity toward his adversaries, has been a guiding power, and has engraved his name in letters more durable than brass or marble on the tablets of history. To this rank of partisanship may be properly assigned the honored name of him whose death we mourn.

Much has been said and written, and often without wisdom or point, on the subject of leadership among men. No man was ever a leader of his fellow-men in a free country by self-assertion or the spirit of dictation. He who controls the reason, convinces the judgment, enlightens and satisfies the conscience, is a leader of the people mightier far than he who relies on the sword. Strong argument, elaborate research, and eloquent persuasion have been, and will ever continue to be, more potent factors in the world's long annals than the gleaming bayonet and the shotted cannon. By their peaceful but powerful instrumentalities Governor Hendricks won his way to a high and very commanding political leadership.

In his repeated, long-sustained, and severe contests in Indiana he always led his followers with consummate judgment, perfect courage, and a brilliant display of intellectual force. Sometimes on the eve of a political battle he paused and weighed the issues at stake with such care and prudence that those who knew but little of the quality of his mind thought he hesitated to go to the front. Nothing could be more incorrect than such a conclusion. While others were at times more aggressive, and more rapid in their decisions at the beginning, yet none led more boldly, nor further in advance, when the conflict became fiercest, and when it closed in victory or in defeat.

Governor Hendricks was never so strong, so magnetic, and so irresistible as when under assault or crowded in discussion by an able antagonist. In joint debate before the people from day to day, and from week to week, he has had no superior, and rarely an equal, in the history of the country. His qualities for such an ordeal were of the highest order. A self-possession never for a moment disturbed, a mental concentration no excitement could shake, a memory of facts never losing its grasp, a will which never faltered, and a courage which rose in the presence of danger as certainly as the mercury in the tube under heat, were all his. Added to these gifts and acquirements was a voice rich, musical, and resonant, pealing forth at his pleasure like a bugle call to action, or modulated into the soft, seductive notes of the flute, wooing the affections. A high-bred, classic face of singular manly beauty, lit up by a winning and genial expression, a large head with the contour and poise of an antique model, completed a picture which was never beheld by an audience without emotions of delight.

Five years ago the unremitting labors and the incessant strain of more than the third of a century caused the powerful and compact physical constitution of Governor Hendricks to put forth its first signals of distress, and to reel for a time like a disabled ship in the breakers. In the autumn of 1880, seeking for rest and surcease of toil, he visited that famous cañon of the Ozark mountains, in Arkansas, where magical springs pour forth their hot and healing waters. While there in repose and apparent security, the icy finger of paralysis, sure precursor of skeleton death, touched him with its fatal premonition.

The extent of his danger at that time was never known, except to her whose life was as his own, and to his physicians, who did not conceive it their duty to publish their patient's ailments in the newspapers. He came home, however, to his beloved state, and again took up his public and private duties with serenity and composure, but he knew from that time forward that he walked in the constant shadow of an impending blow. Not a word ever escaped him on the subject outside of his domestic circle. No wail, nor murmur, nor lament ever shook his lofty fortitude or passed his lips. When, two years later, he was stricken with lameness in his foot, and informed that he could rise no more to take part in the affairs of life, he was the only party to the scene unmoved by the great change then apparently so near. He spoke of his work as finished, and quietly waited for the curtains which divide time from eternity to be drawn aside. But medical opinion had erred, and it was reserved for him to receive one more promotion at the hands of his countrymen, to be crowned with another and higher honor, and to fall at last, when his hour did come, within a single step of the summit of human greatness.

At the Chicago convention in 1884, Governor Hendricks made the only appearance of his life in such a body. The old familiar light was in his face, and his mental vision was as clear and penetrating as ever, but he was physically not strong, and the prompt, alert movement and elastic tread which his friends knew so well were wanting. His presence in that convention was contagious, and the vast multitude shouted themselves hoarse and shook the mighty amphitheater with his name whenever he appeared, but no exultation came for a moment into his look or manner. To those near him he simply appeared to enjoy in a quiet, silent way the popular approval of his long and faithful services, under the weight of which he was then wearily walking in the rich and glowing sunset of a great and well-spent life. When he was nominated for vice-president he was seeking repose and sleep on his bed at the hotel at the close of an exciting day. He did not hear the tender words and strains of Auld Lang Syne break forth from ten thousand voices at the mention of his name, exclaiming:

> Should auld acquaintance be forgot,
> And never brought to mind?

The effect of the nomination on Governor Hendricks himself was immediate and remarkable. The position of vice-president was one to which he had never aspired, nor were its duties congenial to his talents or tastes. He knew and accepted the fact that a dread specter was hovering near him and liable to cast its fatal dart at any moment, and more especially in the midst of labor and excitement. He had so often, however, led his party, and had always so fully met the expectations of his devoted friends in Indiana, that his iron will at once determined not to disappoint them on the last field where he was to appear. His resolution seemed to summon up all the vigor of the best years of his manhood.

The energy and activity he displayed were never surpassed in a political contest. He declared himself ready to answer for his state, as he did in 1876, and the response of the people justified his promise and his claim. The brilliant and gifted leader of the republican party, known in the lists of the political tournament as the Plumed Knight, crossed the borders of Indiana, was welcomed with all the pomp and circumstance of a great party long accustomed to national victories, made a tour of the state with his banner full high advanced, inspiring the confidence and kindling into a flame the zeal and devotion of those who believed in his destiny and followed his star. As Mr. Blaine closed his engagements in Indiana and drew off to other fields, it was determined that his dramatic and dazzling expedition into the West should have its bold and effective counterpart.

Governor Hendricks, upon brief announcement, passed rapidly from point to point, and the people rose up to do him honor until the whole state seemed one vast continuous assemblage. It was his farewell engagement on the hustings, and he filled it like a master. Such an ovation was rarely ever given to hero or statesman in ancient or modern times, and the children of this generation will recall its scenes when they are old men and women in the distant future.

But while he moved in the midst of these pageants, honors and allurements, it was known to a chosen and silent few that his mind and heart dwelt apart from them, and were engaged with matters of higher import than those of earth. During the last two years of his life he selected and prepared the beautiful spot where he now reposes. He gave his close personal attention to the finish and erection of the stately marble shaft which bears his name and marks his final abode. His only child died when but three years old, and for more than thirty years had rested at the old home at Shelbyville. As he felt the evening shadows coming on, the strong man, the able lawyer, the distinguished senator, and governor, and vice-president, wished his long lost little boy to sleep by his side. He tenderly transferred the sacred dust from Shelbyville, and when he himself was by loving hands laid to rest, the grave of a child was observed close by covered with flowers. At times he visited this hallowed spot and lingered there while his own name was ringing with applause or provoking fierce controversy. His thoughts were then far away, and with deep emotion he gathered up the broken links of the past, and by a faith that never faltered nor grew dim, reunited them in that high world beyond the sun and beyond the stars.

Governor Hendricks was a believing and practical Christian all the days of his life. His duties to the church were no more neglected nor evaded than his duties to the state. He held official relations with both, but never mingled them. He bore open and public testimony on all proper occasions to his reliance upon the teachings of Christianity for the advancement of civilization and for the happiness of mankind. In his private life he exemplified the beautiful virtues of his religion. He was much given to charity, not merely in the bestowal of alms to the poor, but in the kindness of his heart and the tolerance of his spirit toward all. He obeyed the apostolic injunction, and lived in peace with all men as far as it lay in his power to do so. He never gave the first blow in a personal controversy, and often forbore to return those he received. He loved his neighbors, and was by them beloved.

Sir, we shall see Thomas A. Hendricks no more with our mortal eyes. He is gone from the high place of earth to the higher realms of immortality. He is lost to the senate chamber, to the forum, and to home and friends. We will follow him; he will return no more to us. As long, however, as American history treasures up pure lives and faithful public services; as long as public and private virtue, stainless and without blemish, is revered, so long will his name be cherished by the American people as an example worthy the highest emulation. Monuments of brass and marble will lift their heads toward heaven in honor of his fame, but a monument more precious to his memory and more valuable to the world has already been founded in the hearts of the people whom he served so long, so faithfully, and with such signal ability. In the busy harvest time of death, in the year 1885, there was gathered into eternity no nobler spirit, no higher intelligence, no fairer soul.

THE FLAG ON THE SEA

An address upon the occasion of the unveiling of the Farragut statue, delivered in Farragut Square, Washington, D. C., April 25, 1881.

HIS is an occasion on which the best emotions of the American heart are inspired. We are here to pay ceremonial honors to the memory of one whose deeds of peril, and of high renown, in defense of his country, adorn more than half a century of his country's history. No good life is ever wholly extinguished, even in this world. He who has lived for the welfare of his fellow-men, for the cause of free and enlightened government, and to enlarge the boundaries of human happiness, lives on forever, even here upon the shores of time. For the benefactors of the human race there is no death. The centuries may move on in an endless procession over their graves; human society may be transformed by the storms of revolution; the world may be carried by the spirit of progress from old conditions to new ones, yet the influences of the philanthropist, the hero, and the lawgiver, in eternal strength and beauty, will keep pace with them all, and give color and shape to the conduct of remotest generations.

It is in recognition of this great fact that statues and monuments have arisen all over the face of the civilized globe. The influences of the illustrious dead are always active in the affairs of the world, and the wish has been strong in every age to perpetuate their form and features, and to transmit them to posterity. As the student of antiquity toils amidst the ruins of former civilizations in Rome, Greece, Egypt and Asia, he constantly encounters the forms and the faces of such as were supposed to have had the strongest control over the events of their times. Indeed, the desire of the human heart to keep alive the virtuous examples of those who have passed

THE FARRAGUT STATUE AT WASHINGTON.

away is as widespread and universal as the race of man. In some form or other it is manifest everywhere, on every shore, and in the customs of every tribe and kindred beneath the sun. From the polished works of Phidias to the mounds of the American Indian the idea is the same.

Nor is this principle in its broadest significance confined alone to honors paid to the great. For every worthy life, however humble, that goes out on the ebbing tide into the vast ocean of eternity there are sighs and tears, and some frail memorial is erected as a mark of love and memory. In every human breast there are records which tell of the dead who still live; in every ear there are voices, at times, which no one else can hear, and to every eye there sometimes comes a face not seen by others.

Such is the experience of individual grief and recognition of the honored and beloved dead; but when a nation mourns, and brings forth its laurel wreath of fame to crown the triumphant hero, then the scene changes into the pomp and pageantry of the present hour. This day and hour the government of the United States unveils to the world the statue of Farragut; the statue of a naval commander first in American history and second to no one who has handled ships in battle since the day on which Themistocles beat Xerxes at "Sea-born Salamis." Happy and fortunate is he who stands in brass or marble at the behest of a grateful country, and in time to be gazed upon by those who knew and loved him in life. On but few have such honors been bestowed; but few such monuments as this can be erected, and yet there comes pressing upon my thoughts at this moment a mighty throng whose toil, whose agony, and whose blood made this glorious monument, and all similar ones in the capital of a united country, possible. Those who fought with Farragut, with Porter, and with others whose names are household words of honor, seem to be here. The spirits of those who died for the flag on ocean and river, perhaps now people the air, looking with joy on its peaceful supremacy and unbroken folds. The mighty hosts who sleep in the bosom of Virginia, and from there to the sunset side of the Mississippi and down to the Gulf of Mexico, make their mute appeal for recognition at all times and places of national glory. No monument has been erected to these warriors of the sea and the land, perhaps none will ever be; they need none fashioned by human hands. Did I say they had no monuments? Not so; the existence of the American Union is their monument, and every bay, and stream, and field where they bled has a voice to proclaim that the memory of their lives, and of their deaths shall never perish.

> They fell devoted, but undying;
> The very gale their names seems sighing;
> The waters murmur of their name;
> The woods are peopled with their fame;
> The silent pillar, lone and gray,
> Claims kindred with their sacred clay;
> Their spirits wrap the dusky mountain;
> Their memory sparkles o'er the fountain;
> The meanest rill, the mightiest river,
> Roll mingling with their fame forever.

In estimating the wonderful career, and the splendid achievements of the great admiral whose statue stands before us, we naturally look to the source of his training, and the school of his experience. The American navy presents a most instructive and inspiring theme for thought and investigation. Its history is full of national and individual honor. Indeed the profession of the sailor has developed in all countries and ages the loftiest and most striking qualities of manhood. From those far distant regions of superstition and of song, wherein Homer described the long, black, high-beaked ships, which bore "the fair tress'd sons of Achaia" to "the flowery plains of Scamander" in the Trojan war, to the present time the ocean has been the home of brave men and the theater of immortal achievements. From the restless bosom of the great deep history has obtained its most brilliant examples of human enterprise and endurance. There are reasons, obvious to all, why this should be so.

The dominion of man over the earth and sea, a divine grant of power in the beginning of time, has been more difficult of enforcement on the waters than on the lands. The assistance of science is more necessary to the progress of fleets than to the march of armies, and such assistance was late in coming. The mysteries of the mariner's needle and compass were slow in being revealed. With what eager interest and solicitude we even yet follow Columbus as he sailed from the bar of Saltes, early in the morning of the 3d of August, 1492, and steered boldly into an unknown ocean, experimenting as he went in the first rudiments of navigation, and feeling his way in the uncertain, twilight dawn of nautical science! But the light grew stronger as he sailed on, and his disciples since, at the opposite poles of the earth, and under the equator, and in all the four quarters of the globe, have touched the utmost limits to which human courage inspired by a thirst for knowledge can attain. The waters of the world, however, assume their most practical and historical aspect when considered as the highways and the battle-fields of nations. It is in this respect that they have enriched the annals of mankind more amply than in any other. Exploring expeditions, voyages of discovery, the great currents of commerce, beneficent and glorious as they are in the peaceful progress of the human race, are all subordinated by the pen of the historian to the warlike navies of the world.

The first and leading thought of the student of American history in connection with the navy of the United States is that it has done more, far more in proportion to its strength, to establish and illustrate the American character among the nations of the earth, than any other branch of the public service, and at the same time has not received that fostering care or generous liberality from the government which its record justifies, and indeed demands. While every American heart beats high at the memory of our naval victories, yet, as a rule in our history, whenever the spirit of an extraordinary economy has penetrated our public affairs it has first been found operating on the small, but glorious, American navy. It has never been thought necessary for the American republic to maintain a naval force more than equal to that of a third-rate European power. This is not a policy originating with the people, for their pride and affection would dictate a different course. It is perhaps more due to the geographical position of the United States than to any other cause. Although we are embraced by more than eleven thousand miles of sea-board, yet we have no immediate neighbors sufficiently formidable to call for large armaments for its defense. Emergencies may arise, however, in the future, as they have in the past, when the absence of a respectable naval force for a first-class power will be felt as a criminal neglect of the public safety and the national honor.

The origin of the American navy is full of curious interest now, and strongly illustrates the statement I have just made. When our forefathers were preparing for independence, a little more than a hundred years ago, their thoughts dwelt upon the creation of a navy, rather as it appeared to be a necessary part of an organized government, than as a means of successful warfare. It is true their first steps were taken prior to the declaration of independence, and merely to redress grievances and resist oppression, but they were in reality forming a government for themselves long before the 4th of July, 1776. On the 13th of October, 1775, the continental congress enacted its first legislation on the subject of a navy. It was in the nature of a resolution creating a marine committee, composed of three members, and directing them "to fit out two swift sailing vessels, the one of ten, and the other of fourteen guns, to cruise to the eastward, to intercept the supplies and transports intended for the British army at Boston." Under this resolution two vessels were equipped, one named the Lexington and the other the Providence; one in commemoration of that hallowed spot where men first died for American liberty, and the other in devout recognition of that high power which rules the fate of nations. The Lexington and the Providence! They were the first to ride the waves by American authority, and the Lexington was the first to carry the American flag in a sea fight to victory. The marine committee was afterwards increased to thirteen members, one from each colony, and additional ships of war were ordered to be built.

In October, 1779, a "board of admiralty" was established which superseded the marine committee, and consisted of five commissioners, two members of congress, and three who were not. Major-General Alexander McDougall, of the army, became the first "secretary of the marine" in February, 1781, and in August of the same year the system was again changed by the appointment of an agent of marine, who assumed full control of the whole service. In the meantime a few small vessels crept out from blockaded harbors, and constituted the navy of the infant government. As nearly as can be ascertained there were never more than one hundred and fifty guns afloat at any one time, under the American flag, during the Revolution.

On the other hand, in order that England's claim to be mistress of the sea should continue to be upheld, there were in the service of the crown, according to her own account, an average of over 26,000 seamen employed against her revolted colonies as long as hostilities existed. In the midst, however, of the vast English armament, holding the keys of every outlet on the Atlantic coast, and standing guard, as it were, over an imprisoned people, the American cruiser of the Revolution flitted to and fro, and often struck its quarry like a daring bird of prey. It is astonishing to the modern reader, whose idea of the war for American independence is that of a land fight from Lexington to Yorktown, to find recorded in an English work of credit a list of three hundred and forty-two English vessels captured in the single year of 1776 by American ships of war.

There are names also in connection with this early period of the navy of the United States which call for mention wherever patriots and heroes are honored. Hopkins, styled commander-in-chief, by act of congress, December 22d, 1775: Barron, Wickes, Nicholson, Hazlewood, Barry, Conyngham, Biddle, Saltonstall, Whipple and others filled the morning of our naval history with brilliant and unfading light. But there is another name belonging to that galaxy which, like the most luminous star in the firmament, deserves to be pointed out alone. In the latter part of December, 1775, the first ensign ever displayed by a regular man-of-war was hoisted in the Delaware, on board the Alfred, by John Paul Jones.

This celebrated officer was then twenty-eight years old, and the senior lieutenant ever regularly commissioned in the naval service of the United States. From the opening to the close of his career upon the ocean it was one of unbroken triumph and splendor. Though not native born, yet no American spirit was ever more fierce or vehement for American independence than that which animated his breast. His cruise of the summer and autumn of 1779 in the most familiar and frequented waters of Great Britain and in sight of the shores of England, Scotland and Ireland startled the civilized world with the capacity and courage of American seamanship. Sailing the Bon Homme Richard, not a superior ship, nor well armed, and accompanied by two unreliable vessels, he captured and destroyed twenty-five ships of the enemy, and threw the inhabitants of the three kingdoms into a panic. Macaulay has recorded the fact that the guns of the Holland fleet were heard at the tower of London during the reign of Charles the Second, and the statement, therefore, of James Fennimore Cooper, in his history of the United States navy, touching the presence of these three American armed ships in British waters, is a most striking one. He says: "Perhaps no vessels of war had ever before excited so much local alarm on the coast of Great Britain." Where in all history, before or since, was ever such a tribute of fear paid by a brave and powerful people to a force so small and comparatively insignificant? And yet he who reads afresh the details of that awful death-grapple in the night time between the Richard and the Serapis, in hearing of the firesides of English villages, will not wonder that consternation pervaded the borders of that country.

In all the annals of the sea, more unfaltering and devoted courage was never shown than in this great sea fight of the American Revolution. It was replete also with those incidents of heroic daring which seized the admiration of the world and have held it ever since. The answer of the commander of the Richard to the hail of his adversary in the midst of the conflict will never be lost. An hour of destructive and bloody work at close range in the dark had passed by when the British captain demanded, "Have you struck your colors?" The answer from the dauntless soul of the American came prompt and startling on the night air, "I have not yet begun to fight." And then lashing himself fast to his antagonist, with a desperate determination for victory or death, the American fought on until each ship was a charnel house, and the gallant Englishman at last pulled down his flag. The Richard went to the bottom soon afterwards from the injuries received in this terrible engagement with a vessel one-third superior in effective armament. We need not wonder, therefore, when we read in the histories of that period that great interest was excited throughout Europe when the victor arrived in Holland with his remarkable prize, and the cir-

THE ENGAGEMENT OF THE BON HOMME RICHARD AND SERAPIS.

cumstances of her capture became known. It appears that the British government was deeply mortified and bitterly incensed. A demand was at once made upon the Dutch government for the release of all the English prisoners, and for the delivery of the great American sea-captain as a pirate. British pride was hurt, and thirsted for an ignoble revenge. This foul scheme was thwarted, and in February, 1781, after an absence of more than three years, the commander of the Bon Homme Richard landed in Philadelphia covered with imperishable honor.

I love this great, heroic character, and I have dwelt upon it here because the fact is too often forgotten that, under his command, a battle was fought on the ocean in support of American liberty which impressed the mind of the world as strongly as the battle of Bunker Hill, or of Saratoga. I have dwelt upon it also in order to remind the American people that the American navy, however diminished its resources, has in every crisis of our history, from the very beginning, not only met every duty, but astonished the world with its brilliant and bloody exploits. The officers of the navy by whom I am surrounded to-day, can look proudly back through the achievements of their profession to the very first, finding nothing for shame, nothing for wail nor humiliation. Those who have sealed their devotion to their country with their blood, who have passed away in smoke and flame under the flag at sea, had their eyes fixed upon examples of heroic duty as illustrious as any in the history of the ages. The spirit of the navy was high and fearless from the hour of its creation, and it has ever since remained a conspicuous theater for the development of all manly virtues.

Admiral Farragut was born on the 5th day of July, 1801, within twenty years of the close of the Revolution, and within twelve years after the formation of the government. He was born amidst the associations of the great struggle for liberty, and he listened in his infancy to the then recent glories of the war for American independence. His father was a soldier of 1776, and he heard from him, in childish wonder, the thrilling deeds of our ancestors by land and sea. It is true that the navy of the Revolution had ceased to exist, but its memory was still fresh. It is a strange fact that during a period of more than fifteen years after the close of the

Revolutionary war this government possessed no navy at all. A careful historian on this subject says:

> While Washington and his ministers appeared to be fully sensible of the importance of a navy, the poverty of the treasury alone would have been deemed an insuperable objection to encountering its expense.

It would seem, therefore, that the policy of abandoning the navy on all occasions, and in preference to any other branch of the public service, as a sacrifice to the spirit of economy, has an early and a high origin; and yet I venture to protest, in the light of American history, that it is a policy far more honored in the breach than in the observance. Without a navy our national character abroad speedily sunk into contempt and derision. With what a bitter pang we now read that the miserable pirates of Algiers and other African barbarians for a number of years, and without any attempt at concealment, captured American vessels of commerce and sold American citizens as slaves to the Turks! Cooper, in his "History of the Navy of the United States," makes the following painful and humiliating statement:

> In the meantime, the Dey of Algiers, discovering that a new country had started into existence, which possessed merchant vessels and no cruisers, as a matter of course began to prey on its commerce. On the 25th of July, 1785, the schooner Maria, belonging to Boston, was seized outside of the Straits of Gibraltar, by a corsair, and her crew were carried into slavery. This unprovoked piracy,—though committed under the forms of a legal government, the act deserves this reproach,—was followed, on the 30th of the same month, by the capture of the ship Dolphin, of Philadelphia, Captain O'Brien, who, with all his people, was made to share the same fate. On the 9th of July, 1790, or a twelvemonth after the organization of the federal government, there still remained in captivity fourteen of the unfortunate persons who had been thus seized. Of course, five bitter years had passed in slavery, because at the period named the United States of America, the country to which they belonged, did not possess sufficient naval force to compel the petty tyrant at the head of the Algerine government to do justice! In looking back at events like these we feel it difficult to persuade ourselves that the nation was really so powerless, and can not but suspect that in the strife of parties, the struggles of opinion and the pursuit of gain the sufferings of the distant captives were overlooked or forgotten * * * Algiers and Portugal had long been at war, and though the latter government seldom resorted to active measures against the town of its enemy, it was very useful to the rest of the Christian world by maintaining a strong force in the Straits of Gibraltar, rendering it difficult for any rover to find her way out of the Mediterranean. Contrary to all expectations this war was suddenly terminated in 1793, through the agency of the British consul at Algiers, and, as it was said, without the knowledge of the Portuguese government. This peace, or truce, allowed the Algerine rovers to come again into the Atlantic, and its consequences to the American commerce were soon apparent. A squadron consisting of four ships, three xebecks and a brig immediately passed the straits, and by the 9th of October, 1793, four more American vessels had

fallen into the hands of these lawless barbarians. At the same time the Dey of Algiers, who commenced this quarrel without any other pretense than a demand for tribute, refused all accommodation, even menacing the person of the minister appointed by the American government, should he venture to appear within his dominions! During the first cruise of the vessels mentioned they captured ten Americans and made one hundred and five additional prisoners.

Shortly after these disgraceful humiliations came on also a general maritime war in Europe, in which American merchantmen, as neutrals, were buffeted and captured by the belligerent powers, and especially by France, with scarcely a pretense of respect for our national character. Then at last the young republic awakened to the fact that in order to command respect as a member of the family of nations she must be prepared to enforce her rights, and to punish lawless aggressions in distant parts of the world, as well as at home. These considerations of national necessity launched the old United States, the Constitution, and the Constellation, in 1797; the first three ships of war ever afloat under the present organization of the navy. They carried in all one hundred and twenty-six guns, and were speedily followed by twelve additional vessels which were entitled to carry twenty-two guns each. The creation of the navy department took place under an act of congress of April 27, 1798, and from that time forward the arrogance of civilized nations was, at least to some extent, rebuked, and chastisement instead of tribute was paid to pirates.

Early in the dawn of this revival of the navy, when its glories were blossoming afresh, Farragut imbibed his first lessons of patriotism and invincible courage. It required no astrologer to cast the stars of his nativity, or to divine their influence upon his career. He entered the world, and received his first impressions of its honors and its duties, when our successes in an actual though not a declared war against France were the pride of the navy, when the punishment inflicted by our ships on the Barbary powers was ringing through the world, and when the names of Decatur, Porter, Preble, Bainbridge, Somers, Truxton, Lawrence, Stewart, Hull, McDonough, Rodgers and Perry were rapidly ascending, like a blazing constellation, to the zenith of fame. The omens which presided over the birth and boyhood of Farragut would have rejoiced more rational soothsayers than the Greeks, and, indeed, they presaged a life, in many respects, more a romance than an ordinary reality. It reads like fiction, and yet it is fact that at nine years of age he received the warrant of a midshipman's appointment from the secretary of the navy. Commodore Porter took Farragut aboard ship, and made him literally a child of the sea, at an age when boys are usually wearing short clothes, in their first forms at school. The war of 1812 was near at hand, British aggression and insolence had become unbearable, when, in August, 1811, Porter took command of the Essex, and Farragut, then a boy of ten, accompanied his friend and guardian, destined to become the head of the American navy, and to wear a higher rank than was ever before known in the naval service of his country. It is easily perceived from the start, that this aspiring boy of tender years,

> Undoubtedly
> Was fashioned to much honor from his cradle.

His first experience in the naval service of his country was such as to awaken in a youthful breast all those high resolves and lofty conceptions of duty which marked his life to its close. In October, 1812, the Essex stood out alone from the Delaware, and started on that immortal cruise which gave an imperishable page of glory to American history. She rounded the Horn, and in less than a year was mistress of the Pacific Ocean. A picture of her, as she lay at the Marquesas Islands, in October, 1813, has been drawn by the pen of Cooper, and I can not resist its reproduction on this occasion. He says:

> The situation of the Essex was sufficiently remarkable, at this moment, to merit a brief notice. She had been the first American to carry the pennant of a man-of-war round the Cape of Good Hope, and now she had been the first to bring it into this distant ocean. More than ten thousand miles from home, without colonies, stations, or even really a friendly port to repair to; short of stores, without a consort, and otherwise in possession of none of the required means of subsistence and efficiency, she had boldly steered into this distant region, where she found all she required, through her own activity; and having swept the seas of her enemies, she had now retired to these little-frequented islands to refit, with the security of a ship at home. It is due to the officer, who so promptly adopted, and so successfully executed this plan, to add that his enterprise, self-reliance and skill indicated a man of bold and masculine conception, of great resources, and of a high degree of moral courage; qualities that are indispensible in forming a naval captain. In the way of service to the public, perhaps the greatest performed by the Essex was in protecting the American ships of the Pacific, nearly all of which would probably have fallen into the hands of the enemy but for her appearance in that ocean. But the positive injury done

the English commerce was far from trifling. The Essex had now captured about four thousand tons of its shipping, made near four hundred prisoners, and for the moment had literally destroyed its fisheries in this part of the world. In October, 1812, she had sailed from America alone, with six months provisions and the usual stores in her; and in October, 1813, she was lying in perfect security, at an island of the Pacific, with a respectable consort, surrounded by prizes, and in possession of all the means that were necessary to render a frigate of her class efficient.

But this picture of triumph, repose and security was not to last. That great power whose fleets encircle the earth, and whose ships of war are the bulwarks of her existence and honor, was speedily on the track of the Essex in overwhelming force. Her brief but brilliant career was destined to close in a desperate and sanguinary contest, with the odds of two to one against her. On the 28th of March, 1814, in a disabled condition, the Essex encountered the Phœbe and the Cherub, one a vessel of heavier rate than herself, and the two together carrying five hundred men as against two hundred and fifty-five on board the American. Captain Porter had repeatedly challenged the Phœbe, his superior in guns and men, to single combat, and no higher compliment was ever paid to American valor than the refusal of the English captain to engage except with two ships against one. Farragut, young as he was, had his opinion of the conduct of the captain of the Phœbe, and it is found recorded in his journal. "He was dealing with a far inferior force," says Farragut, "and it was ignoble in the extreme, on his part, not to meet his foe, when he had the ghost of an excuse for doing so, ship to ship."

Porter, however, had taught even British courage the value of discretion, and the chivalry of the ocean was, for once at least, disregarded by British officers in their anxiety to destroy a formidable antagonist. The action which ensued was sublime for its courage and horrible in its details on the part of the American. We read in history that sometimes youthful warriors have been carried to fields of battle in order to receive the baptism of military fire. Not one, in all the long annals of war, was ever made more familiar with the appalling aspects of danger, carnage and death than Farragut became, at Porter's side, on board the Essex, off Valparaiso, when less than thirteen years of age. During nearly three terrific hours he was baptized and consecrated to the service of his country, pistol in hand, and covered with the blood of the wounded and the dead. He saw the ship of his first love become unmanageable; he saw her hulled at almost every shot by the enemy; he saw nearly all her guns disabled; he saw her berth-deck, steerage, ward-room and cock-pit filled with the wounded, who were sometimes shot to death under the hands of the surgeon; he saw but seventy-five men, officers included, left from the havoc of death fit for duty; he saw Lieutenant McKnight when he was the only commissioned officer who could join Porter on the quarter-deck for consultation; he saw the ship on fire and the flames springing up the hatchways; he heard the roar of powder explosions below, and then only he heard the order to cease the unequal fight, and with bitter tears and choking sobs, as he has himself recorded, he saw the flag of his country lowered to the calculating and ungenerous foe. What a school of instruction for one whose last birthday marked but twelve years distance into the world! It is pleasant to read that when Porter returned to New York a great ovation sprang up in his honor, the people went wild over his splendid fame, unhitched the horses from his carriage and with their own hands drew him all over the city. We can easily imagine that the grief of young Farragut over the loss of the Essex found at least some consolation in this patriotic circumstance, which he has carefully recorded.

But the war of 1812 did not teach, merely by any one example, the lesson of duty at home or of respect abroad. The Essex has a twofold right to mention on an occasion like this; she was the training-ship of Farragut's youth, and commanded by David Porter; but the whole line of naval warfare on the American side in the war of 1812 was a blaze of national glory. The very air was redolent with the fame of American men-of-war, and sailors' rights have never since been invaded on their decks. The highest value of war to civilized governments does not consist in mere physical conquest, in the acquisition of territory, the spoliation of cities, the accumulation of wealth from the enemy, or the collection of an indemnifying war debt from the vanquished. The nation which makes war except in defense of its existence, or for the protection of its honor, in the persons and rights of its citizens, organizes murder and robbery. The war, however, which was declared on the 18th day of June, 1812, by the United States against Great Britain, was upheld by causes as sacred as ever inspired men in battle; and the results which it accomplished were more precious to the American name than the treasures of the world or the subjugation of kingdoms.

The history of this country in its relations with Great Britain, during the first twelve years of the present century, even now can not be dwelt upon by an American without feelings of wounded honor and burning resentment. It is obvious at a glance that the young republic was not welcome amongst the monarchies of Europe, and that she was to be brow-beaten and insulted, especially by the English government. The interests of the American people all lay in the direction of peace; at home they were rapidly developing those great industries which insure a nation's progress, while as early as 1807 they had built up a foreign trade which employed seven hundred thousand tons of American shipping alone. They were tasting the sweets of the first period of prosperity after the Revolution, and they did not want war. Their forbearance was great and endured too long. American commerce was made the sport of blockades, maritime decrees, orders in council and the construction of belligerent rights; the right to seize and search American ships was enforced with shot and shell in American waters; native born American seamen were dragged from beneath their country's flag and impressed into the British service, until it is a relief, and the student of history exults in his heart, when he reaches the point at which the congress of the United States threw down the gage of battle.

At that time the English navy consisted of nearly eight hundred efficient war vessels in active service; the American navy consisted of seventeen; and yet we emerged from that war a new power in the eyes of the world, and more indebted for our national prestige to triumphs upon the ocean than to victories on the land. May I not be pardoned for saying that the respect of the world for our foreign policy rests, not so much on the arts of diplomacy as upon the heroism of the navy; not so much on the dispatches of ministers of state as upon bulletins announcing the prowess of American valor at sea; not so much upon the records of the state department as upon those which are filed in the department to which naval warfare belongs. It has long been said that actions speak louder than words, and it is equally true that their memory is more respected and more enduring. The work performed by the guns of the Constitution, the United States, the Essex, the Enterprise, the Hornet, the Wasp, and other American ships, will be remembered longer and with more salutary consideration by foreign cabinets than any diplomatic communications ever received by them from this government. When the colors of England were pulled down under American fire on the Macedonian, the Guerriere, the Frolic, the Java, the Peacock, the Boxer, and numerous other ships of war, the supposed invincibility of the British navy was broken forever, and the American character became, at once, established and respected in every sea, and on every shore. The victories of Perry and McDonough on the lakes taught the nations of the earth a lesson of respect and justice towards the United States, more powerful than was ever conveyed by a circular, diplomatic note from the haughtiest power in history to its weaker neighbors. And for nearly fifty years after the close of the war of 1812, the reputation of these achievements, and the character of the American marine for prompt action and unquailing courage made the American flag a symbol of honor, and the person of an American citizen secure in every civilized quarter of the globe.

The force of the Hulseman letter in 1853, stating the great doctrines of American citizenship, was due far more to the guns of the St. Louis and the high daring of Captain Ingraham in the Mediterranean, than to the powerful logic and caustic satire of Secretary Marcy. The storming of the Canton barrier forts in the Chinese waters in 1856, with but three ships and an assaulting party of two hundred and eighty men, awakened that old and distant empire to her international duties after all other means had failed. We are told that "all these forts were constructed by European engineers, with granite walls seven feet in thickness, and mounted one hundred and sixty-eight guns," and were defended by five thousand men. It is added that "their capture settled the difficulty

DAVID G. FARRAGUT.

with the Chinese, led to the formation of a treaty of amity and commerce, and has caused the American name to be respected by that people." The pirates of the West Indies, the Malays of Sumatra, and even the cannibals of the Fijis were all made to know that a new mistress of the sea was abroad on the waters of the world.

In the meantime, and before the awful era of 1861 had arrived, American science had revolutionized the construction of ships and the modes of naval warfare. In 1841 the Princeton was built under the guidance of Ericcson's genius, and was the first steamship that ever floated with her propelling machinery under water and out of reach of an enemy's shot. This invention increased the value of ships in war beyond the reach of estimate; but when twenty years later the first monitor, the offspring of the same genius, glided into Hampton Roads at the close of a disastrous day, saved all the shipping which was yet afloat, defeated the iron-armored Merrimac, drove her into a blockade, and to destruction, the revolution was complete, and the navies of the world were powerless before us, until they took time to adopt our methods. When Farragut, therefore, in January, 1862, went aboard the Hartford, in command of the gulf squadron, he did so in a day of light and knowledge in his profession, and with the eyes of all nations watching the developments and possibilities of the American navy. In the beginning of the century he had learned the lessons of naval warfare under the old system of wood and sails, and in the open sea; but he had kept pace with the spirit of American progress, and soon showed that. he was master of the problems of steam and iron, and at home in river, bay or harbor.

He embraced within himself all the splendid associations, patriotism, and courage of the navy of the past, together with a full appreciation of the advancements of modern science. To complete his character as a hero, his love of country was not merely a conviction of duty; it was that and more; it was the ruling passion of his soul. He loved the flag with all a sailor's affection, and his allegiance to his government was more a deep reverence for that power in whose service he had fought, and whose name and fame had been his joy from childhood, than an ordinary sense of attachment. With a lofty and stern enthusiasm, but without bitterness of heart, he struck the rebellion its hardest blows, and gave his name to immortality in the restoration of the American Union.

The conception and the execution of Farragut's expedition up the Mississippi river were fatal to the cause of southern independence. The power which holds the mastery of that mighty stream will hold an unbroken union of states from the lakes to the gulf in spite of all sectional antagonisms. Jefferson foresaw its necessity to a united and prosperous country when in 1803, and under threats of impeachment, he purchased Louisiana from the great Napoleon. When Farragut passed forts Jackson and St. Phillip, and anchored before New Orleans, nineteen years ago to-day, he was executing the statesmanship of Thomas Jefferson, which had declared that no foreign government should ever share the Mississippi river with the government of the United States; that its bosom and its banks belonged to us, and that its waters should continue forever to flow to the sea unvexed by custom houses and undisturbed by the keels of foreign crafts. And it appears as one of the compensations of time and history that the system of gunboats, so much denounced and derided in Jefferson's administration, was conspicuous in restoring the Mississippi to the protection of the American flag.

But why dwell in this presence upon the war for the possession of the Father of Waters? Why recount the glories and the dangers of the forts, of New Orleans, and of Vicksburg, on this occasion? Why tell of the dread magnificence of Mobile Bay to those who are listening to me now? I see many here who were in the flame and smoke of those terrific conflicts, and whose names will descend to posterity with that of their great commander. You saw him at his best; you saw him with the light of battle in his face; you saw him intrepid in action and humane in victory; you saw his scorn for personal danger and heard his orders given with coolness and precision when aloft in the rigging of his ship, under a fire as strong and as accurate as ever assailed a fleet. I am speaking to those who were with him from the beginning to the end. You know his deeds and his fame. His place is first amongst the naval heroes of history. His is no second name in the roll-call of the sea kings of the world. Nelson died in the arms of victory, was buried amidst the sobs of the English nation, and has a memorial statue in Westminster Abbey, but there is a loftier niche in the temple of fame for the American admiral than for the British peer. To beat the French and Spanish at sea was an easier task, three-quarters of a century ago, than to reduce batteries and capture ships manned by Americans and defended by all the improvements of modern warfare. In other countries Farragut would have been decorated with honors and worn the title of duke or earl with the income of a prince. We gave him the highest rank known to his profession, and have decreed him a statue in the capital. There is a simplicity and strength in such honors, recalling the days of republican Rome, and far beyond the significance of star or garter, or cross of the legion of honor.

This figure of bronze, so faithful in likeness, and so familiar in features to those who knew and loved him best, is the tribute of the American people. It is also of American origin and workmanship. Who but an American artist should have modeled the great American admiral? Nor does it lessen the pride of this great demonstration to remember that this noble statue will commemorate for all time to come the genius, the courage, and the educated skill of an American woman, as well as the manly virtues and undying fame of an American hero. It was executed by the brilliant and accomplished American artist, Mrs. Vinnie Ream Hoxie. Under the law authorizing it, the work was open to competition for all artists, native and foreign, and models were submitted by twenty-one competitors. The award in favor of the model submitted by Mrs. Hoxie was made by a commission created by act of congress, and composed of the secretary of the navy, the general of the army, and Mrs. Farragut, the honored widow of the admiral. Their judgment has been amply vindicated, and it is now the just compensation of the artist for years of anxious toil to witness her work received and displayed as a work of fidelity to art, and worthy the proud character it is designed to perpetuate.

This day will also be memorable in American history. A hundred years have passed away since our independence was achieved. The American navy, in five different wars, has studded the history of the republic with the most brilliant illustrations of patriotism, genius, and valor. Its officers and seamen have dwarfed the naval victories of other nations and ages, and made them look tame and commonplace by comparison; and yet we are looking now upon the first statue ever erected to a naval character by the government of the United States. The army is full of such honors, and it merits all it has received, but the navy has been unjustly pushed aside.

A people's gratitude to their national benefactors is to be found recorded in bronze and marble rather than in written books. Monuments towering to the sky from every battle-field of freedom, statues of the wise in council and the brave in action, standing in all the cities of the Union, would be a more faithful expression of the popular heart, and do more to cherish patriotic memories and love of country, than the pens of the most gifted historians. There is a vast work in this direction, and as the government grows older it will go on. Farragut leads the way for the navy. Others will soon follow. The face and form of the commander of the Bon Homme Richard will soon or late stand in the capital for the navy of the Revolution; Lawrence, Porter, Decatur, Perry and others will arise in marble and in brass to represent the second war for American independence, while those who fought upon the waters for the flag of the Union twenty years ago will be embalmed by the sculptor's art for the reverence of a grateful posterity. I speak not now of honors for the living. Their time will come, alas! all too soon; but to the dead alone, whose fame is beyond the accidents of time, is due the government's decree of monumental honors.

And now soon these assembled thousands will disappear from this consecrated spot, and Farragut will be left alone, as he stands revealed by the magic power of art. But others will come to look upon his commanding presence in the days, and in the years, and in the far distant centuries of the future. The American youth will here resort to behold one whose boyhood was the bright, heroic dawn of a life so useful, and so inspiring to noble deeds. Old age will pause, and linger here in rapt admiration of one who, with the weight of three-score years and more upon him, crowded the evening of his life so full of glory in the defense of his country. Presidents, law-makers, heads of departments, and public officials of every grade, will visit this spot as long as American patriotism endures, to reverence one whose life was dedicated to public duty in his childhood, and who left the world with no blemish upon any part of his long career. The soldier and the sailor will come to gaze upon the face of the bravest of the brave, and to drink in lessons of courage and fidelity for future wars if they should unhappily befall us. The American citizen of every calling and of every section, as long as the republic exists, will here dwell with emotions of pride upon a character too great for a divided love amongst his countrymen. May every portion of the American Union salute this statue with equal honor, and may that Union stand in justice, peace, fraternity and equality while brass and marble endure!

TRIBUTE TO GOVERNOR JAMES D. WILLIAMS

An address delivered at Wheatland, Indiana, July 4, 1883, upon the occasion of the unveiling of a monument erected to the memory of the Honorable James D. Williams, who died November 20, 1880, while governor of Indiana.

Addresses were also delivered by Ex-President, then senator, Benjamin Harrison, Ex-Governor Conrad Baker, the Honorable Jason B. Brown and others.

Ladies and Gentlemen:

WHEN our ancestors framed the government of the United States they found in ancient history only dim and faint suggestions of the system which they adopted. The nations of the past, it is true, have had their divisions and subdivisions of territory, but they were the mere helpless, dependent wards of a supreme guardianship, governed in all things, from the greatest to the smallest matters of public or private concern, by one central and absolute power. The provinces of Rome were conquered and created to aggrandize the power of centralization and to reward and enrich the leaders of factions. The different departments into which the governments of modern Europe are divided have the same general purposes in view. It was left for the wisdom of American lawgivers to enact and combine national and state sovereignty, and to accurately define the limits and boundaries of each. It was left for them, by all the ages of the past, to ascertain and work out a system of states possessing indestructible national unity, and at the same time holding within themselves, and in trust for their people, the inalienable rights of local self-government. Many sovereignties in one, each with its orbit of power and action fixed; each moving free from dictation or restraint under the law as it is written, and all in harmony, without jar or friction, constitute the

American republic. To have been the chief magistrate of one of these independent sovereignties; to have been chosen governor of one of these United States by the free voice of the people is an honor such as the Greek and Roman never knew, and such as is not now known anywhere on the globe but here. We meet to-day in memorial services over the grave of one who was thus honored and exalted in his life-time, and no grace or courtesy which we can extend to his sleeping dust will exceed the measure due to the governor of a great American state, or to the integrity of mind and heart with which he filled that proud position.

In looking at the career of Governor Williams and in studying the influences under which his character was developed, a long and most striking retrospective view is presented to the mind. Born in 1808, he came to Knox county in 1818. Here, at the age of ten years, he began his life work on the farm, and here, at the close of more than three-score years and ten, he rests in the soil and in the midst of the people he loved so well. He lived in Indiana and in this county sixty-two years, beholding with intelligent observation the growth and development, step by step, of his own state, and of all the northwestern states, until from a nominal beginning he witnessed the glory of their civilization and power fill the whole earth. His life embraced almost three-quarters of the present marvelous century, and covered such a period of human progress as the eye of man had not rested on until then, in all the wide and varied annals of human effort.

It was on the fourth of July in the year 1800, just eighty-three years ago this day, when "The Indiana Territory" was organized under congressional enactment, embracing "all that part of the territory of the United States northwest of the Ohio river which lies to the westward of a line beginning at the Ohio, opposite to the mouth of the Kentucky river, and running thence to Fort Recovery, and thence north until it shall intersect the territorial line between the United States and Canada." The region thus defined by boundaries comprised all of the states of Indiana and Illinois, and the larger portion of the state of Michigan, and yet within all this vast domain the civilized population was estimated at but 4,875, less than the basis of 1,000 voters. It was the organization of a giant wilderness through whose mighty depths stalked the painted and plumed barbarian in the haughty supremacy of his power. Here and there a feeble and scant ray of civilization had penetrated this widespread abode of savage life. Like a small lamp in a great darkness, the settlement at Vincennes had been throwing its feeble but steady and serene light on the surrounding night for nearly a hundred years. According to reliable history, civilized man first took up his abode at the old post in 1710, sixty-five years before the first guns of the Revolution were fired, and ninety years before the Indiana Territory was created by act of congress. But there had been no growth or expansion at the post, as the meager population of the entire territory in 1800 amply proves. It had been as stationary as its name implied. In 1805 the territory of Michigan was organized and separated from the Indiana Territory, and finally, by act of congress, February 3, 1809, the Indiana Territory was again divided by setting off all that part lying "west of the Wabash river and a direct line drawn from the said Wabash river and Post Vincennes due north to the territorial line between the United States and Canada," to be known as the territory of Illinois. In 1808, a year prior to this final division, we find an enumeration of the white population of the Indiana Territory, there being about nineteen thousand inhabitants in that portion which is now the state of Indiana, and about eleven thousand in that portion now the state of Illinois.

This was the year in which Governor Williams was born, and never in the realms of romance or reality have such stupendous changes and such sublime results been crowded into the span of a single life as in his. But the early stages of progress in the Northwest were not swift nor easy; they were slow and painful and the life of the pioneer was full of toil, privation and peril. Emigration from the old states was reluctant to seek new fields of enterprise, environed as they were by every danger which fact or fancy could present to the mind. Settlers came in slowly and tediously over roads of their own construction. When Indiana was admitted as a state into the Union, after sixteen years of important territorial government, after the battles of Fort Harrison and Tippecanoe had been fought, after the battle of New Orleans, and the treaty of peace with Great Britain at the close of the war of 1812, with the Indian titles nearly all extinguished, and the Mississippi river and all its tributaries opened to the unmolested trade and commerce of the American people, she yet showed by a census then taken a population of only 63,897. There were but thirteen organized counties, and Knox headed the list with 8,068 inhabitants. Then came Franklin, Washington, Clark, Harrison, Wayne, Gibson, Dearborn, Jefferson, Switzerland, Perry, Posey and Warrick, in the order I have named them.

And what a small, tame affair the first gubernatorial election appears to us as we look at it from this distance and compare it with some other Indiana elections which we have known! At a general election held on the first Monday in August, 1816, for governor, lieutenant-governor, representative in congress, members of the general assembly and the various county officers, calling out a full vote, Jonathan Jennings received 5,211 votes and was elected governor over Thomas Posey, who received 3,934 votes. With less than 10,000 voters to persuade, and only thirteen county seats to visit, I am inclined to think that some of my friends in both parties would rather have had such a race for governor than the one they are likely to be engaged in twelve months hence.

In the convention which framed the first constitution of Indiana there were forty-three members, and it is both curious and pleasant to find so many names in that body which have remained familiar to the people of Indiana at every stage of her subsequent history. Jonathan Jennings was its president and William Hendricks its secretary; each of whom soon afterwards served the infant state as governor and as senator in congress. James Noble was also there, and Enoch McCarty, Robert Hanna, John DePauw, John Badaliet, Samuel Milroy, Joseph Holman, David H. Maxwell and others, whose honored names adorn the annals of the state. A careful and competent historian of that period has spoken as follows of those who first here laid the foundations of a great and powerful commonwealth:

> The convention that formed the first constitution of Indiana was composed mainly of clear-minded, unpretending men of common sense, whose patriotism was unquestionable and whose morals were fair. Their familiarity with the theories of the Declaration of American Independence; their territorial expe-

rience under the provisions of the ordinance of 1787, and their knowledge of the principles of the constitution of the United States were sufficient, when combined, to lighten materially their labors in the great work of forming a constitution for a new state. * * * In the clearness and conciseness of its style, in the comprehensive and just provisions which it made for the maintenance of civil and religious liberty, in its mandates, which were designed to protect the rights of the people, collectively and individually, and to provide for the public welfare, the constitution that was formed for Indiana in 1816 was not inferior to any of the state constitutions which were in existence at that time.

And with this constitution for the guidance and welfare of her people, Indiana was admitted into the full fellowship of the Union December 11, 1816, and under these bright auspices began her unparalleled career as a state. I trust that this brief glance at the early history of our territory and our state may be found in harmony with the feeling and spirit of this occasion. The first impressions made on the mind of Governor Williams and on his tenacious memory were those produced by the men, the scenes and times to which I have alluded. The influences which surrounded him in his youth never left him. His school-house education was indeed limited, and colleges and universities were sealed mysteries to his boyhood, but there were lessons of higher wisdom and of more value than schoolmaster or professor ever taught engraved upon his mind as he grew to manhood in the receding shadow of the wilderness and in the opening dawn of civilization.

There was but little reading matter in the pioneer settlements. The first newspaper in all that vast region now comprising Indiana, Illinois, Michigan and Wisconsin, was the *Western Sun*, at Vincennes, published by Elihu Stout. In its columns the young and the old of that day eagerly scanned the sayings and doings of those who were entrusted with public affairs. No other people are so deeply interested in good government as those who are not yet strong, rich and self-reliant. In consequence of this fact the inhabitants of the frontiers at every stage of American history have been vigilant observers of their public servants. Turn now to one of the few white-haired fathers who yet remain, and who can recall the closing days of the Indiana Territory and the early years of the state, as Governor Williams could and often did, and you will be filled with astonishment. You will find that the scenes and events of that period of anxiety and determined effort have been painted on his memory in unfading colors. He will repeat, as I have heard in some instances, *verbatim*, the speeches to which he listened more than half a century ago; he will tell you their effect on the audience, describe the personal appearance and manner of the speaker, and inform you as to his fate at the polls. He will recount the various legislatures of that trying time and specify their acts on leading subjects. He will speak of the messages of governors and the influence they had on the public mind; what principles they involved and how they were settled; and in a thousand other ways he will show you that the fountains of knowledge, though not breaking forth in classic grounds or academic shades, were not denied him. And so it was with Governor Williams. His first reading was on grave and serious matters. His youthful mind knew nothing of fiction. His thoughts and life were real. He read the messages of the early governors—Jennings, Hendricks and others, in which there glowed a fervent love of country and a firm faith in the people.

The glorious traditions and the high American flavor of the Revolution were also fresh, and everywhere prevalent, and as a boy Governor Williams often listened in silent wonder to men not much past middle life who had been under fire with Washington and in council with Jefferson, Madison and Monroe. It has been said that from lack of education and travel he had a certain narrowness of view in public affairs. On the contrary, Governor Williams was developed and instructed from youth to robust manhood in a school of thought and action which never yet failed to make broader, stronger and more useful men than the Greek lexicon or a tourist's guide-book. He formed his earliest ideas of government and of public duty from the purest and best sources, and there was not a proscriptive, intolerant or narrow sentiment in his nature. His love of country was of the old-fashioned kind, inspired by the spirit of 1776, and it was broad enough to embrace every star of the flag, and every foot of American soil beneath its folds. But there was still another powerful reason why Governor Williams carried into the discharge of his duties a sound judgment and a staunch heart. He lived and died a practical farmer. He knew the laboring people better than any public man Indiana ever produced. He was born in their ranks and remained there to the end. He was at home in the broad and wholesome field, and he was familiar with the wants and ways, the hardships, and the hopes of those who eat their bread in the sweat of their faces.

From the days of Cincinnatus to the present time, men seeking popular favor have been paraded and eulogized as farmers, who could not tell a field of wheat from a field of oats, but the farmer in whose memory we are here to-day drove his team and held the plow; planted the corn, attended its growth and gathered it in; sowed his small grain, and reaped his harvests; raised horses, cattle, sheep and hogs, and fed them with his own hands. He made more than two blades of grass grow where none grew before, and thus advanced the general welfare. In the pursuit of these labors he became deeply imbued with sympathy for the agricultural classes, and with an earnest desire for their improvement. At an early period of his life he became actively identified with agricultural associations, and for more than thirty years was a controlling member of the Indiana state fair organization. This tribute, so long continued, and coming as it did from the tillers of the soil, was peculiarly grateful, and I doubt if any political honor was ever as pleasant to him or as highly prized as his prominent connection with the county and state fairs of Indiana. He delighted to interview a herd of blooded cattle as keenly as a reporter delights to interview a string of candidates for the presidency. His enjoyment over a bunch of fine sheep, or a lot of cultivated hogs, looking comfortable from high living, and handsome from high breeding, was very great and very genuine. In his admiration of the horse he had, without reading Bacon, adopted the Baconian philosophy. He looked to utility rather than to style and speed. His pride was in the farmer's horse rather than in the flying courser of the race track. Growing grain, the tall, dark corn, the rich, golden wheat, the clover fields and broad meadow lands were to him a source of unfailing interest and continuous comment.

While traversing every part of the state a few years ago, and as the bright and beautiful farms seemed to glide by like a painted panorama on exhibition, how often have I heard his exclamations of delight, and listened to his comments on the more than magical changes he had witnessed. He had, indeed, in his own day and generation seen the wilderness put off its savage garb and array its waste places in the richest robes of progress, culture and refinement. I have heard him recall the fact that within his recollection not a tree of the primeval forest had been disturbed by the white man's ax where now stands the splendid capital of our state. George Pogue, the first settler of Indianapolis, was massacred by a squad of Shawnee Indians, at a point not far from the Governor's Circle, in April, 1821, and Governor Williams, then an intelligent boy thirteen years old, could easily remember the painful excitement as the news traveled from settlement to settlement along the banks of White river, and down here to his own home. It is not any wonder, therefore, that he looked with peculiar emotions on the present condition of Indiana, the happy home of two million healthy, prosperous people, her fields yielding more agricultural wealth in proportion to area than any other state in the Union; her coal, timber, stone and fine clays giving employment at good wages to nearly one hundred thousand laborers, the products of her manufactories reaching the annual value of $200,000,000; and all these elements of wealth and diversified industries in no necessary conflict, but capable, under wise legislation, of being made to promote, foster and encourage each other.

He also saw the cause of education move forward with a force and rapidity unknown in any other commonwealth; he beheld the whole face of the state adorned and lit up with commodious free schools, with colleges, seminaries, high-schools and universities; he exulted in the fact that rising generations had abundant access to pathways of learning and science, and that there were so few left in Indiana who were unable to read and write their mother tongue.

In all these stupendous developments, Governor Williams, whether in private or public life, always bore an active and honorable part. In 1843, then being thirty-five years of age, he was first elected to the Indiana legislature as a member of the house, and from that time to the day of his death he was rarely, if ever, out of public employment. During a period of thirty years he was almost continuously elected and re-elected to the legislature, either as a member of the house or the senate. Such long and unbroken confidence on the part of those who knew him best is a far more eloquent eulogy than can be uttered over his grave on this occasion. He who in state or nation has legislated faithfully and wisely for the homes and the fireside happiness of his people, needs not the aid of the orator or sculptor to be remembered by his own and by future generations. Governor Williams took a prominent part in all important legislation in Indiana for more than a quarter of a century, and he was the best informed man in the legislative history of the state I have ever had the good fortune to know. The grasp of his memory was strong and reliable, and he was an authority on disputed points in reference to the action of different legislatures.

After long distinction as a capable and an honest official in the management of state affairs, he was elected in 1874 to a seat in the congress of the United States. He was known and respected in Washington as an industrious member, safe and reliable in his judgment and prudent in action. He was not permitted, however, to serve out his term, but was called upon by the people of Indiana, in the memorable year of 1876, to serve them as governor.

There is no party spirit in my heart to-day, nor will there be any in my words, but I am sure I will be pardoned a brief reference to the campaign of that year, for the purpose simply of illustrating the personal qualities of one who is now an historic character. A protracted and exciting canvass of important issues on which a candidate seeks the suffrages of a numerous and intelligent constituency is an ordeal which ascertains and exhibits every element of his strength as well as his weakness; it tries to the utmost all his resources of mind and body; it reveals to himself, as well as to others, exactly what mental, moral and physical forces he has to draw on when put to his highest spread of thought and action. A strong, safe judgment is required to stand sentinel all the time—a judgment cool in the midst of heat and passion, never blinded by party zeal nor warped by hostility to an adversary, and prompt to decide in the face of frightened friends or aggressive enemies the wise and proper thing to say and to do. Such a judgment as this does not spring alone from intellectual capacity. It arises from a combination embracing the moral and mental qualities alike. The only safe leader of the people is one whose judgment is inspired by convictions of principle and duty, so honest and determined that they can not be shaken by the temptations of wealth and power on the one hand nor by the aspect of danger and death on the other. An honest man is not only the noblest, but he is also the strongest work of God. He moves people and guides their minds because of the absolute conviction by which he is himself moved and controlled.

Under great responsibilities, confronted by sudden emergencies, pressed often by imprudent suggestions from over-zealous friends, and at all times on the front line of battle with an able and powerful foe, I never knew Governor Williams at fault in his judgment, because he was never at fault in the truth and honor of his purposes. His native ability and his great common sense were illuminated by an integrity of conviction so pure and so clear that he saw his way plainly under the darkest and most difficult circumstances. If I was permitted to recall his grand tour of the state seven years ago, to review again the mighty processions as they passed on with music and banners, to look into the faces and listen to the shouts of the swelling multitudes, there would appear at every point the same tall, quiet figure, clad in genteel homespun, with a manner composed and self-reliant, his open hand extended hour after hour to all without weariness or impatience, and with a look and voice so full of truth and kindness that he won the personal affections of even his political opponents. And in all that long and stormy contest who ever heard a word of invective or bitterness fall from his lips? Although himself constantly assailed and often grossly reviled, yet those who listened to him every day in public, and were his closest companions in private, never heard him personally assail anyone, nor disparage his adversaries. He felt keenly, and had a strong will and temper, but he put a curb on his tongue and measured what he said in a way worthy of all imitation. In his habitual self-control, in his reticence, and in a certain wariness of observation and manner, he seemed to have imbibed some leading Indian qualities with which he was familiar in his youth. I never knew a man calmer in scenes of confusion, or less open to surprise or panic than Governor Williams. In hot and conflicting councils, amongst those having the same end in view, he always spoke with the composure and good sense of a chief who had first smoked his pipe in careful meditation. Nor did any change of position or social surroundings make any change in his deportment. He entered the drawing-rooms of wealthy and fashionable life with the same mingled dignity, gentleness and reserve which he displayed in the halls of legislation, in the governor's office, or here at home on his farm. He was easy, correct and polite in address and conversation in whatever presence he stood.

The administration of Governor Williams as chief magistrate of Indiana is too recent and fresh in the public mind to call for discussion or extended notice at this time. It is an honorable part of the history of a magnificent state; a state whose career in all the elements of greatness has been with the speed and strength of the eagle's wing in his flight toward the sun. Governor Williams loved Indiana, and has left no blot on her name. He was her thirteenth executive elected by the people, and in the noble fraternity of his predecessors in that high office he stands a peer. Others were more learned in books, but none were wiser in the principles of self-government, nor purer in administering them for the welfare of the laboring, producing, business interests of the state. Others filled the public ear with higher notes of eloquence, but no one, as governor of Indiana, ever filled the hearts of the people with more approbation for his official conduct or greater love for his personal character. But two of those who preceded him in the executive chair are amongst the living, one of whom is here to join in honor to the dead. Long, long may their useful and honorable lives be spared, and at last, when the final hour of rest shall come to them, as it will to us all, may the memories which cluster around their names in the hearts of all their fellow-countrymen, without respect to creed or party, be as kind, as free from reproach and as gentle in their judgment as those which now gather around the name of James D. Williams and hallow the spot where he sleeps!

On this great day of liberty and of American glory; on this high, heroic day, dedicated to an eternity of fame as the beginning of an era in which the people should govern and the humble poor become exalted by virtue and talent to stations once held by kings; on this day we appropriately unveil a monument of everlasting marble in honor of one who, in all the circumstances of early trial, simplicity of life and eminent success, was a most striking and most worthy illustration of the true meaning of American institutions. While this monument will commemorate great personal virtues, it will also proclaim to the present and to future generations the beauty and the glory of our system of government. It will stand here, not only as an incentive to aspiring youth, but also as an enduring evidence that the avenues of honorable distinction are open and free to the laborer as well as to the magnate of millions, to the farmer with hard hands and homely garb as well as to those who wear purple and fine linen.

TRIBUTE TO PRESIDENT GARFIELD

Remarks made at the opera house at Terre Haute, Indiana, September 21, 1881, at a citizens' meeting assembled for the purpose of taking appropriate action upon the tragic death of President James A. Garfield.

R. MAYOR—I can not remain silent on such an occasion as this. All that is mortal of him who a few hours ago was the living head of the most powerful government on the globe, now lies cold and still in death. The sounds and emblems of mourning are encircling the earth to-day. Throughout the boundaries of the republic the bells are tolling for the illustrious dead, and following the track of the sun, wherever the dread intelligence finds the American flag, whether on the stately squadron or coasting schooner; whether over the proud embassy or the humble consulate, there it will droop at half-mast, and its brilliant folds will be shadowed with crape, and with American sorrow will be mingled the sorrow of the whole civilized world. Every nation will be a mourner at this saddest of all funerals in American history. The president of the United States died in public, with the world looking on from hour to hour, counting his pulse-beats and his breathings, and in all the long tragedy he faced death so well, bore himself so manfully, without murmur of complaint, or word of vengeance, that civilized nations of every clime and kindred will stand uncovered as his funeral train carries him back to his beloved western home.

Sir, I knew James A. Garfield well, and except on the political field, we had strong sympathies together. It is nearly eighteen years since we first met, and during that period I had the honor to serve seven years in the house of representatives with him. I have been asked, in this hour of universal grief, to place some

estimate upon his character. The kindness of his nature and his mental activity were his leading traits. In all his intercourse with men, women and children, no kinder heart ever beat in human breast than that which struggled on until half-past ten o'clock Monday night, and then forever stood still. There was a light in his face, a chord in his voice, and a pressure in his hand which were full of love for his fellow-beings. His manners were ardent and demonstrative with those to whom he was attached, and he filled the private circle with sunlight, and with magnetic currents. He had the joyous spirits of boyhood and the robust intellectuality of manhood more perfectly combined than any one I ever knew. Such a character was necessarily almost irresistible with those who knew him personally, and it accounts for that undying hold which, under all circumstances, bound his immediate constituents to him, as with hooks of steel. Such a nature, however, always has its dangers as well as its strength and its blessings. The kind heart and the open hand never accompany a suspicious, distrustful mind. Designing men mark such a character for their own selfish uses, and General Garfield's faults, for he had faults, as he was human, sprang more from this circumstance than from all others combined. He was prompt and eager to respond to the wishes of those he esteemed his friends, whether inside or outside of his own political party. That he made some mistakes in his long, busy career is but repeating the history of every generous and obliging man who has lived and died in public life. They are not such, however, as are recorded in heaven, nor will they mar or weaken the love of his countrymen. The poor, laboring boy, the self-made man, the hopeful, buoyant soul in the face of all difficulties and odds, constitute an example for the American youth which will never be lost nor grow dim.

The estimate to be placed on the intellectual abilities of General Garfield must be a very high one. Nature was bountiful to him, and his improvements were extensive and solid. He was an industrious, judicious student, and his rapidity of thought and activity of mind were, at times, amazing. He grasped a subject as quickly as any man who ever took part in the public affairs of the world. He had that fine mental courage which shrinks from no investigation. His acquirements were consequently rich and various. If I might make a comparison, I would say that, with the exception of Jefferson and John Quincy Adams, he was the most learned president, in what is written in books, in the whole range of American history. This, in my judgment, will be the rank assigned him by the historian of the future.

The Christian character of General Garfield can not, with propriety, be omitted in a glance, however brief, at his remarkable career. Those who knew him best in the midst of his ambition, and his worldly hopes, will not fail now at his tomb to bear their testimony to his faith in God, and his love for the teachings of the blessed Nazarene. Though upon the summit of human greatness, he avowed his Master's cause and accepted the kingdom of heaven in the spirit of a child. His chamber of death adds one more conspicuous illustration of the serenity and peace with which a Christian meets his fate. As the earth with all its honors, its loves, and its hopes receded and disappeared, he was comforted by sights and sounds which this world can neither give nor take away.

It seems but yesterday that I saw him last, and parted from him, in all the glory of his physical and mental manhood. His eye was full of light, his tread elastic and strong, and the world lay bright before him. He talked freely of public men and public affairs. His resentments were like sparks from the flint. He cherished them not for a moment. Speaking of one who he thought had wronged him, he said to me, that sooner or later he intended to pour coals of fire on his head by acts of kindness to some of his kindred. He did not live to do so, but the purpose of his heart has been placed to his credit in the book of eternal life.

Sir, as to the public measures, and the recent vivid occurrences connected with his brief administration, I am not here now to speak. At other times, and in another forum, that task may perhaps be required, but not on this occasion of grief and commemoration.

General Garfield's career at the head of the government was sad, stormy and tragic. He drank a bitter cup to its dregs. He realized, within his own party, in fullest measure, the harsh reward of an honorable and successful ambition.

> He who ascends to mountain tops shall find
>   The loftiest peaks most wrapped in clouds and snow;
> He who surpasses or subdues mankind
>   Must look down on the hate of those below.
> Though high *above* the sun of glory glow,
>   And far *beneath* the earth and ocean spread,
> *Round* him are icy rocks, and loudly blow
>   Contending tempests on his naked head,
>   And thus reward the toils which to those summits led.

But at last he has found rest and peace, the rest and peace of eternity to a Christian soul. As president, loving husband and father, affectionate son, and faithful friend, he will walk this earth no more. Alas! how pathetic was his death. At the high noon time of life, not quite fifty years of age, with a career already made, which would read like romance in any other country than this, and with a mission just before him in which he believed, and for which he longed to live, he fell by the hand of a wretch who had voted for him and wanted some poor office in return. And then the long struggle with slowly approaching but certain death! Whose eye has not wept, as the brave man was seen during the last eighty dreadful days, fighting his last great battle, and fighting it in vain? Like the strong swimmer in the surf of the sea, striving for the shore, he sometimes seemed to be nearing a point of safety, but with each ebbing wave he was carried further out, until at last he was gone forever from our anxious gaze on that tide which breaks alone on the high shores of immortality. How gladly would a million of lives have been ventured for his rescue; but it could not be, and we bow our heads and our hearts in helpless submission. May God in his loving mercy have the bereaved wife and the orphaned children in his holy keeping.

I have no heart now to speak of the future administration of the government. I have faith in the American people, and all will be well. They are a source of power and of safety within themselves, and they can be trusted that no harm shall happen to the republic. He who takes the place, under the constitution, of the dead president has my profound sympathy, and he will have my earnest support in all his efforts to promote the welfare and glory of our common and beloved country.

Sir, I have the honor to move the adoption of the resolutions which have been offered, and are now pending before this meeting.

THE LOUISIANA PURCHASE AND THE SOUTH-LAND OF THE REPUBLIC

An address delivered at Memphis, Tennessee, May 12, 1892, upon the occasion of the opening to traffic of the great bridge across the Mississippi river.

Mr. President, Ladies and Gentlemen:

THE brilliant and imposing demonstrations in which the people of Tennessee, and of surrounding states, are here engaged, mark an event of national interest and enduring importance. You celebrate an achievement in the progress of mankind which has the sanction of divine command. In the dawn of creation man was decreed and proclaimed the master of the planet on which he was placed. To him dominion was given, and the right of conquest, over the earth and all that within it dwelt; over the plains, the mountains, the rivers, the wide oceans, and the inland seas. It has been his high mission to ascertain, develop and subjugate the illimitable treasures of the physical world to his control; and according to the measure of his success in this great task has been the measure of human progress, civilization and glory. There has been no lack of toil in any age of history, but, until within the present century, the world has moved slowly from want of knowledge. The physical sciences, throughout the annals of the human race, remained practically a sealed book until modern intellect and invention discovered and utilized them. By their aid now, as the twentieth century draws near, the declared dominion of man in the fields of nature is no longer a theory, but a stupendous, overwhelming fact. By the light and power of knowledge, the valleys and plains are teeming with fourfold productiveness; mountain, gulch

THE BRIDGE ACROSS THE MISSISSIPPI RIVER AT MEMPHIS.

and cañon are rifled of their precious contents; the loneliest waters of the great deep are made familiar with ships of commerce; the earth is girdled with tracks of steel and iron, on which the merchandise of nations outtravels the birds of the air; the angry and burning element of the clouds in a storm is tamed into a common carrier of the business messages, the domestic interchanges, and the whispered loves of every civilized people on the globe; and the mightiest rivers that pour their torrents to the sea, and on whose banks armies have stood powerless to cross, while the destinies of nations depended on their movements, are spanned, and rendered as free from obstruction to travel, commerce, and the march of men, as the humblest rivulets over which we step in an evening walk.

The place where we stand this hour, illuminated as it is by festivities more glorious and honorable than ever adorned a Roman triumph, has witnessed in past centuries, as well as in the present, many high, heroic struggles for ascendency over the opposing forces of gigantic nature. Here came, three hundred and fifty years ago, the Spanish adventurer, in quest of a new El Dorado, a land of gold; from these bluffs he beheld the Father of Waters, and revealed to the pages of history the existence of the mighty river for the first time since its floods came down from the North in the dim eternity of the past. De Soto lingered on its banks, crossed its turbid tide with difficulty and danger, explored its western valleys and the mountains beyond, in his vain pursuit of fabulous deposits of the precious metals. He wandered back at last to die of a broken heart in sight of its majestic bosom, and to be buried in its restless depths. His career ended, and his eyes closed in death, with no consciousness in his active, eager brain that he had discovered a realm, and a river which ruled it, in comparison with whose boundless and fathomless wealth the gold and silver, the diamonds and the precious stones of the whole earth sink into utter insignificance.

The El Dorado was here, unseen by the ignorant Spaniard, but waiting for the touch of scientific knowledge and enlightened statesmanship to pour forth its treasures, and to glow with a splendor hitherto unknown to the children of men. The most munificent gifts, the bounties of the physical universe were here, then as now, and ready to surrender to the domination and control of man whenever he approached them properly equipped for the contest. What an unparalleled empire of wealth and human abode it was; then dormant, idle, and listless, awaiting the magic wand of science, invention, energy, industry and Christian civilization. The map of the world, displayed in all its parts most renowned for their magnificence and power, discloses no other such formation of the earth's surface, for the prosperous habitation, the growth and progress of the human family, as the Mississippi valley. Within its vast embrace, twenty American states, distinct in their domestic sovereignties, united in their federal relations, contribute in whole or in part to its strength and matchless development.

The Mississippi river, and its far branching tributaries, touch upon twenty-three degrees of latitude and thirty degrees of longitude; draining more than 2,500,000 square miles; an area greater in extent, and richer and more inexhaustible in the endowments of nature, than Great Britain, France, Germany, Austria, Italy, Spain, Portugal, Denmark, Belgium, Greece and European Turkey all combined. In all the ages of the past, and in every clime beneath the sun, population has gathered to the banks of the great rivers of the earth, and swarmed into their fertile valleys. Empire has followed the waterways of the world; cities have lined the tracks of navigation; hives of human energy and industry have been most crowded, active and fruitful in the vicinity of oceans, lakes and running streams. But where on the face of the globe, in all things past, or in the present, are such allurements of wealth and happiness to be found as in the mighty region where we stand to-day? Where else has nature beckoned with such a bountiful hand, or smiled so sweet and hospitable a welcome? Not in the valley of the Nile, carrying the waters of the table-lands of Central Africa to the Mediterranean Sea; not from the banks of the Indus, or the Ganges; not from the plains of the Yangtsekiang, the great artery of the Chinese empire; nor from the broad savannahs of the Amazon as they repose in indolent luxuriance within the tropics and close to the equator. Every climate adapted to the health and activity of a laboring, progressive people, and every species of production known to the wants of mankind, are the gifts of generous nature to the valley of the Mississippi. From the cool springs and fountains of the great river in the freezing zones of the North, to its warm, wide-open mouth into the gulf, nothing is wanting for the support and aggrandizement of a self-reliant, self-governing, dominant race.

An absolute harmony of interests is stamped upon the entire valley. The cedar and pine of the far North wave their branches in kindly salutation to the magnolias and the palms of the furtherest South. The winds and the waters are not sectional, nor are the interests, the associations, the hearts of those who line the banks of the Ohio, the Wabash, the Illinois, the Missouri and all the other water-courses from the western slopes of the Alleghanies to the eastern foot-hills of the Rocky Mountains. The great cities of the valley, with Chicago, queen city, between the two oceans at their head, and soon to be the metropolis of the American continent, extend their hands and hopes in friendly greeting to all the in-dwellers of the lower river countries. The great laws of homogeneity of race, and unity of purpose and destiny, govern throughout all the borders of this vast seat of present and of future empire. In this great valley of the Mississippi, where waters mingle that have their sources in mountains two thousand miles apart, with its many fertile valleys and rich table-lands, with its forests and mines and quarries, this nation is to find its greatest development. Here will be its densest population, here the seat of its great and diversified industries.

With a population now of thirty millions, it is not the work of the imagination, nor a stretch of fancy, but of cool, intelligent calculation, to ascertain at the close of the next century, more than a hundred millions of inhabitants in this great middle belt of the continent. In fact there are those now born who will realize the fulfillment of this vision, and behold in the Mississippi valley the governing power of their own country, and one of the most potent factors in the affairs of civilization throughout the world. This is no dream which needs interpretation. The future ascendency and overwhelming greatness of this vast basin, between far distant mountain ranges, are as fixed and certain as the coming of the morning and the evening star in the sky. Nor can this dazzling, and more than imperial destiny, be checked, or stayed by human agency, any more than the impotent hand of man can "bind the sweet influences of the Pleiades, or loose the bands of Orion."

But a specific cause connected with and marking the swift and stalwart progress of the Mississippi valley, has assembled this great and jubilant concourse of people; a specific triumph of intellect, science and enterprise electrifies the country, and demands our more specific attention. You have thrown a giant causeway across an inland sea, as John C. Calhoun, in high descriptive phrase, forty years ago, styled the august river which flows by your doors. You have here built, and to-day declared open and ready for the commerce of states and nations, the most extensive structure of the kind in the western hemisphere; and at a point further down the swift, inspiring current, and rich alluvial banks of the mighty river, than the science of engineering had hitherto deemed possible. By the side of the work here accomplished, other great bridges of the world are dwarfed in comparison, and grow puny by actual measurement. The St. Louis bridge, noble creation of the genius of James B. Eads, and noble forerunner of what has here occurred, beholds itself surpassed; while the bridges of Brooklyn, Havre de Grace, Montreal, and other proud structures, are left far in the distance as triumphs of modern science. Nor can we in this connection be blind to the different honors which belong to different actions and services in the tremendous drama of life.

To those who have planned and constructed the great and durable public works of the world, more glory is due than to the leaders of victorious armies for the purpose of conquest. When battlefields are forgotten, when the lines where brave men contended and died midst "death shots falling thick and fast" can no longer be found, the bridge at Memphis and the bridge at St. Louis, and others of their kind, will be hailed by other generations as among the most brilliant and beneficial achievements of the wonderful century now drawing to its close. No one now cares or inquires for the places in Gaul, or in Britain, where Cæsar's legions bore the eagles of Rome into the stormy fight, but the solid highways, the aqueducts, the bridges, and even the baths they constructed, have in many instances survived the ravages of more than two thousand years, and still remain to instruct the historian and to delight the antiquarian. The most useful and durable triumph of Roman power over the resisting and obstructive forces of nature were in the marvelous roads she built, leading from her distant conquered possessions to her haughty capital on the Tiber. They were links in the powerful chain which bound the provinces to the center. "They united the subjects of the most distant provinces by an easy and familiar intercourse, but their primary object had been to facilitate the marches of the legions, nor was any country considered as completely subdued till it had been rendered in all its parts pervious to the arms and authority of the conqueror." The objects of pagan Rome in her grandest public improvements were baleful and destructive; the ends which Christian civilization have in view are those of peace on earth and good-will. The gigantic structure with which you have here arched the river secures not only a convergence and a crossing at this point of all transcontinental lines of travel south of the 37th degree of north latitude, but it likewise constitutes a massive link of fraternity, of association, of interchange of affections, as well as of commodities, between the people of the states; an indissoluble tie wrought here in the heart of the South, by which the inhabitants of the seaboards on the east and the west are made nearer neighbors than ever before; a bond of brotherhood and of union, shortening the distance and brightening the intercourse which now prevails between the peaceful homes of kindred commonwealths.

May we not, however, pause in our joyous congratulations to look for a few moments into the causes which have made possible such an occasion as the present. The early policies of this government not only gave form and life and interpretation to its constitution and laws, but also to its physical extent, its geographical boundaries. The fathers of the republic not only traced the principles of free government in our organic laws; they also traced the lines within which the American flag was to be unfurled. The constitution was adopted in convention, ratified by the states, and went into force, with the Mississippi river mainly as the western boundary of the United States, and every inch of the mighty domain beyond was a foreign country.

In the treaty with Great Britain in 1783, after our independence had been achieved, sword in hand, the boundaries of the United States were defined to be the Atlantic Ocean on the east, the Gulf of Mexico on the south, the Great Lakes on the north, and the Mississippi river on the west. These boundaries, however, were subject to a condition which still further, and in a most important and dangerous particular, contracted our western frontier. At that time the Floridas and that portion of Louisiana lying east of the Mississippi river belonged to Spain, as well as all that vast and undefined region, then known as the Louisiana territory, on the sunset side of the Father of Waters.

At the opening of the present century the west end of your bridge would have rested on French soil under the sway of the great Napoleon. When Thomas Jefferson delivered his immortal inaugural on the 4th of March, 1801, the powers of France and Spain held undisputed title to all the western banks and tributaries of the Mississippi river, and to all the intermediate territory between its waters and the Pacific coast. The bosom of the river itself was claimed as a common highway, open to navigation for the Spaniard and the Frenchman, as well as the Island of Orleans, as the Crescent City was then styled, and also the Floridas were in the exclusive grasp of foreign domination. It was on this mutilated map of the future ocean-bound republic that Jefferson looked with a wisdom of statesmanship, and a prophetic foresight of coming events, never before nor since given to man in shaping the policies and the conduct of a free government. He at once gave the alarm to his own countrymen, and at the same time sounded a note of warning to foreign nations that the Mississippi river was purely and exclusively an American channel of commerce, where their presence would not be tolerated. As soon as the intelligence of the cession of Louisiana, and probably of the Floridas, by Spain to France, was received by Jefferson, he sought to open negotiations for the acquisition of New Orleans and the territory thereby implied, but his correspondence shows that if unsuccessful by negotiation, he was prepared to pursue his purpose by other and more forcible means. He seized upon the subject with profound personal zeal, passing by his secretary of state, and conducting the most important features of the correspondence on the American side with his own hands. Napoleon was then first consul over that transition state of government, from anarchy to empire, then existing in France, and Robert Livingston, the distinguished chancellor, was the American minister to his anomalous court. On the 18th of April, 1802, Jefferson wrote to Mr. Livingston the following remarkable letter:

> The cession of Louisiana and the Floridas, by Spain to France, works most sorely on the United States. On this subject the secretary of state has written to you fully, yet I can not forbear recurring to it personally, so deep is the impression it makes on my mind. It completely reverses all the political relations of the United States and will form a new epoch in our political course. Of all nations, of any consideration, France is the one which, hitherto, has offered the fewest points on which we could have any conflict of right, and the most points of a communion of interests. From these causes we have ever looked to her as our natural friend, as one with which we never could have an occasion of difference. Her growth, therefore, we viewed as our own—her misfortunes ours. There is on the globe one single spot, the possessor of which is our natural and habitual enemy. It is New Orleans, through which the produce of three-eighths of our territory must pass to market, and from its fertility it will ere long yield more than half of our whole produce, and contain more than half our inhabitants. France, placing herself in that door, assumes to us the attitude of defiance.
>
> Spain might have retained it quietly for years. Her pacific dispositions, her feeble state, would induce her to increase our facilities there, so that her possession of the place would be hardly felt by us, and it would not, perhaps, be very long before some circumstances might arise which might make the cession of it to us the price of something of more worth to her. Not so can it ever be in the hands of France ; the impetuosity of her temper, the energy and restlessness of her character placed in a point of eternal friction with us, and our character, which, though quiet and loving peace and the pursuit of wealth, is high-minded, despising wealth in competition with insult and injury, enterprising and energetic as any nation on earth ; these circumstances render it impossible that France and the United States can continue long friends, when they meet in so irritable a position. They, as well as we, must be blind if they do not see this ; and we must be very improvident if we do not begin to make arrangements on that hypothesis.
>
> The day that France takes possession of New Orleans, fixes the sentence which is to restrain her forever within her low-water mark. It seals the union of two nations, who, in conjunction, can maintain exclusive possession of the ocean. From that moment we must marry ourselves to the British fleet and nation. We must turn all our attention to a maritime force, for which our resources place us on very high ground; and, having formed and connected together a power which may render reinforcement of her settlements here impossible to France, make the first cannon which shall be fired in Europe the signal for tearing up any settlement she may have made, and for holding the two continents of America in sequestration for the common purposes of the United British and American nations.
>
> This is not a state of things we seek or desire. It is one which this measure, if adopted by France, forces on us, as necessarily as any other cause, by the laws of nature, brings on its necessary effect. It is not from fear of France that we deprecate this measure proposed by her. For however greater her force than is ours, compared in the abstract, when to be exerted on our soil, it is nothing in comparison to ours. But it is from a sincere love of peace, and a firm persua-

47

sion, that bound to France by the interests and the strong sympathies still existing in the minds of our citizens, and holding relative positions which insure their continuance, we are secure of a long course of peace. Whereas, the change of friends, which will be rendered necessary if France changes that position, embarks us necessarily as a belligerent power in the first war of Europe. In that case, France will have held possession of New Orleans during the interval of a peace, long or short, at the end of which it will be wrested from her. Will this short-lived possession have been an equivalent to her for the transfer of such a weight into the scale of her enemy? Will not the amalgamation of a young, thriving nation continue to that enemy the health and force which are at present so evidently on the decline? And will a few years' possession of New Orleans add equally to the strength of France? She may say she needs Louisiana for the supply of her West Indies. She does not need it in time of peace, and in war she could not depend on them, because they would be so easily intercepted.

I should suppose that all these considerations might, in some proper form, be brought into view of the government of France. Though stated by us, it ought not to give offense; because we do not bring them forward as a menace, but as consequences not controllable by us, but inevitable from the course of things. We mention them, not as things which we desire by any means, but as things we deprecate; and we beseech a friend to look forward and prevent them for our common interests.

Jefferson was more familiar with European politics than any other American. While minister to France, from 1784 to 1789, he had been a close and vigilant student, not only of the critical and dangerous condition of the French government, but also of the public affairs of all the leading governments of Europe, and the relations they bore to each other. He was a master of the principal foreign languages, and after his return home kept up his correspondence with the best thinkers and writers abroad, and watched with zealous interest the convulsive struggles there taking place. With his own eyes he had witnessed the opening scenes of the French Revolution. He had driven through the streets of Paris between a mob of infuriated people on one hand and trained cavalry on the other, who closed in bloody conflict as soon as he disappeared. He had seen the mob, on fire with animosities of five hundred years of oppression, compel Louis the Sixteenth to wear the tri-colored cockade in his hat, and crouch with fear in its presence. He, therefore, spoke with personal knowledge, in his letter to Livingston, of the impetuous temper, and the restless energy of the people of France. He foresaw that with such a people colonized on our frontier, three thousand miles in extent, peace would be impossible. The inevitable friction between two races, separate and distinct in blood, language, traditions and destiny, would have been the basis of lasting war; of long lines of fortifications, and bloody fields of armed conflict. The banks of the great river would have frowned at each other in hostile array, and its waters would have been crimson with strife.

But whether peace could have been maintained or not, the vision of a great European power standing across the pathway of western empire, and closing forever the natural routes for the American flag to travel from one ocean to the other, aroused Jefferson as no other event had done since the first guns of the Revolution were heard at Lexington and Concord. He boldly determined to make the issue, and meet it, before France had entered upon her projected scheme of American colonization, and while Napoleon needed money for the outburst of war with Great Britain and the allied powers, which, to the eye of Jefferson, was plainly at hand. He knew the hour for action had come; that the fulfillment of time was at hand; and he did not hesitate, on behalf of a government yet in its early infancy, to hold high language to the most powerful and warlike nations then on the globe. In a letter to M. De Nemours, a distinguished citizen of France, he wrote, to be seen by Napoleon, the following startling sentences:

> I wish you to be possessed of the subject, because you may be able to impress on the government of France the inevitable consequences of their taking possession of Louisiana; and though, as I here mention, the cession of New Orleans and the Floridas to us would be a palliation, yet I believe it would be no more, and that this measure will cost France, and perhaps not very long hence, a war which will annihilate her on the ocean, and place that element under the despotism of two nations, which I am not reconciled to the more because my own would be one of them. I am thus open with you, because I trust that you will have it in your power to impress on that government considerations, in the scale against which the possession of Louisiana is nothing. In Europe, nothing but Europe is seen, or supposed to have any weight in the affairs of nations; but this little event of France possessing herself of Louisiana, which is thrown in as nothing—as a mere make-weight in the general settlement of accounts—this speck which now appears as an almost invisible point on the horizon, is the embryo of a tornado which will burst on both sides of the Atlantic, and involve in its effects their highest destinies. That it may yet be avoided is my sincere prayer.

Throughout all the negotiations for the acquisition of the Louisiana territory, and up to their very close, the government of France was open and pronounced in their opposition to the measure. Peaceful relations had been strained and broken between the United States and France in the years just preceding Jefferson's administration, and Napoleon did not even affect a favorable temper toward American interests. In January, 1802, Livingston wrote to Jefferson, saying:

> The evil our country has suffered by its rupture with France is not to be calculated. We have become an object of jealousy both to the government and the people.

In October of the same year, Jefferson, in replying to Livingston, said:

> It is well, however, to be able to inform you, generally, through a safe channel, that we stand completely corrected of the error, that either the government or the nation of France has any remains of friendship for us.

During the year 1802 Livingston at different times wrote from Paris—

> That the colonization of New Orleans was a darling object of the first consul; that he saw in it a means of gratifying his friends and disposing of his enemies; that it was thought that New Orleans must command the trade of our whole western country; that the French had been persuaded that the Indians were attached to France and hated the Americans; that the country was a paradise, and hence it should remain forever a province of France.

In April, 1802, he wrote—

> That the French minister would give no answer to any inquiries he made on the subject of Louisiana; that the government was at that moment fitting out an armament to take possession, consisting of between five thousand and seven thousand men, under the command of General Bernadotte, who would shortly sail for New Orleans, unless the state of affairs at St. Domingo should change their destination.

As late as March, 1803, the American minister again wrote "that Talleyrand had assured him no sale would be heard of," and further, stating in an official dispatch to his government at home, that, "with respect to a negotiation for Louisiana, I think nothing will be effected here."

In the meantime, so eager and resolute was Jefferson to attain the priceless end in view, that he appointed James Monroe as minister extraordinary to the French government, to act in concert with Mr. Livingston in the pending negotiations. In his letter to Monroe, of January 13, 1803, Jefferson, amongst other things, says:

> If we can not by a purchase of the country, insure ourselves a course of perpetual peace and friendship with all nations, then, as war can not be distant, it

behooves immediately to be preparing for that course, without, however, hastening it, and it may be necessary on our failure on the continent to cross the channel.

For the American minister to cross the English channel after negotiations had failed, meant an alliance with Great Britain, if such a *dernier resort* was necessary, in order to rescue the Mississippi river, and all its territory and tributaries, from the occupancy and the arrogance of the French empire. Jefferson made no concealment of his purpose or his instructions on this point. Napoleon knew them as well as the American minister, to whom they were written. Within ninety days after Jefferson's words of great import to the new minister were put on paper, Monroe was in Paris, and within seventeen days after his arrival, April 30, 1803, a treaty was signed by the French and American ministers, whereby the entire Louisiana province was ceded to the United States for the sum of sixty million francs. It is not necessary to claim that Napoleon was intimidated by the tone of Jefferson's correspondence, but it will be readily seen that Jefferson made no mistake in his judgment of the European situation, nor in the manner of his instructions, nor as to the time when Monroe carried his ultimatum. Only seven days after the treaty was concluded for the cession of Louisiana, war was declared between France and Great Britain, and Napoleon started again on his warlike career, free from danger of embarrassment on account of American hostility, and with a timely assistance to his meager financial resources. It was Edmund Burke who declared that statesmanship arose from the science of circumstances; and Jefferson and Napoleon, the great civilian and the great soldier, both accepted this definition and acted upon it to their own separate interests.

But how different the careers and the destinies of these two imposing characters. The Corsican emperor of the French made conquests and camping grounds of the proudest kingdoms of Europe; he played with ancient thrones as foot-balls in his military festivities; he humiliated the haughtiest dynasties of the world into the dust at his feet; and then, he lost all, and fell, like Lucifer, the bright son of the morning, to hope no more and to perish miserably, chained to a rock in the desolate ocean. The American chief magistrate, lawgiver and sage peacefully and permanently enlarged the boundaries of his country nearly fourfold; his acquisitions were more extensive, without causing a drop of blood or a tear to be shed, than all the regions of the earth combined over which Alexander, Cæsar and Napoleon ever waved their ruthless swords, and at last he died at his own Blue Ridge home, full of years and full of an imperishable glory.

Nor must it be overlooked in estimating the lofty courage and statesmanship of Jefferson that he purchased the Louisiana country under threats of impeachment for a violation of the constitution. The leaders of the federal party assailed him at every step he took in his glorious work. And what is more, Jefferson himself so much doubted the technical constitutionality of his act that he conceded the whole point in controversy, and was ready to join congress in an appeal to the nation, as he says, "for an additional article to the constitution approving and confirming an act which the nation had not previously authorized." In his strict construction of the constitution, and in his view of its limited and express powers, he was led to say:

> The constitution has made no provision for our holding foreign territory, still less for incorporating foreign nations into our own. The executive, in seizing the fugitive occurrence which so much advances the good of the country, has done an act beyond the constitution. The legislature, in casting behind them metaphysical subtleties and risking themselves like faithful servants, must ratify and pay for it and then throw themselves on their own country for doing for them, unauthorized, what we know they would have done for themselves had they been in a situation to do it. It is the case of a guardian investing the money of his wards in purchasing an important adjacent territory and saying to them when of age, "I did this for your good; I pretend to no right to bind you; you may disavow me and I must get out of the scrape as I can; I thought it my duty to risk myself for you." But we shall not be disavowed by the nation, and their act of indemnity will confirm and not weaken the constitution by more strongly marking out its line.

With all our deep veneration for the wisdom of Jefferson, and without questioning his construction of the constitution, it is yet pleasant to know that the American people did not concur in these admissions against himself; that no act of indemnity was needed; no impeachment followed; and that in after years the great Chief Justice John Marshall decided the principles involved in the purchase of the Louisiana territory in Jefferson's favor. In the case of the American and the Ocean insurance companies against David

Canter, decided in first Peters, the chief justice held that "the constitution confers absolutely on the government of the Union the powers of making war and of making treaties; consequently that the government possesses the power of acquiring territory, either by conquest or by treaty."

And thus we behold the Louisiana territory of 1803 legitimately born into the embrace of the American republic, under the sanction of the constitution, as interpreted by the highest judicial authority, not only of this country but of the world. May we not now, with a proud and grateful feeling, look for a few moments at the lines of the map wherein it lay? Its immense extent and infinite resources were practically unknown at the time of its purchase. In the light of the present day, however, with the banners of civilization full high advanced and streaming throughout all its borders, what a revelation arises to our view! What a constellation of states we now see blazing across our whole western sky! From the mouth of the Mississippi river to the strait of Fuca, and from St. Louis to the Pacific ocean, the American flag was planted on the 30th day of April 1803. Under the ample folds are clustered the states of Louisiana, Arkansas, Missouri, Iowa, Minnesota, Nebraska, Kansas, Oregon, Washington, Montana, North Dakota, South Dakota, Idaho, Wyoming, portions of Colorado and Nevada, and of the territory of Utah; all secured to the United States by treaty with France.

But the influences arising from this act of consummate statesmanship did not cease nor perish by the wayside upon its completion; they rapidly grew in force and in far-reaching and marvelous consequences. Only forty years later the lone star of Texas was illuminating the horizon of the Southwest in the revolt against Mexico, and guided toward the United States by the example and precedent of the Louisiana acquisition. The policy of Jefferson's administration in 1803 was the herald, the forerunner of the annexation of Texas, and of all the gigantic and glorious results which followed. Constitutional difficulties no longer barred the way— they had been put forever at rest by judicial authority of the highest and last resort; and when the American people saw the citizens of a neighboring republic fighting for liberty against overwhelming odds, they flew to their aid at the Alamo, and at San Jacinto, and then welcomed them to honored seats in the Union of the American states.

The war with Mexico, which followed, has been the prolific theme of party invective and sectional animosity. Eloquent tongues in high places denounced its prosecution while our soldiers, on a foreign soil, and in conflict with a foreign foe, were engaged at Buena Vista, Monterey, Churubusco, Chapultepec, Molino del Rey, and the city of Mexico. The Mexican government, in its avowed determination to subjugate Texas, and in its aggressive arrogance toward American citizens and their rights, had a powerful party in the United States. For many years the purposes of the war were misrepresented, and the motives of those who declared and prosecuted it, on the American side, were maligned and slandered by the powerful leadership and press of a powerful, sectional prejudice, and party. But we hail now a brighter, better and happier day. The darkness of sectional prejudice, and the bitterness of party, on the subject of the Mexican war, have disappeared forever, along with vast heaps of odious rubbish, connected in the past with other and kindred questions. We are no longer in the uncertain twilight of national progress where the raven's croak is heard; where bats and owls, and all unclean birds are found breeding suspicion, distrust, aversion, alienation and strife. We are at last in the clear and kindly sunlight of a peaceful noonday; and objects of national import no longer appear in distorted and unnatural shapes. With unclouded eyes, and fraternal hearts, the results of the Mexican war are now viewed by the whole American people, as chief among all of the great agencies whereby this republic is to fulfill its high destiny; to run its race and be glorified.

We may pass the acquisitions of New Mexico, Arizona, the southern parts of Colorado, Nevada and Utah, with brief but appreciative comment. They alone are more richly endowed by the prodigal hand of nature than the proudest conquests of antiquity; but when we turn to Texas, that colossus of the Union, which came as a condition precedent, and to California, which fell to us as a condition subsequent to the war with Mexico, the mind is filled with awe, and the boldest imagination is baffled in its conceptions of the future. The fate of nations, the rise and fall of empires, the voice and teachings of the ages, the manifest destiny of the race, all proclaim a providence in history, a Divinity which shapes the conduct of human affairs, and determines the ultimate ends to be attained. The treasures of California, richer and more alluring far than the hoarded contents of all the other gold-bearing regions of the earth combined, belonged to the gold-hunting Spaniard nearly three centuries, but they were hidden from his eager, cruel, and rapacious eye. Spanish adventurers, by the authority of their government, repeatedly thronged the California coast in search of the land of gold that lay open to their sight, to their touch, to their possession, and to their insatiate avarice. Had the Spaniard discovered the gold of California, the face of the world would have been changed, and the American republic of to-day would have been an impossibility. Such a rush of all the evil elements of the Spanish race, and of the whole world, would have followed; such wars between nations would have taken place for the possession of the Pacific coast; such colonies would have been planted there, and such cruel and unsparing slavery practiced, as nowhere else had hitherto blackened the earth, or shocked heaven. Wrecked, exhausted, worn out, and desolate, the mighty gold and silver belt of the Pacific would have been abandoned at last by the Spaniard, or held as a worthless appendage to the home government it had enriched. In any event its part in the providence of history would have been played and lost. Such, however, was not to be, and the baleful Spaniard wandered through a wide wilderness of gold and silver, but found them not; he walked over their lurking places, but did not discover them; he looked upon their thinly covered habitations, but saw not their shining dust. They were not to be surrendered to the greed, and to the accursed uses of the most despotic, bigoted, non-progressive, reactionary power then on the globe.

As controlling factors of commerce and civilization, and for the elevation and prosperity of the laboring millions on the farms and in the workshops of the world, the gold beds and the silver lodes of the Pacific states and territories have been given in trust to the American people, whose sacred duty it is to see that they are coined and put into circulation as money, on terms of absolute equality, and in strict accordance with the constitution and the laws, as framed by the fathers of the republic. We need not dwell to-day on the results already accomplished in our history by the precious metals of the coast regions of the West. Like irresistible magnets they attracted the surveying chain of the engineer as he first marked the line of the Union Pacific railway across the desert and waste places of the continent. To their more than magic power is due that development of nature's resources west of the ninetieth meridian of longitude, which causes the fictions and fables of all times past to seem tame and commonplace in comparison. Without the gold and silver of California, Colorado, Nevada, Arizona, New Mexico, Montana, and their incentive to the growth, wealth, and transportation of the West, the bridge you have opened here would not have been built; locomotives and railway trains would not have sought a crossing at this point during the present generation, if ever. The land of Ophir on the shores of the Indian Ocean was the ancient emporium of Indian and Arabian trade and commerce, and attracted the fleets of Solomon, and Hiram, king of Tyre, which carried back cargoes of gold, of sandal-wood, and of precious stones; but you are in swift and constant communication with richer realms, and more powerful agents of the world's advancement, than Solomon ever knew, or prophet of God proclaimed. Let the honors of history be paid to whom they belong; let a giant statue of Thomas Jefferson stand at the west end of the Memphis bridge, his face to the setting sun; let him look out, as it were, upon the domain he secured for his countrymen, and that which followed in the line of his policy. There will rise up before him an abode for future generations more numerous than the inhabitants of all Europe combined; and it will there remain a monument to his wisdom and statesmanship, as eternal as the mountains that tower up from the plains.

But, Mr. President, there remains yet another lesson for our recognition, instruction, and profit in connection with the present occasion. We are in the southland of the republic; on all hands we behold its vast and inexhaustible plains; its varied, thronging, active industries. History salutes us here, and more especially the history of the last thirty years. I shall speak not now of the contrast between stern-visaged war and the angel of smiles and peace; of the change from plunging shot and screaming shell on southern rivers, to the illuminations which now light up their waters in the celebration of peaceful victories, far more renowned than those of war. I turn to dwell for a few moments on the noblest of them all, the glorious resurrection of the South. In no other quarter of the habitable globe, and nowhere else in the long annals of the human race, was there ever before displayed the high Christian courage, the sublime devotion to duty, the steady nerve and the recuperative energy and strength which have guided the southern people from the profoundest depths of adversity and ruin to the assured and glowing prosperity of the present hour. Every fair and honest-minded man and woman in the world concedes you this glory; the impartial historian of the future will write it down to your imperishable honor; and every heart fit to animate the breast of an American citizen, or to beat beneath the American flag, rejoices now, and will rejoice evermore that it is so. Aided by the manifest hand of an over-ruling Providence, you have caused the calamities and curses of war to become the foremost blessings of peace. You have removed the rubbish left by the most destructive tornado that ever swept the earth, and on their old foundations you have rebuilt states, now more powerful, progressive and full of present and future greatness than ever before. You have risen superior to the most unjust and injurious system of national legislation that ever cursed a people, not excepting English laws for Ireland; and that system, in its day called reconstruction, with all its proclamations, military orders and edicts of unconstitutional usurpation, has totally perished, leaving only its memory, despised alike throughout the North as it is throughout the South. I speak not of a new South; it is the old South that is moving in connection with the revolution that has taken place; the old blood and brain power of the South, transmitted from generation to generation, are now aroused and working out the problem of her splendid destiny. The old South is young again; she has renewed her mighty youth, and henceforth she will tower in her pride of place, regardless of the mousing owls that may hawk at and seek to destroy her.

A glance at the cold statistics of the South at this time is more stirring to the American heart than the richest strains of patriotic music. The forthcoming eleventh census shows a population of nearly 23,000,000 in the states of the South, an increase of more than twenty per cent. in the ten years between 1880 and 1890. From the same source we learn that the assessed value of the property of southern states, two years ago, amounted to $5,442,-835,202—an increase of nearly $2,000,000,000 over the assessment of 1880. In the production of cotton, that great staple which, with wool, constitutes the wearing apparel of the human family, and which was once supposed to depend upon a form of labor now no longer in existence, southern progress has amazed the world, and, indeed, the South itself. When the war between the sections broke out, 4,000,000 bales was the very greatest point to which cotton production had reached. In 1879, fourteen years after the conflict closed, the cotton states counted 5,744,359 bales; in 1889, ten years later, 7,452,281 bales, and it is now estimated that the present yield will closely approach 9,000,000 bales. When, and where, the limit to cotton-growing in this country will be found, can only be answered by the demands of the civilized people of the world. Those demands, however great they may be, can here be met, without the aid of a single cotton-field anywhere else on earth.

But the rapid and extensive construction of railroads in the southern states tells more fully of development, in all particulars, perhaps, than any other one feature of enterprise which could be cited. They tell of that trade, and travel, and interstate commerce which demand transportation only where intelligent industry and permanent prosperity prevail. By the census of 1860 there were 10,865 miles of railroads in the South, and at the close of the war every track was a wreck, and every corporation bankrupt. In 1890 there were 44,466 miles in running order, and since then the number has increased.

In order, however, to clearly comprehend how much greater, stronger, richer and better developed the South now is than in her period of greatest pride and glory before the war, a look at the subject of railroads by states is most instructive.

According to the census statistics of the United States, the following facts appear: In the year 1860 Arkansas, your honored neighbor across the river, had 38 miles of railroad; she has now 2,071 miles. Alabama had 734; she now has 3,214 miles. Florida had 402; she now has 2,192 miles. Georgia had 1,420; she now has 4,263 miles. Kentucky had 534; she has now 2,707. Louisiana had 335; she has now 1,595. Mississippi had 862; she has now 2,446. Missouri had 817; she has now 5,897. North Carolina had 937; she has now 2,878. South Carolina had 973; she has now 2,108. Tennessee had 1,253; she has now 2,643. Texas had 307; she has now 8,247. Virginia had 1,379; she has now 3,327. Maryland had 386; she has now 1,208. Delaware had 127; she has now 334. And West Virginia, though untimely born, still a southern state, had 352; she has now 1,336.

Here is an increase of 33,601 miles of railroad construction, over the limit which the South had reached before war had wasted her resources, or confiscated large portions of her property. Here is an increase of more than 309 per cent. beyond the best she had done when at the zenith of her former prosperity. Sir, who shall say that your people are laggards in the race; that they slumber while others are speeding on? Who shall say that they waste their time and dissipate their energies in party strife, race conflicts, or lawless pastimes? The world is looking on these closing years of the nineteenth century in the American republic. The enemies of free government have made loud predictions that one section of the Union had been ruined by the other; that chronic aversion, strained relations and ill-disguised hostility between the United States and the people of the states would follow the close of the war, never to be superseded by mutual esteem, affection, and a common prosperity. These predictions are already proven false; and at the bar of history, and before the bar of God, the South can claim with truth that she has done, and is still doing, her part nobly and faithfully for that perfect reconciliation, and that full development of a united country, which constitute the highest honor, the value, and glory of American citizenship.

While every part of the American Union is interested in the welfare of the southern states, yet the most natural allies and friends on the maps, not only of the United States, but of the world, bound together by geographical and topographical laws, as well as by ties of blood and kindred, are the inhabitants of the Mississippi valley, without reference to the line where the South begins and the North ends, or where the North begins and the South ends. Every single and separate interest this valley contains is tributary to all its other interests; and the line of transportation which has been thrown across the river at this point has its direct affinity with the most extensive railway system now in existence. We learn from official figures that in 1890 there were 80,538 miles of railway in the Mississippi valley. Like a vast net-work, they intersect each other, penetrate to the most distant homes of the people, and halt at millions of stations to carry them and their productions, whithersoever their wishes or their interests may tend. Taking his seat in a car at Memphis, the traveler is now distant but four or five days from great cities, which a little while ago were unknown, and whose sites in the wilderness he could only have reached after many months of hardship and danger. The triumphs of science which we celebrate this bright, happy day, have placed the people of the United States, and more especially of this valley, not only in calling distance, but as next door neighbors. Let us gratefully accept, each for himself, our places in the grand brotherhood which embraces our homes, our united destiny and our posterity.

The dazzling and tempting possibilities of the future we may not dwell on now. A vision of the next hundred years of American genius, energy, industry, courage, and endurance, and of the coming centuries still further on, if it was indulged in, would overawe the mind as if gazing into the starlit depths of space, when "The heavens declare the glory of God, and the firmament sheweth his handiwork." We may not know the future either of time or eternity, but dreams will sometimes come in our most wakeful hours, and wear the features of glorious, though distant realities. Once the star of empire took its western way; its orbit in that direction is now closed forever. Shall this star, which signifies American progress and destiny, stand still in the sky, or fall, and expire like a transient exhalation? It seems not so to me. I see it in the events of these later days, and in the swift approaching achievements of the future, and the rivers of the South and of the Southwest. The march of empire is here; the empire of Christian civilization, of agricultural wealth, of diversified labor, of human well-being, repose and happiness. The generations of the future will behold this march of empire next towards the Isthmus of Darien; not in columns of conquest, nor with swords in hand, but, with knowledge and science, winning its way, and scattering the blessings of liberty, peace, and justice as it moves on.

Already, in fact, American empire is far on its way in that direction. The acquisition of the republic of Texas was a stride towards Central America, the extent of which it is difficult to realize. That majestic commonwealth contains 265,780 square miles of territory, which can be more clearly perceived and understood by comparison than in any other way. The state of Texas is larger in area than France, England and Wales combined; larger than Germany, Belgium, Denmark, Holland and Switzerland; larger by 2,780 square miles than Maine, New Hampshire, Vermont, Massachusetts, Rhode Island, Connecticut, New York, New Jersey, Pennsylvania, Delaware, Maryland, Virginia, West Virginia, half of North Carolina, and the District of Columbia; and it is more than eight times larger than the state of Indiana, now the abode of more than two millions and a quarter of intelligent people, and the center of the entire population of the United States. Who shall attempt to foretell the influences and the power of such a commonwealth as this? There are comfortable homes within its vast boundaries for a population of more than 50,000,000, and when they are full, as some day they will be, Mexico and countries still further South, will be benefited and blessed and perhaps absorbed by the swarming millions which will go forth from this unparalleled hive of humanity.

In view of that supreme event, so plainly in the pathway of American destiny, we should now, and for all time to come, deal with our neighboring people and their governments along our southern borders so fairly, kindly, liberally and generously, that they may feel that each step which brings us closer together will be for their peace, happiness, elevation and progress. Already the construction of an international railway, no longer from the east to the west, but from the north to the south, traversing the three Americas, is under discussion in practical minds, and is being pressed, from time to time, on the attention of the law-making powers of the different governments interested. If this seems now a visionary dream, far more so seemed the talking cable on the bottom of the ocean only one generation ago. North America, South America and Central America were designed, by the unrepealable laws of their creation, to be helpful neighbors to each other, and the day is not far distant when a reciprocity will be established between them, genuine in all its parts, fair to every industry; with no protected monopolies behind it; no bogus metal in its composition; no party intrigue in its arrangements.

Nor can we fail to behold that the vital point in the western hemisphere for the commerce, the progress and the independence of the three Americas, is the isthmus—that mighty ligature which has bound them together since the morning star first took its place in the sky. No power, not American, can ever be permitted its control, nor can it much longer stand an unbroken barrier to the navigation of the two oceans. The intercourse of the American nations and people, the commerce of the world, the enlightened spirit of the age in which we live, will not much longer submit to brave the tempests of Cape Horn, or to creep through the narrow and dismal straits of Magellan, in passing from one ocean to the other. The waters of the Atlantic and the Pacific are too near to each other to be kept apart in this sublime era of science, invention and energy. It is true the grand old Frenchman, De Lesseps, failed at Panama, but it is also true that it was right for him to fail. It is not given in the providence of history to any European hand to do this work, and such an attempt will never again be made. It belongs to the Americas, with their stalwart Saxon brother of the North at their head, and in chief control, to unite the two oceans and to annihilate the distances and dangers which now interpose between them. Those who behold the opening day of the twentieth century, now but a little more than seven years away, will also behold the flag of the United States carried on ships of commerce across the isthmus, navigating the waters of the canal now under process of construction, by the Nicaragua route. This is not a question of foreign policy; it is a question of American policy, and, so far as diplomacy is concerned, it is a question to be settled by American councils alone. The Monroe doctrine, which was simply the reassertion of the policy of Jefferson against European influence in American affairs, is here involved, and it will stand the test of statesmanship and of time.

And now, Mr. President, we will soon leave these proud scenes of patriotic festivity and go our several ways, many of us to meet no more, but here will remain for the wonder and admiration of future generations, the glorious public work, springing from private means and enterprise, which you have this day dedicated to American advancement toward manifest destiny The travelers of the world for forty centuries have gathered around the pyramids of Egypt and marveled at the useless, unmeaning toil which reared them; the curious antiquarian has gazed upon the sphinx amidst the sands of the desert, and conjectured in vain as to its origin and purpose; but no such doubts or uncertainties will ever haunt the Memphis bridge over the Mississippi river. Nor is the time far in the future when here on this left bank of the American river will stand the American city of Memphis, far greater than the Memphis of Egypt, as it once stood on the left bank of the Nile, and where now its ruins lie. We are told that the Egyptain city was connected by channels with surrounding lakes and became the great center of Egyptain commerce; that in the time of its splendor it is said to have been one hundred and fifty stadia in circumference, and a half day's journey in every direction; that of the splendid buildings with which it was adorned the chief were the palace of the Pharaohs, the temple palace of the god-bull, Apis, the temple of Serapis, with its avenue of sphinxes, now covered by the sands of the desert, and the temple of Vulcan, the Egyptain Phtha, of whose worship Memphis was the chief seat.

In the Memphis of the Mississippi no palaces for kings will be erected, no temples for heathen gods nor altars for their worship;

but here will accumulate the wealth and all the great agencies of civilization; here will continue to come the strong business men of a dominant, governing race; here will arise a center of trade, and here will concentrate the commerce of the railroads and the rivers of a continent; here will continue the temples of a Christian people for the worship of the living God; here will stand great seats of learning and science to refine, cultivate and illuminate the minds of the generations coming on, and here may the American citizen, wherever his home may be, and for all time to come, find in the hearts of this people the same spirit of fraternity, of union, of devotion to the flag, the honor and the glory of their country, that we have found here to-day.

TRIBUTE TO SENATOR MORTON

An address on the death of Oliver P. Morton, a senator from Indiana, delivered in the senate of the United States, January 17, 1878.

MR. PRESIDENT—The proprieties of this sad occasion and the usages of this body do not permit me to remain silent. We are paying the last tribute of respect to one who was long a senator from Indiana, and whose name will be forever associated with her history. We are saying the last few words over the grave of one who played a bold and leading part here, and identified himself with every prominent measure in national affairs for the past ten years.

I knew Oliver P. Morton from my first entrance upon the duties of manhood. We met at the beginning of our acquaintance both as personal and political friends, and although we afterward became as widely separated as the poles of the earth in our views of public affairs, yet our personal relations were never disturbed. There were periods of great excitement in our state when we met but seldom, but when we did it was always with civility and courtesy.

Senator Morton was without doubt a very remarkable man. His force of character can not be overestimated. His will power was simply tremendous. He threw himself into all his undertakings with that fixedness of purpose and disregard of obstacles which are always the best guarantees of success. This was true of him whether engaged in a lawsuit, organizing troops during the war, conducting a political campaign or a debate in the senate. The same daring, aggressive policy characterized his conduct everywhere. He made warm, devoted friends and bitter enemies. His followers were intense in their support and admiration, and his enemies were often unrelenting and unsparing. It is always so with such a nature as his. Small men of neutral temperaments escape the conflicts of life through which the strong, bold man passes to fame and power.

The motives which actuated Senator Morton in his public conduct are not now open to discussion. I shall ask the same charity for mine when I am gone that I extend to his. That he was sincere in his convictions no one will ever question. That the general tenor of his convictions upon the relations between the North and the South was erroneous, I think history will fully establish.

Senator Morton's life contains one great lesson to young men commencing a career of honorable ambition. He entered upon the ordeal of life with nothing on which to rely but his own intellect and his indomitable will. The position from which he started to achieve all his success was humble and unpromising. It is hard to recall any other American whose career better proves that industry and talents will overcome all things than his. He became a power in the land. He was a party leader second to none in our history. If he could not be president himself, he did much to make others so, and to dictate their policies. And now that he is gone a large portion of the American people regard his loss as irreparable.

Sir, Oliver P. Morton is no more, and in his death there is a solemn lesson to us. How small and insignificant appear all the asperities, the heart-burnings, and personal alienations of the hour when we measure them by the side of our responsibilities in that world to which he has gone! We are as evanescent and fleeting here as the insect tribes of the air. Over the river, "in the land to which we are drifting," there is life forever. Let us so use the little margin we have on the shores of time that eternity will open as a joy and not as a terror on our liberated spirits. And may those we leave behind us do for our memories what we now do for the memory of Oliver P. Morton.

I move the adoption of the resolutions.

CONSTANTINO BRUMIDI.

CONSTANTINO BRUMIDI

Remarks made in the senate of the United States, February 24, 1880, upon a bill, introduced by Mr. Voorhees, providing for the payment of certain moneys to the heirs of Constantino Brumidi.

R. PRESIDENT—The reason for the introduction of this bill grows out of the following facts: The government made a contract with Mr. Brumidi for the painting, in fresco, on the canopy of the dome of the capitol. The scaffolding necessary to enable the artist to do his work was furnished by the government. When the painting was finished and the scaffolding removed, the secretary of the interior withheld the sum of five hundred dollars of the contract-price as a guarantee for any retouching which the work might need after it dried out and became thoroughly seasoned to the air. This amount was held back, to be paid to Mr. Brumidi for such future attention on his part as the painting might be found to require. He was at all times in readiness to comply with the wishes of the government on this subject. No scaffolding, however, was ever replaced on which to work in the canopy of the dome, nor was he ever called on by the officials having this matter in charge to give his painting there any further attention. After waiting several years, Mr. Brumidi addressed a letter on the subject to the senator from Massachusetts (Mr. Dawes), as chairman of the committee on public buildings and grounds, asking to be allowed to retouch his work, if necessary, and to draw the balance due him on his contract. This letter was referred by the senator from Massachusetts to the architect of the capitol, who returned the following answer. I will ask the secretary to read it.

The chief clerk read as follows:

ARCHITECT'S OFFICE, UNITED STATES CAPITOL,
WASHINGTON, D. C., February 12, 1879.

SIR: I have the honor to return herewith the letter of C. Brumidi, relative to his claim for $500, retained from his last payment for painting in fresco the picture on the canopy of the dome.

The statement of Mr. Brumidi in relation to the retention of the $500 is correct. As it is desirable to have the picture finished, I respectfully recommend that an appropriation of $700 be made to pay the balance due him on the picture when finished and for the expense of constructing the necessary scaffolding for the purpose of such completion. Very respectfully,

EDWARD CLARK,
Architect United States Capitol.

HON. H. L. DAWES,
Chairman Committee on Public Buildings and Grounds, United States Senate.

MR. VOORHEES. Of course the five hundred dollars withheld by the secretary of the interior, as above stated, had been covered into the treasury under the general law as an unexpended balance, and was no longer available. Hence the necessity for a new appropriation. In response to the recommendation of Mr. Clark, the committee on appropriations, and subsequently both branches of congress, made the following provision in the sundry civil act for the fiscal year ending June 30, 1880:

To pay C. Brumidi for retouching and blending the picture in fresco on the canopy of the dome of the capitol and for constructing a scaffolding under said picture, $700.

The money thus appropriated has been available nearly a year, yet no steps were taken by the proper authorities to enable Mr. Brumidi to ascend again into the canopy of the dome of this capitol, and none now ever will be. In the exact and legal fulfillment of a contract, it is our duty to pay this sum of five hundred dollars to his heirs. On this point I conceive there can be no difference of opinion. I have ventured, however, in the bill just introduced, to ask congress to apply the remaining two hundred dollars of the appropriation of March 3, 1879, to the payment of the funeral expenses of the great artist who has just passed away. May I not be pardoned some brief mention of the wonderful genius, so long, so gently, and so beautifully associated with this capitol? He died poor, without money enough to bury his worn-out body, but how rich the inheritance he has left to the present and succeeding ages! During more than a quarter of a century he hovered along these walls from the basement to the dome, leaving creations of imperishable beauty wherever his touch has been. Wherever he paused by a panel, or was seen suspended to a ceiling, there soon appeared the brilliant conceptions of his fertile and cultivated mind. We can form no correct idea of the extent, the variety, and the perfection of his taste and skill as an artist without sometimes forgetting our pressing cares, and looking in detail over his field of labor.

Almost every committee room announces to the eye by historical or allegorical paintings in fresco the duties to which it is dedicated. Whoever passed through the room of the committee on military affairs without feeling that the very genius of heroism had left there its immortal inspirations? Who would mistake in after ages the use to which the room for the committee on naval affairs had been devoted? The painter has told the whole story in a silent but in an undying language. Who would not know that he approached the room of the committee on patents when glancing up he beholds Robert Fulton over the door, with his little steamboat in the distance plying in a small stream as it once did in Rock creek, between this city and Georgetown? As you seek the committee on Indian affairs you find Columbus, Las Casas, and the hapless Indian, recalling the whole history of the Indian race. Looking down from the ceiling of the library committee room are paintings denoting belles-lettres, painting and history, science and architecture. And so I might continue through the whole range of public affairs, showing that to the unrivaled skill of the painter Mr. Brumidi added the resources of the historian and a full knowledge of the workings of our government.

The poetry of the artist, if I may so express it, had also its field of display. To one who recalls the great forests of the West before they were swept away, the birds and the specimens of American animals with which he has adorned a portion of this capitol must be a source of unceasing enjoyment. The birds, especially, are all there, from a humming-bird at an open flower to the bald eagle with his fiery eye and angry feathers. I have been told that the aged artist loved these birds as a father loves his children, and that he often lingered in their midst as if a strong tie bound him to them. Doubtless he heard, or seemed to hear, their woodland voices. He loved the beautiful objects and forms of this beautiful world and—

> To him who in the love of Nature holds
> Communion with her visible forms, she speaks
> A various language; for his gayer hours
> She has a voice of gladness, and a smile
> And eloquence of beauty; and she glides
> Into his darker musings with a mild
> And healing sympathy, that steals away
> Their sharpness ere he is aware.

Mr. Brumidi was engaged at the time of his death on what he regarded as the greatest work of his life. He was unfolding with the magic of genius in the dome of the capitol the scroll of American history, from the landing of Columbus to the present day. He earnestly desired to live long enough to complete this vast conception. But he has left an empty chair, and his great design unfinished, as others have done and will continue to do in other places. At no distant day some memorial will be erected in some appropriate place in this capitol to his memory. He who beautifies the pathway of life, who creates images of loveliness for the human eye to rest upon, is a benefactor of the human race. He will be crowned by the gratitude of his own and of succeeding generations. In the older countries of Europe, where the profession of art has a higher rank than here, Brumidi would have had a public funeral, and his remains would have been deposited in ground set apart for persons of distinction. In England he would have had a place and a tablet in Westminster Abbey. It matters little, however, whether we or those who come after us do anything to perpetuate his memory. The walls of this capitol will hold his fame fresh and ever increasing as long as they themselves shall stand.

The painter and the sculptor live in their works and achieve an immortality which belongs to no other class. When you and I, Mr. President, and all who hear me, have passed away and been forgotten; when these active times in which we now strive with each other are looked back to as a remote period of antiquity, and viewed through the mist and haze of perhaps a thousand years; when this capitol, like the capitol of Rome, may have gone to decay and been covered by the mold and dust of far-reaching centuries, the antiquarian will be found revealing to a wondering world the frescoed beauties of these walls, and with them the name of Constantino Brumidi.

JOHN MARSHALL.

MAGNA CHARTA

An address delivered upon the occasion of the annual meeting of the State Bar Association of South Carolina, at Charleston, April 29, 1892.

MR. PRESIDENT—In addressing an annual meeting of the bar association of your great, historic commonwealth, I realize, with a keen sense of embarrassment, that others, with greater gifts, and under more auspicious circumstances, have often been here before me. With elaborate discussion, and sweeping review, they have made it difficult for the humble gleaner to gather even a few sheaves for the present occasion, or to discover new fields where harvesters have not already been, and garnered up the fruits, and plucked the flowers, which enrich and adorn the brotherhood to which we belong. I bow, also, with a deep veneration before the legal fraternity of one of the charter states of the American Union; one of the original subscribers to the constitution of 1789; a state which in her colonial condition cradled American independence in its perilous infancy, and in aftertimes has maintained liberty by the wisdom and force of law, throughout all her borders.

I venture, however, to turn to the constitution of the South Carolina Bar Association itself for assistance, assurance, and guidance. Amongst other objects in view, it is there declared that your "Association is formed to maintain the honor, dignity, and courtesy of the profession of the law." May we not salute these three majestic and immortal graces, and make them our theme for this passing hour? Honor, dignity, courtesy! These are not only the graces of our profession, but also the cardinal elements of human progress and civilization.

Lawyers have been defined to be those who are versed in the

laws, and the part they have borne, and the work they have accomplished in the affairs of men, is not left in doubt on the pages of history. The best governments ever known, the most liberal and enlightened institutions, insuring social order and domestic tranquillity, have in every age been devised and established by the great lawyers of the world. Those who have made themselves masters of the laws of their country, studied the science of jurisprudence, and comprehended the spirit and meaning of justice administered in the courts, have possessed a power in human affairs, far reaching, and as enduring as time itself.

The imposing structure of the Mosaic law, towering over the vast gulf of unnumbered centuries, though ascribed to divine inspiration, yet stands as the work of the lawgivers of Israel, educated and toiling as the agents of the Most High. The pen that wrote Leviticus and Deuteronomy, and indeed all the five books of Moses, was the pen of one versed in the law, the pen of a lawyer. There may be found nearly every germ of the common law, and a large proportion of the principles which are now embodied in the statutes of modern nations. There too, in that Hebraic tome of legal learning, may be found those strong, acute, and discriminating traits of intellect, so brilliantly displayed in after ages, and in our own day, by members of the Hebrew race, standing at the head of the legal profession in Europe and in America. To but one name in fact belongs the honor of an acknowledged leadership at both the American and the English bar. Judah P. Benjamin, an American lawyer of the blood of Moses, and of David, and of the judges, stands alone in his glory.

What traveler in the far East now seeks to trace the battle fields of Judea, or is curious to know who commanded her armies? On the other hand what student of history, of the science of jurisprudence, of the great principles of law on which commonwealths have been founded and civilizations upheld, fails to drink at the Mosaic fountains, and to profit by the example of those whose genius, as well as their lineage, comes from that high and distant period? To no one race, kindred, or blood, and to no one era in human progress, has the majesty of the law been confined, or its honor, dignity and courtesy entrusted. The profession of the law in its true scope breaks down all provincialisms, sweeps away all barriers of prejudice, and enforces a cosmopolitan equality of rights in its presence. Its triumphs, too, have in every age dwarfed all other human achievements. Wherever cultivated intellect and civilized courage have combined to produce the loftiest and the most brilliantly illuminated periods of history, towering over long intervals of the lower and more obscure annals of mankind, like giant peaks springing up from ordinary mountain ranges, there the student will find the law, which distributes and secures individual rights to the citizen, has done its most perfect work.

What curious antiquarian of the present day would wander back to the period of Lycurgus, the Spartan lawgiver, more than seven hundred years before the dawn of the Christian era, except for the purpose of examining his system of laws, and of obtaining a better knowledge of his monumental labors? A classic author, writing of that period, and of Lycurgus, says:

> Sparta was in a state of anarchy and licentiousness, and he was considered as the man who alone could cure the growing diseases of the state. He undertook the task, yet before he set to work, he strengthened himself with the authority of the Delphic oracle, and with a strong party of influential men at Sparta. The reform seems not to have been carried altogether peaceably. The new division of the land among the citizens must have violated many existing interests. But all opposition was overborne, and the whole constitution, military and civil, was remodeled. After Lycurgus had obtained for his institutions an approving oracle of the national god of Delphi, he exacted a promise from the people not to make any alteration in his laws before his return. And then he left Sparta to finish his life in voluntary exile, in order that his countrymen might be bound by their oath to preserve his constitution inviolate forever. Where and how he died nobody could tell. He vanished from the earth like a god leaving no traces behind but his spirit, and he was honored as a god at Sparta with a temple and yearly sacrifices down to the latest times.

Such is the historic picture of the man and of his life work in general terms. May we not, however, in this assemblage of lawyers, take for a few moments, and without impropriety or waste of time, a somewhat closer look at the principles and details of the laws that came from his hands? The analogies which exist between them and the most enlightened governments of modern ages, will be found in leading instances to be most striking and instructive. The following statement rests upon safe authority:

> The Spartan constitution was of a mixed nature; the monarchical principle was represented by the kings, the aristocracy by the senate, and the democratical

element by the assembly of the people, and subsequently by their representatives, the ephors. The kings had originally to perform the common functions of the kings of the heroic age. They were high priests, judges, and leaders in war, but in all these departments they were in course of time superseded more or less. As judges they retained only a particular branch of jurisdiction, that referring to the common succession of property. As military commanders they were restricted and watched by commissioners sent by the senate; the functions of high priest were curtailed least, perhaps because least obnoxious. In compensation for the loss of power, the kings enjoyed great honors, both during life and after death. Still the principle of monarchy was very weak among the Spartans. The powers of the senate were very important. They had the right of originating and discussing all measures before they could be submitted to the decision of the popular assembly; they had, in conjunction with the ephors, to watch the due observance of the laws and institutions; and they were judges in all criminal cases, without being bound by any written code. For all this they were not responsible, holding their office for life. But with all these powers the elders formed no real aristocracy. They were not chosen senators either for property qualification, or for noble birth. The senate was open to the poorest citizen, who, during sixty years, had been obedient to the laws, and zealous in the performance of his duties.

The mass of the people, that is, the Spartans of pure Doric descent, formed the sovereign power of the state. The popular assembly consisted of every Spartan of thirty years of age, and of unblemished character; only those were excluded who had not the means of contributing their portion to the syssitia. They met at stated times to decide on all important questions brought before them, after a previous discussion in the senate. They had no right of amendment, but only that of simple approval or rejection, which was given in the rudest form possible, by shouting. The popular assembly, however, had neither frequent nor very important occasions for directly exerting their sovereign power. Their chief activity consisted in delegating it; hence arose the importance of the ephors, who were the representatives of the popular element of the constitution. The ephors answer in every characteristic feature to the Roman tribunes of the people. Their origin was lost in obscurity and insignificance, but at the end they engrossed the whole power of the state.

The system of government here described, with whatever imperfections it contains, is far superior to the constitutional monarchy of England to-day. If the Spartan senate appears to have had too much power, and its members were chosen for life, still it was not filled by hereditary rank, and consequently hereditary imbecility and hereditary corruption, which now degrade and disgrace the British house of lords. The principle embodied in the election of the Spartan ephors is the same which, in the nineteenth century, sends representatives to the congress of the United States. And though the constitution of Sparta was framed twenty-seven hundred years ago, for a region no larger than an ordinary county in an American state, a mere speck on the map of the globe, yet the light of that great legal instrument has never gone out; it has continued to shine across the vast and turbulent centuries, like the imperishable beacon of a giant light-house, streaming far out over the ocean as a warning, a guide, and a hope.

Two hundred years later came Solon, the Athenian lawyer, to whose hands, as in the case of the great Spartan, was entrusted the preservation of his country through the revision of her laws, and the enactment of new ones, as they were found necessary. "He was chosen archon, B. C. 594, and under that legal title was invested with unlimited power for adopting such measures as the exigencies of the state demanded. In fulfillment of the task entrusted to him, Solon addressed himself to the relief of the existing distress." His labors were severe, and the details of his legal system extensive. He established a constitution and laws under which peace and prosperity again returned to his country, but at the same time it is related that he was himself aware that he had been compelled to leave many imperfections in his system and code. He is said to have spoken of his laws as being not the best, "but the best which the Athenians would have received."

But the legal structure reared by Solon yet remains, in its outlines and in many of its details, for the use of the historian and the instruction of the student, while the lines of battle on the fields of Marathon are lost, and the ground occupied by the two armies which met there can not be identified. And when Rome, expanding her dominion by military power, absorbed the Grecian states, she was more enriched by Grecian civilization, springing from the imperishable principles of Grecian constitutions, codes, and legal safeguards, than by all the plunder and spoliation of all other nations and peoples against whom her ruthless sword was drawn. The conquests of the Roman republic, and also of the empire, extended to all the then known abodes of the human race. The legions of Rome, sent out from the Tiber, and from that narrow coast of the Mediterranean which modern travelers look at with wonder, carried their eagles wherever human prey could be found, and marked the earth with the footprints of their devastating victories. Roman sway was absolute from the straits of Gibraltar on the west, to the Euphrates and the Persian gulf on the east; from the Rhine and from beyond the Danube on the north, to the torrid sands of the interior of Africa on the south, embracing an extent of country far greater than that over which the American flag flies to-day. A look at the boundaries of ancient Rome, as they are explained by the modern maps of the world, reveals such a startling grasp of dominion as never before nor since has belonged to any one of the powers of the earth. The greatest kingdoms and nations of the eastern hemisphere, as they stand outlined at the present day, were her obedient provinces. Spain, Portugal, France, England, Belgium, Switzerland, Turkey, Greece, and large portions of Austria and Russia, comprised her European possessions, outside of Italy, her rightful home. In Africa she was mistress of Morocco, Algeria, Tunis, Tripoli and Egypt, the five states of Barbary, constituting a productive belt nearly three thousand miles long, with an average of one hundred miles wide, lying in the temperate zone, and between the destructive sands of Sahara on the south, and the sea on the north. In Asia her arms embraced all now known as Asiatic Turkey, together with extensive regions of Persia and Arabia. Those admitted to the citizenship of Rome, with their wives and children, numbered twenty millions, the inhabitants of her provinces forty millions, and her slaves more than sixty millions; making the enormous aggregate population of over one hundred and twenty millions, nearly, if not quite, double the present population of the United States.

As the enlightened, modern historian, however, explores that vast field of gigantic conflict and conquest, what does he find of value to the human race, save the free institutions of the Roman republic, the laws which made the Roman citizen a sovereign at home and abroad, and the intellectual products in the forum, in letters, and in the arts, which always adorn a period and a country where liberty secured by law prevails? Forgotten now, or but dimly remembered, are the long marches, the distant invasions, and the bloody battles. The achievements of Roman warriors, from Cæsar down to the lieutenant, have perished in the dust of ages, while the labors of Roman lawyers, those versed in the laws, have survived the wrecks of time, and confront us to-day with the aspect of perpetual youth. For seven hundred years the lawgivers and lawmakers of Rome maintained a republic in name and in form, and secured to the citizen an independence, a dignity, and a security, never since equaled in the history of nations. Under the banner of the republic too all her mighty conquests were made except Britain, Dacia, and the eastern provinces that submitted to the sword of Trajan; but nothing is now left to signify her greatness and glory, except the principles of her government, her codes, her laws, her jurisprudence, and her masterpieces of eloquence, literature, and art, which were created and fostered in an atmosphere of freedom. The productions of Cicero, the leader of the Roman bar, and of the historians and poets, Tacitus, Livy, Virgil, Juvenal, and other illustrious men of genius, all clustering near the dawn of the Christian era, have survived; all else is a dreary waste of ruin and desolation.

And when we take our stand six centuries further down the stream of time, and explore the era of Justinian the Great, the same lesson is borne in upon us as to the durability and power of legal principles, and the perishable and evanescent character of all other human achievements. Who now recalls his splendid reign, or delves curiously into the history of his mighty empire except for the purpose of studying and admiring the immortal labors of his great lawyers. Justinian wore the imperial purple thirty-eight years; his armies were victorious in Asia, Africa, and Europe; he restored the ancient boundaries of the Roman empire, and reunited the East and the West under his rule; he constructed and maintained a vast line of fortifications on the eastern and southeastern frontier of the empire, which at that time filled the world with its power; he decorated the city of Rome with public buildings of costly and magnificent architecture; he built fountains, and planted groves, and displayed his cultivated taste by a lavish patronage of statuary, painting, and letters; yet of all this long and luminous reign, what is there now gathered up and preserved as a part of the treasure trove of civilized nations, save and except the Justinian code, the Institutes, and the Pandects? The robust, stalwart, and powerful genius of ancient Rome seemed to blaze up in all its splendor and glory under the sway of Justinian, and for the last time, before it flickered low and died on the murky confines of the dark ages. But his claim to remembrance and honor rests alone, and will forever rest, on his contributions to the legal knowledge of subsequent, and still more powerful nations than his own. His works have been thus briefly described:

> Immediately on his accession he set himself to collect all previous legislative enactments which were still in force, and in order to do this thoroughly he first compiled a code which comprised all the constitutions of his predecessors. The authoritative commentaries of the jurists were next harmonized, and published under the title, Digesta Pandecta. The code was republished A. D. 534, with the addition of Justinian's own constitution. His third great legal undertaking was the composition of a systematic treatise on the laws for the guidance of students, and lawyers. This was published a short time before the Pandects under the title of Institutes. All these works were accomplished under the careful superintendence and direction of Tribonian, and were written originally in Latin.

Forgotten now is the military glory of Justinian; his triumphs have passed away, as evanescent as the clouds in an April sky, and his fortifications have turned to dust, leaving no trace, while the labors of Tribonian and his associate lawyers still live in all their primeval vigor and far-reaching influences. When the downfall of Rome brought chaos and darkness on the face of civilization, the principles of social order, public safety and private right, were found securely embodied and preserved in her written laws. They were the strong material with which governments were again constructed and society protected. The civil law of Rome spanned the dark ages, and brought to modern Europe, and still later to the new world, and to American states, a system of jurisprudence sufficient for another and higher civilization than that which gave it birth. Napoleon spoke it into existence in imperial France, and there it has remained unchanged through stormy revolutions, while the results of Marengo and Austerlitz have vanished forever. When Jefferson, with wise prophetic foresight, purchased from France the Louisiana territory, he brought into active fellowship with the laws of the United States the principles of the Pandects, the Institutes, and the code of Justinian, and there they control now, as they did more than thirteen centuries ago in the regions of the Mediterranean.

It is to the English speaking people of the world, however, that the chief glory of the law belongs. A glance at English and American history brings us face to face with the honor, the dignity, and the courtesy of the profession of the law, more clearly defined, and standing out more boldly than anywhere else in the annals of the world. For a thousand years the race to which we belong has been the lawmaker and the lawgiver of the highest, proudest types of Christian civilization. When the historian speaks of England's "best and greatest king," he speaks of Alfred, and designates him as "the lawgiver." He ascended the throne A. D. 872, when twenty-three years of age, and died prematurely at fifty-two. He was at war with the invaders of his country from the start. In bloody and desperate engagements he repeatedly drove the ruthless Danes and the Northmen from his shores, and beat them on the seas. His place as a soldier fighting for independence and self-government is amongst the foremost who have lived. It was also true of him that "in an age of ignorance and barbarism he was an accomplished scholar and a zealous patron of learning. No prince of his age did so much for the diffusion of knowledge, and few monarchs at any time have shown an equal zeal for the instruction of their people. He caused many manuscripts to be translated into Anglo-Saxon from the Latin, and himself translated several works, such as Bœthius on the Consolations of Philosophy, the history of Orosius, Bede's Ecclesiastical History, and selections from the Soliloquies of St. Augustine." He is known, however, to posterity as Alfred the Great more because of his work as a lawgiver than from all other achievements combined. "The fact that he compiled a code of laws, divided England into counties, hundreds and tithings, and thoroughly reformed the administration of justice," and the further fact that he was himself the author of valuable original law books, written in the Anglo-Saxon language, have given him his loftiest and most permanent position in the temple of fame.

The origin of trial by jury was also ascribed, during many centuries, to Alfred the Great, but his claim is now doubted; and this imperishable monument of personal liberty seems to have been evolved in the twilight councils of men, at an earlier date. On this point one of the greatest and most gifted legal minds of his own country, and of the world, Jeremiah S. Black, of Pennsylvania, has spoken, and enriched the law literature of his times. In *Ex parte* Milligan in the supreme court of the United States, and in defense of the right of his client to a trial by jury instead of being put to death by a military commission, Judge Black said:

> I might begin with Tacitus and show how the contest arose in the forests of Germany more than two thousand years ago; how the rough virtues and sound common sense of that people established the right of trial by jury, and thus started on a career which has made their posterity the foremost race that ever lived in all the tide of time. The Saxons carried it to England, and were ever ready to defend it with their blood. It was crushed out by the Danish invasion, and all that they suffered of tyranny and oppression during the period of their subjugation resulted from the want of trial by jury. If that had been conceded to them the reaction would not have taken place which drove back the Danes to their frozen homes in the North. But those ruffian sea kings could not understand that, and the reaction came. Alfred, the greatest of revolutionary heroes, and the wisest monarch that ever sat on a throne, made the first use of his power, after the Saxons restored it, to re-establish their ancient laws. He had promised them that he would, and he was true to them, because they had been true to him. But it was not easily done; the courts were opposed to it, for it limited their power—a kind of power that everybody covets—the power to punish without regard to law. He was obliged to hang forty-four judges in one year for refusing to give his subjects a trial by jury. When the historian says that he hung them, it is not meant that he put them to death without a trial. He had them impeached before the grand council of the nation, the Wittenagemote, the parliament of that time. During the subsequent period of Saxon domination no man on English soil was powerful enough to refuse a legal trial to the meanest peasant. If any minister, or any king, in war or in peace, had dared to punish a freeman by a tribunal of his own appointment, he would have roused the wrath of the whole population; all orders of society would have resisted it; lord and vassal, knight and squire, priest and penitent, bocman and socman, master and thrall, copyholder and villain, would have risen in one mass and burned the offender to death in his castle, or followed him in his flight and torn him to atoms. It was again trampled down by the Norman conquerors, but the evils resulting from the want of it united all classes in the effort which compelled King John to restore it by the great charter.

It is an obvious, and a glorious fact, that the history of English law at every stage, and in every struggle, marks the growth and increased strength of personal liberty and personal security. Lawyers by profession, and men learned in the law, have been prone to the side of liberty in every age and country, but more especially so when in their veins flowed the blood of the Saxon. This proud and dominating race has held a still curb on arrogant, encroaching power wherever it has taken the reins of government.

Nearly seven hundred years ago there was lying about twenty miles from London, a piece of meadow land, through which a small stream ran its winding course; and hence this place was called Runningmead. Here the people of England, not merely the barons, but also the armed masses, met their corrupt and faithless king, and extorted Magna Charta from his most unwilling hands. Every detail connected with this immortal instrument must always remain of undying interest. An author of great merit, in an essay on Magna Charta, says:

> Between Staines and Windsor is a large tract of meadow land, where this meeting between the king and his peers was appointed to be held; a stream which flowed through it gave to it the name of Running-mead, or Runnimede, but the same spot also bore the name of Council Meadow, because in former times it was devoted to such purposes. Here, then, on the 5th of June, appeared the conflicting parties, and while John was attended with but few supporters, the barons were followed by such vast multitudes that had the king again endeavored to retract, the attempt would have been as unavailing as it would have been deceitful.

Prior to this meeting King John had made repeated and desperate efforts to avoid the guarantees demanded of him. He had even offered to mortgage his kingdom to foreign powers, in order to obtain the means with which to resist the demands of his oppressed people for a reform of government abuses. The Great Charter of Liberties, as the old writers style it, did not fall easily, and as ripe fruit, into the laps of our stalwart, remote ancestors, but was plucked by force and with strong, warlike hands. Nor should the effects of Runnimede on the tyrant king himself be overlooked in estimating the mighty revolution there accomplished. Holingshed, a celebrated English historian, speaks in the following terms concerning the manner in which the grant of Magna Charta preyed upon the health and the disposition of John:

> Great rejoicings were made for this conclusion of peace betwixt the king and his barons, the people judging that God had touched the king's heart and molified it, whereby happy days were come for the realm of England, as though it had been delivered out of the bondage of Egypt; but were much deceived, for the king, having condescended to make such grant of liberties, far contrary to his mind, was right sorrowful in his heart, cursed his mother that bare him the hour that he was born, and the paps that gave him suck, wishing that he had received death by violence of sword or knife, instead of natural nourishment. He whetted his teeth; he did bite now on one staff and now on another as he walked, and oft broke the same in pieces when he had done, and with such disordered behavior and furious gestures he uttered his grief in such sort that the noblemen very well perceived the inclination of his inward affection concerning these things, before the breaking up of the council, and therefore sore lamented the state of the realm, guessing what would come of his impatience and displeasant taking of the matter.

It is a relief to know, even at this remote period, that the miserable being here described perished from the earth only four months after his hand and the great seal had been affixed to the imperishable charter. The impotent rage of a defeated tyrant, baffled and bound down by law, broke his life, and drove him to the refuge of the grave.

A close look at the contents of the Great Charter of Liberties shows them to be far more extensive, and even more precious, than is generally understood by the hurried student of modern times. The world has been so illuminated and electrified by one well known article, and succeeding ages have been so enchanted by its bugle call for freedom, that the general, comprehensive, and thorough character of the charter secured from the perfidious John, is too often overlooked. Two sentences in this mighty instrument of legal reform and free government have resounded down the centuries, as if all-sufficient within themselves for the establishment and security of the natural rights of man.

> No freeman shall be seized, or imprisoned, or dispossessed, or outlawed, or in any way destroyed; nor will we condemn him, nor will we commit him to prison, excepting by the legal judgment of his peers, or by the laws of the land.
>
> To none will we sell, to none will we deny, to none will we delay right or justice.

The stars over our heads, the bright emblazonry of God, are not more eternal or more glorious in the heavens, than are these few and simple words in the history of legal liberty. But in its inspiration and in its details the Great Charter extended to every phase of the laws of England, and to every branch of English jurisprudence. It treated of every relation between the subject and his king; of every right and duty belonging to domestic life, of the relative rights of creditors and debtors, of principals and sureties, of landlords and tenants, of rents and distraints, of county assizes, and justices of the peace, of the rights of merchants to buy and sell without unjust exactions, and on the principles of free trade; of unequal taxation, of military duty and service, and of the entire ecclesiastical establishment which then prevailed in England. On all these vital questions, and many more, the work done at Runnimede was a legal revolution, limitless in its results, boundless in duration, and priceless in the value of its blessings. Sir Edward Coke says:

> It is called Magna Charta, not that it is great in quantity, for there be many voluminous charters commonly passed, specially in these later times, longer

than this is; nor, comparatively, in respect that it is greater than Charta de Foresta, but in respect of the great importance and weightiness of the matter as shall hereafter appear.

As the gold-finer will not out of the dust, threads, or shreds of gold, let pass the least crumb, in respect of the excellency of the metal, so ought not the learned reader to let pass any syllable of this law in respect of the excellency of the matter.

Nor indeed have any of the words or syllables of this law, more precious than all the dust, threads, and shreds of gold in the universe, been lost or allowed to pass away. They are to be found clustered together in the constitution of the United States, and from there blazing out over all the nations like a constellation of the first magnitude in the firmament on high. Their light is also beheld in the constitutions and the laws of the individual states of the American Union. In the proud and noble history of South Carolina nothing is more to her honor, or more significant of her devotion to constitutional freedom, than the fact that her legislature in 1712, one hundred and eighty years ago, incorporated into the body of her laws, not only Magna Charta, but likewise the petition of right, the *habeas corpus* act, and the bill of rights of the reign of James the Second. They are all embraced in the statutes at large of South Carolina, as compiled and published by Thomas Cooper, under resolution of her legislature of December, 1834.

Lingering, however, a few moments more over the Great Charter, as the fountain of all legalized liberty, a curious, an eager inquiry asserts itself in the lawyer's mind, and will not down at any one's bidding. Who wrote this indestructible document? Whose hand traced its luminous lines? It is consecutive and coherent in its order of thought, the same in style of composition in all its parts, and with no break in the unity which belongs to the production of a single mind. Whose brain wrought it out? History nowhere gives his name? It is the work of a legal mind, the production of an educated and accomplished lawyer. The barons, leading the multitude, and surrounding King John with their hands on their swords, brought it not with them, nor could they have conceived its superb structure. Education, and especially legal learning, were confined to the few at that early and hazy period of English history. For the discovery of the actual author of Magna

Charta we are forced to rely on circumstantial evidence. In this field of research, however, there are strong and peculiar indications of the true authorship. The name of Stephen Langton is the one first mentioned in the opening lines of the charter, as a counselor and adviser in its concessions, and promulgation by the king. In the short but instructive essay on Magna Charta, by Richard Thompson, published in London in 1829, Langton is six times mentioned as a leading, ardent, and fearless promoter of the movement for redress and reform. His education was of the highest order, and it strikes the modern mind strangely to find that he was, at one and the same time, archbishop of Canterbury, primate of all England, cardinal of the Holy Roman Church, and lord chancellor of English jurisprudence. He was a scholar of the cloisters, and a trained lawyer in the highest ranks of the judiciary. Thompson, amongst other things concerning Langton, in his essay says:

> The year 1214 continued to pass away without any appearance of the liberties of Magna Charta being instituted, or King Edward's laws being recalled, but about the month of November, or as some authors have supposed, on the 20th, Saint Edmund's day, a second meeting of the peers and clergy took place at Saint Edmund's Bury, to take into consideration the most effective methods for the obtaining of their demands. This convocation being made under pretense of devotion, but little suspicion could be excited of its real purpose. Before the barons was laid the charter for which they contended, whilst Langton stood behind the high altar in the midst of the assembly to receive their protestations, and to give their proceedings all the sanction which ceremonial services could impart. It was then, irritated by the unexpected delay which they had found, with their actions calling on the prelate to witness their oaths, and their voices entreating heaven to confirm them, the barons of England swore to support the Charter of Liberties on these terms: That the king should immediately grant and confirm the said laws and liberties by a charter under his seal, or they would withdraw themselves from his fealty until they gained the satisfaction they desired. And at length it was agreed that, after the nativity of our Lord, they should come to the king in a body, to desire a confirmation of the liberties before mentioned. And that in the meantime they were to provide themselves with horses and arms in like manner; that if the king should perchance break through that he had specially sworn, which they well believed, and recoil by reason of his duplicity, they would instantly, by capturing his castles, compel him to give them satisfaction.

What a marvelous picture is here presented! It can have but one interpretation as to the brain and pen that produced Magna Charta. The leaders of the movement against legalized oppression and crime are here seen convoked in religious assemblage. Their priest, a scarlet-robed cardinal, and likewise a lord chancellor of the realm, stands behind the high altar in their midst, and in this situation lays the charter, for which they contended, before the barons. There, with solemn protestations, and oaths appealing to God, they are sworn by their prelate-chancellor to defend and support it, with their honor, their estates, and their lives. This imposing spectacle occurs in 1214, showing that the charter was maturely and carefully prepared in advance, and was not the sudden production of Runnimede nearly a year later. The conclusion appears irresistible that to a lord chancellor of England, and a cardinal archbishop, both distinctions combined in the same person, the world is indebted for the old and sacred first Latin draft of the immortal parchment, whereon are engraved the liberties of that and of all subsequent ages. Stephen Langton, "Stephen, Archbishop of Canterbury," as the charter styles him, greets the student of English and American freedom, as a most pleasing and glorious factor in the history of his times. To the broad, liberal thought of the present high noon-tide of civil and religious liberty, it is a gracious and enjoyable fact, that so early in the very dawn of the coming day, after the long night of the middle ages, it was demonstrated that the cause of free government was upheld without respect to creed, canon, faith or church distinctions. The work and zeal of the liberty-loving lawyer were not controlled or impeded by any reactionary or despotic tendencies in the breast of the ecclesiastic. This is a lesson of history in itself, worth finding out and commemorating when the profession of the law is under review. In all of human effort and progress in the cause of self-government since June, A. D. 1215; in every struggle, whether in the high councils of statesmen, or on the field of warriors for the natural rights of man; in every epoch of aroused thought and action, marking the advance of the world as certainly as the log book marks the speed of the ship at sea, the great legal work of the priestly lawyer, the law-priest of England, and his associates and followers in the thirteenth century has guided the way.

When, in 1628, Sir Edward Coke, at nearly eighty years of age, and the great lawyer to the last, drew the petition of right, leveled against the lawless prerogatives of the first Charles, he kept his eye on the Great Charter, then more than four centuries old, as steadily as the mariner watches the north star, with its undeviating light and its eternity of wisdom. The king had arrested Hampden, Darnel, and three others, and thrown them in prison for refusing to pay certain taxes. They applied to the court of king's bench for the writ of *habeas corpus* in order that it might be known whether their commitment was "by the law of the land." We are told that "the writ was granted; but the warden of the prison made return that they were detained by a warrant from the privy council, informing him of no particular cause of imprisonment, but that they were committed by the special command of his majesty." Bold and fearless discussion followed, until the illegal arrest and imprisonment of five Englishmen produced another clear and explicit affirmation of the principles of Magna Charta, and the application of them to existing grievances. The petition of right merely claimed to be a re-assertion, a corroboration, and an explanation of the ancient guarantees and constitution of the kingdom. The weight of the law was again laid on a perfidious monarch by the lawyers of the lawgiving race of the world, and it was in his efforts to evade and throw off its just powers and restraints that he brought his head to the block.

A period of usurpation and oppression in the history of the Saxons has always been the opportunity of legal liberty. The reigns of the Stuarts are all decorated by great achievements, made in resistance to the tyrannical instincts of that ill-fated family. The brief and disgraceful ascendency of James the Second produced the bill of rights in 1688; another protest against the despotic and reactionary spirit of monarchical government. Even the writ of *habeas corpus*, that mighty muniment of liberty, emerged from the Stuart dynasty with renewed and increased strength and glory. And may I not be pardoned if, in this presence of lawyers, I linger for a moment over this, the greatest of all safeguards of personal freedom?

In perilous times, now nearly thirty years ago, I discussed the immortal writ and its high and sacred mission in the house of representatives at Washington, and I venture now to recall a few sentences not unsuited to an occasion like the present.

Magna Charta, as I have shown, declared a mighty principle in the science of just government, and it has been repeated over and over again many times since, and at last finds a polished and detailed embodiment in the American constitution; but something more is necessary and indispensable in order to carry it out and confer its practical benefits on mankind. The barons said that the executive should not take, imprison, or punish any citizen of the realm, except according to the law of the land; the subjects of every English king have repeated it, and our constitution asserts the same thing with great particularity and care; but what would all this be worth if no means had been provided to enforce this often reiterated principle of liberty? It would simply stand as an expression, a sublime one it is true, in favor of immutable justice and right, but, without the machinery of some active process of administrative law, it would be powerless to extend succor to the oppressed. Therefore all the proud declarations against the infringement of personal liberty by the executive, from Runnemede to the present hour, have been accompanied by that messenger of speedy justice, the writ of *habeas corpus*. It executes what they declare. It gives motion and efficacy to the laws of a free government. It is the active agent by which the will of the people, as expressed in the constitution and laws made for their own protection, are enforced. Without it, the tyrant may laugh to the winds every doctrine of Magna Charta, every provision of our own constitution. Without it, an executive ruler is beyond legal restraint or coercion, and can with impunity substitute his own will for the constitution and the laws.

Sir, the *habeas corpus* is the life of liberty. It is of ancient origin. It was born amid the opening struggles of our remote ancestors for popular freedom. It was recognized as a law of necessity by a race unwilling to be slaves. It sprang from no statute. It depends on no enactment. It is one of those high, self-existing, unrepealable laws which liberty writes on the hearts of her worshipers; which, without the aid of legislation, became a part of the common law of England, simply because of that rule in God's providence which prescribes an eternal fitness of things. It is perhaps older than Magna Charta itself. Hallam, in his History of the Middle Ages, referring to the period when Magna Charta was obtained, says: "Whether courts of justice framed the writ of *habeas corpus* in conformity to the spirit of this clause, or found it already in their register, it became from that era the right of every subject to demand it."

The most important question, however, connected with this great legal key to prison doors, relates to the power which may suspend it, and where that power belongs. In view of the last thirty-one years of American history, and in view of the fact that within the last seven years, the governor of an American territory was sustained by the federal administration, in declaring martial law, and suspending the writ of *habeas corpus*, because of a very temporary anti-Chinese disturbance, it becomes as refreshing as a tonic to indulge in the language of Blackstone on this vital feature of the British and of the American constitution. This profound commentator, writer, and delineator of the law says:

Of great importance to the public is the preservation of this personal liberty, for if it once were left in the power of any, the highest, magistrate to imprison arbitrarily whomever he or his officers thought proper, as in France it is daily practiced by the crown, there would soon be an end of all other rights and immunities. Some have thought that unjust attacks, even upon life or property, at the arbitrary will of the magistrate, are less dangerous to the commonwealth than such as are made upon the personal liberty of the subject. To bereave a man of life, or by violence to confiscate his estate, without accusation or trial, would be so gross and notorious an act of despotism as must at once convey the alarm of tyranny throughout the whole kingdom; but the confinement of the person, by secretly hurrying him to gaol where his sufferings are unknown or forgotten, is a less public, a less striking, and therefore a more dangerous engine of arbitrary government. And yet sometimes, when the state is in real danger, even this may be a necessary measure. But the happiness of our constitution is that it is not left to the executive power to determine when the danger of the state is so great as to render this measure expedient; for it is the parliament only, or legislative power, that, whenever it sees proper, can authorize the crown, by suspending the *habeas corpus* act for a short and limited time, to imprison suspected persons without giving any reason for so doing; as the senate of Rome was wont to have recourse to a dictator, a magistrate of absolute authority, when they judged the republic in any imminent danger.

In turning at this point to the legal frame-work of our own government, and viewing it in the light of what had already been accomplished for personal liberty and security by the English speaking race prior to 1787, certain curious facts confront us, and give rise to curious and instructive reflections. The vast treasure-house of English history wherein were stored the accumulations of more than a thousand years in behalf of free government, was wide open to those who constructed the American constitution. The men who composed the convention of 1787, at Philadelphia, were learned in the written laws of every period of human history. From the enactments on Mount Sinai, in the great Mosaic epoch, down to their own revolutionary times, they were familiar with every code of laws ever framed for the establishment and administration of governments. Magna Charta, the petition of rights, the bill of rights, and the *habeas corpus* writ, were as well known to them as their own recent Declaration of Independence. And yet when the constitution of the United States came from their hands, on the 17th day of September, A. D. 1787, it contained no mention of any one of the guarantees of personal liberty, and personal protection, so long and so well known to the common law of England, with the single exception of a brief provision against the suspension of the writ of *habeas corpus*. It was accompanied by no bill of rights; it was adorned by none of the resounding assertions and principles of the Great Charter. It contained that matchless system of fundamental law, at whose magic touch arose a mighty commonwealth as the offspring of many; a federal government resting on states retaining all of their sovereignty and independence, not voluntarily and specifically granted by them and conveyed away.

Such an achievement of statesmanship was hitherto unknown to any age or people, and it still remains the wonder of the world. To have made harmonious relations between thirteen sovereign states, and between them and the national government in the beginning, and to maintain such relations now in a Union of forty-four, is a tribute to the constitution of the United States, and to the wisdom of its framers, never before due to the legal work of men. But with all this, and more, conceded, it still remains a problem of profound interest, why the constitution as signed and put in force, was totally barren of all the ancient landmarks and safeguards of liberty for the citizen; why the natural rights of man were not asserted, and declared secure from assault by the executive or by any other department of the government. Contemporaneous correspondence shows that this wonderful omission was urged against the constitution as soon as it was promulgated. The moment a copy of it reached Jefferson at his post of duty in Paris, as minister to France, he wrote to leading men at home, urging, not its rejection, but its amendment. He expressed his amazement at the "omission of a bill of rights, providing clearly," as he says, "and without the aid of sophism, for freedom of religion, freedom of the press, protection against standing armies, restriction of monopolies, the eternal and unremitting force of the *habeas corpus* laws, and trials by jury in all matters of fact triable by the laws of the land, and not by the laws of nations." Jefferson declared further, "that a bill of rights was what the people were entitled to against every government on earth, general or particular, and what no just government should refuse or rest on inference."

As the foremost political thinker and writer of his own age, if not of any age in history; as the author of the Declaration of Independence, and of the famous statutes of Virginia for religious freedom, Jefferson's voice was a potent one, and his words on all subjects were eagerly caught up and heeded. The first congress convened, acted promptly, and on the 25th day of September, 1789, proposed to the legislatures of the several states the first ten amendments, as they now stand embodied in the constitution of the United States. By the middle of the following June they were all ratified by a sufficient number of states to put them in force, and in less than two years by all the states. In these amendments are to be found those high and vital principles without which free government is impossible, and personal liberty a mockery. They ring out on listening ears, and stir the souls of men like strains of martial music. Here in these amendments are the old, immutable, and eternal guarantees, in small space, and in brief, sententious phrase: Freedom of religion, freedom of speech, freedom of the press; the right of the people to assemble and petition for a redress of grievances, to keep and bear arms, to be secure in their persons, houses, papers and effects; their right to presentment or indictment for a capital or otherwise infamous crime, and their security in life, liberty and property unless taken away by due process of law; their right to speedy and public trial by an impartial jury, assisted by counsel, and confronted by witnesses; with excessive bail, excessive fines, and cruel and unusual punishments sternly prohibited. All these, and other cardinal and indispensable safeguards of freedom, are here for the repose and wellbeing of the citizen, while as a glorious aftermath, the tenth and last amendment of this immortal series declares:

> The powers not delegated to the United States by the constitution, nor prohibited by it to the states, are reserved to the states respectively or to the people.

But again; what shall the conclusion be as to the omission of these all-powerful and all-essential provisions of legal liberty from the constitution as it was wrought out, and submitted through congress to the states for ratification? No answer is to be found in the debates which took place in the convention. The proceedings of that august body are silent on this problem, and leave the mind to fall back for its solution on reasons which must have actuated such men as were there engaged. It will not do to say that the omission was an oversight; that James Madison, Benjamin Franklin, Alexander Hamilton, John Rutledge, Pierce Butler and the Pinckneys totally forgot the liberties of the citizen, or purposely left him naked to the usurpations of executive, legislative, and military power. It will not do to assume that the wisdom of Jefferson, great as it was, discovered that the signers of the constitution were in default on account of ignorance or neglect of duty. Is it not, therefore, apparent and conclusive that in article five of the constitution, providing for its own amendment by the action of the states, it was intended that the individual states should be regarded as the special repositories of personal freedom, and that to them should be left the duty and the honor of making it secure? Article five provides that two-thirds of the representatives of the people, and of the states in congress, shall propose amendments to the constitution, and that the legislatures of three-fourths of the states shall ratify the same, thus more fully embodying an expression of state rights than in any other act required by the state governments. Thus, too, is shown the perfect reliance of the fathers of the republic on the states as the chief bulwarks of freedom, and the first and the last citadels for the protection of life, liberty, and the pursuit of happiness. The ten amendments were the ten commandments of the law, delivered by the states to the federal government, to the end that the American citizen should never be touched, or harmed by the hand of despotic power.

One more achievement of legal minds, Mr. President, in connection with the constitution, challenges the attention, respect, and veneration of lawyers wherever and whenever assembled. The creation of the supreme court of the United States, as provided for in the third article of that hallowed instrument, can never be passed in silence when the question of what the world owes to the profession of the law is under consideration. As the chosen interpreter of the constitution, and the highest, and the last resort for the peaceful arbitrament of every conflict of rights that can arise within its scope, we bow with uncovered heads before the lofty history, and the luminous landmarks, with which it has lighted up the world, and measured the progress of human freedom. No sectional thought can exist in contemplating the supreme court of the American Union, and yet here under a southern sun, and in a state decorated with the names of great lawyers, from John Rutledge to James L. Petigru, it seems as if we inhale, in a peculiar manner, the atmosphere of that great tribunal. To southern states, to southern lawyers, belong its highest honors. John Rutledge, **born** in this beautiful city in 1739, won distinction at the bar prior to the Revolution. During the struggle for independence he was governor of South Carolina, and commander-in-chief of her forces. He was a member of the convention which framed her temporary state constitution, and also a member of the congress of the confederation. Under the first act of the congress of the United States, passed September, 1789, to provide for judicial courts, Washington sent his name to the senate, first on the list of associate justices of the supreme court, and his appointment was at once confirmed. This position he afterwards resigned to become chief justice of his native state. In the meantime, upon the resignation of John Jay in 1794, Washington promoted Rutledge to the chief justiceship of the supreme court of the United States. To this position he was not confirmed because of broken health, mentally and physically, which retired him from public life, and, five years later, laid him in his honored grave.

After a brief interval, in January, 1801, another southern lawyer was appointed chief justice, and began a judicial career without a parallel in any age or country. John Marshall, of Virginia, was forty-six years old when he ascended the bench in the beginning of the century. He had been a colonel in the Revolution, and a member of congress after independence was achieved, but these distinctions are almost blotted out and forgotten in the blaze of his judicial fame. For thirty-four years this man of transcendent intellect, endowed with the very genius of jurisprudence, and yet with the guileless simplicity of childhood, addressed himself to the task of finding out and making known the meaning of the constitution of his country, in all its parts, and in all its bearings on the complex system of government, then, for the first time in history, put in operation. The constitution was a new and untried experiment, an infant in age, undeveloped in strength, and assailed with predictions from high quarters of its early overthrow, when Marshall first bent over its provisions, and evoked their power, their wisdom, and their perpetual glory.

The record shows that but two decisions of the supreme court, involving constitutional questions, had been made during its brief existence before Marshall became its chief justice, and that more than fifty of the gravest constitutional character were afterwards rendered during his service, the large majority of them being delivered personally by himself. He had no precedents to guide him. A written constitution of government was a thing hitherto unknown to the nations of the earth. No decided cases of courts could be produced, throwing light on such a system as ours. The relations between the states and the general government, and between the states themselves, and between the citizens of different states, were all as novel and untried as a Utopian dream. Marshall touched them, and they stood forth practical realities; assuming shape, order, harmony, strength, symmetry, and imposing grandeur. The difficult and often obscure boundaries of jurisdiction were first surveyed by his penetrating vision, and traced by his unerring hand. "During this period also the calendars of his court teemed with abstruse questions growing out of the wars with which the young country had been visited, or threatened; the maritime jurisdiction, the powers of admiralty, the law of prize, the force of treaties, were all to be defined."

It is not an over-claim, nor too much to say, that for the constitution as it now stands, in substance and in spirit, and as it has executed its high mission, the American people are indebted to the great Virginia lawyer, the peerless chief justice, John Marshall. What the constitution would have been in the hands of a different interpreter we may not conjecture, but what it became, and still remains, as the result of his giant grasp of the law, all the world knows. For more than the third of a century he stood at the legal helm, and the ship weathered every storm, outrode every tempest. And when death in 1835 relaxed his hold, and closed his immortal career on earth, his successor in the judicial department of the government found the laws of the republic, and the widespread and various rights and interests by them controlled, moving in such harmony as the heavenly bodies display when the music of the spheres is said to be heard.

Roger B. Taney, of Maryland, put on Marshall's robes and walked in his footsteps. Learned, upright, conscientious, Christian jurist! As the heavens grew dark, and the storm of sectional, fratricidal war broke with all its fury on the land, he was misunderstood by some, and assailed, maligned, slandered, traduced by others, because he was faithful to the constitution as it was written and adopted by the states. After twenty-eight years of pure, illustrious service, his brave, benignant soul found peace and rest, in a world beyond the reach of malice or party rage.

It will be seen that the terms served by Marshall and Taney, both southern lawyers, and at the same time thoroughly national jurists, embrace a continuous period of sixty-two years of history under the constitution. The terms served by all the other chief justices from the beginning of the government—seven in number—aggregate thirty-one years, and their labors are in the same disproportion in extent, and in importance, to the work performed by the great jurists from Virginia and Maryland. Illustrious names in the legal profession shine from every quarter of the American firmament, but in upholding the honor, the dignity, the courtesy, the utility, the power, and the glory of the law, it has been given to the genius, the states, and the people of the South, to lead the way, and to secure an amplitude of fame beyond the reach of envy or reversal. May the bonds of the law, administered in the spirit of justice, liberty, and equality for all the states of the American Union, hold it together in everlasting peace; and may the broad, catholic fraternity of the American bar and bench contribute more and more, as the years move on, to the harmonious and affectionate relations of the American people; to their complete unity in heart, mind, and purpose as they go forward to a common destiny; all at home, in the house their fathers built; under the flag, waving evermore in the future, as an emblem of love and good will towards men!

SAMUEL F. B. MORSE.

TRIBUTE TO PROFESSOR MORSE

On the evening of Tuesday, April 16, 1872, a meeting was held in commemoration of the great philosopher and discoverer, Samuel F. B. Morse, in the hall of the United States house of representatives. Speaker James G. Blaine occupied the chair. After an appropriate prayer by Rev. Dr. W. Adams, of New York, remarks were made by Speaker Blaine, Dr. C. C. Cox, Senator Patterson, Hon. Fernando Wood, General James A. Garfield, Hon. S. S. Cox, Hon. D. W. Voorhees, and Hon. N. P. Banks; and telegraphic dispatches from this country and abroad were read, testifying sympathy in the great loss sustained by America in the death of this brilliant light of science. After the reading of a message of sympathy from the operators of England, Ireland, and Scotland, Speaker Blaine introduced Mr. Voorhees, who spoke as follows:

HONORS paid by the living to the dead are as old and as universal as the races of mankind. They follow the bereavements of the cabin and the palace. Simple ceremonies attend the humble and the lowly, and frail memorials mark their resting-places; while the long procession, the solemn and lofty dirge, the crowded assemblage, and the voice of eulogy, all wait on departed eminence and glory. The barbarian chants a requiem over the grave of his fellow-mortal, and the Christian celebrates the virtues of his fallen comrade. No one ever dies all forgotten, and no one ever wholly perishes from the face of the earth. The influences of a life, even in this world, are eternal. The tomb can not inclose them. They escape from its portals, and continue to pervade the daily walks of men, like unseen spirits, guiding and controlling human thought and action. Who is free from their touch? Whose life and destiny have not been colored and fashioned by the influences of those who have passed away, even unknown to fame? The greatest actors on the broad stage of human affairs have pointed back from the loftiest points of their elevation to the mother with her prayers,

to the father with his toil and devotion, to unselfish kindred, to self-sacrificing friends, and bowed with reverence before the living power associated forever with their names and memories. Every mind and heart reproduces some of its achievements and some of its qualities in the minds and hearts of others, after it has gone to far-off spheres and realms. And this is the average of human influence—the silent, but mighty stream of causes producing effects, on which mankind, from its birth, has been borne gradually and steadily forward in its vast career of progress and development.

Now and then, however, the current of this stream receives a new and startling velocity. Some intellectual force, towering over all others of its period, occasionally imparts to all the world at once an impulse, which condenses the ordinary advancement of centuries into the thrilling compass of a single day. Then nations and generations, and not merely individuals, become the subjects of an irresistible and everlasting influence. A new era is then noted on the page of the historian, and new gateways are opened for the onward movement of humanity. Such an event happened in this capital, when, only twenty-eight years ago, a single wire was drawn through the air as a messenger of thought, as swift and unfailing as the light of the sun. It was a period of mental activity and pride, and men were boastful of the light and knowledge which the world already possessed; but the results which followed this achievement were as the awakening of dawn after long and heavy darkness. A revolution, forward and upward in the progress of the world, was at once accomplished, of greater practical consequence to the human family than any other known in history. The toils, the penury, and the hopes deferred, which had darkened many years of the life of the student and the philosopher, were succeeded by a triumph whose proportions will continue to swell and expand until time shall be no more. The influence of this one man has taken to itself the wings of the morning, and visited the uttermost parts of the earth. It dwells in all the four quarters of the globe, and shapes the destinies of men and nations with a power second only to the omnipresent omnipotence of God himself.

Professor Morse, in one sense, is dead. His body, after its labors of fourscore years, has lain down to rest, and to sleep until the voice of the Master shall awaken it again. But, even in this world, his life has just begun. As his great soul enters upon its new career in the regions of immortality, so does the influence which he left behind him here move forward each day to new developments of glory and of power. We are here to-night because he lives in his works, and because his undying genius still sways and governs our conduct. Forty million people, whose representatives we are bow reverently at his tomb for the same reason. All the civilized races of the earth are his mourners, because his great discovery has testified of him in their midst. Memorial services, however, can not reach him. He is beyond the sounds of praise or the fragrance of its incense.

> Can honor's voice provoke the silent dust,
> Or flattery soothe the dull, cold ear of death?

No; we simply honor ourselves on this occasion by recognizing the gigantic power of the mighty dead, and attesting his immortality here on earth. Thus I interpret the meaning of these imposing national solemnities.

If we pause here for a moment to reflect upon the class to which the discovery of Professor Morse belongs, we find it in that field which has produced nearly all there is of useful knowledge. The physical sciences alone can place man in his true relation to the material universe. He arose from the dust, in the hour of his creation, a master and a conqueror by divine right, in the world of nature. Dominion was given to him over all. Power was granted him as the lord of a domain and all it contained; but it was a power which had to be reduced to possession by knowledge. He who is ignorant of the proper ties and laws of the physical world, can have no control of its tremendous agencies. The most polished nations of antiquity, therefore, rose to no higher fame than that which is acquired in wars and conquests. The shape and motion of the heavenly bodies, the electricity of the clouds, the magnetism of metals, the qualities and power of steam, were to them almost entirely sealed mysteries. If they sometimes caught a glimpse of an element of science they applied it to no useful purpose. Cicero, it is true, with that universal wisdom which distinguished him, admits the importance to the human understanding of physical investigation. "*Est animorum ingeniorumque nostrorum naturale quoddam quasi pabulum considerato contemplatique naturæ.*" But in this he stood almost, if not quite alone, and it was left for modern ages to produce those wonderful results which attend a revelation of the secret forces and principles of nature. They are numerous and beneficent to the wants and comfort of the human family; but the discoveries which caused the steamer to plow the deep in safety, and the railroad train to fly across a continent, and which led to the instantaneous transmission of thought to the opposite regions of the globe, stand unrivaled in the history of mental triumphs over the elements of physical creation. And these sublime achievements are American! Fortunate and glorious as our history has in many things been, it has no page so bright as this. Fulton, and Franklin, and Morse are American names. We have lived as a nation less than a century, and yet, in the realms of useful philosophy, practical art and beneficial science, all the centuries of all the past furnish no parallel to our glory. The American mind has contributed more in these walks to the elevation and happiness of mankind than all the other nations and ages of the world combined. All else may fail us, but this will never fail. Our liberties may be lost, our free form of government may fall to the ground, our very name may be blotted from the map of nations; but the inventions of American genius will continue to illuminate the world with a light as imperishable as the stars in the heavens.

There is another reflection, however, which presents itself for brief mention on this occasion. In the brilliancy of the discoverer's fame, after his success is complete, the world is apt to forget the price he paid for his immortality. It is often a most melancholy task to trace the weary and painful struggles which men of science have made, in order to be permitted to bless mankind. Looking behind the sweet hour of their triumphs, we usually behold a dismal plain of poverty, and an almost friendless life of vigilant, unremitting and exhaustive labor. The feverish, throbbing brain; the anxious, sleepless nights; the longing, sick, and disappointed heart—all are there. The sneers of dullness, the opposition of envious intelligence, and the cold and stinted patronage of the timid and doubting also attend the efforts of every daring explorer in unknown regions after new truths. Columbus was fifty-seven years of age when he at last sailed on the fulfillment of his long and troubled dream. In the prosecution of his vast design, he had begged bread and water at the gates of the convent of Santa Maria de Rabida, and encountered the malevolent superstition of Spain in the fifteenth century before the council at Salamanca.

He followed the camp of Ferdinand and Isabella for years, and fought in their bloodiest battles against the Moors, in order to be near the court and solicit its aid in the discovery of a new world. He borrowed money to buy suitable apparel in which to appear in the presence of his sovereigns. He journeyed, foot-sore and travel-stained, with the peasants on the highways. But in the midst of it all, whether in want or in humiliation, in fatigue or in danger, whether battling under the cross against the crescent, or lingering in the antechamber of royalty for an audience, he never for an instant lost sight of the mission on which he had embarked his life. He was present when the last Moorish king surrendered the keys of the Alhambra, and he was a spectator when the whole court and army of Spain were abandoned to jubilee—when the air resounded with shouts of joy, with songs of triumph, and hymns of thanksgiving. Yet, at this great moment, an old Spanish writer thus describes him:

> A man, obscure and little known, followed at this time the court. Confounded in the crowd of unfortunate applicants, feeding his imagination in the corners of antechambers with the pompous project of discovering a world, melancholy and dejected in the midst of the general rejoicing, he beheld with indifference, and almost with contempt, the conclusion of a conquest which swelled all bosoms with jubilee, and seemed to have reached the utmost bounds of desire.

So, too, perhaps, might the great American whose deeds we commemorate to-night, have been seen in the halls of this capitol, when, at the age of fifty-two years, he witnessed general rejoicings over the success of small events in comparison to that which was so clear and so immeasurably great to his view. In some niche or corner or gallery he watched and waited for the succor he had so long sought in vain. It came at last, as did the three small ships to Columbus, and similar results followed, to a certain extent, in both instances. Success was immediate and glorious. One delivered a new hemisphere to the knowledge of mankind, and the other compelled the lightning to carry instant communication between both hemispheres. They rose from adversity and culminated in conquests alike, but their fates and fortunes there diverged. The mighty Genoese admiral realized the anguish of those who hang on princes' favors. He drained the cup of his country's ingratitude to its dregs. His great heart was broken in prison and in chains. He was three hundred years in advance of the powers whom he served. He died in sorrow, and with the unpropitious clouds of his early life again lowering over his head.

Not so with Professor Morse. Happy and bright was the age in which he achieved his triumph. He was shorn of none of its honors or its profits. He took his place permanently in the temple of fame, and received the well-earned rewards of his toils and his genius. He lived with the affections of the world clustering about him, and died honored, revered, and mourned by the human race. The world has advanced, and it still advances.

END OF VOLUME II.

www.ingramcontent.com/pod-product-compliance
Lightning Source LLC
Chambersburg PA
CBHW020739020526
44115CB00030B/223